Lecture Notes in Computer Science 8919

Commenced Publication in 1973
Founding and Former Series Editors:
Gerhard Goos, Juris Hartmanis, and Jan van Leeuwen

T0236374

Ina Schaefer   Ioannis Stamelos (Eds.)

Software Reuse
for Dynamic Systems
in the Cloud and Beyond

14th International Conference on Software Reuse, ICSR 2015
Miami, FL, USA, January 4-6, 2015
Proceedings

 Springer

Volume Editors

Ina Schaefer
Technische Universität Braunschweig
Institut für Softwaretechnik und Fahrzeuginformatik
Mühlenpfordtstr. 23
38106 Braunschweig, Germany
E-mail: i.schaefer@tu-braunschweig.de

Ioannis Stamelos
Aristotle University of Thessaloniki
Department of Informatics
54124 Thessaloniki, Greece
E-mail: stamelos@csd.auth.gr

ISSN 0302-9743   e-ISSN 1611-3349
ISBN 978-3-319-14129-9   e-ISBN 978-3-319-14130-5
DOI 10.1007/978-3-319-14130-5
Springer Cham Heidelberg New York Dordrecht London

Library of Congress Control Number: : 2014956679

LNCS Sublibrary: SL 2 – Programming and Software Engineering

Typesetting: Camera-ready by author, data conversion by Scientific Publishing Services, Chennai, India

Printed on acid-free paper

Springer is part of Springer Science+Business Media (www.springer.com)

Preface

The 14th International Conference on Software Reuse took place in Miami, Florida, USA, during January 4–6, and was hosted by the University of Miami. ICSR is the premier event in the field of software reuse research and technology. The main goal of ICSR is to present the most recent advances and breakthroughs in the area of software reuse and to promote an intensive and continuous exchange among researchers and practitioners.

The specific theme of the 2015 conference was "Reuse for Dynamic Systems in the Cloud and Beyond." Software applications are allowing desktop computers and single servers to become more "mobile" and pervasive as required, for example, for the Internet of Things and the cloud. This phenomenon increases the demand for practical software reuse and generative approaches that avoid "reinventing the wheel" on different platforms over and over again. In this context, non-functional aspects (such as performance and data security) are of special importance to guarantee a satisfying experience for users of cloud-based and other distributed systems.

Responding to the call for papers that was centered around the conference theme, 60 papers were submitted by authors all around the world. All papers went through a thorough review process, examined by three reviewers, all members of the Program Committee. In several cases, a discussion followed the reviews to consolidate the review results, steered by the Program Chairs. As a result, 24 high-quality papers were selected, of which 21 were full and three were short papers, with an acceptance ratio of 40%.

The accepted papers cover several software engineering areas where software reuse is important, such as software product lines, domain analysis, open source, components, cloud, quality. Both empirical and theoretical research works were presented during the event. Overall, ICSR 2015 provided an overview of the recent developments in software reuse to interested researchers and practitioners. The program chairs wish to thank all authors for their contribution to a successful conference. Special thanks go to Oliver Hummel, Conference Chair, and all members of ICSR 2015 committes for their invaluable support.

November 2014

Ina Schaefer
Ioannis Stamelos

Organization

ICSR 2015 was organized by ISASE – the International Society for the Advancement of Software Education.

Organizing Committee

General Chair

Oliver Hummel   iQser (formerly KIT), Germany

Program Co-chairs

Ina Schaefer   TU Braunschweig, Germany
Ioannis Stamelos   Aristotle University of Thessaloniki, Greece

Workshops and Tutorials Chair

Eduardo Santana de Almeida   Universidade Federal da Bahia, Brazil

Doctoral Symposium Co-chairs

Stan Jarzabek   National University of Singapore
Hassan Gomaa   George Mason University, USA

Tools and Demo Chair

Werner Janjic   Fraunhofer Institute for Experimental Software
                                 Engineering, Germany

Publicity Chair

Robert Walker   University of Calgary, Canada

Local Arrangements Chair

Iman Saleh Moustafa   University of Miami, USA

Steering Committee

Ted J. Biggerstaff	Software Generators, USA
John Favaro	INTECS, Italy
William B. Frakes	Virginia Tech, USA
Chuck Lillie	ISASE, USA (Finances)

Sponsors

Software Generators, LLC
University of Miami Graduate School

Table of Contents

Software Product Lines

Solving Reuse Problems

Empirical and Industrial Studies

Reuse for the Web/Cloud

Reuse Based Software Development

Reuse Metrics

Reuse in Object-Oriented

Evaluating Feature Change Impact
on Multi-product Line Configurations
Using Partial Information

Nicolas Dintzner[1], Uirá Kulesza[2], Arie van Deursen[1], and Martin Pinzger[3]

[1] Software Engineering Research Group, Delft University of Technology,
Delft, The Netherlands
{N.J.R.Dintzner,Arie.vanDeursen}@tudelft.nl
[2] Department of Informatics and Applied Mathematics,
Federal University of Rio Grande do Norte, Natal, Brazil
uira@dimap.ufrn.br
[3] Software Engineering Research Group, University of Klagenfurt,
Klagenfurt, Austria
martin.pinzger@aau.at

Abstract. Evolving large-scale, complex and highly variable systems is known to be a difficult task, where a single change can ripple through various parts of the system with potentially undesirable effects. In the case of product lines, and moreover multi-product lines, a change may affect only certain variants or certain combinations of features, making the evaluation of change effects more difficult.

In this paper, we present an approach for computing the impact of a feature change on the existing configurations of a multi-product line, using partial information regarding constraints between feature models. Our approach identifies the configurations that can no longer be derived in each individual feature model taking into account feature change impact propagation across feature models. We demonstrate our approach using an industrial problem and show that correct results can be obtained even with partial information. We also provide the tool we built for this purpose.

Keywords: software product line, variability, change impact, feature.

1 Introduction

Evolving large-scale, complex and variable systems is known to be a difficult task, where a single change can ripple through various parts of the system with potentially undesirable effects. If the components of this system are themselves variable, or if the capabilities exposed by an interface depend on some external constraint (i.e. configuration option), then engineers need extensive domain knowledge on configuration options and component implementations to safely improve their system [8]. In the domain of product line engineering (PLE), an approach aiming at maximising asset reuse in different products [14], this type

I. Schaefer and I. Stamelos (Eds.): ICSR 2015, LNCS 8919, pp. 1–16, 2014.

of evolutionary challenge is the norm. Researchers and practitioners have looked into what variability modeling - and feature modeling specifically - can bring to change impact analysis on product lines (PLs). Existing methods can evaluate, given a change expressed in features, how a feature model (FM) and the composition of features it allows (configurations) are impacted [13], [7], [19]. However, FMs grow over time in terms of number of features and constraints and safe manual updates become unmanageable by humans [4]. Moreover, automated analysis methods do not scale well when the number of configurations or feature increases [7].

To mitigate this, *nested product lines, product populations*, or *multi-product lines* (MPL - a set of interdependent PLs) approaches recommend modularizing FMs into smaller and more manageable pieces [11], [18], [12]. While this solves part of the problem, known FM analysis methods are designed for single FMs. A common approach is to recompose the FMs into a single one. To achieve this, existing approaches suggest describing explicitly dependencies between FMs using cross-FM constraints, or hierarchies [1] to facilitate model composition and analysis. Such relationships act as vectors of potential change impact propagation between FMs. However, in [9] Holl et al. noted that the knowledge of domain experts about model constraints is likely to be only partial (both intra-FMs or extra-FMs). For this reason, we cannot assume that such relationships will be available as inputs to a change impact analysis.

In this context, we present and evaluate an approach to facilitate the assessment of the impact of a feature change on existing configurations of the different PLs of an MPL using partial information about inter-FMs relationships. After giving background information regarding feature modelling and product lines (Section 2), we present the industrial problem that motivated this work and detail the goals and constraints of this study (Section 3). We then present our approach to enrich the variability model of an MPL using existing configurations of individual FMs, and the heuristic we apply when analyzing the effect of a feature change on existing configurations of an MPL (Section 4). In Section 5, we assess our approach in an industrial context. We present and discuss how we built the appropriate models, the output of our prototype implementation and the performance of the approach with its limitations. Finally, Section 6 presents related work and we elaborate on possible future work in Section 7.

2   Background

In this paper, the definition of *feature* given by Czarnecki et al. in [5] is used: "a feature may denote any functional or nonfunctional characteristic at the requirement, architectural, component, platform or any other level". A feature model (FM) is a structured set of features with selection rules specifying the allowed combinations of features. This is achieved through relationships (optional, mandatory, part of an alternative or OR-type structures) and cross-tree constraints - arbitrary conditions on feature selection. The most common types of cross-tree constraints are "excludes" (e.g. "feature A excludes feature B") and

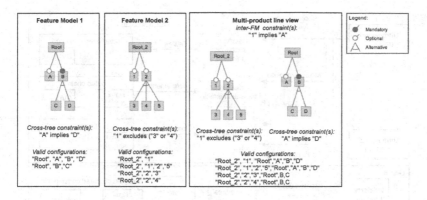

Fig. 1. Example of FMs in a SPL and MPL context

"implies" [10]. With a FM, one can derive configurations: a set of features which does not violate constraints established by the FM. An example of simple FMs with their valid configurations are depicted on the left hand side of Figure 1.

In the context of a multi-product line, several inter-related FMs are used to describe the variability of a single large system. This can be achieved by creating "cross-feature model" constraints or through feature references [3] - where a given feature appears in multiple FMs. The constraints between FMs can be combination rules referring to features contained within different models. Those constraints can also be derived from the hierarchy (or any imposed structure [15], [3]) of the FMs involved in an MPL. In those cases, the combination rules can refer to both features and FMs. A product configuration derived from an MPL is a set of features which does not violate any constraints of individual FMs nor the cross-FM constraints that have been put in place. An example of combined FMs with a constraint between two FMs can be seen on the right hand side of Figure 1.

3 Motivation: Change Impact in an Industrial Context

Our industrial partner builds and maintains high-end medical devices, among which an x-ray machine. This x-ray machine comes in many variants, each differing in terms of hardware (e.g. tables, mechanical arms) and software (e.g. firmware version, imaging system). Certified third party products can be integrated through different types of external interfaces: mechanical (e.g. a module placed on the operating table), electrical (inbuilt power supply), data related (image transfer). As an example, three main subsystems of the x-ray machine (data/video exchange, video chain, and display) and three main interfaces (display interface, video signal, and data/video exchange) are shown in Figure 2. The two working modes of a given 3rd party product ("mode 1" and "mode 2") use the same interfaces in slightly different ways. In "mode 1", the 3rd party product reuses the x-ray machine display to show images ("shared display") while in

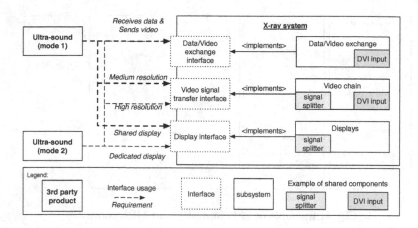

Fig. 2. X-ray machine system overview

"mode 2" a dedicated display is used. Sharing an existing display implies using a signal splitter/merger in the display subsystem. But the splitter/merger also plays a role in the video processing chain and is only available in certain of its variants.

Following any update, engineers must validate if the new version of the system can still provide what is necessary for 3rd party product integration. This leads to the following type of questions: *"Knowing that 3rd party product X uses the video interface to export high resolution pictures and import patient data, is X supported by the new version of the x-ray machine?"*. Let us consider the following scenario: a connection box, present in the video chain and data/video exchange subsystems, is removed from the list of available hardware. Some specific configurations of the video chain and of the data/video exchange subsystems can no longer be produced. The data/video exchange interface required the removed configurations to provide specific capabilities. Following this, it is no longer possible to export video and import data and the integration with the 3rd party product is compromised.

Currently, engineers validate changes manually by checking specification documents (either 3rd party products requirements or subsystem technical specifications) and rigorous testing practices. Despite this, it remains difficult to assess which subsystem(s) and which of their variant(s) or composition of variants will be influenced by a given change. Given the rapid evolution of their products, this error-prone validation is increasingly time consuming. Our partner is exploring model-driven approaches enabling early detection of such errors.

While this example is focused on the problems that our industrial partner is facing, enabling analysis for very large PLs and MPLs is a key issue for many companies. Recently, Schmid introduced the notion of variability-rich eco systems [17], highlighting the many sources of variability that may influence a software product. This further emphasizes the need for change impact analysis approaches on highly variable systems.

4 Feature-Change Impact Computation

Given the problem described in the previous section, we present here the approach we designed to assist domain engineers in evaluating the impact of a change on their products. We first describe the main goal of our approach and our contributions. Then, we detail the approach and illustrate it with a simple example. Finally, we consider the scalability aspects of the approach and present our prototype implementation.

4.1 Goals and Constraints

For our industrial partner, the main aim is to obtain insights on the potential impacts of an update on external interfaces used by 3rd party products. However, we have to take into account that domain engineers do not know the details of the interactions of the major subsystems [9] nor all components included in each one - only the ones relevant to support external interfaces. As an input, we rely on the specifications of each major subsystem and their main components in isolation as well as their existing configurations. Because of the large number of subsystem variants and interface usages (choices of capabilities or options), we consider each of them as a product line (PL) in its own right. Features then represent hardware components, (non-)functional properties, software elements, or any other relevant characteristic of a subsystem or interface. Using a simple feature notation and cross-tree constraints [10], we formalize within each subsystem the known features and constraints between them. By combining those PLs, we obtain a multi-product line (MPL) representation of the variability of the system.

With such representation, a change to a subsystem or interface can be expressed in terms of features: adding or removing features, adding, removing or modifying intra-FM constraints. Once the change is known, we can apply it to the relevant FM and evaluate if existing configurations are affected (no longer valid with respect to the FM). Then, we determine how the change propagates across the FMs of the MPL using a simple heuristic on configuration composition. As an ouput, we provide a tree of configuration changes, where nodes are impacted FMs with their invalid configurations.

Our work brings the following main contributions. We present a novel approach to compute feature change impact on existing configurations of an MPL. We provide a prototype tool supporting our approach, available for download.[1] We demonstrate the applicability of the approach by applying it to a concrete case-study executed in cooperation with our industrial partner.

4.2 Approach

We describe here first how the model is built. Then, we show how we enrich the model with inferred information and finally the steps taken for simulating

---

[1] The tool is available at
   http://swerl.tudelft.nl/bin/view/NicolasDintzner/WebHome

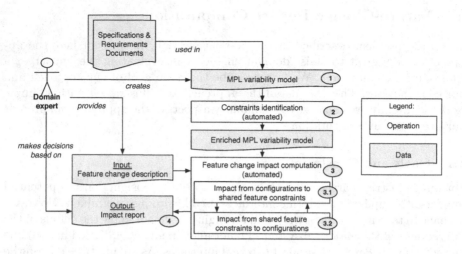

Fig. 3. Approach overview

the effects of a feature change on existing configurations. An overview of the different steps are shown in Figure 3.

Step 1: Describe subsystem variability. The first step of our approach consists in modelling the various subsystems using FM notation. This operation is done by domain experts, using existing documentation. When a subsystem uses a feature that has already been described in another subsystem, we reference it instead of creating a new one [1]. We associate with each FM its known configurations.

Step 2: Enrich the model with inferred composition rules. Once all FMs and configurations have been described, we use the configurations to infer how pairs of subsystems can be combined. We identify, in FMs sharing features, which features are shared and then create a list of existing partial configurations containing only them. Partial configurations appearing in existing configurations of both FMs constitute the whitelist of partial configurations enabling composition of configurations between the involved FMs. For two given FMs, the number of feature involved in shared feature constraints is equal to the number of features shared between them. Those partial configurations are the *shared feature constraints* relating pairs of FMs: two configurations, from two different FMs sharing features, are "compatible" if they contain exactly the same shared features. In order to apply such heuristic, shared feature constraints must be generated between every pairs of FMs sharing features. An example of such constraints is shown in Figure 4, where FMs 1 and 2 share features E and D.

Step 3: Compute the impact of a feature change. We use the enriched model to perform feature change impact computation at the request of domain experts. A feature change can be any modification of a FM (add/remove/move/modify features and constraints) or a change in available configurations (add/remove). We assess the impact of the change of the configurations of a modified FM by re-validating them with respect to the updated FM, as suggested in [7].

This gives us a first set of invalid configurations that we use as a starting point for the propagation heuristic.

Step 3.1: Compute impact of configuration changes on shared feature constraints. We evaluate how a change of configuration of a FM affects the shared feature constraints attached to it. If a given shared feature constraint is not satisfied by at least one configuration of the FM then it is invalidated by the change. For each FM affected by a configuration change, we apply the reasoning presented in Algorithm 1. In the case a change does not modify existing configurations, this step will tell us that all existing constraints are still valid, but some can be added. Otherwise, if all configurations matching a constraint have been removed then that constraint is considered invalid (i.e. does not match a possible combination of configurations). Given a list of invalid shared feature constraints and the FMs to which it refers to, we can execute Step 3.2. If no shared feature constraints are modified, the computation stops here.

Data: a FM fm with an updated set of configurations
Result: a list of invalidated shared feature constraints $lInvalidConstraints$

foreach *shared feature constraint of fm: sfc* **do**
    $allowedFeatures \leftarrow$ selected features of sfc;
    $forbiddenFeatures \leftarrow$ negated features of sfc;
    foreach *configuration of fm: c (list of feature names)* **do**
        if *allowedFeatures $\subseteq$ c* **then**
            if $c \cap forbiddenFeatures == \emptyset$ **then**
                | c is compliant;
            end
        end
    end
    if *no compliant configuration found* **then**
        | add sfc to $lInvalidConstraints$;
    end
end

Algorithm 1. Configuration change propagation

Step 3.2: Compute impact of shared feature constraint changes on configurations. Given a set of invalid shared feature constraints obtained in the previous step, we evaluate how this invalidates other FMs configurations. If a configuration of an FM does not match any of the remaining shared feature constraints, it can no longer be combined with configurations of other FMs and is considered invalid. We apply the operations described in Algorithm 2. If any configuration is invalidated, we use the output of this step to re-apply Step 3.1.

Step 4: Consolidate results. We capture the result of the computation as a tree of changes. The first level of the tree is always a set of configuration changes. If more than one FM is touched by the initial change (e.g. removal of a shared feature) then we have a multi-root tree. Each configuration change object describes the addition or removal of any number of configurations. If a

---

Data: fm: a FM with updated shared feature constraints
Result: $lInvalidConfs$: a list of invalidated configurations of fm

foreach *configuration of fm: c (list of feature names)* **do**
   | **foreach** *shared feature constraint of fm: sfc* **do**
   | | *allowedFeatures* ← selected features of sfc;
   | | *forbiddenFeatures* ← negated features of sfc;
   | | **if** *allowedFeatures* $\subset c$ **then**
   | | | **if** $c \cap forbiddenFeatures == \emptyset$ **then**
   | | | | c is compliant;
   | | | **end**
   | | **end**
   | **end**
   | **if** *no compliant constraint found* **then**
   | | add c to $lInvalidConfs$;
   | **end**
end

Algorithm 2. Shared feature constraint change propagation

configuration change triggered a change in shared feature constraints, a shared feature constraint change is added as its child. A shared feature constraint change references the two FMs involved and any number of constraints that were added or removed. The configuration changes following this shared feature constraint modification are then added as a child "configuration change object". This structure allows us to describe the path taken by the impact propagation through the different FMs.

4.3   Example

Let us consider the example shown in Figure 4, where two FMs share two features: D and E. The model is enriched with the "shared feature constraints" deduced from existing configurations. Those constraints state that, for a configuration of FM1 and FM2 to be combined, both of them need to have shared features that are either (E,D), (D, not E) and (not E, not D). The resulting data structure is shown on the left hand side of Figure 4.

We consider the following change: Configuration 1.2 is removed, operation marked as 1 in Figure 4. We apply the algorithm described in Step 3.1, using FM1 as a input, and with Configurations 1.1 and 1.3 (all of them except the removed one) and the associated 3 shared feature constraints. For Constraint 1, the allowed features are "E" and "D", and there are no forbidden features. We search for existing configurations of FM1 containing both "E" and "D" among Configurations 1.1 and 1.3. We find that Configuration 1.3 satisfies this constraint. The Constraint 2 (allowing "D" and forbidding "E") is not matched by any configurations, since the only configuration containing "D" and not "E" is Configuration 1.2 has been removed. Constraint 3 forbidding features "D" and

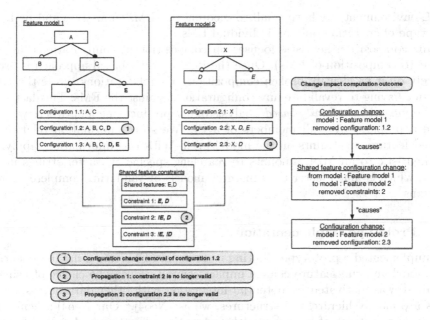

Fig. 4. Change impact propagation example

"E" is satisfied by Configuration 1.1. The resulting list of invalid constraints contains only one element: Constraint 2 (marked as operation 2 in the diagram).

We then apply 2 presented in Step 3.2 to assess the effect of that change on the configurations of other FMs (FM2 only in this case). With the remaining Constraints 1 and 3, we run through the configurations of FM2 to identify which configurations no longer satisfy any constraints. We find that Configuration 2.1 satisfies Constraint 3 (does not contain "D" nor "E"), and Configuration 2.2 satisfies Constraint 1 (contains both "E" and "D"). However, configuration 2.3 does not satisfy any of the remaining constraints and for this reason, is marked as invalid (shown as operation 3 on the diagram).

On the right hand side of Figure 4, we present the resulting tree (a branch in this case). The intial change (removal of configuration 1.2 of FM1) is captured by the first "configuration change" object. Changes to shared features constraints are directly attached to this configuration change: the "shared feature configuration change" object. Finally, the last node of the tree is the invalidation of Configuration 2.3 of FM2.

4.4 Scalability Aspects

The initial step of our approach replicates what Heider suggests in [7]: reinstantiating existing configurations. Such approaches are known as *product-based* approaches [20]. They have known drawbacks: as the number of configurations and features increases, the solution does not scale. By placing ourselves in an

MPL environment, we have small to medium size FMs to analyze and perform this type of operation only on individual FMs.

Our composition heuristic focuses on composition of configurations (as opposed to composition of FMs). Once the local product-based approach is used, we rely on it to identify broken compositions of configurations across the FMs without having to revalidate any configurations against the FMs. This last step can be viewed as a *family-based* analysis of our product line [20], where we validate a property over all members of a PL. We store information relative to shared feature constraints on the model itself. With this information, applying the heuristic to an MPL amounts to searching specific character strings in an array, which is much faster than merging models or validating complete configurations.

4.5   Prototype Implementation

We implemented a prototype allowing us to import FMs into a database, enrich the model and run feature change impact computations. The choice of using a database was motivated by potential integration with other datasources. Since FMs are mostly hierarchical structures, we use Neo4j.[2] Our Neo4j schema describes the concepts of feature model, feature, configuration and shared feature constraint with their relationships as described in the previous section. This representation is very similar to other FM representations such as [21] with one exception. The mandatory, optional or alternative nature of a feature is determined by its relationship with its parent; as opposed to be a characteristic of the feature itself. This allows to have an optional feature in a FM, referenced by another FM as part of an alternative.

We leverage the Neo4j *Cypher* query language to retrieve relevant data: shared features, configurations containing certain features as well as interconnected feature models and the features which links them. We use FeatureIDE [21] as a feature model editor tool. We import models in their xml format into our database using a custom java application. A basic user interface allows us to give the name of a feature to remove, run the simulation, and view the result.

5   Industrial Case Study

As mentioned in Section 3, this paper is motivated by an industrial case study proposed by our partner. The end-goal of this case study is to assess the applicability of our approach in an industrial context. To do so, we reproduce a past situation where a change modified the behaviour of some products of their product line on which a 3rd party product was relying, and where the impact was detected late in the development process. We present and discuss the main steps of our approach and their limitations when applied in an industrial context: the construction of the model, the feature change impact computation with its result, and the performance of our prototype implementation.

---

[2] http://www.neo4j.org

5.1   Modelling a X-Ray MPL

We start by gathering specification documents of the main subsystems identified in Section 3, as well as 3rd party product compatibility specifications. With the domain experts, we identify relevant components and existing configurations of each subsystem. Using this information, we model the three interfaces and three subsystems presented in Figure 2 as six distinct feature models (FMs). The three interfaces are (i) the video/data transfer interface (data and video transfer capabilities), (ii) the video export interface specifying possible resolutions and refresh rates, and finally (iii) the display interface representing a choice in monitor and display modes. 3rd party product interface usages are modeled as the configurations associated to those FMs. The three subsystems of the x-ray machine are (i) the data/video transfer subsystem, (ii) the video chain used to transport images from a source to a display, and finally (iii) display subsystem. Configurations of those subsystems are the concrete products available to customers (between 4 and 11 configurations per FM). Each FM contains between 10 and 25 features, with at most 5 cross-tree constraints. The "data transfer", "video chain", and "screen" FMs share features relating to hardware components, and reuse features from interface FMs. We use FeatureIDE to create FMs and configurations. We then import them into a Neo4J database and use our prototype implementation to generate the necessary shared feature constraints as described in Section 4.

The main challenge of this phase is to ensure that shared features represent the same concept in all FMs. For instance, a feature "cable" refers to one specific cable, in a specific context, and must be understood as such in all FMs including it. Misreferencing features will lead to incorrect shared feature constraints and incorrect change impact analysis results. We mitigated this effect by carefully reviewing FMs and shared features with domain expert.

5.2   Simulating the Change

We studied the effect of the removal of a hardware component used to import video into the system. To simulate this with our prototype, we provide our tool with the name of the feature to remove ("Connection box 1"). "Connection box 1" is included in both the "data/video transfer" and "video chain" FMs, so its removal directly impacts those two FMs. The tool re-instantiates all configurations of those two FMs and find that 6 configurations of the "video chain" FM, and 1 from the "data transfer" FM are invalid. Then, the prototype executes the propagation heuristic. A shared feature constraint between the "data transfer" and "data transfer interface" FMs is no longer satisfied by any configuration of the "data transfer" FM, and is now invalid. Without this shared feature constraint, one configuration of the "data transfer interface" FM can no longer be combined with the "data transfer" FM and is considered as invalid. The removal of a configuration in an interface FM tells us that the compatibility with one 3rd party product is no longer possible. The modifications of the "data transfer" FM also invalidated a shared feature constraint existing between the "data transfer" and "video chain" FMs. However, the change of "shared feature

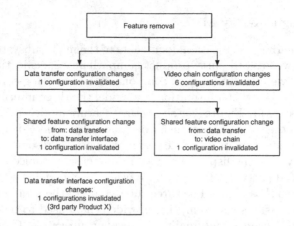

Fig. 5. Output of the feature removal simulation

constraint" did not propagate further; the configurations that it should have impacted had already been invalidated by a previous change.

The result of this impact analysis, reviewed with 3 domain experts, showed the impact of interfaces that had been problematic in the past. We ran several other simulations on this model (removal of features, removal of configurations). On each occasion, the result matched the expectations of domain experts - given the data included in the model. In this context, the approach proved to be both simple and successful. This being said, by using information from existing configurations, we over-constrain inter-FMs relationships. If a shared optional feature is present in all configurations of a given FM, it will be seen as mandatory during impact computation. However, if a feature is present in all of existing configurations, it is mandatory with respect to what is available - as opposed to mandatory in the variability model. As long as we reason about existing configurations only, using inferred shared feature constraints should not influence negatively the result of the simulation.

5.3 Performance Analysis

We provide here a qualitative overview of performance measurements that were performed during this case study. For our main scenario, our approach checked all configurations of 2 of the FMs, and the change propagated to 2 others. 2 of the 6 FMs did not have to be analyzed. In this specific context, our implementation provided results in less than a few seconds, regardless of the scenario that was ran. We then artificially increased the size of the models (number of features and number of configurations) to evaluate how it influences the computation time of the propagation algorithm. Given a set of invalid configurations, we measure how long it takes to assess the impact on one connected FM. For 2 FMs with 20 features each and 20 configurations each, sharing 2 features, the propagation from 1 FM to the other and impact its configurations takes approximately 450ms.

With 200 configurations in each FMs, the same operation takes 1.5s; and up to 2.5s for 300 configurations.

During the industrial case study, the performance of the prototype tool was sufficient to provide almost real-time feedback to domain engineers. The size of the models and the number of configurations affect negatively the computation time of the change impact analysis, because the first step of our approach is product-based: we do check all configurations of the initially impacted FMs. However, using an MPL approach, individual FMs are meant, by design, to be relatively small. Then, computing the propagation of those changes, if any, depends on the number of affected FMs as defined by our propagation heuristic. The heuristic itself is the validation of a property over all members of the product family ("family-based" approach), so its performance is less influenced by model size [20]. This operation consists in searching for strings in an array, which should remain manageable even for large models. Our naive implementation, using Neo4j, already provided satisfactory performance.

5.4   Threats to Validity

With respect to *internal validity*, the main threat relates to the construction of the models used for the industrial case study. We built the different FMs and configurations of the case study using existing documentation while devising the approach. To avoid any bias in the model construction, we reviewed the models several times with domain experts, ensuring their representativeness.

Threats to *external validity* concern the generalisation of our findings. For this study, we used only the most basic FM notation [10]. Our approach should be applicable using more complex notations as long as those notation do not change the representation of the configurations (list of feature names, where each name appear once). If, for instance, we use a cardinality-based notation, the heuristic will have to be adapted to take this cardinality into account. The extracted information from existing configurations was sufficient for this case study, but more complex relationships between FMs might not have been encountered. Applying our approach on a different PL would confirm or infirm this.

6   Related Work

The representation of variability in very large systems, using multiple FMs, has been studied extensively during the past few years. Several composition techniques have been devised. Composition rules can be defined at an FM level, specifying how the models should be recombined for analysis. Otherwise, cross-FM constraints can be defined. Examples can be found in the work of Schirmeier [16] and Acher [1, 2]. In our context, we chose not to follow those approaches as we do not know a priori the over-arching relationships between FMs, nor can we define cross-FM constraints since we work with partial information. Moreover, those techniques would then require us to re-compose models before validating the various configurations which, as noted in [6], is complex to automate.

Recent work on MPLs showed that there is a need to specialise feature models to segregate concerns in MPL variability models. Reiser et al. [15] propose the concept of "context variability model" for multi-product lines, which describes the variability of the environment in which the end product resides. In our study, we classified our FMs as either interface or subsystem. This classification also allows us to qualify the configurations (as interface usage or product implementation), which proved to be sufficient for our application. Schröter et al. present the idea of interface FMs where specific FMs involved in an MPL act as interfaces between other FMs [18]. They propose a classification of the characteristics that can be captured by such models (syntactic, behavioral, and non-functional). While we did not use this approach directly, we noted that for non-interface FMs, we used specific branches of the model to organize reused shared features. It is interesting to note that the designs of (non-interface) FMs share a common structure. We used specific branches of their respective FM to organise features shared with interface FMs. Doing so, we specialized a branch of a FM instead of creating dedicated FMs and we do not restrict the type of features it contains (functional and non-functional alike).

Heider et al. proposed to assess the effect of a change on a variability model by re-instantiating previously configured products [7], and thus validating non-regression. Our approach applies similar principles, as we will consider a change safe as long as the existing products can be re-derived. We apply those concepts in a multi-product line environment, where change propagation is paramount. Thüm et al. [19] proposed to classify changes occurring on feature models based on their effect on existing product configurations. The change is considered as a "generalisation" if the set of valid products has been extended, "specialisation" if it has been reduced, "refactoring" if it has not changed, and "arbitrary edit" in all other cases (when some configurations were removed and others added). This initial classification gave us some insight into the potential impact of a change, but only for a single FM. Their methodology could be applied during the initial step of our approach to identify changes that do not affect existing configurations, avoiding extra computation later on.

7   Conclusion

Understanding the full extent of the impact of a change on a complex and highly variable product is a difficult task. The main goal of this research is to facilitate the evolution of such systems by assisting domain experts in assessing the effects of changes on multi-product line variability models. In this paper, we presented an approach to compute the impact of a feature change on a multi-product line for non-regression purposes, leveraging information contained in existing product configurations to infer feature model composition constraints. We described how our modelling approach can be used in a practical context, using an industrial case and provide a qualitative review of the performance of our prototype tool. With partial information, we were able to accurately identify which configurations of an MPL were rendered invalid by a feature change.

As industrial products grow more complex and become more variable, managing their evolution becomes increasingly difficult. Approaches supporting domain experts' activities will have to be adapted to meet new challenges. As a step in that direction, we released our implementation as an open source project[3] as well as the dataset we used for the performance evaluation. We then plan to integrate it into existing feature modelling tools. We intend to explore how we can make the best use of the promising graph database technologies such as Neo4J for feature model checking. With such technology, we will be in a position to consider more complex models, with potentially more complex FM composition constraints, further facilitating the design, analysis and maintenance of highly variable systems.

Acknowledgements. This publication was supported by the Dutch national program COMMIT and carried out as part of the Allegio project under the responsibility of the Embedded Systems Innovation group of TNO in partnership with Philips Healthcare.

References

1. Acher, M., Collet, P., Lahire, P., France, R.: Comparing approaches to implement feature model composition. In: Kühne, T., Selic, B., Gervais, M.-P., Terrier, F. (eds.) ECMFA 2010. LNCS, vol. 6138, pp. 3–19. Springer, Heidelberg (2010)
2. Acher, M., Collet, P., Lahire, P., France, R.: Managing multiple software product lines using merging techniques. Research report, Laboratoire d'Informatique de Signaux et Systèmes de Sophia Antipolis - UNSA-CNRS (2010)
3. Acher, M., Collet, P., Lahire, P., France, R.: Managing variability in workflow with feature model composition operators. In: Baudry, B., Wohlstadter, E. (eds.) SC 2010. LNCS, vol. 6144, pp. 17–33. Springer, Heidelberg (2010)
4. Bagheri, E., Gasevic, D.: Assessing the maintainability of software product line feature models using structural metrics. Software Quality Journal 19(3), 579–612 (2011)
5. Czarnecki, K., Helsen, S., Eisenecker, U.: Staged configuration through specialization and multilevel configuration of feature models. Software Process: Improvement and Practice 10(2), 143–169 (2005)
6. Hartmann, H., Trew, T.: Using feature diagrams with context variability to model multiple product lines for software supply chains. In: 12th International Software Product Line Conference, pp. 12–21. IEEE Computer Society, Washington (2008)
7. Heider, W., Rabiser, R., Grünbacher, P., Lettner, D.: Using regression testing to analyze the impact of changes to variability models on products. In: 16th International Software Product Line Conference, pp. 196–205. ACM, New York (2012)
8. Heider, W., Vierhauser, M., Lettner, D., Grunbacher, P.: A case study on the evolution of a component-based product line. In: 2012 Joint Working IEEE/IFIP Conference on Software Architecture (WICSA) and European Conference on Software Architecture (ECSA), pp. 1–10. IEEE Computer Society, Washington (2012)

---

[3] The tool is available at
http://swerl.tudelft.nl/bin/view/NicolasDintzner/WebHome

9. Holl, G., Thaller, D., Grünbacher, P., Elsner, C.: Managing emerging configuration dependencies in multi product lines. In: 6th International Workshop on Variability Modeling of Software-Intensive Systems, pp. 3–10. ACM, New York (2012)
10. Kang, K.C., Cohen, S.G., Hess, J.A., Novak, W.E., Peterson, A.S.: Feature-oriented domain analysis (FODA) feasibility study. Tech. rep., Software Engineering Institute, Carnegie Mellon University (1990)
11. Krueger, C.: New methods in software product line development. In: 10th International Software Product Line Conference, pp. 95–99. IEEE Computer Society, Washington (2006)
12. van Ommering, R., Bosch, J.: Widening the scope of software product lines - from variation to composition. In: Chastek, G.J. (ed.) SPLC 2002. LNCS, vol. 2379, pp. 328–347. Springer, Heidelberg (2002)
13. Paskevicius, P., Damasevicius, R., Štuikys, V.: Change impact analysis of feature models. In: Skersys, T., Butleris, R., Butkiene, R. (eds.) ICIST 2012. CCIS, vol. 319, pp. 108–122. Springer, Heidelberg (2012)
14. Pohl, K., Böckle, G., van der Linden, F.J.: Software Product Line Engineering: Foundations, Principles and Techniques. Springer, Secaucus (2005)
15. Reiser, M.O., Weber, M.: Multi-level feature trees: A pragmatic approach to managing highly complex product families. Requirements Engineering 12(2), 57–75 (2007)
16. Schirmeier, H., Spinczyk, O.: Challenges in software product line composition. In: 42nd Hawaii International Conference on System Sciences. IEEE Computer Society, Washington (2009)
17. Schmid, K.: Variability support for variability-rich software ecosystems. In: 4th International Workshop on Product Line Approaches in Software Engineering, pp. 5–8. IEEE Computer Society, Washington (2013)
18. Schröter, R., Siegmund, N., Thüm, T.: Towards modular analysis of multi product lines. In: Proc. of the 17th International Software Product Line Conference Co-located Workshops, pp. 96–99. ACM, New York (2013)
19. Thüm, T., Batory, D., Kästner, C.: Reasoning about edits to feature models. In: 31st International Conference on Software Engineering, pp. 254–264. IEEE Computer Society, Washington (2009)
20. Thüm, T., Apel, S., Kästner, C., Schaefer, I., Saake, G.: A classification and survey of analysis strategies for software product lines. ACM Computing Surveys 47(1), 1–45 (2014)
21. Thüm, T., Kästner, C., Benduhn, F., Meinicke, J., Saake, G., Leich, T.: FeatureIDE: An extensible framework for feature-oriented software development. Science of Computer Programming 79, 70–85 (2014)

Recovering Architectural Variability of a Family of Product Variants

Anas Shatnawi[1], Abdelhak Seriai[1], and Houari Sahraoui[2]

[1] UMR CNRS 5506, LIRMM, University of Montpellier II, Montpellier, France
{shatnawi,seriai}@lirmm.fr
[2] DIRO, University of Montreal, Montreal, Canada
sahraoui@iro.umontreal.ca

Abstract. A Software Product Line (SPL) aims at applying a pre-planned systematic reuse of large-grained software artifacts to increase the software productivity and reduce the development cost. The idea of SPL is to analyze the business domain of a family of products to identify the common and the variable parts between the products. However, it is common for companies to develop, in an ad-hoc manner (e.g. clone and own), a set of products that share common functionalities and differ in terms of others. Thus, many recent research contributions are proposed to re-engineer existing product variants to a SPL. Nevertheless, these contributions are mostly focused on managing the variability at the requirement level. Very few contributions address the variability at the architectural level despite its major importance. Starting from this observation, we propose, in this paper, an approach to reverse engineer the architecture of a set of product variants. Our goal is to identify the variability and dependencies among architectural element variants at the architectural level. Our work relies on Formal Concept Analysis (FCA) to analyze the variability. To validate the proposed approach, we experimented on two families of open-source product variants; Mobile Media and Health Watcher. The results show that our approach is able to identify the architectural variability and the dependencies.

Keywords: Product line architecture, architecture variability, architecture recovery, product variants, reverse engineering, source code, object-oriented.

1 Introduction

A Software Product Line (SPL) aims at applying a pre-planned systematic reuse of large-grained software artifacts (e.g. components) to increase the software productivity and reduce the development cost [1–3]. The main idea behind SPL is to analyze the business domain of a family of products in order to identify the common and the variable parts between these products [1, 2]. In SPL, the variability is realized at different levels of abstraction (e.g. requirement and design). At the requirement level, it is originated starting from the differences in users'

I. Schaefer and I. Stamelos (Eds.): ICSR 2015, LNCS 8919, pp. 17–33, 2014.
© Springer International Publishing Switzerland 2014

wishes, and does not carry any technical sense [2] (e.g. the user needs *camera* and *WIFI* features in the phone). At the design level, the variability starts to have more details related to technical senses to form the product architectures. These technical senses are described via Software Product Line Architecture (SPLA). Such technical senses are related to which components compose the product (e.g. *video recorder*, and *photo capture* components), how these components interact through their interfaces (e.g. *video recorder* provides a *video stream* interface to *media store*), and what topology forms the architectural configuration (i.e. how components are composited and linked) [2].

Developing a SPL from scratch is a highly costly task since this means the development of the domain software artifacts [1]. In addition, it is common for companies to develop a set of software product variants that share common functionalities and differ in terms of other ones. These products are usually developed in an ad-hoc manner (e.g. clone and own) by adding or/and removing some functionalities to an existing software product to meet the requirement of a new need [4]. Nevertheless, when the number of product variants grows, managing the reuse and maintenance processes becomes a severe problem [4]. As a consequence, it is necessary to identify and manage variability between product variants as a SPL. The goal is to reduce the cost of SPL development by first starting it from existing products and then being able to manage the reuse and maintenance tasks in product variants using a SPL. Thus, many research contributions have been proposed to re-engineer existing product variants into a SPL [5, 6]. Nevertheless, existing works are mostly focused on recovering the variability in terms of features defined at the requirement level. Despite the major importance of the SPLA, there is only two works aiming at recovering the variability at the architectural level [7, 8]. These approaches are not fully-automated and rely on the domain knowledge which is not always available. Also, they do not identify dependencies among the architectural elements. To address this limitation, we propose in this paper an approach to automatically recover the architecture of a set of software product variants by capturing the variability at the architectural level and the dependencies between the architectural elements. We rely on Formal Concept Analysis (FCA) to analyze the variability. In order to validate the proposed approach, we experimented on two families of open-source product variants; Mobile Media and Health Watcher. The evaluation shows that our approach is able to identify the architectural variability and the dependencies as well.

The rest of this paper is organized as follows. Section 2 presents the background needed to understand our proposal. Then, in Section 3, we present the recovery process of SPLA. Section 4 presents the identification of architecture variability. Then, Section 5 presents the identification of dependencies among architectural-element variants. Experimental evaluation of our approach is discussed in section 6. Then, the related work is discussed in Section 7. Finally, concluding remarks and future directions are presented in section 8.

2   Background

2.1   Component-Based Architecture Recovery from Single Software: ROMANTIC Approach

In our previous work [9, 10], *ROMANTIC*[1] approach has been proposed to automatically recover a component-based architecture from the source code of an existing object-oriented software. Components are obtained by partitioning classes of the software. Thus each class is assigned to a unique subset forming a component. *ROMANTIC* is based on two main models. The first concerns the object-to-component mapping model which allows to link object-oriented concepts (e.g. package, class) to component-based ones (e.g. component, interface). A component consists of two parts; internal and external structures. The internal structure is implemented by a set of classes that have direct links only to classes that belong to the component itself. The external structure is implemented by the set of classes that have direct links to other components' classes. Classes that form the external structure of a component define the component interface. Fig. 1 shows the object-to-component mapping model. The second main model proposed in *ROMANTIC* is used to evaluate the quality of recovered architectures and their architectural-element. For example, the quality-model of recovered components is based on three characteristics; composability, autonomy and specificity. These refer respectively to the ability of the component to be composed without any modification, to the possibility to reuse the component in an autonomous way, and to the fact that the component implements a limited number of closed functionalities. Based on these models, *ROMANTIC* defines a fitness function applied in a hierarchical clustering algorithm [9, 10] as well as in search-based algorithms [11] to partition the object-oriented classes into groups, where each group represents a component. In this paper, *ROMANTIC* is used to recover the architecture of a single object oriented software product.

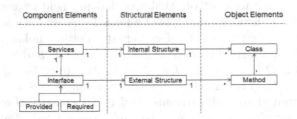

Fig. 1. Object-to-component mapping model

2.2   Formal Concept Analysis

Formal Concept Analysis (FCA) is a mathematical data analysis technique developed based on lattice theory [12]. It allows the analysis of the relationships

---

[1] *ROMANTIC*: Re-engineering of Object-oriented systeMs by Architecture extractioN and migraTIon to Component based ones.

between a set of objects described by a set of attributes. In this context, maximal groups of objects sharing the same attributes are called formal concepts. These are extracted and then hierarchically organized into a graph called a concept lattice. Each formal concept consists of two parts. The first allows the representation of the objects covered by the concepts called the extent of the concept. The second allows the representation of the set of attributes shared by the objects belonging to the extent. This is called the intent of the concept. Concepts can be linked through sub-concept and super-concept relationship [12] where the lattice defines a partially ordered structure. A concept A is a sub-concept of the super-concept B, if the extent of the concept B includes the extent of the concept A and the intent of the concept A includes the intent of the concept B.

Table 1. Formal context

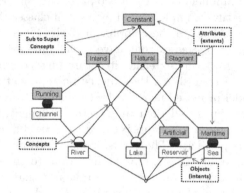

	Natural	Artificial	Stagnant	Running	Inland	Maritime	Constant
River	X			X	X		X
Sea	X	X				X	X
Reservoir		X	X		X		X
Channel				X	X		X
Lake	X		X		X		X

Fig. 2. Lattice of formal context in Table 1

The input of FCA is called a formal context. A formal context is defined as a triple $K = (O, A, R)$ where O refers to a set of objects, A refers to a set of attributes and R is a binary relation between objects and attributes. This binary relation indicates to a set of attributes that are held by each object (i.e. $R \subseteq OXA$). Table 1 shows an example of a formal context for a set of bodies of waters and their attributes. An X refers to that an object holds an attribute.

As stated before, a formal concept consists of extent E and intent I, with E a subset of objects O ($E \subseteq O$) and I a subset of attributes A ($I \subseteq A$). A pair of extent and intent (E, I) is considered a formal concept, if and only, if E consists of only objects that shared all attributes in I and I consists of only attributes that are shared by all objects in E. The pair ("river, lake", "inland, natural, constant") is an example of a formal concept of the formal context in Table 1. Fig. 2 shows the concept lattice of the formal context presented in Table 1.

3   Process of Recovering Architectural Variability

The goal of our approach is at recovering the architectural variability of a set of product variants by statically analyzing their object-oriented source code. This is obtained by identifying variability among architectures respectively recovered from each single product. We rely on *ROMANTIC* approach to extract the architecture of a single product. This constitutes the first step of the recovery process. Architecture variability is related to architectural-elements variability, i.e. component, connector and configuration variability. In our approach, we focus only on component and configuration variability[2]. Fig. 3 shows an example of architecture variability based on component and configuration variability. In this example, there are three product variants, where each one diverges in the set of component constituting its architecture as well as the links between the components. Component variability refers to the existence of many variants of one component. *CD Reader* and *CD Reader / Writer* represent variants of one component. We identify component variants based on the identification of components providing similar functionalities. This is the role of the second step of the recovery process. Configuration variability is represented in terms of presence/absence of components on the one hand (e.g. *Purchase Reminder*), and presence/absence of component-to-component links on the other hand (e.g. the link between *MP3 Decoder / Encoder* and *CD Reader / Writer*). We identify configuration variability based on both the identification of core (e.g. *Sound Source*) and optional components (e.g. *Purchase Reminder*) and links between these components. In addition, we capture the dependencies and constraints among components. This includes, for example, require constraints between optional components. We rely on FCA to identify these dependencies. These are mined in the fourth step of the recovery process. Fig. 4 shows these steps.

4   Identifying the Architecture Variability

The architecture variability is mainly materialized either through the existence of variants of the same architectural element (i.e. component variants) or through the configuration variability. In this section, we show how component variants and configuration variability are identified.

4.1   Identifying Component Variants

The selection of a component to be used in an architecture is based on its provided and required services. The provided services define the role of the component. However, other components may provide the same, or similar, core services. Each may also provide other specific services in addition to the core ones. Considering these components, either as completely different or as the same, does not allow the variability related to components to be captured. Thus, we consider them as component variants. We define component variants as a set of components providing the same core services and differ concerning few secondary ones. In Fig. 3, *MP3 Decoder* and *MP3 Decoder / Encoder* are component variants.

We identify component variants based on their similarity. Similar components are those sharing the majority of their classes and differing in relation to

---

[2] Most of architectural description languages do not consider connector as a first class concept.

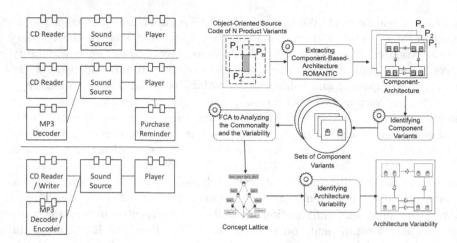

Fig. 3. An example of architecture variability

Fig. 4. The process of architectural variability recovery

some others. Components are identified as similar based on the strength of similarity links between their implementing classes. For this purpose, we use cosine similarity metric [13] where each component is considered as a text document composed of the names of its classes. We use a hierarchical clustering algorithm [13] to gather similar components into clusters. It starts by considering components as initial leaf nodes in a binary tree. Next, the two most similar nodes are grouped into a new one that forms their parent. This grouping process is repeated until all nodes are grouped into a binary tree. All nodes in this tree are considered as candidates to be selected as groups of similar components. To identify the best nodes, we use a depth first search algorithm. Starting from the tree root to find the cut-off points, we compare the similarity of the current node with its children. If the current node has a similarity value exceeding the average similarity value of its children, then the cut-off point is in the current node. Otherwise, the algorithm continues through its children. The results of this algorithm are clusters where each one is composed of a set of similar components that represent variants of one component.

4.2   Identifying Configuration Variants

The architectural configuration is defined based on the list of components composing the architecture, as well as the topology of the links existing between these components. Thus the configuration variability is related to these two aspects; the lists of core (mandatory) and optional components and the list of core and optional links between the selected components.

Identification of Component Variability: To identify mandatory and optional components, we use Formal Concept Analysis (FCA) to analyze architecture configurations. We present each software architecture as an object and each member component as an attribute in the formal context. In the concept lattice, common attributes are grouped into the root while the variable ones are hierarchically distributed among the non-root concepts.

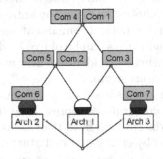

Fig. 5. A lattice example of similar configurations

Fig. 5 shows an example of a lattice for three similar architecture configurations. The common components (the core ones) are grouped together at the root concept of the lattice (the top). In Fig. 5 *Com1* and *Com4* are the core components present in the three architectures. By contrast, optional components are represented in all lattice concepts except the root. e.g., according to the lattice of Fig. 5, *Com2* and *Com5* present in *Arch1* and *Arch2* but not in *Arch3*.

Identification of Component-Link Variability: A component-link is defined as a connection between two components where each connection is the abstraction of a group of method invocation, access attribute or inheritance links between classes composing these components. In the context of configuration variability, a component may be linked with different sets of components. A component may have links with a set of components in one product, and it may have other links with a different set of components in another product. Thus the component-link variability is related to the component variability. This means that the identification of the link variability is based on the identified component variability. For instance, the existence of a link *A-B* is related to the selection of a component *A* and a component *B* in the architecture. Thus considering a core link (mandatory link) is based on the occurrence of the linked components, but not on the occurrence in the architecture of products. According to that, a core link is defined as a link occurring in the architecture configuration as well the linked components are selected. To identify the component-link variability, we proceed as follows. For each architectural component, we collect the set of components that are connected to it in each product. The intersection of the sets extracted from all the products determines all core links for the given component. The other links are optional ones.

5   Identifying Architecture Dependencies

The identification of component and component-link variability is not enough to define a valid architectural configuration. This also depends on the set of dependencies (i.e. constraints) that may exist between all the elements of the architecture. For instance, components providing antagonism functionalities have an exclude relationship. Furthermore, a component may need other components to perform its services. Dependencies can be of five kinds: alternative, OR, AND, require, and exclude dependencies. To identify them we rely on the same concept lattice generated in the previous section.

In the lattice, each node groups a set of components representing the intent and a set of architectural configurations representing the extent. The configurations are represented by paths starting from their concepts to the lattice concept root. The idea is that each object is generated starting from its node up going to the top. This is based on sub-concept to super-concept relationships (c.f. Section 2.2). This process generates a path for each object. A path contains an ordered list of nodes based on their hierarchical distribution; i.e. sub-concept to super-concept relationships). According to that, we propose extracting the dependencies between each pair of nodes as follows:

- **Required dependency.** This constraint refers to the obligation selection of a component to select another one; i.e. component B is required to select component A. Based on the generated lattice, we analyze all its nodes by identifying parent-to-child relation (i.e. top to down). Thus node A requires node B if node B appears before node A in the lattice, i.e., node A is a sub-concept of the super-concept corresponding to node B. In other words, to reach node A in the lattice, it is necessary to traverse node B. For example, if we consider lattice of the Fig. 5, $Com6$ requires $Com2$ and $Com5$ since $Com2$ and $Com5$ are traversed before $Com6$ in all paths including $Com6$ and linking root node to object nodes.
- **Exclude and alternative dependencies.** Exclude dependency refers to the antagonistic relationship; i.e. components A and B cannot occur in the same architecture. This relation is extracted by checking all paths linking root to all leaf nodes in the lattice. A node is excluded with respect to another node if they never appear together in any of the existing paths; i.e. there is no sub-concept to super-concept relationship between them. This means that there exists no object exists containing both nodes. For example, if we consider lattice of Fig. 5, $Com6$ and $Com7$ are exclusives since they never appear together in any of the lattice paths.
  Alternative dependency generalizes the exclude one by exclusively selecting only one component from a set of components. It can be identified based on the exclude dependencies. Indeed, a set of nodes in the lattice having each an exclude constraint with all other nodes forms an alternative situation.
- **AND dependency.** This is the bidirectional version of the REQUIRE constraint; i.e. component A requires component B and vice versa. More generally, the selection of one component among a set of components requires

the selection of all the other components. According to the built lattice, this relation is found when a group of components is grouped in the same concept node in the lattice; i.e. the whole node should be selected and not only a part of its components. For example if we consider lattice of the Fig. 5, *Com2* and *Com5* are concerned with an AND dependency.

- **OR dependency.** When some components are concerned by an OR dependency, this means that at least one of them should be selected; i.e. the configuration may contain any combination of the components. Thus, in the case of absence of other constraints any pair of components is concerned by an OR dependency. Thus pairs concerned by required, exclude, alternative, or AND dependencies are ignored as well as those concerned by transitive require constraints; e.g. *Com6* and *Com7* are ignored since they are exclusives. Algorithm 1 shows the procedure of identifying groups of OR dependency.

Input: all pairs (ap), require dependencies (rd), exclude dependencies (ed) and
  alternative dependencies (ad)
Output: sets of nodes having OR dependencies (orGroups)
OrDep = ap.exclusionPairs(rd, ed, ad);
OrDep = orDep.removeTransitiveRequire(rd);
ORPairsSharingNode = orDep.getPairsSharingNode();
for *each pairs p in ORPairsSharingNode* **do**
  if *otherNodes.getDependency() == require* **then**
    | orDep.removePair(childNode);
  else if *otherNodes.getDependency()= exclude || alternative* **then**
    | orDep.removeAllPairs(p);
end
orGroups = orDep.getpairssharingOrDep();
return *orGroups*

Algorithm 1. Identifying OR-Groups

6   Experimentation and Results

Our experimentation aims at showing how the proposed approach is applied to identify the architectural variability and validating the obtained results. To this end, we applied it on two case studies. We select two sets of product variants. These sets are Mobile Media[3] (MM) and Health Watcher[4] (HW). We select these products because they were used in many research papers aiming at addressing the problem of migrating product variants into a SPL. Our study considers 8 variants of MM and 10 variants of HW. MM variants manipulate music, video and photo on mobile phones. They are developed starting from the core implementation of MM. Then, the other features are added incrementally for each variant. HW variants are web-based applications that aim at managing health

---

[3] Available at: http://ptolemy.cs.iastate.edu/design-study/#mobilemedia
[4] Available at: http://ptolemy.cs.iastate.edu/design-study/#healthwatcher

records and customer complaints. The size of each variant of MM and HW, in terms of classes, is shown in Table 2. We utilize *ROMANTIC* approach [9] to extract architectural components from each variant independently. Then, the components derived from all variants are the input of the clustering algorithm to identify component variants. Next, we identify the architecture configurations of the products. These are used as a formal context to extract a concept lattice. Then, we extract the core (mandatory) and optional components as well as the dependencies among optional-component.

In order to evaluate the resulted architecture variability, we study the following research questions:

- **RQ1: Are the identified dependencies correct?** This research question goals at measuring the correctness of the identified component dependencies.
- **RQ2: What is the precision of the recovered architectural variability?** This research question focuses on measuring the precision of the resulting architecture variability. This is done by comparing it with a pre-existed architecture variability model.

Table 2. Size of MM variants and HW ones

Name	1	2	3	4	5	6	7	8	9	10	Avg.
MM	25	34	36	36	41	50	60	64	X	X	43.25
HW	115	120	132	134	136	140	144	148	160	167	136.9

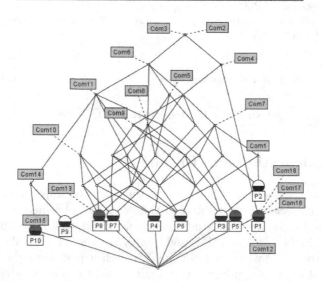

Fig. 6. The concept lattice of HW architecture configurations

6.1   Results

Table 3 shows the results of component extraction from each variant independently, in terms of the number of components, for each variant of MM and HW.

The results show that classes related to the same functionality are grouped into the same component. The difference in the numbers of the identified components in each variant has resulted from the fact that each variant has a different set of user's requirements. On average, a variant contains 6.25 and 7.7 main functionalities respectively for MM and HW.

Table 3. Comp. extraction results

Name	1	2	3	4	5	6	7	8	9	10	Avg.	Total
MM	3	5	5	5	7	7	9	9	X	X	6.25	50
HW	6	7	9	10	7	9	8	8	7	6	7.7	77

Table 4. Comp. variants identification

Name	NOCV	ANVC	MXCV	MNCV
MM	14	3.57	8	1
HW	18	4.72	10	1

Table 4 summarizes the results of component variants in terms of the number of components having variants (NOCV), the average number of variants of a component (ANVC), the maximum number of component variants (MXCV) and the minimum number of component variants (MNCS). The results show that there are many sets of components sharing the most of their classes. Each set of components mostly provides the same functionality. Thus, they represent variants of the same architectural component. Table 5 presents an instance of 6 component variants identified from HW, where X means that the corresponding class is a member in the variant. By analyzing these variants, it is clear that these components represent the same architectural component. In addition to that, we noticed that there are some component variants having the same set of classes in multiple product variants.

Table 5. Instance of 6 component variants

Class Name	Variant 1	Variant 2	Variant 3	Variant 4	Variant 5	Variant 6
BufferedReader	X	X	X	X	X	X
ComplaintRepositoryArray	X	X	X	X	X	X
ConcreteIterator	X	X	X	X	X	X
DiseaseRecord	X					
IIteratorRMITargetAdapter	X	X	X	X	X	X
IteratorRMITargetAdapter	X	X	X	X	X	X
DiseaseType		X				
InputStreamReader	X	X	X	X	X	X
Employee		X		X		
InvalidDateException			X	X	X	X
IteratorDsk	X	X	X	X	X	X
PrintWriter	X	X	X		X	X
ObjectNotValidException		X			X	X
RemoteException	X	X		X		
PrintStream			X		X	X
RepositoryException	X	X				
Statement	X	X	X	X	X	X
Throwable	X	X		X		
HWServlet					X	
Connection					X	X

The architecture configurations are identified based on the above results. Table 6 shows the configuration of MM variants, where X means that the component is a part of the product variants. The results show that the products are similar in their architectural configurations and differ considering other ones. The reason behind the similarity and the difference is the fact that these products are common in some of their user's requirements and variable in some others. These architecture configurations are used as a formal context to extract the concept lattice. We use the Concept Explorer[5] tool to generate the concept lattice. Due to limited space, we only give the concept lattice of HW (c.f. Fig. 6). In Table 7, the numbers of core (mandatory) and optional components are given for MM and HW. The results show that there are some components that represent the core architecture, while some others represent delta (optional) components.

Table 6. Arch. configuration for all MM variants

Variant No.	Com1	Com2	Com3	Com4	Com5	Com6	Com7	Com8	Com9	Com10	Com11	Com12	Com13	Com14
1	X		X		X									
2	X		X		X			X	X					
3	X		X		X			X	X					
4			X		X			X	X		X			
5	X		X		X			X	X		X	X		
6			X		X		X	X	X		X	X		
7		X		X	X		X	X	X	X	X	X		
8		X		X	X	X	X	X		X			X	X

Table 7. Mandatory and optional components

Product Name	MM	HW
Mandatory	1	2
Optional	13	16

The results of the identification of optional-component dependencies are given in Table 8 (*Com 5* is excluded since it is a mandatory component). For conciseness, the detailed dependencies among components are only shown for MM only. The dependencies are represented between all pairs of components in MM (where R= Require, E= Exclude, O= OR, RB = Required By, TR = Transitive Require, TRB = Transitive Require By, and A = AND). Table 9 shows a summary of MM and HW dependencies between all pairs of components. This includes the number of direct require constrains (NRC), the number of exclude ones (NE), the number of AND groups (NOA), and the number of OR groups (NO). Alternative constrains is represented as exclude ones. The results show that there are dependencies among components that help the architect to avoid creating invalid configuration. For instance, a design decision of AND components indicates that these components depend on each other, thus, they should be selected all together.

To the best our knowledge, there is no architecture description language supporting all kinds of the identified variability. The existing languages are mainly focused on modeling component variants, links and interfaces, while they do not support dependencies among components such as AND-group, OR-group, and require. Thus, on the first hand, we use some notation presented in [15] to represent the concept of component variants and links variability. On the other hand, we propose some notation inspired from feature modeling languages to model the

---

[5] Presentation of the Concept Explorer tool is available in [14].

Table 8. Component dependencies

	C1	C2	C3	C4	C6	C7	C8	C9	C10	C11	C12	C13	C14
Com1	X		R		E	E				O	E	E	E
Com2		X	E	A	RB	R	TR		A			RB	RB
Com3	RB	E	X	E	E		O		E			E	E
Com4		A	E	X	RB	R	TR		A			RB	RB
Com6	E	R	E	R	X	TR	TR	E	R	E	E	A	A
Com7	E	RB		RB	TRB	X	R	O	RB			TRB	TRB
Com8		TRB	O	TRB	TRB	RB	X	RB	TRB	TRB	TRB	TRB	TRB
Com9					E	O	R	X		RB	TRB	E	E
Com10		A	E	A	RB	R	TR		X			RB	RB
Com11	O				E		TR	R		X	RB	E	E
Com12	E				E		TR	TR		R	X	E	E
Com13	E	R	E	R	A	TR	TR	E	R	E	E	X	A
Com14	E	R	E	R	A	TR	TR	E	R	E	E	A	X

Table 9. Summarization of MM and HW dependencies

Name	NDR	NE	NA	NO
MM	17	20	6	3
HW	18	62	3	11

dependencies among components. For the purpose of understandability, we document the resulting components by assigning a name based on the most frequent tokens in their classes' names. Figure 7 shows the architectural variability model identified for MM variants, where the large boxes denote to design decisions (constraints). For instance, core architecture refers to components that should be selected to create any concrete product architecture. In MM, there is one core components manipulating the base controller of the product. This component has two variants. A group of *Multi Media Stream*, *Video Screen Controller*, and *Multi Screen Music* components represents an AND design decision.

RQ1: Are the Identified Dependencies Correct? The identification of component dependencies is based on the occurrence of components. e.g., if two components never selected to be included in a concrete product architecture, we consider that they hold an exclude relation. However, this method could provide correct or incorrect dependencies. To evaluate the accuracy of this method, we manually validate the identified dependencies. This is based on the functionalities provided by the components. For instance, we check if the component functionality requires the functionality of the required component and so on. The results show that 79% of the required dependencies are correct. As an example of a correct relation is that *SMS Controller* requires *Invalid Exception* as it performs an input/output operations. On the other hand, it seems that *Image Util* does not require *Image Album Vector Stream*. Also, 63% of the exclude constrains are correct. For AND and OR dependencies, we find that 88% of AND groups are correct, while 42% of OR groups are correct. Thus, the precision of identifying dependencies is 68% in average.

RQ2: What is the Precision of the Recovered Architectural Variability? In our case studies, MM is the only case study that has an available architecture model containing some variability information. In [16], the authors presented the aspect oriented architecture for MM variants. This contains information about which products had added components, as well as in which product a component implementation was changed (i.e. component variants). We manually compare both models to validate the resulting model. Fig. 8 shows

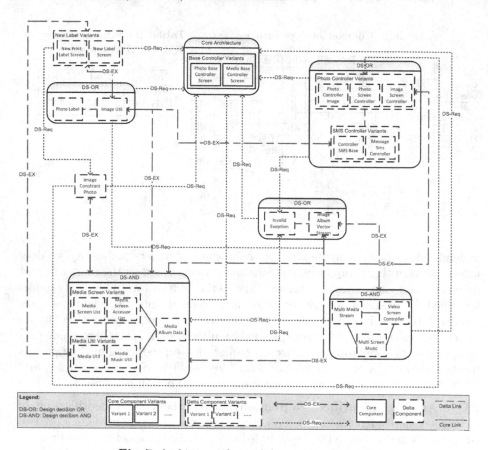

Fig. 7. Architectural variability model for MM

the comparison results in terms of the total number of components in the architecture model (TNOC), the number of components having variants (NCHV), the number of mapped components in the other model (NC), the number of unmapped components in the other model (NUMC), the number of optional components (NOC) and the number of mandatory ones (NOM). The results show that there are some variation between the results of our approach and the pre-existed model. The reason behind this variation is the idea of compositional components. For instance, our approach identifies only one core component compared to 4 core components in the other model. Our approach grouped all classes related to the controller components together in one core components. On the other hand, the other model divided the controller component into *Abstract Controller*, *Album Data*, *Media Controller*, and *Photo View Controller* components. In addition, the component related to handling exceptions is not mentioned in the pre-existed model at all.

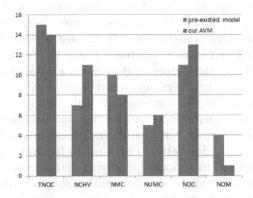

Fig. 8. The results of the MM validation

7 Related Work

In this section, we discuss the contributions that have been proposed in two research directions; recovering the software architecture of a set of product variants and variability management.

In [7], an approach aiming at recovering SPLA was presented. It identifies component variants based on the detection of cloned code among the products. However, the limitation of this approach is that it is a semi-automated, while our approach is fully automated. Also, it does not identify dependencies among the components. In [8], the authors presented an approach to reconstruct Home Service Robots (HSR) products into a SPL. Although this approach identifies some architectural variability, but it has some limitation compared to our approach. For instance, it is specialized on the domain of HSR as the authors classified, at earlier step, the architectural units based on three categories related to HSR. These categories guide the identification process. In addition, the use of feature modeling language (hierarchical trees) to realize the identified variability is not efficient as it is not able to represent the configuration of architectures. Domain knowledge plays the main role to identify the architecture of each single product and the dependencies among components. In some cases, domain knowledge is not always available. The authors in [6] proposed an approach to reverse engineering architectural feature model. This is based on the software architect's knowledge, the architecture dependencies, and the feature model that is extracted based on a reverse engineering approach presented in [5]. The idea, in [6], is to take the software architect's variability point of view in the extracted feature model (i.e. still at the requirement level); this is why it is named architecture feature model. However, the major limitations of this approach are firstly that the software architect is not available in most cases of legacy software, and secondly that the architecture dependencies are generally missing as well. In [5], the authors proposed an approach to extract the feature model. The input of the extraction process is feature names, feature descriptions and dependencies among features. Based on this information, they recover ontological constraints (e.g. feature groups) and cross tree constrains. A strong assumption behind this approach is that feature names, feature descriptions, and dependencies among features are available. In [17], the authors use FCA to generate a feature model. The input of their approach is a set of feature configurations. However, the extraction of the feature model elements is based on NP-hard problems (e.g. set cover to identify or groups). Furthermore, architecture variability is not taken into account in this approach. In [18], an approach was presented to visually analyze the distribution of variability and commonality among the source code of product variants. The analysis includes multi-level of abstractions (e.g. line of code, method, class, etc.). This aims to facilitate the interpretation of variability distribution, to support identifying reusable entities. In [19], the authors presented an approach to extract reusable software components from a set of similar software products. This is based on identifying similarity between components identified independently from each software. This approach can be related only to the first step of our approach.

8   Conclusion

In SPLA, the variability is mainly represented in terms of components and configurations. In the case of migrating product variants to a SPL, identifying the architecture variability among the product variants is necessary to facilitate the software architect's tasks. Thus, in this paper, we proposed an approach to recover the architecture variability of a set of product variants. The recovered variability includes mandatory and optional components, the dependencies among components (e.g. require, etc.), the variability of component-links, and component variants. We rely on FCA to analyze the variability. Then, we propose two heuristics. The former is to identify the architecture variability. The latter is to identify the architecture dependencies. The proposed approach is validated through two sets of product variants derived from Mobile Media and Health Watcher. The results show that our approach is able to identify the architectural variability and the dependencies as well.

There are three aspects to be considered regarding the hypothesis of our approach. Firstly, we identify component variants based on the similarity between the name of classes composing the components, i.e., classes that have the same name should have the same implementation. While in some situations, components may have very similar set of classes, but they are completely unrelated. Secondly, dependencies among components are identified based on component occurrences in the product architectures. Thus, the identified dependencies maybe correct or incorrect. Finally, the input of our approach is the components independently identified form each product variants using *ROMANTIC* approach. Thus. the accuracy of the obtained variability depends on the accuracy of *ROMANTIC* approach.

Our future research will focus on migrating product variants into component based software product line, the mapping between the requirements' variability (i.e. features) and the architectures' variability, and mapping between components' variability and component-links' variability.

References

1. Clements, P., Northrop, L.: Software product lines: practices and patterns. Addison-Wesley, Reading (2002)
2. Pohl, K., Böckle, G., Van Der Linden, F.: Software product line engineering. Springer, Heidelberg (2005)
3. Tan, L., Lin, Y., Ye, H.: Quality-oriented software product line architecture design. Journal of Software Engineering & Applications 5(7), 472–476 (2012)
4. Rubin, J., Chechik, M.: Locating distinguishing features using diff sets. In: IEEE/ACM 27th Inter. Conf. on ASE, pp. 242–245 (2012)
5. She, S., Lotufo, R., Berger, T., Wasowski, A., Czarnecki, K.: Reverse engineering feature models. In: Proc. of 33rd ICSE, pp. 461–470 (2011)
6. Acher, M., Cleve, A., Collet, P., Merle, P., Duchien, L., Lahire, P.: Reverse engineering architectural feature models. In: Crnkovic, I., Gruhn, V., Book, M. (eds.) ECSA 2011. LNCS, vol. 6903, pp. 220–235. Springer, Heidelberg (2011)
7. Koschke, R., Frenzel, P., Breu, A.P., Angstmann, K.: Extending the reflexion method for consolidating software variants into product lines. Software Quality Journal 17(4), 331–366 (2009)
8. Kang, K.C., Kim, M., Lee, J.J., Kim, B.-K.: Feature-oriented re-engineering of legacy systems into product line assets - a case study. In: Obbink, H., Pohl, K. (eds.) SPLC 2005. LNCS, vol. 3714, pp. 45–56. Springer, Heidelberg (2005)
9. Kebir, S., Seriai, A.D., Chardigny, S., Chaoui, A.: Quality-centric approach for software component identification from object-oriented code. In: Proc. of WICSA/ECSA, pp. 181–190 (2012)
10. Chardigny, S., Seriai, A., Oussalah, M., Tamzalit, D.: Extraction of component based architecture from object-oriented systems. In: Proc. of 7th WICSA, pp. 285–288 (2008)
11. Chardigny, S., Seriai, A., Oussalah, M., Tamzalit, D.: Search-based extraction of component-based architecture from object-oriented systems. In: Morrison, R., Balasubramaniam, D., Falkner, K. (eds.) ECSA 2008. LNCS, vol. 5292, pp. 322–325. Springer, Heidelberg (2008)
12. Ganter, B., Wille, R.: Formal concept analysis. Wissenschaftliche Zeitschrift-Technischen Universitat Dresden 47, 8–13 (1996)
13. Han, J., Kamber, M., Pei, J.: Data mining: concepts and techniques. Morgan Kaufmann (2006)
14. Yevtushenko, A.S.: System of data analysis "concept explorer". In: Proc. of the 7th National Conf. on Artificial Intelligence (KII), vol. 79, pp. 127–134 (2000) (in Russian)
15. Hendrickson, S.A., van der Hoek, A.: Modeling product line architectures through change sets and relationships. In: Proc. of the 29th ICSE, pp. 189–198 (2007)
16. Figueiredo, E., Cacho, N., Sant'Anna, C., Monteiro, M., Kulesza, U., Garcia, A., Soares, S., Ferrari, F., Khan, S., et al.: Evolving software product lines with aspects. In: Proc. of 30th ICSE, pp. 261–270 (2008)
17. Ryssel, U., Ploennigs, J., Kabitzsch, K.: Extraction of feature models from formal contexts. In: Proc. of 15th SPLC, pp. 1–4 (2011)
18. Duszynski, S., Knodel, J., Becker, M.: Analyzing the source code of multiple software variants for reuse potential. In: Proc. of WCRE, pp. 303–307 (2011)
19. Shatnawi, A., Seriai, A.D.: Mining reusable software components from objectoriented source code of a set of similar software. In: IEEE 14th Inter. Conf. on Information Reuse and Integration (IRI), pp. 193–200 (2013)

A Feature-Similarity Model
for Product Line Engineering

Hermann Kaindl[1] and Mike Mannion[2]

[1] Institute of Computer Technology, Vienna University of Technology, Vienna, Austria
`kaindl@ict.tuwien.ac.at`
[2] Executive Group, Glasgow Caledonian University, Glasgow, UK
`m.a.g.mannion@gcu.ac.uk`

Abstract. Search, retrieval and comparison of products in a product line are common tasks during product line evolution. Feature modeling approaches do not easily support these tasks. This vision paper sets out a proposal for a *feature-similarity model* in which similarity metrics as used for example in *case-based reasoning* (CBR) are integrated with feature models. We describe potential applications for Product Line Scoping, Domain Engineering and Application Engineering.

Keywords: Product line engineering, feature-based representation, case-based reasoning, similarity metric, feature-similarity model.

1 Introduction

Software Product Line Engineering (SPLE) consists of: Product Line Scoping, Domain Engineering and Application Engineering (though in some frameworks [1] Product Line Scoping and Domain Engineering are both considered a part of a single core asset development activity). During these activities, we are interested in comparing the similarity of:

- a target product specification against existing product specifications;
- two or more existing product specifications against each other;
- how close an existing product matches the target market.

The information structure and content of feature models (regardless of notation) does not readily lend itself to compare similarity. Understanding what features are similar across different products, or what products are similar to other products, becomes very difficult as a product line evolves into tens, hundreds, maybe even thousands of products each with many features.

Case-based reasoning (CBR) is a development approach in which *software cases* are stored in a repository and new product development involves retrieving the most similar previous case(s) to the problem to be solved and then adapting it (them). Similarity matching, e.g. [2], is achieved by comparing some combination of *surface* features i.e. those provided as part of its description, *derived* features (obtained from a

I. Schaefer and I. Stamelos (Eds.): ICSR 2015, LNCS 8919, pp. 34–41, 2014.

product's description by inference based on domain knowledge) and *structural* features (represented by complex structures such as graphs or first-order terms). An overall similarity measure is computed from the weighted similarity measures of different elements. Efficient implementations for commonly used similarity metrics are readily available, so that the computational effort for search and retrieval of similar products has little impact on the efficiency of this approach. The key issue is the (manual) effort for adapting similar cases found and retrieved.

This vision paper sets out a proposal for a *feature-similarity model* in which similarity metrics as used in *case-based reasoning* (CBR), *information retrieval* or *service discovery* are integrated with feature models. We describe potential applications for Product Line Scoping, Domain Engineering and Application Engineering.

2   Related Work

Much work on feature models (see [3]) has focused on modelling representations and traversal algorithms that lend themselves to automation, and there has been little work on the relationships between product line feature models and similarity metrics.

The ReDSeeDS project (http://www.redseeds.eu) developed a specific similarity metric including textual, semantic and graph-based components [4]. Requirements *representations* are compared (e.g. requirements specifications or models) rather than requirements [5]. Reuse can be based on a *partial* requirements specification rather than a "complete" requirements specification [6]. The specification of new requirements can be facilitated by reusing related requirements from a retrieved software product, and the implementation information (models and code) of (one of) similar problems can be taken for reuse and adapted to the newly specified requirements. There are well-defined reuse processes, tightly connected with tool support (in parts) [7].

Similarity-based *(Web) service discovery* and *(Web) service retrieval* are also based on similarity metrics, see e.g. [8, 9]. *(Web) service matchmaking* uses additional heuristics [10], which may be adopted for whole software cases, and *semantic* service annotations and the use of ontologies allow for metrics apart from those based on text similarity [11]. Some approaches for an automated construction of feature models, based on similarity metrics, have been proposed [12, 13].

3   Contrasting SPLE and CBR

SPLE and CBR both support software product line engineering but address it differently. Table 1 summarizes these differences. In SPLE, the premise underlying feature model construction is that the rigour and consistency of the model structure can be used to derive new products from existing product elements. Model construction and maintenance costs (structure and content) are large but significantly reduce the costs of new product development and thus have large benefits for *reuse*. In CBR, the premise is that each product is constructed by retrieving and adapting similar cases already built. Product description construction costs are small whilst the cost of adapting an existing case can vary. So, SPLE and CBR have differences in the costs of making software assets *reusable* and the benefits for *reusing* them. More details on this comparison can be found in [14].

Table 1. Costs vs. Benefits

	SPLE	CBR
Costs of Making *Reusable*	Substantial	Negligible
Benefits for *Reuse*	Facilitates automated product derivation	Facilitates finding similar cases for reuse

4   A Feature-Similarity Model

A *feature-similarity model* combines a feature model for managing and deriving new products and provides similarity values for several purposes. Figure 1 shows a small feature model for a mobile phone in which the *ability to make a call* and the *ability to display* are mandatory features. To make a call there are one or more alternatives and the display can be in black and white or in colour. Figure 1 also shows four products that contain different combinations of these features, and whilst the model shows only examples of functional features, it can be extended to include non-functional features.

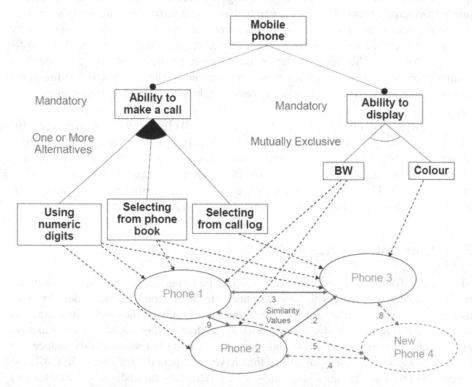

Fig. 1. Integrated Model of a Mobile Phone Worked Example

The scores attached to the bidirectional links between the ellipses signify similarity scores between products e.g. Phone 1 has 2 features for making a call, using numeric digits or from a phone book, and a black and white display. Phone 2 has one way of making a call, using numeric digits, and a black and white (BW) display. Phone 3 has three ways of making a call and has a colour display. Intuitively Phone 1 and Phone 2 are more similar to each other than Phone 1 and Phone 3, or Phone 2 and Phone 3. This is played out in the similarity values Phone 1/Phone 2 (.9), Phone 1/Phone 3 (.3), Phone 2/Phone3 (.2). *New Phone 4* is not yet fully specified, but similarity scores compared to the other phones can be determined (cf. [5]) independently of whether this new product is derived from the given feature model or not.

The solid lines of the (standard) feature model are explicit, while the bidirectional links between the product ellipses are implicit i.e. they are computed on demand, not necessarily stored, especially not upfront. The dotted lines to the product ellipses should be stored, to enhance traceability during product derivation from the feature model thus clarifying which features are in which product.

A *feature-similarity* model (i) combines features and similarities (ii) provides direct similarity values between *features* (iii) facilitates comparing *feature combinations* in different products) (iv) facilitates comparing *entire product specifications*. The added value of an integrated model is the influence it will have during feature model construction on an engineer's deeper thinking about the extent to which one product is different to another, particularly when the overall similarity differences are small, why that is, and whether it is necessary or not. Each product line specification becomes a *searchable* asset and the similarity metrics enhance the search function.

The construction process for a feature-similarity model is (i) construct a feature model (ii) allocate features to products (iii) calculate similarity values between features (iv) calculate similarity values between specific feature combinations in different product specifications (v) calculate similarity values between entire product specifications. In practice these steps might be used iteratively to help with the construction of a product line to ensure that derivable products are sufficiently distinctive.

4.1   Product Line Scoping

Product Line Scoping is the process of identifying and bounding capabilities (products, features) and areas (subdomains, existing assets) of the product line where investment into reuse is economically useful and beneficial to product development [15]. The output is a scope definition, which can be seen as part of the specification the product line engineering project must eventually satisfy.

A feature-similarity model for product line scoping will focus on the features that represent the distinguishing characteristics of the product line, which are important for the market that is being targeted and which represent the product line boundary. That information will come from a variety of sources e.g. industry forecasts, sales and marketing intelligence, customer feedback, technology advances. Feature description detail and the complexity of the corresponding feature model structure will depend on the niche of the target market. For example in the fashion mobile phone market, the emphasis is on the shape, size and colour of the casing to reflect the values of a fashion brand name, rather than the phone's functionality (often an existing model with minor modifications). By calculating the similarity value of the casing feature compared to a new target casing feature (step (iii) in the process above) we can inform the judgment about whether the product should be in the product line or not and how it might be best positioned in a market where look-and-feel govern distinctiveness.

When the number of target market characteristics and the number of products is small, product line scoping is tractable without much need for tool support. When the size or the level of complexity significantly increase, an automated similarity matching tool can become very valuable. Whilst scoping is normally an activity undertaken at the start of product line development it should continue as a product line evolves.

4.2 Domain Engineering

Domain Engineering encompasses domain requirements definition, domain analysis, domain design, domain implementation. Our focus here is domain requirements definition. Finding domain requirements can be difficult because existing requirements specifications (where they exist) can be written in different ways. A tool implementing a feature-similarity model (step (v)) can provide some support for identifying similarity between concepts across requirements specifications.

A feature-similarity model for Domain Engineering sets out all the features of the product line model. Adding new variability to an existing product line model can be difficult, and may not be required if there is already an existing alternative that seems close enough. Finding this alternative quickly in a large model can be very difficult and time-consuming. Making a judgment about the level of similarity of an existing alternative can help with making a commercial judgment on whether to proceed or not with including a new alternative. For example mobile phone product lines are becoming increasingly feature-rich and complex: the number of different ways of making a call is rapidly increasing beyond those set out in Figure 1. The ability to scan a number from a Quick Response code and the ability to scan a number from a jpeg image is similar. However if one of these alternatives is already available then a decision may be made not to include the other. Here we are calculating the similarity value of two alternative features (step (iii)), such as different ways of making a phone call. In practice it is highly unlikely that this approach would be adopted for all alternatives across all features, but rather, effort will be targeted on features that are valued by the customer but expensive to produce, and similar cheaper alternatives are available.

Feature-based SPLE most often lacks explicit representation of *non-functional* characteristics (e.g. performance, security, safety). In CBR, specific (text) searches based on similarity metrics can be an effective approach to uncovering such *cross-cutting concerns*.

4.3 Application Engineering

Application Engineering is the construction of a new product drawing on the assets that were developed during Domain Engineering. If a new product cannot be derived from a given product line model then often the model needs to be adapted so that derivation can follow a defined process. Exceptionally, if the "new" features required are not going to be required in any other product, they can be added solely to the new product, and the product line model is not adapted. A feature-similarity model for Application Engineering sets out the features of the product line model that have been derived, through a selection process, for the new product.

In large-scale product lines a challenge is to know whether a new product being derived is similar to an existing one. The overall difference can be small but for a particular feature or feature combination it can be significant. Knowing the degrees of similarity can help with commercial judgments e.g. whether to introduce a new product into the market, use an existing product, or remove a product. Suppose there is a mobile phone product line targeted at teenagers, where the feature focus is the ability to make a call, the ability to display, the ability to take pictures and the ability to play music but the product line manager has decided to add a multi-person video-conferencing feature to the feature model. It will be sensible to know if this combination of features exists already in a different product line. By calculating the similarity value of the entire product specification (step (v)) against phones targeted at small-to-medium business enterprises (SMEs) that have all of these features, and by calculating the similarity values of a feature combination (step (iv)) of playing music and making multi-person video conference calls, we may discover that in the product line targeted at SMEs the phone we want already exists, albeit that the quality of the ability to play music is a little lower than desired but the quality of the multi-person video-conference facility is a little higher than desired.

In practice, there may not always be enough time for adapting a product line model so that the product derivation can take place, or there is insufficient time to complete the detailed selection process from the model. Then, the most similar products may be looked up to see whether the new product may be adapted directly based on them (so one attribute of a search tool for Application Engineering is to enable search by similarity threshold either for individual features and/or for entire products). In effect, this can lead to CBR reuse instead of working with feature models.

5   Discussion and Open-ended Questions

We do not prescribe here which set of specific similarity metrics to be used or how those metrics should be computed. Commonly-used general-purpose similarity metrics could be enhanced by other approaches e.g. it is possible to indicate whether a feature is a distinguishing characteristic of a product (e.g. display size) or not (e.g. number of default screen savers). We can distinguish between *alignable* differences and *non-alignable* differences [16] where alignable differences have the larger impact on people's judgments of similarity. Electronic Tablets and Mobile Phones have memory, processing power and a display (albeit of different sizes) which are recognized as *alignable* differences because they are characteristics defining computers. However, Mobile Phones provide the ability to make a telephone call without accessing the Internet, which Electronic Tablets usually do not, making this a non-alignable difference.

Placing a numerical value on the significance of alignable and non-alignable differences could be factored into the overall similarity metric.

Another approach is structural similarity i.e. a syntactic approach to matching normally based on the structure of a feature model. For example products having mutually exclusive features such as BW and colour display, respectively, e.g. *Phone 2* and *Phone 3*, may be considered less similar than products with the same feature, such as BW, e.g. *Phone 1* and *Phone 2*. Mutually exclusive features will make more of a difference in this regard than having one more feature of a kind where all the others are shared, e.g. *Phone 1* can make a call from a phone book, while *Phone 2* cannot.

We envisage that such similarity metrics of a feature-similarity model may also serve as objective functions for automated search in the space of systems defined by its feature model. Depending on what is to be optimised in terms of similarity, these may serve as cost functions or utility functions, respectively. Such approaches would fit into *search-based software engineering*, see [17].

A set of open ended questions includes:

- What are the thresholds for "similar" and for "different"?
- Which combination of similarity approaches might be suitable and when?
- What similarity metrics are worth computing and how should they be calculated ?
- How can similarity metrics be factored into existing process models for Product Line Scoping, Domain Engineering, and Application Engineering?

The deployment of similarity metrics for SPLE requires a degree of caution and prudence as with the use of any other software development metrics. Metrics provide a data reference point and will best serve managers and engineers when they are used in conjunction with data from other reference points. Be clear on what you are using the metric for, get general agreement in the organization on which metrics to use, and focus on only a few metrics – less is more.

6   Conclusion

A feature model does not facilitate search, retrieval or comparison of products in a product line, common tasks during product line evolution. To address this, we have set out ideas for enhancing feature models with similarity metrics in a new feature-similarity model. However we recognize that whatever metrics are used there will always be a need to map these numerical values on to an organisation's collective conceptual understanding of what similar and difference means in each context in which the metrics are being used.

References

1. A Framework for Software Product Line Practice, Version 5.0, http://www.sei.cmu.edu/productlines/frame_report (last accessed October 6, 2014)

2. Cover, T.M., Hart, P.E.: Nearest Neighbour Pattern Classification. IEEE Trans. on Information Theory 13, 21–27 (1967)
3. Benavides, D., Felfernig, A., Galindo, J.A., Reinfrank, F.: Automated Analysis in Feature Modelling and Product Configuration. In: Favaro, J., Morisio, M. (eds.) ICSR 2013. LNCS, vol. 7925, pp. 160–175. Springer, Heidelberg (2013)
4. Bildhauer, D., Horn, T., Ebert, J.: Similarity-driven software reuse. In: Proceedings of CVSM 2009, pp. 31–36. IEEE (2010)
5. Kaindl, H., Svetinovic, D.: On confusion between requirements and their representations. Requirements Engineering 15, 307–311 (2010)
6. Kaindl, H., Smialek, M., Nowakowski, W.: Case-based Reuse with Partial Requirements Specifications. In: 18th IEEE International Requirements Engineering Conference (RE 2010), pp. 399–400 (2010)
7. Kaindl, H., Falb, J., Melbinger, S., Bruckmayer, T.: An Approach to Method-Tool Coupling for Software Development. In: Fifth International Conference on Software Engineering Advances (ICSEA 2010), pp. 101–106. IEEE (2010)
8. Botelho, L., Fernández, A., Fires, B., Klusch, M., Pereira, L., Santos, T., Pais, P., Vasirani, M.: Service Discovery. In: Schumacher, M., Helin, H., Schuldt, H. (eds.) CASCOM: Intelligent Service Coordination in the Semantic Web, ch. 10, pp. 205–234. Birkhäuser, Basel (2008)
9. Czyszczoń, A., Zgrzywa, A.: The MapReduce Approach to Web Service Retrieval. In: Bǎdicǎ, C., Nguyen, N.T., Brezovan, M. (eds.) ICCCI 2013. LNCS, vol. 8083, pp. 517–526. Springer, Heidelberg (2013)
10. Klusch, M.: Semantic Web Service Coordination. In: Schumacher, M., Helin, H., Schuldt, H. (eds.) CASCOM: Intelligent Service Coordination in the Semantic Web, ch. 4, pp. 59–104. Birkhäuser, Basel (2008)
11. Becker, J., Oliver Müller, O., Woditsch, M.: An Ontology-Based Natural Language Service Discovery Engine – Design and Experimental Evaluation. In: 18th European Conference on Information Systems (ECIS 2010) (2010)
12. Itzik, N., Reinhartz-Berger, I.: Generating Feature Models from Requirements: Structural vs. Functional Perspectives. In: REVE 2014. SPLC Proceedings – Volume 2: Workshops, Demonstrations, and Tools, pp. 44–51 (2014)
13. Weston, N., Chitchyan, R., Rashid, A.: A framework for constructing semantically composable feature models from natural language requirements. In: 13th International Software Product Line Conference (SPLC 2009), pp. 211–220 (2009)
14. Mannion, M., Kaindl, H.: Using Similarity Metrics for Mining Variability from Software Metrics. In: REVE 2014. SPLC Proceedings – Volume 2: Workshops, Demonstrations, and Tools, pp. 32–35 (2014)
15. John, I., Eisenbarth, M.: A Decade of Scoping: A Survey. In: 13th International Software Product Line Conference (SPLC 2009), pp. 31–40 (2009)
16. McGill, A.L.: Alignable and nonalignable differences in causal explanations. Memory Cognition 30(3), 456–468 (2002)
17. Harman, M., Jia, Y., Krinke, J., Langdon, W., Petke, J., Zhang, Y.: Keynote: Search based software engineering for software product line engineering: a survey and directions for future work. In: 18th International Software Product Line Conference (SPLC 2014), pp. 5–18 (2014)

Evaluating Lehman's Laws of Software Evolution within Software Product Lines: A Preliminary Empirical Study

Raphael Pereira de Oliveira[1,2], Eduardo Santana de Almeida[1],
and Gecynalda Soares da Silva Gomes[1]

[1] Federal University of Bahia, Campus Ondina
Av. Adhemar de Barros, s/n, 40.170-110, Salvador - Bahia, Brazil
[2] Federal Institute of Sergipe, Campus Estância
Rua Presidente João Café Filho, S/N, Estância - Sergipe, Brazil
{raphaeloliveira,esa}@dcc.ufba.br, gecynalda@yahoo.com

Abstract. The evolution of a single system is a task where we deal with the modification of a single product. Lehman's laws of software evolution were broadly evaluated within this type of systems and the results shown that these single systems evolve according to his stated laws over time. However, when dealing with Software Product Lines (SPL), we need to deal with the modification of several products which include common, variable and product specific assets. Because of the several assets within SPL, each stated law may have a different behavior for each asset kind. Nonetheless, we do not know if the stated laws are still valid for SPL since they were not yet evaluated in this context. Thus, this paper details an empirical investigation where four of the Lehman's Laws (LL) of Software Evolution were used in an SPL industrial project to understand how the SPL assets evolve over time. This project relates to an application in the medical domain developed in a medium-size company in Brazil. It contains 45 modules and a total of 70.652 bug requests in the tracking system, gathered along the past 10 years. We employed two techniques - the KPSS Test and linear regression analysis, to assess the relationship between LL and SPL assets. Finally, results showed that three laws were supported based on the data employed (continuous change, increasing complexity, and declining quality). The other law (continuing growth) was partly supported, depending on the SPL evaluated asset (common, variable or product-specific).

Keywords: Software Product Lines, Software Evolution, Lehman's Laws of Software Evolution, Empirical Study.

1 Introduction

Software evolution is a very important activity where the software must have the ability to adapt according to the environment or user needs, to keep its satisfactory performance, [1] given that if a system does not support changes, it will gradually lapse into uselessness [2].

I. Schaefer and I. Stamelos (Eds.): ICSR 2015, LNCS 8919, pp. 42–57, 2014.

Back in the 1970s, Meir Lehman started to formulate his laws of software evolution, after realizing the need for software systems to evolve. These laws, shown in Table 1, stressed that a system needed to evolve due to its requirement to *operate in or address a problem or activity in the real world*, what Lehman called *E-type Software*.

According to Barry et al. [3], these laws can be ordered into three broad categories: (i) laws about the evolution of software system characteristics; (ii) laws referring to organizational or economic constraints on software evolution; and (iii) meta-laws of software evolution. However, the laws were evaluated in the context of single systems.

Table 1. Lehman's Laws of Software Evolution [4]

Software Evolution Laws	Description
Evolution of Software System Characteristics (ESSC)	
(1974) Continuous change	E-type systems must be continually adapted else they become progressively less satisfactory.
(1980) Continuing growth	The functional content of an E-type system must be continually increased to maintain user satisfaction with the system over its lifetime.
(1974) Increasing complexity	As an E-type system evolves, its complexity increases unless work is done to maintain or reduce it.
(1996) Declining quality	Stakeholders will perceive an E-type system to have declining quality unless it is rigorously maintained and adapted to its changing operational environment.
Organizational/Economic Resource Constraints (OERC)	
(1980) Conservation of familiarity	During the active life of an evolving E-type system, the average content of successive releases is invariant.
(1980) Conservation of organizational stability	The average effective global activity rate in an evolving E-type system is invariant over a products lifetime.
Meta-Laws (ML)	
(1974) Self regulation	The evolution process of E-type systems is self regulating, with a distribution of product and process measures over time that is close to normal.
(1996) Feedback System	The evolution processes in E-type systems constitute multi-level, multi-loop, multi-agent feedback systems and must be treated as such to achieve significant improvement over any reasonable baseline.

In contrast to single systems, a Software Product Line (SPL) represents a set of systems sharing a common, managed set of features that satisfy the specific needs of a particular market or mission. The products which compose an SPL are developed from a common set of core assets in a prescribed way [5], aiming to achieve benefits such as large scale reuse, reduced time to market, improved quality and minimized costs, large-scale productivity, maintain market presence, enable mass customization, and so on [5] [6].

In order to achieve the above mentioned benefits, an SPL's evolution needs special attention, since the sources of SPL changes can be targeted to the entire product line (affecting common assets), targeted to some products (affecting variable assets), or targeted to an individual product (affecting product-specific assets) [7] [8] [9].

In this study, our objective is to examine whether Lehman's Laws (LL) are reflected in the development of SPLs, where common, variable and product specific assets are built. The hypothesis we put forward is that there is a relationship between LL of Software Evolution and the software evolution in SPL environments. In this context, in order to understand whether there is a relationship between the LL of software evolution and the SPL evolution process, we carried out an empirical investigation in an industrial software product line project. As a preliminary study, we selected the first group of laws (Evolution of Software System Characteristics - ESSC, which includes the Continuous change, Continuing growth, Increasing complexity and Declining quality laws) to perform our evaluation. We evaluated each one of the laws from the ESSC group for common, variable and product-specific assets in the context of an industrial SPL. To the best of our knowledge, this is the first study stating that most of evaluated LL of software evolution can be applied in the context of SPL. Thus, results of this study can help in understanding and improving SPL evolution process.

The remainder of this paper is organized as follows: Section 2 presents related work and uses it as context to position this work. Section 3 describes the empirical investigation, followed by the discussion of key findings and contributions from our preliminary empirical study in Section 4. Finally, Section 5 presents the conclusions and future directions.

2   Related Work

Since the publication of Lehman's work on software changes, other researchers have investigated his laws within the context of open source and industrial projects. Israeli and Feitelson [10] examined Lehman's Laws (LL) within the context of the Linux kernel. They selected the Linux kernel because of its 14 years data recording history about the system's evolution, which includes 810 versions. Only two out of the eight laws were not supported in this experiment (i.e., *self-regulation* and *feedback system*). Barry et al. [3] also investigated LL; however within the context of industrial projects. They proposed some metrics as dependent variables, which were also related to six LL (the *self-regulation* and the *feedback system* laws were not investigated in this study). We have adapted some of the metrics proposed by Barry et al. [3] to support and evaluate the LL in an industrial SPL project.

Lotufo et al. [11] studied the evolution of the Linux kernel variability model. This model is responsible for describing features and configurations from the Linux kernel. They found that the feature model grows together with the code. Besides the growth of the number of features, the complexity still remains the same. Most of the evolution activity is related to adding new features and there is a necessity for tool support, mainly regarding constraints. Their results showed that evolving large variability models is feasible and does not necessarily deteriorate the quality of the model. Godfrey and Tu [12] found a similar conclusion after studying the evolution of the Linux kernel. They explored the evolution of the Linux kernel both at the system level and within the major subsystems and found out that the Linux has been growing in a super-linear rate over the years. However, as will be detailed later, within the context of our study we found a different behavior. The complexity within the assets has grown over the years and the quality has decreased. It is important to notice that the number of maintainers in a private context is smaller compared to maintainers of the Linux kernel and also the time-to-market pressure in a private context influences the overall software product quality.

Xie et al. [13] also investigated LL by studying 7 open source applications written in C and several laws were confirmed in their experiment. Their analysis covered 050 releases in total and sum 69 years of software evolution including the 7 applications. According to the authors, the definition of the *increasing complexity* and *declining quality* laws may lead to misinterpretations, and the laws could be supported or rejected, depending on the interpretation of the law definition. In our study, to avoid this misinterpretation, we consider that the increasing of complexity and the declining of quality must happen to support these laws.

The investigations assessing LL available in the literature are related to single systems and not to SPL. In our empirical study, we evaluated four laws of software evolution (ESSC group of laws) in an SPL industrial project, which can be considered as a first work in this direction. This project has a long history of data with more than 10 years of evolution records, as many of the related work. Nevertheless, it is a private system developed using the SPL paradigm, allowing the evaluation of the laws for the common, variable and product-specific assets.

3   Empirical Study

This empirical study focuses on investigating the relationship between LL (ESSC group of laws) of software evolution and the common, variable and product-specific assets, based on data from an industrial SPL project.

The industrial SPL project, used as basis for the investigation described herein, has been conducted in partnership with a company located in Brazil, which develops for more than 10 years strategic and operational solutions for hospitals, clinics, labs and private doctor offices. This company has $\sim$ 50 employees, of which six are SPL developers with a range of 4 to 19 years of experience in software development.

The company builds products within the scope of four main areas (hospitals, clinics, labs and private doctor offices). Such products comprise 45 modules altogether, targeting at specific functions (e.g., financial, inventory control, nutritional control, home care, nursing, and medical assistance). Market trends, technical constraints and competitiveness motivated the company to migrate their products from a single-system development to an SPL approach. Within SPL, the company was able to deliver its common, variable and product-specific assets. To keep the company name confidential, it will be called *Medical Company (MC)*. During the investigation, MC allowed full access to its code and bug tracking system.

Regarding the bug tracking system, we collected a total of 70.652 requests over 10 years, allowing an in-depth statistical data analysis. MC uses a bug tracking system called *Customer Interaction Center (CIC)*, which was internally developed. CIC allows MC's users to register requests for adaptations, enhancements, corrections and also requests for the creation of new modules.

The empirical study presented herein was planned and executed according to Jedlitschka et al.'s guidelines [14].

3.1 Planning

All the products at MC have some assets (called modules) in common (commonalities), some variable assets (variabilities) and also some specific assets (product-specific), enabling the creation of specific products depending on the combination of the selected assets.

Figure 1 shows the division of modules between the areas supported by MC. Four (4) modules represent the commonalities of the MC SPL, twenty-nine (29) modules represent the variabilities of the MC SPL and, twelve (12) modules represent the product-specific assets, totaling forty-five (45) modules in the MC SPL.

Based on those modules, some of the laws could be evaluated with the records from CIC. However, other ones required the LOC of these modules. From CIC and LOC, we collected data since 1997. Nevertheless, data related to the three types of maintenance (adaptive, corrective and perfective) just started to appear in 2003.

The GQM approach [15] was used to state the goal of this empirical study, as follows: the goal of this empirical study is *to analyze Lehman's Laws of Software Evolution (ESSC group of laws)* for the purpose of *evaluation* with respect to *its validity* from the point of view of *the researcher* in the context of *an SPL industrial project*. Based on the stated Goal, the following research questions were defined:

RQ1.) Is there a relationship between the *Continuous Change* law and the evolution of common, variable and product-specific assets?

RQ2.) Is there a relationship between the *Continuous Growth* law and the evolution of common, variable and product-specific assets?

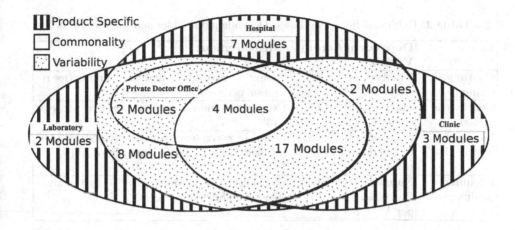

Fig. 1. Modules (assets) per Areas Supported by MC

RQ3.) Is there a relationship between the *Increasing Complexity* law and the evolution of common, variable and product-specific assets?

RQ4.) Is there a relationship between the *Declining Quality* law and the evolution of common, variable and product-specific assets?

The term relationship used in the RQs seeks for evidences of each evaluated law in the SPL common, variable, and product specific assets. In order to answer those questions, some metrics were defined. Since the SPL literature does not provide clear metrics directly associated to the laws, the metrics extracted from Barry et al. [3], Xie et a. [13], Kemerer and Slaughter [16], and Lehman et al. [17] were used herein. Barry et al. defined some dependent variables and some metrics for measuring each dependent variable. Based on their work, in order to evaluate each LL of software evolution, we have adapted the relationship among laws, dependent variables and the measurements (as shown in Table 2), according to the available data in the private industrial environment. Moreover, instead of using the Cyclomatic Complexity [18] as in Barry's work, we decided to use the LOC metric, since LOC and Cyclomatic Complexity are found to be strongly correlated [19].

For each one of the dependent variables, we have stated one null and one alternative hypothesis. The hypotheses for the empirical study are shown next:

H_0 : There is no growth trend in the data during the years (Stationary);

H_1 : There is a growth trend in the data during the years (Trend);

To corroborate Lehman's Laws of Software Evolution, *Continuous Change, Continuous Growth, Increasing Complexity* and *Declining Quality*, we must reject H_0. Thus, if there is a trend of growth in the data during the years, there is evidence to support these four laws.

The next subsection describes how the data were collected and grouped to allow the evaluation of the defined hypotheses.

Table 2. Relationship among Laws, Dependent Variables and Measurement

Law	Dependent Variable	Acronym	Measurement
Continuous change	Number of Activities	NA	Count of *corrective, adaptive* and *perfective* requests per year [3]
Continuous growth	Lines Of Code	LOC	Number of lines of code of modules per year [13]
Increasing complexity	Number of Corrections per LOC	NCLOC	Total of *correction* requests divided by LOC of modules per year (adapted from [16])
Declining quality	Number of Corrections per Module	NCM	Total *correction* requests divided by the number of modules per year [3]

3.2   Execution

The object of this study was the MC SPL. To collect the necessary data (from source code and the bug tracking system), we defined an approach composed of three steps. In the first step, we were able to collect data from *Customer Interaction Center (CIC)*, in the second one we collected LOC data and at the third step, MC clarified some doubts, through interviews, that we had about the collected data.

After collecting all the data, we started to group them according to an CIC filed. When registering a new request at CIC, the user must fill a field called *request type*. Based on this request type, the records from CIC were grouped according to the types of maintenance [20] [21]. The records were grouped in three types of maintenance, according to Table 3.

It was possible to relate each request from the bug tracking system to either adaptive, corrective or perfective maintenance since each request has a field for its type, and each type is related to a maintenance type. The preventive maintenance type was not used because none of the records corresponded to this type. We also show other records not related to maintenance types from CIC, since MC also use CIC to register management information. These other records had a null request type field or their request type field was related to commercial proposals, visiting requests or training requests. Thus, they were not used in the analysis. We found a total of 70.652 requests in the CIC system.

Based on this classification and the LOC, we were able to investigate each dependent variable and also perform the statistical analysis as discussed in the next section.

3.3   Data Analysis and Discussion

For analyzing the evolution at MC, in the first step, we collected data related to all assets and we did not distinguish common, variable and product-specific records. This step can be seen in each graph from Appendix A as the

Table 3. Maintenance Types Groups

Maintenance Type	Request Type in CIC	Total of Records
Adaptive	Reports and System Adaptation Request	22,005
Corrective	System Error, Database Error, Operating System Error, Error Message of type General Fail in the System, Error Message (Text in English) and System Locking / Freezing	14,980
Perfective	Comments, Suggestions and Slow System	2,366
Other	Doubts, Marketing - Shipping Material, Marketing Presentation, Marketing Proposal, Marketing Negotiation, Training and Visit Request	31,301

Total line. As our objective was to evaluate the evolution in software product lines, we grouped the records into commonalities, variabilities and product-specific, facilitating the understanding of the evolution at MC.

The period in which the data were collected was not the same to evaluated the laws. The continuous growth law was evaluated using data from the period between 1997 and 2011. The other laws (continuous change, increasing complexity, and declining quality) were evaluated using data from the period between 2003 and 2011.

In order to evaluate the hypotheses we applied the KPSS Test [22]. This test is used to test a null hypothesis for an observable time series. If the series is stationary, then we do not reject the null hypothesis. Otherwise, if the series has a trend, we reject the null hypothesis. In this study, the level of confidence used was 5% (p-value). We could evaluate all assets (common, variable and product-specific) for all the laws using this statistical test.

We applied also a linear regression analysis [23] to the collected data to evaluate the variance between the assets of the SPL at MC (see Appendix B). Through this variance, we could understand which assets evolve more and should receive more attention. We have checked the variance $(Y = \beta_0 + \beta_1 X)$ for each dependent variable and for each asset (Common = comm, Variable = var, Product-Specific = ps) of the SPL.

The descriptive statistics analysis and the discussion of the empirical study results are shown next grouped by each research question.

RQ1.) Is there a relationship between the *Continuous Change* law and the evolution of common, variable and product-specific assets?

For this law, the number of activities (adaptive, corrective and perfective) registered in CIC from January 2003 up to December 2011 were used, corresponding to the *Number of Activities* dependent variable as shown on Appendix A(a). The plot shows a growth for the commonalities and variabilities, however, for the product-specific activities a small decrease can be noticed for the last years. The number of activities related to the variabilities are greater than the activities related to the commonalities. For the product-specific activities, as expected, there is a smaller number of activities, since it corresponds to the small group of assets from the MC SPL.

Besides the small decrease for product-specific assets activities for the last years, we could identify a trend of growing in the number of activities for all assets (common, variable and product-specific) by applying the KPSS Test. Based on the confidence intervals analysis, Appendix B(a) indicates that the different assets from the SPL have different amounts of activities. The number of activities related to the variabilities are bigger in the SPL because *"variability has to undergo continual and timely change, or a product family will risk losing the ability to effectively exploit the similarities of its members"* [24].

RQ2.) Is there a relationship between the *Continuous Growth* law and the evolution of common, variable and product-specific assets?

Regarding this law, it was possible to identify similar behaviors for each of the SPL assets. Appendix A(b) shows the lines of code from 1997 up to 2011, corresponding to the *Lines Of Code* dependent variable. For common, variable and product-specific assets, we can observe a tendency to stabilization over the years. They grow at a high level in the first years, but they tend to stabilize over the next years.

Due to the growth in the number of activities for common and variable assets according to the *Continuous Change* law, these activities had an impact on the LOCs. By using the KPSS Test, the commonalities and variabilities showed a trend of increasing. Despite the continuous change observed for the commonalities and variabilities in the SPL, MC does not worry about keeping the size of its common and variable assets stable, contributing with the increase of complexity.

For the product-specific assets, the KPSS Test showed a stationary behavior. Therefore, the *Continuos Growth* law to the product-specific assets is rejected. This happens because similar functions among the product-specific assets are moved to the core asset of the SPL [25].

Moreover, through the confidence intervals analysis, Appendix B(b) shows that the variabilities from the SPL have more LOC than other assets. This could be one of the reasons why variabilities have more activities (Continuous Change).

RQ3.) Is there a relationship between the *Increasing Complexity* law and the evolution of common, variable and product-specific assets?

The total number of corrections per line of code, corresponding to the *Number of Corrections per LOC* dependent variable is shown in Appendix A(c). As it can be seen, the complexity for commonalities, variabilities and product-specific assets is increasing up to 2007. This increase was bigger for the commonalities because at that time MC had to evolve the SPL to support new government laws. However, variable and product-specific assets have also grown up to 2007, since modifications within common assets also had an impact on variable and product-specific assets [7] [8] [9]. After 2007, MC started to try to reduce the complexity and prevent the system from breaking down.

However, we could also identify a trend of growing in the complexity for the commonalities, variabilities and product-specific assets by applying the KPSS Test in the *Increasing Complexity* law. Hence, considering that the complexity is always growing, the *Increasing Complexity* law is supported for all the assets in the SPL at MC.

Confidence intervals analysis (see Appendix B(c)) indicates that the complexity inside the commonalities raises more than inside other assets. It happens because the commonalities have to support all the common assets from the products of the SPL and any change can affect the entire product line [7] [8] [9] [26].

RQ4.) Is there a relationship between the *Declining Quality* law and the evolution of common, variable and product-specific assets?

The number of corrections per total of modules in the year, corresponding to the *Number of Corrections per Module* dependent variable, is shown in Appendix A(d). The number of corrections for the variabilities and for the specific assets follow almost the same pattern. However, for the common assets of the product line, we can notice a higher number of corrections per module in 2007, also caused by the adaptation of the system to the government laws. A small increase in the variabilities and in the specific assets also can be observed in the same year. From 2007, the number of corrections per module starts to decrease because of the feedback from users and corrections of problems related to the evolution to deal with the new government laws.

Besides the decrease after 2007, a trend of growing in the number of corrections per modules could be identified for the commonalities, variabilities and product-specific assets by using the KPSS Test. Hence, considering that the number of corrections per module is always growing, the *Declining Quality* law is supported for all the assets in the SPL at MC.

Based on the confidence intervals analysis, Appendix B(d), we could conclude that the number of corrections per module inside the commonalities is bigger than the other assets. As stated for commonalities the increasing complexity law, this happens because the commonalities have to support all the common assets from the products of the SPL and any change can affect the entire product line [7] [8] [9] [26].

The results of the KPSS test are shown in Appendix C. The next section discusses the threats to validity of the empirical study.

3.4 Threats to Validity

There are some threats to the validity of our study. They are described and detailed as follows.

External Validity threats concern the generalization of our findings. In the analyzed medical domain, government laws are published constantly. This may affect the generalizability of the study since those laws affect both common, variable and product-specific assets. Hence, it is not possible to generalize the results to other domains, however, the results maybe considered to be valid in the medical domain.

This empirical study was performed in just one company and only one SPL was analysed. Thus, it needs a broader evaluation in order to try to generalize the results. However, this was the first study in this direction evaluating each of the four laws of software evolution (ESSC group of laws) in an SPL industrial company with more than 10 years of historical data, which is not always available for researchers.

Internal Validity threats concern factors that can influence our observations. The period in which the data were collected was not the same. We evaluated some laws using the period between 1997 and 2011. Others were evaluated using the period between 2003 and 2011. Also, the requests from the bug tracking system were used in the same way no matter of their quality, duplication or rejected requests. Nevertheless, the available data period is meaningful because it is an industrial SPL project and both periods can be considered long periods, where statistical methods could be successfully applied.

Construct Validity threats concern the relationship between theory and observation. The metrics used in this study may not be the best ones to evaluate some of the laws, considering that there is no baseline for those metrics applied to SPL. However, metrics used to evaluate Lehman's laws of software evolution in previous studies were the basis for our work. For some metrics, we based on LOC. Even though LOC can be considered a simplistic method, LOC and Cyclomatic Complexity are found to be strongly correlated [19], thus we decided to use LOC since MC had this information previously available.

4   Key Findings and Contributions for SPL Community

In this section, we present the key findings and also discuss what is the impact of each finding for industrial SPL practitioners, according to each law.

a. *Continuous Change Law. Finding*: Variable assets are responsible for the greater number of activities performed in the SPL project. Practitioners should be aware of making modifications within those assets, since there are several constraints among them. Also we could realize that the number of product-specific activities decreases starting 2007 while the number of activities on common and variable assets increases. It could be that there are so many activities on the variable and common assets (compared to the product-specific assets) because their scope has not been chosen well (or has changed significantly in 2007), implying that more and more specifics assets have to be integrated into commonalities. This would be a typical product line behavior. Also, another reason for increasing the number of activities on common and variable assets is that in SPL more attention is by definition given to the commonalities and variabilities for the sake of reuse.

b. *Continuous Growth Law. Finding*:Variable assets had also the biggest growth in LOCs during the years. Practitioners should search, among the variable assets, those that share behavior and can be transformed into common assets. Transforming variable assets into common assets will reduce the total growth of variable assets and also it will reduce their complexity. However, within this study, the transition from variability to commonality does not happen at all, however, it should happen. For example, when a variability is been used in almost all the products of the SPL.

c. *Increasing Complexity Law. Finding*: Complexity within common assets is bigger that for other assets. Practitioners should be aware of complexity in common assets since they have to support all the products from the SPL [26]. This makes any kind of change in common assets to be considered as critical, since they may affect the whole SPL.

d. *Declining Quality Law. Findings*: The number of corrections per modules were higher for common assets. In fact, for this empirical study we also have to consider the number of maintainers at MC, which was a small number and maybe they were overload with work and left behind quality issues. In a further study, we will check if there is any relationship between complexity and quality, because in this study, higher complexity is related with poor quality.

Based on the results of this empirical study, we propose the following initial items to improve the evolution within SPLs:

. *Creation of guidelines for evolving each SPL artifact*. Guidelines supporting evolution steps for SPL artifact should exist to systematize the evolution of common, variable and product-specific assets. These guidelines should consider why, when, where and how the SPL assets evolve.

. *For each evolution task, keep constant or better the quality of the SPL*. Measurements within the SPL common, variable and product-specific assets (including requirements, architecture, code, and so on) should be part of the SPL evolution process.

. *For each evolution task, try to decrease the complexity of the SPL*. After evolving the SPL code, measurements should be applied to check if the new change in the code increases or not the complexity of the SPL;

These are some improvements that can be followed according to the findings of the empirical study at MC. Next Section presents our conclusions and future work.

5   Conclusions and Future Work

Lehman's Laws of Software Evolution were published in the seventies and still are evaluated in recent environments, such as the one used in this empirical study. From this empirical study, commonalities, variabilities and product-specific assets seems to behave differently regarding evolution. Three laws were completely supported (continuous change, increasing complexity and declining quality) in this empirical study. The other law (continuous growth) was partly supported, depending on the SPL asset in question.

According to this study, all assets from the SPL industrial project are changing over the time. However, there is an increasing of complexity and a decrease of quality during the years. Changes in all assets will always happen, therefore, dealing with the complexity and quality in evolving an SPL needs special attention. To deal with the declining quality and increase complexity during the SPL evolution, we intend to propose guidelines. These guidelines will help during the whole SPL evolution starting from the SPL requirements up to the SPL tests.

This empirical study within an industrial SPL project was important to reveal findings not confirmed within open source projects where the complexity keeps the same, the quality is not deteriorated [11] and system grows in a super-linear rate [12].

As future work, we would like to confirm if those laws (Continuous Change, Increasing Complexity, Declining Quality) also happen for other industrial SPL projects. Moreover, we would like to have more insights about the reason why continuous growth law is not supported to product-specific assets. In our opinion, we believe that the LL are also applicable in the SPL context, since most of the laws could be confirmed for most of the SPL assets (eleven at the total).

In addition, we would like to confirm some findings from this empirical study, such as: to confirm if the number of activities and LOC for variable assets are bigger than for other assets; investigate if the commonalities have a higher number of corrections related to other assets and; check if there is any relationship between complexity and quality, because in this study, higher complexity is related with poor quality. Hence, we intend to replicate this study in another company using SPL. For replicating this empirical study, any kind of bug tracking system can be used, since the replicated empirical study can use the same research questions, metrics, hypotheses and statistical methods. After synthesizing the results from both empirical studies, we will try to elaborate some insights of how Lehman's laws of software evolution occur in the SPL environment and propose some guidelines to the SPL evolution process. Based on these guidelines, it will be possible to evolve each SPL asset (common, variable or product-specific) according to its level of complexity, growth and desired quality.

Acknowledgement. This work was partially supported by the National Institute of Science and Technology for Software Engineering (INES[1]), funded by CNPq and FACEPE, grants 573964/2008-4 and APQ-1037-1.03/08 and CNPq grants 305968/2010-6, 559997/2010-8, 474766/2010-1 and FAPESB. The authors also appreciate the value-adding work of all reviewers of this paper and some colleagues: Silvia Abrahão, Emilio Insfrán, and Emilia Mendes who made great contributions to the current work.

---

[1] INES - http://www.ines.org.br

Appendix A. Plotted Graphs from CIC data and LOC

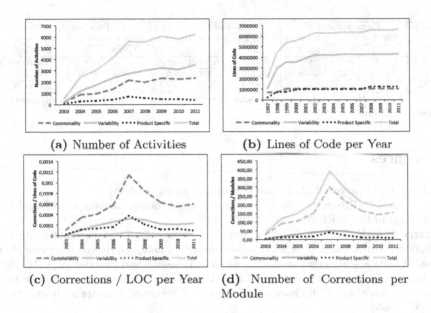

(a) Number of Activities

(b) Lines of Code per Year

(c) Corrections / LOC per Year

(d) Number of Corrections per Module

Appendix B. Confidence Intervals (Regression Coefficients)

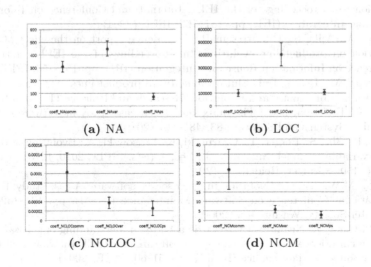

(a) NA

(b) LOC

(c) NCLOC

(d) NCM

Appendix C. KPSS Test and Hypotheses Results

Variable	Commonalities			Variabilities			Product-Specific		
	KPSS Test	p-value	Decision	KPSS Test	p-value	Decision	KPSS Test	p-value	Decision
NA	0.1651	0.0341	Reject H_0	0.2187	0.0100	Reject H_0	0.1979	0.0168	Reject H_0
LOC	0.2125	0.0113	Reject H_0	0.2400	0.0100	Reject H_0	0.1354	0.0697	Do Not Reject H_0
NCLOC	0.1856	0.0214	Reject H_0	0.2252	0.0100	Reject H_0	0.1764	0.0249	Reject H_0
NCM	0.1856	0.0214	Reject H_0	0.2274	0.0100	Reject H_0	0.1799	0.0236	Reject H_0

H_0: Stationary; H_1: Trend. The gray shading represents the supported laws/assets for this empirical study.

References

1. Mens, T., Demeyer, S.: Software Evolution. Springer (2008)
2. Lehman, M.: Programs, life cycles, and laws of software evolution. Journal Proceedings of the IEEE 68, 1060–1076 (1980)
3. Barry, E.J., Kemerer, C.F., Slaughter, S.A.: How software process automation affects software evolution: A longitudinal empirical analysis: Research articles. Journal of Software Maintenance and Evolution: Research and Practice 19, 1–31 (2007)
4. Cook, S., Harrison, R., Lehman, M.M., Wernick, P.: Evolution in software systems: foundations of the SPE classification scheme. Journal of Software Maintenance 18, 1–35 (2006)
5. Clements, P.C., Northrop, L.: Software Product Lines: Practices and Patterns. In: SEI Series in Software Engineering. Addison-Wesley (2001)
6. Schmid, K.: A comprehensive product line scoping approach and its validation. In: Proceedings of the 24th International Conference on Software Engineering (ICSE), pp. 593–603. ACM, New York (2002)
7. Ajila, S., Kaba, A.: Using traceability mechanisms to support software product line evolution. In: Proceedings of the IEEE International Conference on Information Reuse and Integration (IRI), pp. 157–162. IEEE (2004)
8. Bailetti, A., Ajila, S., Dumitrescu, R.: Experience report on the effect of market reposition on product line evolution. In: Proceedings of the IEEE International Conference on Information Reuse and Integration (IRI), pp. 151–156. IEEE (2004)
9. Svahnberg, M., Bosch, J.: Evolution in software product lines: Two cases. Journal of Software Maintenance and Evolution: Research and Practice 11, 391–422 (1999)
10. Israeli, A., Feitelson, D.G.: The linux kernel as a case study in software evolution. Journal of Systems and Software 83, 485–501 (2010)
11. Lotufo, R., She, S., Berger, T., Czarnecki, K., Wąsowski, A.: Evolution of the linux kernel variability model. In: Bosch, J., Lee, J. (eds.) SPLC 2010. LNCS, vol. 6287, pp. 136–150. Springer, Heidelberg (2010)
12. Godfrey, M.W., Tu, Q.: Evolution in open source software: A case study. In: IEEE International Conference on Software Maintenance (ICSM), pp. 131–142. IEEE Computer Society, Washington (2000)
13. Xie, G., Chen, J., Neamtiu, I.: Towards a better understanding of software evolution: An empirical study on open source software. In: IEEE International Conference on Software Maintenance (ICSM), pp. 51–60. IEEE (2009)

14. Jedlitschka, A., Ciolkowski, M., Pfahl, D.: Reporting experiments in software engineering. In: Shull, F., Singer, J., Sjøberg, D.I.K. (eds.) Guide to Advanced Empirical Software Engineering, pp. 201–228. Springer, London (2008)
15. Marciniak, J.J.: Encyclopedia of Software Engineering. In: Basili, V.R., Caldiera, G., Rombach, H.D. (eds.) Goal Question Metric Approach 2, pp. 528–532. Wiley-Interscience, Hoboken (1994)
16. Kemerer, C., Slaughter, S.: An empirical approach to studying software evolution. Journal IEEE Transactions on Software Engineering (TSE) 25, 493–509 (1999)
17. Lehman, M.M., Ramil, J.F., Wernick, P.D., Perry, D.E., Turski, W.M.: Metrics and laws of software evolution - the nineties view. In: Proceedings of the 4th International Symposium on Software Metrics, pp. 20–32. IEEE Computer Society, Washington (1997)
18. McCabe, T.J.: A complexity measure. IEEE Transactions on Software Engineering (TSE) 2, 308–320 (1976)
19. Kan, S.H.: Metrics and Models in Software Quality Engineering. Addison-Wesley, Boston (2002)
20. Gupta, A., Cruzes, D., Shull, F., Conradi, R., Rønneberg, H., Landre, E.: An examination of change profiles in reusable and non-reusable software systems. Journal of Software Maintenance and Evolution: Research and Practice 22, 359–380 (2010)
21. Lientz, B.P., Swanson, B.E.: Software Maintenance Management: A Study of the Maintenance of Computer Application Software in 487 Data Processing Organizations. Addison-Wesley (1980)
22. Kwiatkowski, D., Phillips, P.C.B., Schmidt, P., Shin, Y.: Testing the null hypothesis of stationarity against the alternative of a unit root. How sure are we that economic time series have a unit root? Journal of Econometrics 54, 159–178 (1992)
23. Yan, X., Su, X.G.: Linear Regression Analysis: Theory and Computing. World Scientific Publishing, River Edge (2009)
24. Deelstra, S., Sinnema, M., Nijhuis, J., Bosch, J.: Cosvam: a technique for assessing software variability in software product families. In: 20th IEEE International Conference on Software Maintenance (ICSM), pp. 458–462. IEEE (2004)
25. Mende, T., Beckwermert, F., Koschke, R., Meier, G.: Supporting the grow-and-prune model in software product lines evolution using clone detection. In: 12th European Conference on Software Maintenance and Reengineering (CSMR), pp. 163–172. IEEE (2008)
26. McGregor, J.D.: The evolution of product line assets. Technical Report, Software Engineering Institute, CMU/SEI-2003-TR-005 (2003)

Experiences in System-of-Systems-Wide Architecture Evaluation over Multiple Product Lines

Juha Savolainen[1], Tomi Männistö[2], and Varvana Myllärniemi[3]

[1] Danfoss Power Electronics A/S, Global Research and Development, Graasten, Denmark
JuhaErik.Savolainen@danfoss.com
[2] Department of Computer Science, University of Helsinki, Helsinki, Finland
tomi.mannisto@cs.helsinki.fi
[3] School of Science, Aalto University, Espoo, Finland
varvana.myllarniemi@aalto.fi

Abstract. Software architecture evaluation, both for software products and software product lines, has become a mainstream activity in industry. Significant amount of practical experience exists in applying architecture evaluation in real projects. However, most of the methods and practices focus on evaluating individual products or product lines. In this paper, we study how to evaluate a system-of-systems consisting of several cooperating software product lines. In particular, the intent is to evaluate the system-of-systems-wide architecture for the ability to satisfy a new set of crosscutting requirements. We describe the experiences and practices of performing a system-of-systems-wide architecture evaluation in industry: the system-of-systems in question is a set of product lines whose products are used to create the All-IP 3G telecommunications network. The results indicate there are significant differences in evaluating the architecture of system-of-systems compared with traditional evaluations targeting single systems. The two main differences affecting architecture evaluation were the heterogeneity in the maturity levels of the individual systems, i.e., product lines, and the option that instead of simply evaluating each product line individually, responsibilities can be moved from one product line to another to satisfy the system-of-systems level requirements.

Keywords: Architecture evaluation, System-of-systems, Industrial Experience.

1   Introduction

Architecture evaluations are typically used when there is a need to evaluate the qualities of an existing product against future requirements. The intent of the evaluation process is to understand the suitability of the current architecture to the future needs and estimate the cost of the changes needed to the architecture. Alternatively architecture assessments can be used during a development project to identify and analyze architectural risks so that they can be managed for that particular product. In both cases, the focus is on evaluating single products or product lines.

However, there are situations in which an architectural evaluation should encompass several products and product lines, that is, the evaluation should cover

I. Schaefer and I. Stamelos (Eds.): ICSR 2015, LNCS 8919, pp. 58–72, 2014.
© Springer International Publishing Switzerland 2014

system-of-systems. In the telecommunication domain, the vendors avoid commoditization and competition from other manufacturers by introducing various services and features that crosscut the whole telecommunication network. Such features can differentiate manufacturers and encourage their customers to buy all network equipment from the same manufacturer to get the new features deployed easily. However, the ability to create new telecommunication system-of-systems-wide features is difficult, as it requires a collaboration of many network elements to realize the functionality. At the same time a manufacturer must guarantee that none of the functionality covered by the standards is jeopardized. All this requires the ability to conduct a system-of-system-wide architectural evaluation.

Therefore, instead of just evaluating single products or product lines separately, there is a need to evaluate the entire systems of systems, which consists of several software-intensive product lines. The aim of such evaluation is to ensure that new system-of-systems-wide features can be realized. We report the experiences of conducting a system-of-systems-wide architecture evaluation in the telecommunication industry. In particular, we address the following research questions:

RQ1: What practices to use in system-of-systems-wide evaluation over multiple product lines?
RQ2: How does the system-of-systems-wide architecture evaluation differ from the architecture evaluation of a single product line?

We conducted an experience-based case study on the system-of-systems-wide architecture evaluation that took place in Nokia Networks during the first six months of year 2002. The evaluation studied the All-IP 3G network, which can be considered as a system-of-systems consisting of cooperating products from several product lines.

The results indicate there are significant differences in making an architecture evaluation to a system-of-systems compared with architecture evaluations targeting a single product. When evaluating a system-of-systems, the individual systems are typically in a different phase of their lifecycle. That is, some systems have existed as products for a long time and their capabilities can be exactly determined. Others may be under development and their exact capabilities can thus only be estimated. Another significant difference is that in a system-of-systems-wide architecture evaluation one can change the roles of the individual systems to satisfy the capabilities of the whole. From the evaluation perspective, this means that not only does an evaluator try to find if a single system can satisfy its requirements, but may also try to come up with different scenarios how the system-of-systems-wide requirements could be satisfied by changing the way the different systems participate in achieving the overall functionality.

This paper is organized as follows: Section 2 presents related work on architecture evaluation methods, particularly for different levels of maturity, and how architecture evaluation is relevant across the lifecycle of a product. Section 3 describes the case study research method used. Section 4 describes the results to the research questions, whereas Section 5 discusses and Section 6 concludes.

2   Previous Work on Architecture Evaluation Methods

Architecture evaluations can be divided into early and late methods based on at which stage in the design process they are suitable for evaluating the architecture or architecture decisions [1]. An early architecture evaluation need not rely on the existence of architecture documentation, but can utilize other sources of information, such as interviews of architects.

For early architecture evaluation methods it is typical that the design, or making the design decisions, is intertwined with the evaluation [2]. As at the early design stages of the commitment to the decisions is still at least partly open, it is natural for the evaluation to be suggestive and discussing rather than formally assessing. An early architecture evaluation method, such as Global Analysis [3], may thus be partly or even more clearly about architecture design than evaluation per se.

Svanhberg [2] have classified the scenario-based methods, such as Software Architecture Analysis Method [4] and Architecture Trade-Off Analysis Method (ATAM) [5], as early evaluation methods, as they are typically conducted without tangible artifacts suitable, for example, for simulation. Nord and Tomayako [6] addressed the use of architecture evaluation methods ATAM and Cost-Benefit Analysis Method (CBAM) within agile software development and argued for their usefulness and applicability as early architecture evaluation methods.

Tyree and Akerman [7] have proposed an architecture description template for capturing the important early design decisions. One particular benefit of concentrating on decision by means of the template comes from more effective reviewing when the reviewers can easily see the decision's status and rationale more effectively than from the descriptions of architecture structure. In addition, the decisions can be discussed earlier within the team.

Along similar lines of thought, the early evaluation can be alleviated by architecture documentation that better supports the essential decision making process. One idea is to collect and represent the crosscutting concerns from multiple architecture views in perspectives [8]. One more step further is to create specific conflict-centric views with the purpose of concentrating on the conflicts between stakeholders' concerns [9].

As many architecture evaluation methods concentrate on evaluating a given architecture, there are also those aimed towards making a selection from a set of architecture candidates [2,10]. Instead of trying to evaluate the architecture in absolute means, such a method is based on relative evaluation of the candidates under discussion. One aim of the discussions is to increase and share understanding among the participants on the architecture and design choices related to it [2].

Moreover, architecture evaluation in the context of software product lines may have its implications. For software product lines, two levels of evaluation of can distinguished: evaluation of the product line architecture and evaluation of the product architecture [12]. Although it is possible to evaluate product line architectures with methods meant for single products, it has been argued that this is difficult to do for large, complex product lines where the products differ from each other significantly [13].

Therefore, a number of product-line specific evaluation methods have been proposed: a survey of methods is given in [12]. Several methods utilize scenarios in the evaluation process, for example, in the method that adapts ATAM to the product line context [13].

3   Research Method

This study was conducted as a light-weight qualitative case study [14] based mainly on first-hand experiences. We selected qualitative case study approach, since we wanted to gain in-depth understanding on systems-of-systems-wide architecture evaluation. The unit of analysis in the case study was the system consisting of several product lines. Data collection took mainly place via the first author participating in the evaluation of the case study, thus drawing participant observation and first-hand experiences. Additionally, documentation about the evaluation results was used as additional data source. The data was analyzed in an informal and light-weight way with the intention of providing a rich narrative on how the actual evaluation was conducted and seeking specific characteristics that differentiate the system-of-systems-wide evaluation from single product line evaluation.

The case covers an All-IP 3G telecommunication network in Nokia Networks, and in particular, the evaluation project that focused on studying how to realize crosscutting software features. The case organization is a large company providing networking solutions globally. The unit of analysis was purposefully selected as being information rich with non-trivial system-of-systems characteristics spanning multiple product lines.

4   Results

To answer RQ1, the following describes the practices and the process of performing a system-of-systems-wide architecture evaluation over multiple product lines. Thereafter, we highlight the differences to evaluating single product lines to answer RQ2.

Background of the Evaluation Project

Right after 2000, many of the telecommunication manufacturers realized that selling only products, would in the long run lead into commoditization of the basic network equipment. This was true especially for those products being pursued heavily by competition from China and other emerging economies. Therefore, it was seen that most opportunities were arising from services, such as operating the networks for the customers and by selling software features.

This strategic need was seen by the management of the Nokia Networks. To understand how selling new software features could be facilitated, the management initiated an effort to run a software architecture evaluation over all of the network elements that participated to the All-IP radio access network, which is a complex system-of-systems shown in Fig. 1. This case study focused on the architecture evaluation of this system-of-systems.

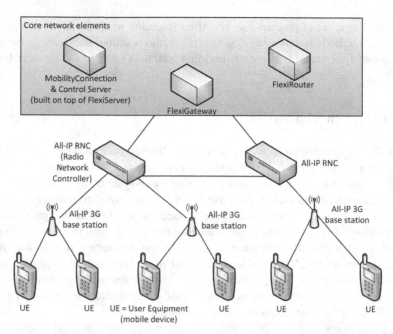

Fig. 1. The network elements in the All-IP 3G network that comprise the system-of-systems in this case study. One software product line produces each element, yet many e-business features cross-cut over several network elements.

The need to perform a system-of-systems-wide architecture evaluation was born out of a need to understand how to realize e-business model, that is, "software as business" business model. As historically network sales have been focusing on large contracts selling hardware, the ability to sell individual system-of-systems-wide software features was seen to allow finer granularity of monetizing the software and tailoring the offering towards clients' different needs.

Before the actual evaluation project started, a short survey of architecture evaluation methods was conducted to guarantee that the team was aware of the recent software architecture evaluation methods. As the team found no guidance on the system-of-systems-wide evaluation from the literature, the original intent was to treat the evaluation as a series of single system or singe product line evaluations and simply combine the evaluated architecture solutions later.

Staffing and Roles in the Evaluation

To investigate the feasibility of e-business model and to conduct architecture evaluation, a *project manager* from Nokia Networks was appointed to lead the investigation. Thereafter, two persons from the Software Architecture group of Nokia Research Center (NRC) were allocated to the project as *primary and secondary investigators*. The investigators had significant previous experiences in performing architecture evaluations for single systems and individual product lines, and thus acted as architecture evaluation experts. Together, the project manager and primary and secondary investigators formed the *core team* for the evaluation.

Table 1. Roles and responsibilities in the system-of-systems-wide architecture evaluation project

Role	Org.	Responsibilities
Project manager	NET	Define the system-of-systems-level requirements as use cases. Define the initial view on how the use cases could be realized by the coordinated behavior of network elements.
Primary Investigator (architecture evaluation expert)	NRC	Lead the architecture evaluations. Pursue on the consensus of the evaluation results. Help in technical communication towards the stakeholders.
Secondary Investigator (architecture evaluation expert)	NRC	Perform the initial survey of architecture evaluation methods. Document the evaluation sessions. Support the primary investigator in architecture evaluation process.
Experts (for quality attributes)	NRC	Participate to the architecture review and provide support for the particular area of expertise.
SW architects (for product lines)	NET	Describe the capabilities of the system. Provide answers to the questions and agree on the evaluation results.

In addition to the core team, a number of *software architects for each product line* participated in the evaluation. Their main function was to give details about the capabilities and design of the product lines.

Finally, a number of additional *experts* from NRC were utilized during the evaluation. There was intent to do as much as possible preparation by the core team and additional experts to reduce the time required from the persons representing the product lines. The NRC experts were highly competent in understanding and analyzing a particular quality attribute. In particular, the core team used experts of telecommunication network performance and dependability. While most the e-business use cases targeted flexibility and extendibility characteristics, it was crucial to see that the proposed solutions did not negatively affect the primary characteristics of the telecommunication networks, i.e., performance (throughput) and dependability (high availability). The intent of the specific experts was to investigate the documentation and participate in the relevant reviews to see that the primary characteristics were not violated.

Step 1: Select and Refine the Use Cases to be Evaluated, Identify the Involved Product Lines

Firstly, the core team discussed and iterated the requirements that would enable the ideal e-business being used by the Nokia Networks. The project manager created initial *system-of-systems-level use cases* for the whole system behavior, which described the needs for the e-business. The main intent was to allow developing, selling, and deploying new system-of-systems-wide network features during the system operations. Some of the features were new functionalities, such as advanced analytics of the data usage across the network, while others, such as capacity increases, were based on the license keys that the customer could buy [15].

Thereafter, the core team identified all network elements that participated in selected the e-business scenarios. As a result, four different product lines (PL1-4) needed to be involved into the evaluation, and respective organizations were identified.

Step 2: Decompose the System-of-Systems-Level Use Cases

The system-of-systems-level use cases were broken down into collaboration diagrams that described how the identified product lines were envisioned to participate in the system-of-systems-level use case realizations. This process required considerable insight into the telecommunications system design and the roles in which the product lines participate in it. An experienced project manager performed this work. Initial system-of-systems-level use case realizations were then discussed with the respective experts to confirm assumptions made during this step.

As a result, each system-of-systems-level use case was decomposed into *product line specific use cases*.

The initial breakdown of system-of-systems-level use cases into product line specific ones was developed over the email and the plan for an architecture evaluation process was created. The plan provided the overview of the process use cases that apply to each particular network element.

Additionally, *explicit assessment questions* were derived from the use cases for each product line. A question could be, for example, "Please explain how your network element can support runtime upgrade of the SW without hindering the normal operations of the system?"

Step 3: Collect Initial Evaluation from the Product Lines, Identify the Product Line Maturity

After the initial breakdown of the use cases, the product line organizations were contacted, and the product line specific use cases were given along with the explicit assessment questions. The architects were encouraged to provide any documentation that would further explain how their system supports the identified use cases. The architects responsible for each of the network elements would provide the answers back to the core team.

After receiving the answers, it became apparent that the maturity levels of the systems were highly varied. Some provided detailed a complete SW feature description that fully described the design of the use case, whereas others did not provide anything that an evaluator could use. The core team then decided to represent the product line maturity as its own characteristics to emphasize the risk involved in dealing with unfinished specifications.

Based on the answers the core team categorized the different levels of maturity of the product line. The following levels were identified:

A *mature product line that is designed, implemented and deployed to customers*. During the evaluation, one of the product lines (PL2) was well established and had been released to the customers. Thus the evaluators could have a clear idea of the main characteristics. In these cases, making an architecture evaluation was fairly straightforward and resembled making an architecture evaluation for any implemented product line against some change cases, that is, making a late architecture evaluation.

A product line that is at an advanced level of maturity, but not yet delivered to the customers. Another product line had been released (PL3), but the actual release covered only partially the functionality described in the use cases. In this case, one needed to evaluate for one part the existing implementation and for another part the plan for the future iterations of the product line.

A product line that has design, but not significant implementation. In the evaluation, one of the product lines was in fairly early maturity stage (PL4) and only some initial descriptions and ideas how to address the requirements were available.

A product line that is in very early maturity stage. Finally, one of the product lines (PL1) was in an early maturity stage, thus many of the requirements had not yet been specifically considered. This meant that part of the architecture evaluation session concentrated on idea generation rather than architecture evaluation. The evaluation commonly tried to find ways and approach how the system could fulfill the requirements. This process resembled an early architecture evaluation.

Step 4: Classify the Product Line Use Cases Based on the Uncertainty of the Design

In addition to recording the maturity of the product line, also the *uncertainty related to a specific product-line use case and its design* was recorded. As the evaluations were performed when many of the design choices especially for e-business use cases remained open, it was important to also document if the evaluation for a particular product line specific use case was based on very early information of the architectural ideas or on decisions implemented on a customer deployed software. To capture this information a classification was created as described in Table 2.

Table 2. Source information classification for the product line use cases and related design

Tag	Rationale
CURRENT	The answer and the description are based on the current design and implementation of the architecture.
PLAN	The answer and the description are based on the chosen strategy address the question in context. But the implementation does not exist yet.
IDEA	The current answer and the description are based on the current proposal to address this concern but it has not been yet chosen as a solution. (Note that it is possible to provide alternative ways to solve a problem.)
NONE	The topic has not been addressed by the architecture and no solution idea exists.

Documenting uncertainty information was a good choice. We realized that there is no direct mapping between the maturity of a product line and the uncertainty classification of a use case. Even for PL2 many of the evaluations were defined to be in the level of IDEA. This was because many of the e-business use cases were out of the scope of the current release of the PL2.

Step 5: Conduct Evaluation Sessions for Each Product Line

For each product line (PL1-4), one face-to-face meeting was organized as a three hour session. Between 3-9 representatives from each network participated to meeting with two to four evaluators. The number of product line software architects from Nokia Networks (NET) and evaluators (NRC) are shown in Fig. 2 for each meeting of the different product line (PL1-PL4).

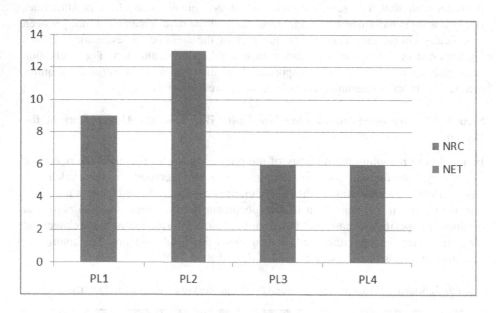

Fig. 2. Participants of the architecture evaluation meetings

As described in Fig. 2, the number of participants in the meetings varied between 6 and 13. PL2 was a platform project for creating a basis for a number of network elements each of which would form their own product lines. This made the PL2 very complex with a need to cover many different quality attributes. Therefore, no single person was able to answer all evaluation questions and a large number of participants were needed from the business side. This also meant that all specific experts from NRC (see Table 1) participated in the evaluation. Other product lines were simpler and could thus be successfully evaluated by a smaller group. PL1 and PL2 projects were based in Finland, which made it easier to meet in the same location. PL3 and PL4 were distributed globally and in both cases one remote participant took part in the evaluation over a phone conference.

All evaluation meeting followed the same overall plan. After the introduction to the e-business requirements and use cases, the primary evaluator went through all of the questions derived from the product line specific use cases. The architects explained briefly their answers to each question (they had provided initial answers in the pre-documentation to the evaluation team). The primary evaluator then investigated the answers also based on the insight generated by the documentation previously provided to the evaluators.

Thereafter, any comments or disagreements about the requirements were identified. While the evaluation team had asked comments already when the product line use cases were initially provided - it became obvious that typically the product line representatives would raise concerns only during this initial overview of the requirements. This happened partially because the way how the requirements were recorded. As the splitting of the system-of-systems-level use cases were done by the project core team – sometimes the product line had different view on how responsibilities among the network elements should be distributed.

The disagreements about the product line use cases happened for three main reasons. First, for certain aspects the product line representatives had significantly more insight into the solutions and based on this insight they would see a different way how to distribute the system-of-systems-level functionality into their system. Second, in other cases the product line representatives had so little knowledge on the emerging e-business requirements that they misunderstood the requirements. Third, in some cases the product line representatives had not taken sufficient time to familiarize with the use cases so they were then discussed during the face-to-face meeting more extensively than originally predicted.

After agreeing on the product line use cases, the intent was to reach a common understanding on the extent to which the current product line architecture fulfilled the PL-specific use cases. We used an existing results classification scheme from [11], shown in Table 3.

Table 3. Evaluation result classification [11]

Tag	Rationale
IDEAL	Subject is explicitly addressed, and receives best possible treatment.
GOOD	Sound treatment of the subject relative to the expectations.
MARGINAL	Treatment of the subject meets minimal expectations.
UNACCEPTABLE	Treatment of subject does not meet minimal expectations.
INCOMPLETE	Treatment of subject exhibits a level of detail, which is insufficient to make a judgment.
NON-APPLICABLE	This measure is not applicable to the subject of interest.

By combining the source information classification in Table 2 and the evaluation results classification in Table 3 it was possible to get a reasonable understanding on the proposed solutions. This classification was done for each product line for every use case.

The approach made it also possible to have more than one solution described. For example, an implemented solution in an established system could be classified as CURRENT and UNACCEPTABLE, but at the same time as an IDEA level solution to how to address the use case at a MARGINAL level. After the product line level evaluations were all collected, a summary was done to explain how well the system-of-systems-wide requirements were fulfilled by the combination of the product lines.

During the product line evaluation sessions, one goal was to avoid the design for any use case to remain in stage NONE (see Table 2). Thus, the meetings were also used for idea creation. In the meetings, the core team pushed for creating at least some ideas to address the use cases, even if some of the architects were initially reluctant to do so. The ability to record multiple ways to address the requirements at the IDEA level made it easier to generate discussions and better reflected the uncertainty that was contained in these envisioned design decisions. The strong emphasis on idea creation had the consequence that the roles of the architects and the evaluators become mixed during the meetings. However, the mixing of roles was found beneficial, because the intent of the e-business evaluation was to find out if the uses cases can be implemented across the network elements. Therefore, generating even initial ideas that might support the requirements was needed to understand, if indeed the implementation was possible for the network element in question.

Step 6: Collect the Results at the System-of-Systems-Level

After each meeting, the results were collected and the summary was send to the whole team to guarantee that everyone agrees on the results.

After the of the evaluations were done and verified with the architects, the primary investigator created the final report that collected the results in the level of the e-business use cases. There the ability to implement the use cases was described together with high level estimates what was needed to realize the requirements. This was then communicated towards the top management by the project manager on behalf of the core team.

The classification of the design uncertainty in Table 2 was also important when considering the conclusions of the overall evaluation. If the most of the material is in the level of ideas of possible design choices, then the evaluation is mostly based on verbal explanation and changes to the chosen solutions is likely. However, analyzing software architectures in the early phase of the lifecycle can be very useful, since no large investments have been made and the suggested changes can be often fairly easily accepted.

Changing and Adding New Responsibilities during the Evaluation

Additionally, the case revealed an issue that was specific for the system-of-systems-wide architecture evaluations: it is possible to change the responsibilities among product lines to facilitate achieving system-of-systems-wide requirements, or even to add completely new responsibilities to certain product lines.

As a concrete example, one of the system-of-systems-level uses cases was to make a system-of-systems-wide software update that would deliver a new feature. This would require a collaboration of many of the product lines implementing this new system functionality. As the telecommunications network needs to be functioning continuously, it is important to deploy software updates during the runtime of the products without disconnecting calls or preventing access to the telecommunications network.

This use case was initially decomposed into a set of product line specific use cases requiring runtime upgradeability of all of the products that create the telecommunications network. For most of the telecommunication servers facilitating this requirements was easy. Most of these systems employ high reliability hot-standby configuration, which is realized through duplicated hardware that can take over in a matter of milliseconds if a hardware failure occurs. This allows continuing the operation of the system without disconnecting current calls.

Realizing the need for runtime upgrade for these kinds of systems is easy. One can first update the software in the backup hardware card. Then verify the correctness of the update by comparing its output to the currently operational card running the old software release. After the correctness is verified, the updated backup is switched to become the operational card and so the system is running the new software. Thereafter, the still old software on the other card is updated as well.

However, soon after starting the architecture evaluation for the base station, it became apparent that this strategy was not applicable to base stations. Because of the price constraints base stations tend not to have duplicate hardware for all parts of the system. This required another approach to be envisioned, and consequently, a number of ideas were generated during the software architecture evaluation meeting. One of the possible solutions relied on the change of responsibilities among the product lines and therefore changing the product line specific use case of another product line.

To upgrade the software of a base station one could rely on the functionality of a radio network controller (RNC) depicted in Figure 1. A typical telecommunications network is designed in such a way that there are significant overlaps among the coverage of the base stations. Some overlap is simply needed for the network to function, as a mobile device must be able to move geographically. A moving mobile device will eventually reach the limit of the coverage of one base station and a handover to another base station needs to happen.

To prevent dropping calls, there needs to be an overlap of coverage areas of the base stations. That is, at any given point a mobile device can receive calls and data from multiple base stations. In practice, the overlaps in modern networks are much more than what is required for the handovers. This is because the distance to the base station has a significant effect on the speed of the data transmission, power consumption of the mobile devices, and to the overall capacity and the reliability of the telecommunications network.

These observations were used to create a new idea how to address the base station upgrade problem. One could shut down one base station at the time and use the RNC to transfer all calls to the adjacent base stations. This would allow, during low traffic situations (e.g. during the night), to upgrade all base stations.

This basically created a new requirements and a use case for the RNC without needing the base station to change any implementation. Later it was evaluated with the RNC team that creating this functionality would be easy and straightforward.

Identified Differences of the System-of-Systems-Wide Evaluation

To address RQ2, we summarize the differences of the system-of-systems-wide architecture evaluation to the architecture evaluation of a single product line highlighted in the utilized practices.

First, when evaluating a system (over multiple product lines), then the product lines are typically in a different phases of their lifecycle. Some product lines have existed for a long time and their capabilities can be exactly determined. It is more costly to change the design or responsibilities of these product lines. Other product lines are under development and their exact capabilities can only be estimated. Their design and capabilities are easier to change. Second, when evaluating a system over multiple product lines), not just the design, but also the responsibilities and requirements of those product lines can be changed.

The benefit of this kind of evaluation is the openness across teams and organizations: it is easier to convince open dialog in system-of-systems-wide evaluations. Further, reliance on the openness limits the effort needed for all parties.

5   Discussion

The architecture evaluations were performed at the product line level. None of the product specific software was investigated. Many recent research results argue that the evaluations may need to be done in both product line and product level [12].

We believe that there were a number of reasons that contributed to the fact that we found it feasible to perform the evaluation only on the product line level. First and foremost, the use cases represented aspects that need to be supported by all products. Therefore, they naturally should be implemented as part of the platform functionality. Thus evaluating only the platform architecture is sufficient to understand how well the architecture supports realizing the use cases.

Second, the traditional way to create network system product lines was to utilize the platform approach where the shared product characteristics were implemented in the pre-integrated platform. Typically a separate platform existed for different types of system. Switching system requiring extreme performance and highly reliable behavior would be implemented on top of a different software platform than a network management system that would have requirements for flexibility and extensibility.

In this way nearly all of the quality attribute requirements of the product line were implemented by the common reference architecture and platform components. This again supported observation that one can evaluate architectures by focusing on the product line part and ignoring product specific details. Even the required performance variability was implemented using a common platform derived mechanism [15].

These two factors were the main reasons why in this case we could perform architecture evaluations only at the product line level using techniques that were initially created to evaluate individual products without variability. We believe that these observations are also valid outside the telecommunication domain. Therefore, when considering architecture evaluations for a product line one should consider whether the requirements needed are required by some or all products of the product line and to what extent quality attribute requirements of the product line are implemented by the reference architecture and common infrastructure or are, at least partially, realized by the product architectures.

6   Conclusions

In this paper, we presented experiences in performing system-of-systems-wide architecture evaluation over a number of product lines. We identified characteristics that make system-of-systems-wide architecture evaluations different from the traditional ones.

First, in a system-of-systems, the individual systems, particularly if they are products, are likely to differ in maturity and therefore one needs to be able to perform both early and late evaluations of architectures. As the techniques for these evaluations are partially different, it is important that the evaluators use correct methods and approaches to perform the evaluation. In order to make the differences in maturity explicit, we proposed using two different classifications. One is to classify the source material of the evaluation in order to distinguish whether to perform an early or late architecture evaluation. Combining this with the evaluation results (the second classification) one can communicate the reliability of the assessment to the outside stakeholders.

Second, one needs to pursue opportunities to satisfy the requirements also through changing the responsibilities of the individual systems realizing the system-of-systems-wide functionality. This requires an ability to think beyond the capabilities of a single system and encouraging the architects to do the same. If such opportunities are identified further iterations are needed to confirm the feasibility of the ideas with other architects of other systems.

While the whole evaluation process was geared towards understanding whether the set of products could meet the wanted system-of-systems-wide requirements, a number of other benefits where observed during the system-of-systems-wide architecture evaluation.

The process helped to communicate the key system-of-systems-wide requirements to product line organizations. This was especially important in the case, as many of the product lines had not considered the requirements of the whole system-of-systems in which their product were to be the individual systems.

The evaluations also assisted to communicate and agree upon the intended division of system-of-systems-wide requirements among the key stakeholders. This allowed unifying towards a common view of how the system-of-systems-wide requirements will be realized as collaboration between all participating product lines.

We believe that this paper helps practitioners to understand how to apply architecture evaluation techniques for evaluating system-of-systems-wide characteristics. We hope that the experiences will be valuable for researchers for finding new ways to combine early and late architecture evaluation methods into a cohesive catalogue of architecture evaluation methods.

References

1. Lindvall, M., Tvedt, R.T., Costa, P.: An empirically-based process for software architecture evaluation. Empirical Software Engineering 8(1), 83–108 (2003)
2. Svahnberg, M.: An industrial study on building consensus around software architectures and quality attributes. Information and Software Technology (46), 818–850 (2004)
3. Hofmeister, C., Nord, R., Soni, D.: Applied Software Architecture. Addison-Wesley, Reading (2000)
4. Bass, L., Clements, P., Kazman, R.: Software Architecture in Practice, 2nd edn. Addison-Wesley (2003)
5. Clements, P., Kazman, R., Klein, M.: Evaluating Software Architectures—Methods and Case Studies. Addison-Wesley, Boston (2002)
6. Nord, R., Tomayko, J.: Software architecture-centric methods and agile development. IEEE Software (2006)
7. Tyree, J., Akerman, A., Financial, C.: Architecture decisions: Demystifying architecture. IEEE Software (2005)
8. Rozanski, N., Woods, E.: Software Systems Architecture: Working With Stakeholders Using Viewpoints and Perspectives. Addison-Wesley (2005)
9. Savolainen, J., Männistö, T.: Conflict-Centric Software Architectural Views: Exposing Trade-Offs in Quality Requirements. IEEE Software 27(6), 33–37 (2010)
10. Svahnberg, M., Wohlin, C., Lundberg, L., Mattsson, M.: A method for understanding quality attributes in software architecture structures. In: Proceedings of the 14th International Conference on Software Engineering and Knowledge Engineering (SEKE 2002), pp. 819–826. ACM Press, New York (2002)
11. Hillard, R., Kurland, M., Litvintchouk, S., Rice, T., Schwarm, S.: Architecture Quality
12. Assessment, version 2.0, MITRE Corporation (August 7, 1996)
13. Etxeberria, L., Sagardui, G.: Product-line architecture: New issues for evaluation. In: Obbink, H., Pohl, K. (eds.) SPLC 2005. LNCS, vol. 3714, pp. 174–185. Springer, Heidelberg (2005)
14. Olumofin, F.G., Mišić, V.B.: A holistic architecture assessment method for software product lines. Information and Software Technology 49(4), 309–323 (2007)
15. Runeson, P., Höst, M.: Guidelines for conducting and reporting case study research in software engineering. Empirical Software Engineering 14(2), 131–164 (2009)
16. Myllärniemi, V., Savolainen, J., Männistö, T.: Performance variability in software product lines: A case study in the telecommunication domain. In: Software Product Line Conference, pp. 32–41 (2013)

A Systematic Literature Review of Software Product Line Management Tools

Juliana Alves Pereira, Kattiana Constantino, and Eduardo Figueiredo

Computer Science Department, Federal University of Minas Gerais, Belo Horizonte, Brazil
{juliana.pereira,kattiana,figueiredo}@dcc.ufmg.br

Abstract. Software Product Line (SPL) management is a key activity for software product line engineering. The idea behind SPL management is to focus on artifacts that are shared in order to support software reuse and adaptation. Gains are expected in terms of time to market, consistency across products, costs reduction, better flexibility, and better management of change requirements. In this context, there are many available options of SPL variability management tools. This paper presents and discusses the findings from a Systematic Literature Review (SLR) of SPL management tools. Our research method aimed at analyzing the available literature on SPL management tools and the involved experts in the field. This review provides insights (i) to support companies interested to choose a tool for SPL variability management that best fits their needs; (ii) to point out attributes and requirements relevant to those interested in developing new tools; and (iii) to help the improvement of the tools already available. As a direct result of this SLR, we identify gaps, such as the lack of industrial support during product configuration.

Keywords: Systematic Literature Review, Software Product Lines, Variability Management, Tools.

1 Introduction

The growing need for developing larger and more complex software systems demands better support for reusable software artifacts [46]. In order to address these demands, software product line (SPL) has been increasingly adopted in software industry [15, 60, 52]. SPL is a set of software systems that share a common and variable set of features satisfying the specific needs of a particular market segment [46]. It is built around a set of common software components with points of variability that allow different product configurations [15, 60]. SPL adoption brings significant improvements to the software development process [46, 48]. Experience already shows that SPL can allow companies to realize order-of-magnitude improvements in time to market, cost, productivity, quality, and flexibility [15]. Large companies, such as Hewlett-Packard, Nokia, Motorola, and Dell have already adopted SPL practices [52].

An important concept of an SPL is the feature model. Feature models are used to represent the common and variable features in SPL [30]. A feature represents an increment in functionality or a system property relevant to some stakeholders [30].

I. Schaefer and I. Stamelos (Eds.): ICSR 2015, LNCS 8919, pp. 73–89, 2014.

It may refer to functional or non-functional requirements, architecture decisions, or design patterns [4]. The potential benefits of SPLs are achieved through a software architecture designed to increase the reuse of features in several SPL products.

In practice, developing an SPL involves feature modeling to represent different viewpoints, sub-systems, or concerns of the software products [5]. Therefore, it is necessary to have tool support to aid the companies during the SPL variability management. Supporting tools provide the companies a guide for the development of SPLs, as well as, a development and maintenance environment of the SPL. However, the choice of one tool that best meets the companies SPL development goals is far from trivial. In particular, this is a critical activity due to a sharp increase in the number of SPL management tools available in the last years. Furthermore, tool support should assist the complete SPL development process, and not just some activities. In this context, this paper contributes with a systematic literature review (SLR) aiming to identify and classify tools that support the SPL management, including the stages from conception until products derivation.

SLR is one secondary study method that has gotten much attention lately in software engineering [32]. An SLR reduces researchers' bias through pre-defined data forms and criteria that limit the room for interpretation [64]. Briefly, an SLR goes through existing primary reports, reviews them in-depth, and describes their methodology and results [45]. Therefore, our SLR represents a significant step forward in the state-of-the-art by deeply examining many relevant tools for feature modeling and management. The general propose of this study is to give a visual summary, by categorizing existing tools. Results are extracted from searching for evidences in journals and conference proceedings since 2000, by the fact that visibility provided by SPL in recent years has produced a higher concentration of research [37].

This study is based on a systematic search of publications from various data sources and it follows a pre-defined protocol during the whole process. Our results contributes specifically with relevant information (i) to support practitioners choosing appropriate tools that best fits their needs in a specific context of SPL, (ii) to point out attributes and requirements relevant to those interested in developing new tools, and (iii) to help with the improvement/extension of existing tools. We expect that both researchers and practitioners can benefit from the results of this SLR.

The rest of this paper is organized as follow. Section 2 presents the steps carried out in this SLR, presenting the research protocol, conduction, and process of data extraction. Section 3 presents the summary and analysis of observed data in the selected studies, answering three research questions. Section 4 presents the threats to validity related to this SLR and how they were addressed prior of the study to minimize their impact. Finally, Section 5 concludes the paper and provides directions for future work.

2   Literature Systematic Review (SLR)

This study has been carried out according to the guideline for SLR proposed by Kitchenham and Charters [32]. We have adapted and applied such techniques in order to identify and classify existing tools to support SPL management. The guidelines [32] are structured according a three-step process for Planning, Conducting, and Reporting the review. Fig. 1 depicts an overview of our research process comprising each step and its stages sequence. The execution of the overall process involves iteration, feed-back, and refinement of the defined process [32]. The SLR steps and protocol are detailed below.

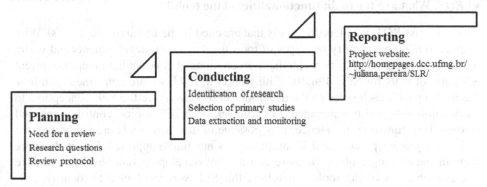

Fig. 1. Overview research process

2.1   Planning the Review

This step has the goal of developing a protocol that specifies the plan that the SLR will follow to identify, assess, and collate evidence [32]. To plan an SLR includes several actions:

Identification of the Need for a Review. The need for an SLR originates from in-crease in the number of SPL management tools made available. In this context, the choice of one tool that best fits the researchers and practitioners needs in a specific context of SPL is far from trivial. Therefore, this SLR aims to give an overall picture of the tools available in the literature for SPL management, in order to find out how they support the variability management process.

Specifying the Research Questions. The focus of the research questions (RQs) is to identify and analyze SPL management tools. The RQs are formulated with the help of Population, Intervention, Comparison, Outcome, and Context (PICOC) criteria [28]. The population is composed of studies that cite SPL management tools. The interven-tion includes search for indications that the SPL conception, development, and main-tenance can be fully supported. The comparison goal is to find evidences on the characteristics and functionalities that differ each tool. The outcome of this study represents how tools support the variability management process. It supports practi-tioners and researchers not only choosing appropriate tools, but also in the develop-ment of new tools and improvement of existing tools. The context is within the domains of SPL management with a focus on tools and their application domain.

The main research question (RQ) of this study is: **How do the available tools for SPL support the variability management process?** To answer this question, a set of sub-questions was derived from the main RQ to identify and analyze the relevant literature discussions. More specifically, we investigate three RQs:

- *RQ1*. **How many SPL management tools have been cited in the literature since 2000?**
- *RQ2*. **What are the main characteristics of the tools?**
- *RQ3*. **What are the main functionalities of the tools?**

To address *RQ1*, we identified tools that are cited in the literature since 2000. With respect to *RQ2*, we identify the types of tools that have been developments and where the tools were developed. Through these descriptions, it is possible to map the current adoption of tools for SPL. Finally, with respect to *RQ3*, we are concerned with how the tool supports each stage of the development process, since the SPL conception, to its development, and maintenance. In particular, what SPL topics, contributions, and novelty they constitute to. Hence, it is possible to map how tools are supporting the SPL management process and if the process is not fully supported, i.e., if there are gaps in the existing tools, or if there is a need of developing functionalities that are not available in existing tools. Therefore, this SLR was conducted to identify, analyze, and interpret all available evidence related to specific RQs.

Developing a Review Protocol. We conducted an SLR in journals and conferences proceedings published from January 1st 2000 to December 31th 2013, by the fact that visibility provided by SPL in recent years has produced a higher concentration of research [37]. Three researchers were involved in this process and all of them continuously discussed and refined the RQs, search strings, inclusion, and exclusion criteria.

2.2   Conducting the Review

Conducting the review means executing the protocol planned in the previous phase. The conduction of this SLR includes several actions:

Identification of Research. Based on the RQs, the keywords were extracted and used to search the primary study sources. The search string used was constructed using the strategy proposed by Chen et al. [13]. Note that, we check preliminarily the keywords in all relevant papers already known [35, 40, 55]. Based on this strategy, this study relies on the following search string.

("tool") AND ("product line" OR "product family" OR "system family") AND ("management" OR "modeling" OR "configuration")

The term *"tool"* ensures that the research is conducted in order to find tools. In addition, the terms *"product line"*, *"product family"* or *"system family"* restrict the search by SPL tools. Finally, the terms *"management"*, *"modeling"* or *"configuration"* refers to the main functions for the development of SPL tools. Note that management is a generic term that includes both the modeling management and the configuration management in SPL. The primary studies were identified by applying the search strings to three scientific databases, namely ACM Digital Library[1], IEEE Xplore[2], and ScienceDirect[3]. These libraries were chosen because they are some of the most relevant ones in the software engineering literature [58]. The search was performed using the specific syntax of each database and considering only the title, abstract, and keywords. The results in each digital library are detailed in the Web supplementary material [2]. In addition to the search in digital libraries, the references of the primary studies were also read in order to identify other relevant primary studies (this technique is called "snowballing") [64].

Selection of Primary Studies. The basis for the selection of primary studies is the inclusion and exclusion criteria [32]. The following two inclusion criteria (IC) were used to include studies that are relevant to answer the RQs.

- *IC1*. The publications should be "journal" or "conference" and only papers written in English were considered.
- *IC2*. We included only primary studies that present tools to support the SPL management process (including one or more phases of the development cycle and maintenance of SPLs, from conception until products derivation). Therefore, the title, abstract, and keywords should explicitly mentions that the focus of the paper contributes with tools to support SPL variability management.

The following three exclusion criteria (EC) were used to exclude studies that we do not consider relevant to answer the RQs.

- *EC1*. We exclude technical reports presenting lessons learned, theses/dissertations, studies that describe events, and studies that are indexes or programming.
- *EC2*. We exclude duplicate papers. If a primary study is published in more than one venue, for example, if a conference paper is extended in a journal version, only the latter instance should be counted as a primary study. The journal version is preferred since it is expected to be the most complete report.
- *EC3*. Papers that do not focus on SPL management tools. Approaches, methods, and other techniques for SPL by itself should be excluded.

After papers inclusion, during the tools selection, we apply the following two EC.

- *EC4*. Tools that are currently discontinued.
- *EC5*. Tools without executable and/or documentation describing its functionalities available. Moreover, the tools with written documentation that does not have usable description about their functionalities were excluded because it would not be possible to understand how the tool works.

Data Extraction and Monitoring. As in the study of Petersen et al. [45], the reviewers first read abstracts and look for keywords and concepts that reflect the contribution of the paper. When abstracts are insufficient to allow meaningful keywords

---

[1] http://dl.acm.org/
[2] http://ieeexplore.ieee.org/
[3] http://www.sciencedirect.com/

to be chosen, reviewers choose to also scan the introduction or conclusion sections of the paper. As in the study of Kitchenham et al. [32], each journal and conference paper was reviewed by one of three different researchers (i.e. Pereira, Constantino and Figueiredo). Pereira coordinated the allocation of researchers to tasks based on the availability of each researcher and their ability to access the specific journals and conference proceedings. The researcher responsible for searching the specific journal or conference applied the detailed inclusion and exclusion criteria to the relevant papers. When the reviewers decided that a paper is not relevant, they provided a short rationale why paper should not be included in the study (for instance, because the paper does not cite a tool that support the SPL management process). In addition, another researcher checked any papers included and excluded at this stage. This step was done in order to check that all relevant papers were selected.

Once the list of primary studies is decided, the data from the tools cited by the papers are extracted. The phase of data extraction aims to summarize the data from the selected studies for further analysis. All available tool documentation served as data sources, such as tutorials, technical reports, industry magazines, dissertations/theses, websites, as well as the communication with authors (e.g., emails exchanged). The data extracted from each tool selected were: (i) date of data extraction; (ii) references to primary studies; (iii) tool name; (iv) main references of the tool; (v) release year; (vi) website tool (if available); (vii) main tools characteristics (graphical user interface, prototype, online, plugin, free for use, open-source, user guide, example solutions, and where the tool was developed); and (viii) main functionalities of each tool.

The data extraction phase involved all authors of this paper. We use Google's search engine to collect the data from the tools. The researcher Pereira extracted the data and the other researchers checked the extraction. Note that, during the data extraction the exclusion criteria (*EC4* and *EC5*) were verified. As in Kitchenham [32] when there was a disagreement, we discussed the issues until we reach an agreement. In this step, we used an Excel table to document the data extraction process. It was done in order to assess the quality of the extraction procedure. The data extraction can be found in the Web supplementary material [2].

2.3   Reporting the Review

The reporting step follows to publish the detailed results in the project website [2] and to write this paper. Its goal is to make it clear to others how the search was, and how they can find the same results. The project website also provides detailed information about the results and the search protocol.

3   Results and Analyses

The primary studies identified by the inclusion criteria were selected individually and summarized in the results. After the selection and data extraction of the tools cited by these papers, we discuss the answers to our RQs.

3.1   SPL Management Tools

Table 1 summarizes the number of papers found in our SLR. Note that, for this analysis, relevant studies (total included) more than doubled after 2007. In the first stage, after applying the inclusion and exclusion criteria, 46 papers were included and 103 papers were excluded (4 are duplicated papers). In the second stage, for each reference of primary studies included, we analyze the title and we included more 6 papers [1, 6, 25, 26, 29, 37] that present additional tools to support the SPL management process (technique called "snowballing"). This technique was necessary in order to have a more complete set of tools. At the end of the search phase, 52 papers were included. Specifically, we included 16 papers of the ACM Digital Library (from 48 papers returned), 19 papers of IEEE Xplore (from 71 papers returned), and 11 papers of Science Direct (from 30 papers returned).

Table 1. Number searched for years 2000-2013

Year	2000	2001	2002	2003	2004	2005	2006	2007	2008	2009	2010	2011	2012	2013	All
Total	1	4	1	3	7	4	6	13	13	9	15	22	30	21	149
Total Selected	0	0	1	1	2	1	3	4	6	2	4	7	6	9	46
Total Snowballing	0	0	0	0	1	0	1	0	1	1	1	0	0	1	6
Total Included	0	0	1	1	3	1	4	4	7	3	5	7	6	10	52

After the papers inclusion process, 60 potentially relevant tools were selected for extracting and analyzing the data. Another search was performed on Google search engine with the particular information of every tool cited by the papers, in order to find out more documentation about these tools. There are two major artifacts analyzed in this review. The first is concerned with the executable, through which the reviewers could test the functionalities of the tool; and the second involves the written documentation found, i.e. websites, tutorials, technical reports, papers, industry magazines and dissertations/theses for data extraction.

During data extraction, 19 relevant tools were excluded as a result of applying the detailed exclusion criteria *EC4* and *EC5*. Two tools was excluded because the project is currently discontinued (*EC4*), and the remaining tools were not possible to characterize how they work due to the lack of information (*EC5*). The 41 tools included are listed in Table 2 in chronological order. Data in this table show that the number of released tools increased in the years 2005, 2007, 2009 and 2012.

3.2   Main Characteristics of the Tools

After a careful selection of documentation about the included tools, we identify their main characteristics. Table 2 shows which characteristics each tool implements. The following characteristics were considered: graphical user interface (GUI), prototype (PRT), online (ONL), plugin (PLG), free for use (FRE), open-source (OPS), user guide available (USG), example solutions available (EXS), and where the tool was developed (DEV). We use "n/a" for information not available. These characteristic was selected inspired by [13, 37, 59].

Table 2. Characteristics each SPL management tool supports

Tool [Ref.]	Year	GUI	PRT	ONL	PLG	FRE	OPS	USG	EXS	DEV
LISA toolkit [25]	2013	●			●	n/a	n/a	n/a	n/a	B
ISMT4SPL [43]	2012	●		●		n/a	n/a	n/a	n/a	A
Sysiphus-IVMM [56]	2012	●		●	●	●	●	n/a	n/a	A
VariaMos [39]	2012	●		●	●		n/a	●	n/a	A
VULCAN [36]	2012	●		●	●	●	●	n/a	n/a	A
Pacogen [27]	2011				●	●	●	n/a	n/a	A
Invar [19]	2010	●	●	●		●	n/a	n/a	●	A
FMT [35]	2009	●			●	●	n/a	●	n/a	A
Hephaestus [6]	2009	●				●	●	n/a	n/a	A
Hydra [47]	2009	●			●	●	●	●	n/a	B
SPLOT [40]	2009	●		●		●	●	n/a	●	A
S²T² [7]	2009	●			●	●	n/a	n/a	●	B
FeatureMapper [26]	2008	●			●	●	●	●	n/a	A
MoSPL [54]	2008	●	●			n/a	n/a	n/a	n/a	A
VISIT-FC [12]	2008	●	●			n/a	n/a	n/a	n/a	A
DecisionKing [17]	2007	●			●	n/a	n/a	n/a	n/a	B
DOPLER [18]	2007	●			●	n/a	n/a	n/a	●	B
FaMa [3]	2007	●			●	●	●	●	●	A
GenArch [14]	2007	●			●	●	●	n/a	n/a	A
REMAP-tool [49]	2006	●	●		●	n/a	n/a	n/a	●	A
YaM [29]	2006	●		●		n/a	n/a	n/a	n/a	B
AORA [61]	2005	●				n/a	●	n/a	●	A
DOORS Extension [9]	2005	●						●	n/a	A
FeatureIDE [55]	2005	●			●	●	●	●	●	A
Kumbang [41]	2005	●			●	●	●	●	●	B
PLUSS toolkit [21]	2005	●						n/a	n/a	B
VARMOD [62]	2005	●			●		n/a	n/a	●	A
XFeature [63]	2005	●			●	●	●	●	●	B
COVAMOF-VS [50]	2004	●			●			●	n/a	A
DREAM [42]	2004	●				n/a	n/a	n/a	n/a	A
ASADAL [31]	2003	●			●		n/a	n/a	n/a	A
Pure::Variants [51]	2003	●			●			●	●	I
Captain Feature [11]	2002	●				●	●	●	n/a	A
DECIMAL [16]	2002	●				n/a	n/a	n/a	n/a	A
Odyssey [8]	2002	●				●		●	●	A
GEARS [33]	2001	●			●			n/a	n/a	I
WeCoTin [1]	2000	●	●	●				n/a	●	I
Holmes [53]	1999	●	●			n/a	n/a	n/a	n/a	A
DARE [23]	1998	●	●					n/a	n/a	I
Metadoc FM [57]	1998	●			●			●	●	I
001 [34]	1993	●						n/a	n/a	A

In this analysis, we identified that only one tool (Pacogen) has no graphical user interface. Most tools are neither prototypes (83%) nor online (90%). Furthermore, we found out that 51% of the tools are plugins. Plugins provide the extension of tools already established and known. Additionally, 46% are free for use and only 34% are open-source projects. However, we highlight that the increased development of free and open source tools could increase the community's interest in adopting the concept of SPL, and promote knowledge sharing and extension. A drawback in this case is that several developers do not make the source code available.

User guide (USG) and example solutions (EXS) are not available for most tools analyzed. User guide and example solutions are mainly important for users that do not have any kind of previous training before the tool usage, because these documents show how the user can start from. They enable novice users to use the tool according to the planned process and the result to be correctly interpreted. Little documentation available and lack of supporting examples are some of the reasons that may end up discouraging the adoption and wide use of these tools since it would requires users to study and guess the tool behavior. Finally, we extract information about where the tool was developed (last column in Table 2). We found out that 66% of the selected tools were developed exclusively in the academic environment (A), while only 12% were developed exclusively in the industry (I), and the remaining 22% tools were developed in both academic and industrial environments (B).

3.3 Main Functionalities of the Tools

Our next analyses in this section extend an existing classification of research approaches by Lisboa et al. [37], summarized in Table 3. This classification schema

Table 3. Explanation functionalities evaluated extended from Lisboa et al. [37]

Functionalities	Explanation
Planning	*It is responsible for collecting the data needed to define domain scope*
(1) Pre-analysis documentation	Stores and retrieves the information
(2) Matrix of the domain	It is represented using rows and columns (features and applications)
(3) Scope definition	Identifies the features that should be part of the reuse infrastructure
Modeling	*It represents the domain scope (commonality, variability and constraint)*
(4) Domain representation	Represents the defined scope
(5) Variability	Represents the variability a feature can have (optional, alternative and or)
(6) Mandatory features	Represent the features that will always be in the products
(7) Composition rule	Create restrictions for representing and relating the features
(8) Relationship types	Provides different types of relationships between the features
(9) Feature attributes	Permits the inclusion of specific information for each feature
(10) Source code generator	Responsible for generating source code based on model
Validation	*This group refers to functionalities responsible to validate the domain*
(11) Domain documentation	Provides documentation about the domain
(12) Manage requirements	Provides support for inclusion of requirements or use cases in the tool
(13) Relationship	Relates the existing features of a domain to the requirements
(14) Reports	Generates reports about the information available in the domain
(15) Consistency check	Verifies if the generated domain follows the composition rules created
Product Configuration and Integration	*Product configuration is built from a common set of reusable asset, and Integration allows the interoperability between other applications.*
(16) Product derivation	Identifies the features that belong to a product
(17) Import/export	Provides the function of Import/export from/to other applications

present a practical approach for analysis based on a well-defined set of guidelines and metrics. We extend the previous classification [37] by analyzing new functionalities, such as source code generation and support for integration. Based on Table 3, Table 4 shows which functionalities each tool offers support to. The numbers refer to the functionalities described in Table 3 and the columns separate each group of functionalities: *Planning, Modeling, Validation,* and *Product Configuration and Integration (PCI),* respectively. The analysis of the results focuses on presenting the frequencies of publications for each functionality. This result facilitates the identification of which functionalities have been emphasized in past research and, thus, to identify gaps and possibilities for future research. In addition, it can help to discover which tool best satisfies the need of a user in a given context.

In Table 4, there is an evident lack of tools to support all stages of SPL development and evolution. In this classification, the majority of the analyzed tools have similar functionalities. Most of the tools available both commercially and freely support the first four functionalities in group *Modeling,* the last functionality in the *Validation* group, and the two functionalities in the *Product Configuration and Integration* group. Therefore, this result identified that the largest gap in the analyzed tools is support the *Planning* group. In the *Planning* group, the identified functionalities were available only in fourteen tools, and only six tools implement all functionalities in this group. The results of this systematic review reveal that 66% of the selected tools stress the need for planning support. A much smaller number of tools (34%) describe concrete support. This seems to indicate that, despite increasing interest and importance, planning is not yet the main focus of the product line research community. Particularly, in *Modeling* group, thirty-five tools (85%) support at least four of the functionalities of this group. Regarding the *Validation* group, only one tool (*YaM*) does not support any functionality. Note that twenty tools (49%) support at least three of the functionalities of this group. In the *Product Configuration and Integration* group, thirty-four tools (83%) support the product derivation functionality, and the import/export from/to other applications functionality is exploited for twenty-nine tools (71%). Integration is a desirable functionality since it allows the interoperability between other applications. The lack of this functionality could hinder the adoption of the tool, as it hampers their integration with other existing tools. Therefore, although the results highlight the lack of tools to fully support SPL management; e.g., much of the analyzed tools do not support the *Planning* group. On the other hand, we found that the tools offer interoperability between other applications. This fact maximizes the reuse within the solution itself and externally, for instance, allowing users to migrate from on technology (e.g., conditional compilation [22]) to another (e.g., feature oriented programming [24]).

4   Threats to Validity

A key issue when performing of the SLR is the validity of the results. Questions we need to answer include: was the study designed and performed in a sound and controlled manner? To which domain can the results generalize? This section presents the

Table 4. Functionalities each SPL management tool supports

Tool	Planning			Modeling							Validation					PCI	
	1	2	3	4	5	6	7	8	9	10	11	12	13	14	15	16	17
LISA toolkit	•		•	•	•	•	•	•	•	•	•		•	•			•
ISMT4SPL	•		•	•	•		•			•		•	•		•	•	
Sysiphus-IVMM	•	•	•	•	•	•	•					•		•		•	
VariaMos				•	•	•	•	•					•	•		•	•
VULCAN				•	•	•	•	•	•		•			•		•	•
Pacogen													•	•			•
Invar											•			•	•	•	
FMT				•	•	•	•		•					•		•	•
Hephaestus											•	•	•	•		•	•
Hydra				•	•	•	•							•		•	•
SPLOT				•	•	•	•					•		•		•	•
S²T²				•	•	•	•				•			•		•	•
FeatureMapper					•	•	•						•	•		•	•
MoSPL					•	•	•					•		•		•	•
VISIT-FC					•	•	•							•		•	
DecisionKing	•		•		•	•	•					•		•			•
DOPLER	•	•	•		•	•	•	•				•		•		•	•
FaMa				•	•	•	•	•	•		•			•		•	•
GenArch				•	•	•	•		•		•			•		•	•
REMAP-tool	•		•	•	•	•	•	•			•		•	•		•	•
YaM			•											•			
AORA	•	•	•	•	•	•	•				•	•		•		•	
DOORS Extens.				•	•	•						•		•		•	
FeatureIDE				•	•	•	•			•				•		•	•
Kumbang		•		•	•	•	•	•				•		•		•	•
PLUSS toolkit				•	•	•	•					•		•		•	
VARMOD	•			•	•	•	•				•		•	•		•	•
XFeature				•	•	•	•	•		•	•			•		•	•
COVAMOF-VS				•	•	•								•		•	
DREAM		•	•	•	•	•						•		•			
ASADAL				•	•	•	•		•					•		•	•
Pure::Variants				•	•	•	•		•					•		•	•
Captain Feature				•	•	•	•							•		•	
DECIMAL				•	•	•	•							•		•	
Odyssey				•	•	•					•		•	•		•	•
GEARS				•	•	•	•	•		•				•		•	•
WeCoTin				•	•	•		•						•		•	
Holmes	•	•	•	•	•	•					•			•		•	•
DARE	•	•	•	•	•	•					•						
Metadoc FM	•	•	•	•	•	•	•						•	•		•	•
001				•	•	•	•	•		•	•			•		•	

different validity threats related to SLR. We presented how the threats were addressed to minimize the likelihood of their realization and impact. We discussed the SLR validity with respect to the four groups of common threats to validity: internal validity, external validity, construct validity, and conclusion validity [64].

External Validity. External validity concerns the ability to generalize the results to other environments, such as to industry practices [64]. A major external validity to this study was during the identified primary studies. The search for the tools was conducted in three relevant scientific databases in order to capture as much as possible the available tools and avoid all sorts of bias. However, the quality of search engines could have influenced the completeness of the identified primary studies. That means our search may have missed those studies whose authors would have used other terms to specify the SPL management tool or would not have used the keywords that we used for searches in the title, abstract, and keywords of their papers.

Internal Validity. Internal validity concerns the question whether the effect is caused by the independent variables (e.g. reviewers) or by other factors [64]. In this sense, a limitation of this study concerns the reliability. The reliability has been addressed as far as possible by involving three researchers, and by having a protocol which was piloted and hence evaluated. If the study is replicated by another set of researchers, it is possible that some studies that were removed in this review could be included and other studies could be excluded. However, in general we believe that the internal validity of the SLR is high given the use of a systematic procedure, consultation with the researchers in the field, involvement, and discussion between three researchers.

Construct Validity. Construct validity reflects to what extent the operational measures that are studied really represent what the researcher have in mind and what is investigated according to the RQs [64]. The three reviewers of this study are researchers in the software engineering field, focused in SPL, and none of the tools was written/developed by us. Therefore, we are not aware of any bias we may have introduced during the analyses. However, from the reviewers perspective, a construct validity threat could be biased judgment. In this study, the decision of which studies to include or to exclude and how to categorize the studies could be biased and thus pose a threat. A possible threat in such review is to exclude some relevant tool. To minimize this threat both the processes of inclusion and exclusion were piloted by the three reviewers. Furthermore, potentially relevant studies that were excluded were documented. Therefore, we believe that we do not have omitted any relevant tool.

Conclusion Validity. Threats to conclusion validity are related with issues that affect the ability to draw the correct conclusions from the study [64]. From the reviewers' perspective, a potential threat to conclusion validity is the reliability of the data extraction categories from the tools, since not all information was obvious to answer the RQ and some data had to be interpreted. Therefore, in order to ensure the validity, multiple sources of data were analyzed, i.e. papers, websites, technical reports, industry magazines manuals, and executable. Furthermore, in the event of a disagreement between the two primary reviewers, the third reviewer acted as an arbitrator to ensure agreement was reached.

5   Conclusion and Future Work

In industry, the development of large software systems requires an enormous effort for modeling and configuring multiple products. To face this problem, several tools have been proposed and used for representing and managing the variations of a system. There are many available options of variability management tools. Therefore, this paper aims to identify and evaluate existing tools in the literature to support the SPL management. To this end, we conducted a SLR, where we follow a guide of systematic review proposed by Kitchenham [32]. To substantiate the findings of the paper, the working group has set up a website [2] where interested people can verify detailed results of the SLR.

Although analysis of existing SPL management tools has been performed in previous studies [5, 10, 20, 59, 44], the purpose of these studies in a general way was to facilitate tool selection in the context of SPL. However, they were aimed at studying only tools very specifics or a small group of tools. Our study differs from others by the fact of being an SLR. In addition, with regard to SLR presented by Lisboa et al. [37], the results confirm that our study analyzes a relatively number higher of tool. Finally, our resulted have impact due to the SLR period, search string, processes of inclusion/exclusion and data extraction.

Our SLR identified 41 tools existing in the literature that provide support to at least one SPL management phase. It provides an overview of tools where it is possible to see which characteristics and functionalities each tool implemented. The contribution of this research covers both the academic and the professional segment. In the academic environment, this research helps to highlight the lack of complete tools in this area, identifying gaps in current research to provide a background for new research activities. In the professional context, this research helps to find possible tools that will assist SPL developers or even help them manage existing SPL.

Through the results obtained, it is clear that the little documentation available and the complexity and/or the unavailability of existing support tools are some of the reasons that may end up discouraging the adoption and wide use of these tools in organizations and academia. Therefore, we intend to use our knowledge to conduct courses in both academia and industry, in order to encourage adoption of these tools. In addition, there are still gaps in the complete process support in all the tools we investigated. Although most of the tools offer interoperability between other applications, such gaps in functionality can make it difficult for industry to adopt a tool, because it would hinder the use of several tools and traceability of information among them. Therefore, our review suggests that there are opportunities for the extension of the existing tools. One of the gaps that we identify with the SLR is that manual method for product configuration adopted by the tools may not be sufficient to support industries during SPL managing. The manual process makes product configuration into a complex, time-consuming, and error-prone task. Therefore, we are working on an extension of a tool with the new functionality [38]. Moreover, as future work, we aim to evaluate (i) notations used in each tool; (ii) tools that can be used together in a complementary way; (iii) some criteria to analyze the tools comparatively, for example, GUI complexity and visualization support; and (vi) characteristics and functionalities relevant for the practitioners and researchers.

Acknowledgements. This work was partially supported by CNPq (grant Universal 485907/2013-5) and FAPEMIG (grants APQ-02532-12 and PPM-00382-14).

References

1. Asikainen, T., et al.: Using a Configurator for Modelling and Configuring Software Product Lines based on Feature Models. In: Workshop on Software Variability Management for Product Derivation, Software Product Line Conference (SPLC), pp. 24–35 (2004)
2. A Systematic Literature Review of Software Product Line Management Tools, http://homepages.dcc.ufmg.br/~juliana.pereira/SLR
3. Benavides, D., et al.: Fama: Tooling a Framework for the Automated Analysis of Feature Models. In: 1st International Workshop on Variability Modelling of Software Intensive Systems (VaMoS), pp. 129–134 (2007)
4. Bernardo, M., et al.: Architecting Families of Software Systems with Process Algebras. ACM Transactions on Software Engineering and Methodology 11(4), 386–426 (2002)
5. Beuche, D., et al.: Variability Management with Feature Models. Journal Science of Computer Programming 53(3), 333–352 (2004)
6. Bonifácio, R., et al.: Hephaestus: A Tool for Managing SPL Variabilities. In: Brazilian Symposium on Components, Architectures and Reuse Software (SBCARS), pp. 26–34 (2009)
7. Botterweck, G., et al.: A Design of a Configurable Feature Model Configurator. In: 3rd International Workshop on Variability Modelling of Software Intensive Systems (VaMoS), pp. 165–168 (2009)
8. Braga, R., et al.: Odyssey: A Reuse Environment based on Domain Models. In: IEEE Symposium on Application-Specific Systems and Software Engineering and Technology (ASSET), pp. 50–57 (1999)
9. Buhne, S., et al.: Modelling Requirements Variability across Product Lines. In: 13th International Conference on Requirements Engineering (RE), pp. 41–50 (2005)
10. Capilla, R., et al.: An Analysis of Variability Modeling and Management Tools for Product Line Development. In: Software and Service Variability Management Workshop - Concepts, Models, and Tools, pp. 32–47 (2007)
11. Captain Feature Tool, http://sourceforge.net/projects/captainfeature
12. Cawley, C., et al.: Interactive Visualisation to Support Product Configuration in Software Product Lines. In: 2nd International Workshop on Variability Modeling of Software-Intensive Systems (VaMoS), pp. 7–16 (2008)
13. Chen, L., Babar, M.A.: A Systematic Review of Evaluation of Variability Management Approaches in Software Product Lines. Journal Information and Software Technology 53(4), 344–362 (2011)
14. Cirilo, E., et al.: A product Derivation Tool based on Model-Driven Techniques and Annotations. Journal of Universal Computer Science 14(8), 1344–1367 (2008)
15. Clements, P., Northrop, L.: Software Product Lines: Practices and Patterns. Addison-Wesley (2001)
16. Dehlinger, J., et al.: Decimal and PLFaultCAT: From Product-Line Requirements to Product-Line Member Software Fault Trees. In: 29th International Conference on Software Engineering (ICSE), pp. 49–50 (2007)
17. Dhungana, D., et al.: Decisionking: A Flexible and Extensible Tool for Integrated Variability Modeling. In: 1st International Workshop on Variability Modelling of Software-intensive Systems (VaMoS), pp. 119–128 (2007)
18. Dhungana, D., et al.: The Dopler Meta-Tool for Decision-Oriented Variability Modeling: A Multiple Case Study. Journal Automated Software Engineering 18(1), 77–114 (2011)

19. Dhungana, D., et al.: Integrating Heterogeneous Variability Modeling Approaches with Invar. In: 7th International Workshop on Variability Modelling of Software-intensive Systems, VaMoS (2013)
20. Djebbi, O., et al.: Industry Survey of Product Lines Management Tools: Requirements, Qualities and Open Issues. In: 15th IEEE International Requirements Engineering Conference (IREC), pp. 301–306 (2007)
21. Eriksson, M., et al.: The Pluss Toolkit: Extending Telelogic Doors and IBM-Rational Rose to Support Product Line Use Case Modeling. In: 20th International Conference on Automated Software Engineering (ASE), pp. 300–304 (2005)
22. Figueiredo, E., et al.: Evolving Software Product Lines with Aspects: An Empirical Study on Design Stability. In: 30th International Conf. on Soft. Eng. (ICSE), pp. 261-270 (2008)
23. Frakes, W.B., et al.: Dare-cots: A Domain Analysis Support tool. In: International Conference of the Chilean Computer Science Society, pp. 73–77 (1997)
24. Gaia, F., et al.: A Quantitative and Qualitative Assessment of Aspectual Feature Modules for Evolving Software Product Lines. In: Science of Computer Programming (SCP), pp. 1–24 (2014)
25. Groher, I., Weinreich, R.: Supporting Variability Management in Architecture Design and Implementation. In: 46th Hawaii International Conference on System Sciences (HICSS), pp. 4995–5004 (2013)
26. Heidenreich, F., et al.: FeatureMapper: Mapping Features to Models. In: International Conference on Software Engineering (ICSE), pp. 943–944 (2008)
27. Hervieu, A., et al.: Pacogen: Automatic Generation of Pairwise Test Configurations from feature models. In: 22nd International Symposium on Software Reliability Engineering (ISSRE), pp. 120–129 (2011)
28. Higgins, J., et al.: Cochrane Handbook for Systematic Reviews of Interventions, vol. 5. Wiley Online Library (2008)
29. Jain, A., Biesiadecki, J.: Yam: A Framework for Rapid Software Development. In: 2nd IEEE International Conference on Space Mission Challenges for Information Technology (SMC-IT), pp. 182–194 (2006)
30. Kang, K., et al.: Feature-Oriented Domain Analysis (FODA) Feasibility Study (1990), http://www.sei.cmu.edu/reports/90tr021.pdf/
31. Kim, K. et al.: Asadal: A Tool System for Co-Development of Software and Test Environment based on Product Line Engineering. In: 28th International Conference on Software Engineering (ICSE), pp. 783–786 (2006)
32. Kitchenham, B., et al.: Systematic Literature Reviews in Software Engineering: A systematic Literature Review. Journal Information and Software Technology 51(1), 7–15 (2009)
33. Krueger, C.: Biglever Software Gears and the 3-tiered SPL Methodology. In: 22nd Conference on Object-Oriented Programming Systems, Languages, and Applications (OOPSLA), pp. 844–845 (2007)
34. Krut, J.R.W.: Integrating 001 Tool Support in the Feature-Oriented Domain Analysis methodology. Technical Report, Software Engineering Institute (SEI) (1993), http://repository.cmu.edu/cgi/viewcontent.cgi?article=1166&context=sei
35. Laguna, M., Hernández, C.: A Software Product Line Approach for Ecommerce Systems. In: 7th International Conference on e-Business Engineering (ICEBE), pp. 230–235 (2010)
36. Lee, H., et al.: VULCAN: Architecture-Model-Based Workbench for Product Line Engineering. In: 16th International Software Product Line Conference (SPLC), pp. 260–264 (2012)

37. Lisboa, L.B., et al.: A Systematic Review of Domain Analysis Tools. Journal Information and Software Technology 52(1), 1–13 (2010)
38. Machado, L., et al.: SPLConfig: Product Configuration in Software Product Line. In: Brazilian Congress on Software (CBSoft), Tools Session, pp. 1–8 (2014)
39. Mazo, R., et al.: Variamos: A Tool for Product Line Driven Systems Engineering with a Constraint Based Approach. In: 24th International Conference on Advanced Information Systems Engineering (CAiSE), pp. 1–8 (2012)
40. Mendonça, M. et al.: S.P.L.O.T.: Software Product Lines Online Tools. In: 24th Conference on Object-Oriented Programming Systems, Languages, and Applications (OOPSLA), pp. 761–762 (2009)
41. Myllärniemi, V., et al.: Kumbang tools. In: 11th Software Product Line Conference (SPLC), pp. 135–136 (2007)
42. Park, J., et al.: Dream: Domain Requirement Asset Manager in Product Lines. In: International Symposium on Future Software Technology (ISFST) (2004)
43. Park, K., et al.: An Integrated Software Management Tool for Adopting Software Product Lines. In: 11th International Conference on Computation and Information Science (ICIS), pp. 553–558 (2012)
44. Pereira, J., et al.: Software Variability Management: An Exploratory Study with Two Feature Modeling Tools. In: Brazilian Symposium on Software Components, Architectures and Reuse (SBCARS), vol. 1, pp. 1–10 (2013)
45. Petersen, K., et al.: Systematic Mapping Studies in Software Engineering. In: 12th International Conference on Evaluation and Assessment in Software Engineering (EASE), pp. 68–77 (2008)
46. Pohl, K., et al.: Software Product Line Engineering: Foundations, Principles and Techniques. Springer (2005)
47. Salazar, J.R.: Herramienta para el Modelado y Configuración de Modelos de Características. PhD Thesis, Dpto. Lenguajes y Ciencias de la Comp. Universidad de Málaga (2009)
48. Santos, A., et al.: Test-based SPL Extraction: An Exploratory Study. In: 28th ACM Symposium on Applied Computing (SAC), Software Engineering Track, pp. 1031–1036 (2013)
49. Schmid, K., et al.: Requirements Management for Product Lines: Extending Professional Tools. In: 10th International Software Product Line Conference (SPLC), pp. 113–122 (2006)
50. Sinnema, M., Deelstra, S., Nijhuis, J., Dannenberg, R.B.: COVAMOF: A Framework for Modeling Variability in Software Product Families. In: Nord, R.L. (ed.) SPLC 2004. LNCS, vol. 3154, pp. 197–213. Springer, Heidelberg (2004)
51. Spinczyk, O., Beuche, D.: Modeling and Building Software Product Lines with Eclipse. In: 19th Conference on Object-Oriented Programming Systems, Languages, and Applications (OOPSLA), pp. 18–19 (2004)
52. SPL Hall of Fame, http://splc.net/fame.html
53. Succi, G., et al.: Holmes: An Intelligent System to Support Software Product Line Development. In: 23rd International Conference on Software Engineering (ICSE), pp. 829–830 (2001)
54. Thao, C., et al.: Software Configuration Management for Product Derivation in Software Product Families. In: 15th International Conference and Workshop on the Engineering of Computer Based Systems (ECBS), pp. 265–274 (2008)
55. Thüm, T., et al.: FeatureIDE: An Extensible Framework for Feature-Oriented Software Development. Journal Science of Computer Programming 79, 70–85 (2014)
56. Thurimella, A.K., Bruegge, B.: Issue-Based Variability Management Information and Software Technology. Journal Information and Soft. Technology 54(9), 933–950 (2012)

57. Thurimella, A.K., Janzen, D.: Metadoc Feature Modeler: A Plug-in for IBM Rational Doors. In: International Software Product Line Conference (SPLC), pp. 313–322 (2011)
58. Travassos, G.H., Biolchini, J.: Systematic Review Applied to Software Engineering. In: Brazilian Symposium on Software Engineering (SBES), Tutorials, p. 436 (2007)
59. Unphon, H.: A Comparison of Variability Modeling and Configuration Tools for Product Line Architecture (2008),
    http://www.itu.dk/people/unphon/technical_notes/
    CVC_v2008-06-30.pdf
60. Van der Linden, F., et al.: Software Product Lines in Action: The Best Industrial Practice in Product Line Engineering. Springer (2007)
61. Varela, P., et al.: Aspect-Oriented Analysis for Software Product Lines Requirements Engineering. In: Proceedings of the 2011 ACM Symposium on Applied Computing (2011)
62. Varmod-Prime Tool. Software Systems Engineering Research Group/University of Duisburg-Essen, http://paluno.uni-due.de/en/varmod-prime
63. XFeature Modeling Tool, http://www.pnp-software.com/XFeature
64. Wohlin, C. et al.: Experimentation in Software Engineering: An Introduction. Kluwer Academic Publishers (2012)

Open Source License Violation Check for SPDX Files

Georgia M. Kapitsaki[1] and Frederik Kramer[2]

[1] Department of Computer Science, University of Cyprus,
1 University Avenue, Nicosia, Cyprus
gkapi@cs.ucy.ac.cy
[2] Otto von Guericke University, Universitaetsplatz 2, D-39106, Magdeburg, Germany
frederik.kramer@ovgu.de

Abstract. The Open Source Software development model has gained a lot of momentum in the latest years providing organizations and software engineers with a variety of software, components and libraries that can be exploited in the construction of larger application systems. Open Source Software is accompanied by licenses that state the conditions under which the intellectual property can be used. Since not all licenses are governed by the same conditions of use, the correct combination of licenses is vital, when different libraries are exploited in newly developed application systems. If this is not adequately handled, license violations might be a consequence of incompatibilities. In this paper we present our work on license violation checking in the framework of Software Package Data Exchange (SPDX). Starting from the modelling of license compatibilities our approach examines potential violations in software package information formatted using the SPDX specification. At the same time alternative solutions in the form of applicable licenses for the software package are proposed. This approach can be a valuable asset for Open Source practitioners in the license decision process assisting in detecting possible violations and in making suggestions on license use.

Keywords: Free Open Source Software, Licensing, License compatibility, Software Package Data Exchange.

1   Introduction

The popularity of Free and Open Source Software (FOSS) among software engineers and enterprises is constantly growing as organizations try to integrate openness in their procedures [5]. FOSS provides new possibilities for engineers to incorporate third party software into their implementations and for organizations to distribute their products as open source embracing open ICT models. In open source software, licenses express how the software can be exploited by the potential users differentiating between user rights and obligations [13]. An open source software license contains *the terms under which the software is made available and under which conditions it can be used, integrated, modified and redistributed.*

I. Schaefer and I. Stamelos (Eds.): ICSR 2015, LNCS 8919, pp. 90–105, 2014.

The problem that many software vendors often face is how to incorporate third party software in their implementations correctly without causing any license violations; remaining hence legally compliant. License violations are a complex issue in FOSS due to the variety of licenses that state different and often contradicting conditions of use referring mainly to conditions for software modification and re-distribution. When software libraries licensed under different terms are jointly used, this license diversity may lead to license incompatibilities. Licenses cover a range from very permissive licenses, such as the MIT license and the Academic Free License (AFL), to highly restrictive licenses, such as the GNU General Public License (GPL) and the Open Source License (OSL). Licenses are categorised as either permissive or copyleft. Permissive licensing allows the software to be part of a larger product under almost any other license. Copyleft licenses are posing more restrictions. Copyleft is further divided into weak and strong copyleft. If the software used is weak copyleft-licensed, the created work can be distributed under another license as long as no changes are made in this weak copyleft-licensed software used. Strong copyleft requires all derivative work that uses strong copyleft-licensed software to be distributed with the very same license.

The Software Package Data Exchange (SPDX) specification addresses the issue of integrating license information into the distribution of software packages that can be formatted according to SPDX [12]. As such it is vital to examine whether the information contained in the SPDX file regarding the license applied on the software package is correct.

In this work we are addressing license violation detection by using SPDX files. Specifically, we have designed and implemented a compatibility tool that assists in: 1) verifying that the information on the license applied on the software package is correct, 2) identifying any license incompatibilities among the licenses of the software package, and 3) making suggestions for licenses that can be applied without causing violations. A side contribution of our work, that is evolving, lies in the modelling of license compatibilities for a popular license set captured in a license graph. This is the first work that approaches license violations in a specification setting that can offer a global solution for license compatibility enforcement. We hope that it will trigger more research on license compatibility and further promote the use of SPDX, as well as contribute to the tools accompanying the specification.

The rest of the paper is structured as follows. Section 2 briefly presents the Software Package Data Exchange specification focusing on parts that are relevant to our work, whereas section 3 is dedicated to the modelling of license compatibilities presenting the license compatibility graph. Section 4 analyses the SPDX tool. This is further demonstrated in section 5 through a proof-of-concept evaluation on existing open source projects. Section 6 gives a brief overview of related work on open source licensing and compatibilities and, finally, section 7 concludes the paper.

2   Describing Software Packages with SPDX

The Software Package Data Exchange specification with 1.2 being its latest formal version can be used in distributing information on the licenses of software packages [10]. According to the specification, it is "*a standard format for communicating the components, licenses, and copyrights associated with a software package.*" SPDX has been initiated by the Linux foundation and its contributors include commercial companies such as BlackDuck, Fujitsu, HP, Siemens, amongst others, as well as non-profit organizations such as the Eclipse and the Mozilla foundations. SPDX covers over 200 licenses including the ones approved by the Open Source Initiative (OSI), an organization dedicated to promoting open-source software. This latter information on whether a license is OSI-approved is also indicated in the SPDX file itself.

The SPDX consortium has introduced a number of tools that assist in the manipulation of SPDX files including file converters and comparators (i.e., SPDX Compare Utility). However, more elaborated tools are missing. Novel tools could collaborate with SPDX files in order to assist software engineers, managers and legal departments in drawing useful conclusions on the use of software licenses in cases, where complicated software architectures prevail. For instance, when a software package contains components with over 10 different licenses it is vital to examine if these are treated correctly from a legal perspective. This is the case addressed in the current work that examines license violation and compliance in SPDX files.

SPDX files appear in various formats. These include RDF (Resource Description Framework) files, a textual key-value pair format referred to as tag format and a spreadsheet format. The latter is provided for better readability and manual changes. With respect to license compatibility and potential conflicts that may appear in an existing SPDX file, we are mostly interested in the content of the following RDF flavour fields:

- *licenseDeclared* (or tag key name *PackageLicenseDeclared* in tag format): indicates the license that has been asserted for the package.
- *licenseConcluded* (or tag key name *PackageLicenseConcluded* in tag format): indicates the license that the creator of the SPDX file concluded. This may differ from the declared license.
- *licenseInfoFromFiles* (or tag key name *PackageLicenseInfoFromFiles* in tag format): indicates the list of all licenses found in the files of the software package.

3   Modelling License Compatibilities

In order to model license compatibility, we need to define what makes two FOSS licenses compatible: we can consider license V_1 to be "one-way compatible" with license V_2, if software that contains components from both licenses can be licensed under license V_2. As an example we assume two artefacts: One smaller artifact licensed under any of the BSD-type licenses and a larger artefact licensed under any of the LGPL licenses. The merged code could than be licensed under any of the LGPL licenses (see also 1). Or: anyone who conforms to license V_1 would also conform to license V_2. Following this rationale, we can represent known licenses and their compatibilities using a directed graph $G(V, E)$ with each vertex V representing a specific license with its version and each edge E connecting two compatible licenses V_1 and V_2 (with direction from V_1 to V_2).

Although in the ideal case the complete set of licenses recognized by the OSI and the Free Software Foundation (FSF) should be examined for compatibility, this is not feasible in practice due to their very large number and the big differences in the respective licenses text. If one considers different license versions the OSI covers 70, the FSF 88 licenses and the SPDX specification maintains as much as 215 licenses. As a starting point we selected the most popular licenses. We considered a license popular, if it were amongst the topmost selected in relevant online repositories, such as SourceForge and the KnowledgeBase originating from BlackDuck. The most popular license in these repositories is the GPL version 2.0 that is used in 58% of the projects hosted at SourceForge and in 33% of the projects hosted on BlackDuck's KnowledgeBase. Following this selection process the license list depicted in Table 1 has derived with 20 licenses from different categories. All have been approved both by OSI and FSF.

We have created a license compatibility graph (Figure 1) based on these licenses. The hard task of compatibility analysis for the construction of the graph was based on various sources. These include Wikipedia article entries on licenses, information from the license texts and forums, as well as the GNU hosted page on license compatibilities with GPL that contains valuable information on the rights and obligations of many FOSS licenses. The license graph that we obtained from this process is directed and acyclic. Directionality is apparent due to the "one way compatibility" between licenses. The second attribute derives from the fact that usually compatibility stems from a less restrictive to a more restrictive license. For instance, although the MIT and the BSD licenses seem equivalent, software that contains both licenses should be licensed entirely under the more restrictive license. In this case this would be the BSD license. Hence, it is not feasible to return to the less restrictive license again through edge reachability.

Public domain appears also on the graph and is connected to the less restrictive permissive license, i.e., MIT/X11. Public domain is applied on work whose intellectual property rights have expired and cannot be claimed anymore [3]. However there is no equivalent for public domain in the European Union. Note that there are cases of ambiguities in license compatibility. This is based on the fact that different organizations provide different interpretations of the license text placing a license in different categories. For instance, the Eclipse Public License 1.0 (EPL-1.0) is generally considered a weak copyleft one, but the German institute for legal issues regarding free and open source software IfrOSS[1] places the license under the strong copyleft category.

---

[1] http://www.ifross.com/

Table 1. Chosen license set

License name	Abbreviation	Category
Academic Free License version 3.0	AFL-3.0	Permissive
Apache License version 2.0	Apache-2.0	Permissive
Artistic License version 2.0	Artistic-2.0	Weak copyleft
BSD 2-clause or "Simplified" or "FreeBSD"	BSD-2-clause	Permissive
BSD 3-clause or BSD New" or "BSD Simplified"	BSD-3-clause	Permissive
Common Development and Distribution License	CDDL-1.0	Weak copyleft
Common Public License	CPL-1.0	Weak copyleft
Eclipse Public License	EPL-1.0	Weak copyleft
GNU Affero GPL version 3.0	AGPL-3.0	Strong copyleft
GNU General Public License version 2.0	GPL-2.0	Strong copyleft
GNU General Public License version 3.0	GPL-3.0	Strong copyleft
GNU Lesser General Public License version 2.1	LGPL-2.1	Weak copyleft
GNU Lesser General Public License version 3.0	LGPL-3.0	Weak copyleft
Microsoft Public License	MS-PL	Weak copyleft
Microsoft Reciprocal License	MS-RL	Weak copyleft
MIT License (X11 is treated similarly)	MIT/X11	Permissive
Mozilla Public License version 1.1	MPL-1.1	Weak copyleft
Mozilla Public License version 2.0	MPL-2.0	Weak copyleft
Open Software License version 3.0	OSL-3.0	Strong copyleft
zlib/libpng License	Zlib/Libpng	Permissive

The rationale behind the use of the license graph is the same as in Wheeler's slide that provide the only available license graph [16], i.e., it can be used to see if different software products licensed under two or more distinctive licenses can be combined in a new application under another license. This can be performed by following the edges coming out of these licenses to see whether they reach the same license at some point or if one of them is reachable from all other licenses of the distinctive set. In comparison to this earlier slide, our work covers a wider range of licenses including licenses that were potentially less popular or did not exist in 2007 (e.g., MPL-2.0), when Wheeler's slide was created.

The compatibility evaluation of FOSS licenses can be really complex. For example the MPL-1.1 and all versions of the GPL are incompatible [13] and cannot be shipped jointly in one single software artefact. However, the problem can be solved by proceeding from MPL-1.1 to MPL-2.0 and subsequent shipping under GPL-2.0 terms for instance. In order to visualise this incompatibility as well as the incompatibility between Apache-2.0 and GPL-2.0 in the graph dashed edges have been used (between MPL-1.1 and MPL-2.0, and between Apache-2.0 and MPL-2.0 that appear in grey). Those denote that transitivity is not applicable

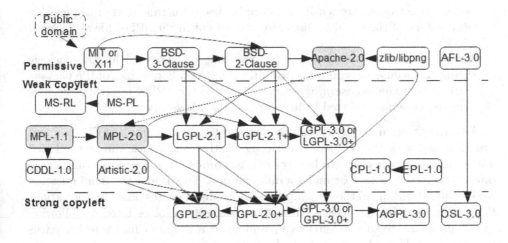

Fig. 1. The current license compatibility graph

when a path contains any of those two edges; hence, license compatibility does not apply for licenses that reach the same node, if the path contains one of the dashed edges. The above does not apply when the dashed edge is the last edge on the path.

Moreover, the type of combination of software artefacts needs to be considered. If, for example, the LGPL library A is dynamically linked to another piece of software B, B is not required to be LGPLed. The same applies to plug-in architectures, since they are considered a type of dynamic linking. If component A is statically linked to B in turn, B is required to be LGPLed as well. For different programming languages, such as Java, C /C++ or PHP, and different scenarios, such as embedded device or web application, development popularity of static and dynamic linking differs. We are not considering these architecture/integration aspects in our prototypical implementation yet. However this extension is of utmost practical relevance and will therefore be considered an important future extension.

4 The SPDX Violation Checker

As aforementioned the main contribution of this work is the SPDX violation checker, a tool that examines the content of a SPDX file in order to verify that the license information contained is accurate and make appropriate suggestions, if necessary. The major design objectives of the SPDX violation checker are to:

- verify whether the correct declared license(s) is/are indicated for the package in the SPDX file by the creator of the software package as indicated in the *licenseDeclared* field,
- check whether any adjustments are feasible in these declared license(s) in case of found violations,

– when adjustments are feasible, determine the adjustments that are feasible as a subset of the set of licenses already present in the SPDX file as declared licenses,
– propose a number of alternate licenses that can be used for the package using the license information encountered in the different files of the package captured in the *licenseInfoFromFiles* fields of the SPDX file (these licenses are subsequently referred to in the paper as *info licenses*).

All aspects examined by the checker exploit the license graph of Figure 1 and are all linked with the problem of deciding whether one license can be combined with another or whether two licenses can be combined in a new package under one of those two licenses or under a different one. This is also the main question asked when deciding on the set of applicable package licenses based on the various licenses present in the package files. This basically resolves into the following graph problem: given two vertices V_1 and V_2 in a graph G find whether paths p_1 from V_1 to V_x and p_2 from V_2 to V_x both exist:

$$comp(V_1, V_2) = true \; if \; V_1 \xrightarrow{p_1} V_x \; AND \; V_2 \xrightarrow{p_2} V_x \tag{1}$$

comp shows the ability to combine licenses V_1 and V_2. In that case V_x would be the applicable license for the info licenses. The above rationale is generalized for the case of more vertices, e.g., when deciding whether three info licenses are compatible or when choosing the applicable license using three info licenses.

This problem falls into graph multiple-source reachability that refers to determining where we can get to in a directed graph. In order to solve this problem assuming that updates (insertions and deletions) are not required on the license graph and that there are no storage restrictions for execution performance purposes it is more convenient to calculate the transitive closure $G^* = (V, E^*)$ of the license graph once and then store this graph and use it for every subsequent query on license compatibility. For the transitive closure creation we are using a variant of the Floyd-Warshall algorithm present in many approaches concerning reachability [15]. Specifically, we have modified the algorithm so that at each step 1) a new edge is added between two nodes for two consecutive edges only if the first edge allows transitivity (covering the transitivity exceptions explained for the license graph), and 2) the new edges contain also the number of licenses that are found on the 'path' of the new edge (helpful in finding the closest compatible license). Moreover, regarding the first change if the second edge does not allow transitivity the new edge added also does not allow it. The Floyd-Warshall algorithm requires in the worst case $O(n^3)$ time for the computation giving the possibility to check after this computation the existence of compatibility between two vertices and hence two licenses in constant time $O(1)$.

With n being the number of vertices in the license graph the worst case hypothesis is to consider having n incoming vertices that need to be checked. If these are connected with all remaining $n - 1$ vertices, then the execution time would rise to:

$$O((n - 1) * n) = O(n^2) \tag{2}$$

However, in practice this complexity would reach $O(n)$, since no license vertex is connected to all other vertices. This execution time is also maintained even though the compatibility between each pair of info licenses also needs to be examined using the same transitive closure graph. This is crucial to guarantee the combination of the info licenses in a common software package. Please note that if in the future updates are expected on the graph (i.e., by adding support for more licenses at frequent intervals), this procedure needs to be improved.

A parameter that is taken into account in the violation checker when more than one licenses are indicated as declared is whether these are mentioned in the SPDX file as disjunctive (any of these licenses can be applied) or as conjunctive (multiple licenses that all need to be applied). In the former case potential license conflicts need to be examined for each declared license. If one or more declared licenses pose no problems for the info licenses, then these licenses X_i can be applied on the package. If these X_i licenses are only a subset of the license in the declared set ($X_i \subseteq X_{declared}$), this indicates a necessary adjustment to the software package and is handled as such by the SPDX violation checker proposing to the user the necessary adjustments (i.e., informing the user that only a specific subset of the declared licenses can be used without violations). In case of a conjunctively declared license again all licenses need to be examined, but all need to adhere to license compatibility principles, i.e., all info licenses need to be compatible with all declared licenses; otherwise, a violation occurs.

Following the above procedure the SPDX violation checker proposes a compatible license or alternate compatible licenses that can be applied on the package. Note that in the current version this does not include the proposal of multiple licenses (i.e., dual licensing or tri-licensing). In the current implementation we also neglect licenses with exceptions; for instance, the GPL linking exception that was found in some projects was treated as a GPL license. According to Wikipedia *"a GPL linking exception modifies the GPL in a way that enables software projects which provide library code to be "inked to" the programs that use them, without applying the full terms of the GPL to the using program."* This is also related with the aforementioned architecture aspects that require further investigation, but are outside the scope of the current work.

Regarding the tool implementation the violation checker has been implemented in Java as a new tool to complement the available list of SPDX tools[2] listed on the website of the specification. The violation checker is using as input the RDF versions of SPDX in order to guarantee the compliance with ontology standards. To this end the following existing SPDX workgroup tools have been exploited: the *Tag to RDF Translator* that converts a tag file to its respective RDF format and the *RDF parser* that parses the information in a RDF file. This violation check can be used along with a license extraction tool that identifies licenses from software packages in source or binary format, such as FOSSology [8] or ASLA [14]. Regarding license information extraction from the source code distribution of the software package we have chosen to use FOSSology and exploit the existing *FOSSology+SPDX* community tool that allows to create a tag

---

[2] https://spdx.org/tools/

SPDX file out of the results of the license analysis performed by the Nomos license scanner of FOSSology. The whole set of transformations performed until the software packages reach the SPDX violation checker are depicted in Figure 2. For the implementation of the algorithms related to the license graph the *JGraphT* graph library for Java was used.

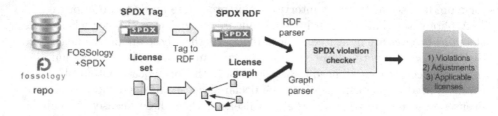

Fig. 2. Main transformations in the violation assessment process

5   Experiments and Discussion

5.1   Testing Set

For evaluating our prototype implementation of the violation checker we created a small testing set with open source projects hosted on SourceForge under the prerequisite that the project should contain an open source license (or more). Not all SPDX licenses are covered in the current implementation; hence, we randomly selected from the repository 15 projects that are distributed under widely used licenses and downloaded their latest version. The majority of chosen projects carry a GPL license, whereas some multi-licensing schemes also appear. More packages will be tested in the future as the license compatibility graph expands.

At the current state of the spread of SPDX it is not possible to find existing SPDX descriptions online, although SPDX has been adopted by some companies internally (e.g., Texas Instruments, Alcatel-Lucent) as indicated also in the Wiki of SPDX. Hence, the software projects are uploaded on a FOSSology repository[3] that we created for this purpose and these are subsequently analysed for license information. The license analysis results performed by the Nomos analyser of FOSSology are initially transformed to a Tag format for SPDX 1.1 using the FOSSology+SPDX tool provided by SPDX and subsequently to an RDF format using the TAG to RDF translator. This RDF format is used as input for the implemented violation checker. The FOSSology+SPDX tool would use the licenses found in the various files of the software package to insert the information on the declared package license (as a conjunctive license set) instead of using the license under which the software package was published by its creator. For this reason we add the declared license information manually in the SPDX files as retrieved from the corresponding software package website or as declared inside the package itself (e.g., in a license.txt or copying file).

---

[3] http://metis.initos.com/repo/

The testing set is shown in Table 2. In the list of projects the applied licenses for the project version we employed in our experiments is indicated. In most cases this was identical to the version of the package hosted on SourceForge. The license list modelled in the graph was augmented by LGPL-2.0 and LGPL-2.0+, since the former was encountered as license applied on two of the projects in the testing set. Although not displayed on the graph, licenses compatible with LGPL-2.1 and LGPL-2.1+ are also compatible with LGPL-2.0+, whereas LGPL-2.0+ is compatible with LGPL-2.0. In essence LGPL-2.1was derived from LGPL-2.0 with minor changes.

Table 2. Testing set for the SPDX violation checker

# Software package	Version	Size	Official license
1 Anomos	0.9.5	824.2 KB	GPL-3.0
2 AresGalaxy	2.2.6 (Beta)	1.05 MB	GPL-2.0
3 CuteFlow	2.11.2	3.8 MB	BSD 3-Clause
4 FCKEditor	4.3	985.39 KB	GPL-3.0, LGPL-3.0, MPL-1.1
5 Fraqtive	0.4.6	342.85 KB	GPL-3.0
6 HandBrake	0.9.9	8.88 MB	GPL-2.0
7 Hunspell	1.3.2	20.84 KB	LGPL-2.0, MPL-1.1
8 Jexcelapi	2.6.12	1.82 MB	LGPL-2.0
9 Joda-Time	2.3	1.23 MB	Apache-2.0
10 Mlpy	3.5.0	1.87 MB	GPL-3.0
11 MrBayes	3.2.2	2.44 MB	GPL-2.0
12 opencsv	2.3	273.93 KB	Apache-2.0
13 Open Programmer	0.8.1	100.25 KB	GPL-2.0
14 py2exe	0.6.9	146.17 KB	MIT
15 VirtualDub	1.10.4	2.1 MB	GPL-2.0

5.2 Main Results

The results of the violation checker are shown in Table 3 and are additionally summarized in percentages in Figure 3. The results indicate the licenses encountered by FOSSology in the different files of the package containing also some license names that were neglected by the violation checker because they do not contain any license-specific information, such as "Same-license-as", "Dual-license", "See-doc(OTHER)." Note also that some licenses encountered by FOSSology state the license name, but do not contain the exact license (i.e., the license version). Such examples can be found in GPL and MIT-style. These license cases were neglected when a specific license indication of the same type existed in the software package; for instance for the GPL case, if GPL-2.0 was found in another file of the software package, then the extraction of GPL by FOSSology would be neglected. For the remaining cases, the license name with no version was replaced by the "closest" license, i.e., the license of the most representative version. For instance, LGPL would be substituted with version 2.1 of the LGPL.

The column referring to adjustment contains information on whether a subset of the existing declared licenses can be used to correct any violations that exist (as explained in the previous section). Proposed licenses column shows the alternate licenses that can be applied on the package based on the examination of its info licenses. For packages without violations these proposed licenses should contain the already declared licenses. When the violation is due to an incompatibility among the info licenses this is also indicated in the Table. No applicable licenses are found in this case.

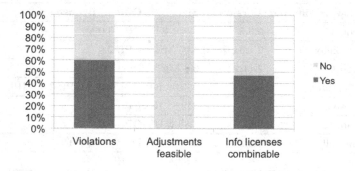

Fig. 3. Evaluation results summary

The results indicate that a significant number of projects contain violations (9 out of 15 packages or 60%) and adjustments in the present licenses are not feasible for any of them. The main violation is encountered in projects that contain the MPL-1.1 license that is incompatible to GPL. No applicable license can be proposed for projects containing both MPL-1.1 and any version of the GPL showing that the licenses from the independent packages used in the application cannot be combined to a new software product. This is the case for AresGalaxy, CuteFlow, FCKEditor, HandBrake and Hunspell. Also other reasons for violations appear, such as in CuteFlow and MrBayes where the presence of GPL-2.0 makes it impossible to propose any applicable license. Conflicts with no possibility for applicable licenses are also found.

Performing a manual investigation of the graph to verify our results we found a case of a false indication in py2exe. No applicable license is indicated for py2exe due to the lack of transitivity on the edge between MPL-1.1 and MPL-2.0, although LGPL-2.1+, LGPL-3.0 or LGPL-3.0+ can be used. To overcome such issues, we intend to consider also the license category in the actions on the license graph. As a general note the fact that many existing open source projects appear to have violations based on the analysis using the implemented tool is not necessarily generalizable. The SPDX input to the violation checker is based on the license identification by FOSSology that might contain false positive

Table 3. Results of violation checker per project

# Licenses found in files (FOSSology results)	Violation found	Adjustment feasible	Info licenses combinable	Proposed licenses
1 Same-license-as, GPL-3.0+, Public-domain-ref, LGPL-3.0+, GPL-3.0	x		✓	GPL-3.0, GPL-3.0+, AGPL-3.0
2 GPL-2.0+, LGPL-2.1, Artistic-1.0, BSD-3-Clause, Dual-license, MPL-1.1	✓	x	x	*NONE*
3 LGPL-2.0+, BSD-3-Clause, GPL-3.0+, GPL-2.0, GPL-2.0+, LGPL-2.1+, MIT, BSD	✓	x	x	*NONE*
4 UnclassifiedLicense, Trademark-ref, LGPL-2.1+, Microsoft-possibility, GPL-2.0+, MPL-1.1	✓	x	x	*NONE*
5 GPL-3.0+, GPL-3.0, BSD-3-Clause	x		✓	GPL-3.0, GPL-3.0+, AGPL-3.0
6 LGPL-2.0+, MIT, See-doc (OTHER), Trademark-ref, MPL-1.1, LGPL-2.1+, FSF, UnclassifiedLicense, GPL2.0+, GPL-2.0, GPL-exception, BSD-3-Clause, BSD-2-Clause	✓	x	x	*NONE*
7 GPL-2.0+, Dual-license, MPL-1.1, LGPL-2.1+	✓	x	x	*NONE*
8 LGPL-2.1+, BSD-style	✓	x	✓	LGPL-2.1, LGPL-2.1+, LGPL-3.0, LGPL-3.0+, GPL-2.0+, GPL-2.0, GPL-3.0, GPL-3.0+, AGPL-3.0
9 Apache-possibility, BSD, Apache-2.0, Public-domain, Apache-1.0	✓	x	x	*NONE*
10 GPL-3.0, BSD-3-Clause, GPL-3.0+	x		✓	GPL-3.0, GPL-3.0+, AGPL-3.0
11 GPL-2.0+, GPL-3.0+, GPL-2.0	✓	x	x	*NONE*
12 BSD-3-Clause, Apache-2.0	x		✓	Apache-2.0, MPL-2.0, LGPL-3.0, LGPL-3.0+, GPL-3.0, GPL-3.0+, AGPL-3.0
13 GPL-2.0, GPL-2.0+	x		✓	GPL-2.0
14 MPL, MIT-style, See-doc(OTHER), LGPL, MPL-1.1, UnclassifiedLicense	✓	x	x	*NONE*
15 UnclassifiedLicense, GPL-2.0	x		✓	GPL-2.0

cases in license identification. For instance, in the case of Joda-Time Apache-1.0 is encountered in some files as indicated in the SPDX file produced by the SPDX tools, although this was not clearly indicated on the FOSSology repository (Apache-1.0 did not appear on the license list of the package in FOSSology). We opted not to remove Apache-1.0 despite this fact. Apache-1.0 is not compatible with Apache-2.0, since the former is more restrictive than the latter and in essence is no longer used (Apache-1.0 does not appear on the license graph).

An additional disadvantage of using a separate license extraction tool like FOSSology is that it is not possible to know whether a license in the package is mentioned by FOSSology because there is a third party library used in the package that carries this license or because this is the license the creators of the package have decided to apply on the package. The above problem appeared for instance in the FCKEditor project that carries the tri-license MPL-1.1, LGPL-3.0, GPL-3.0. All these licenses were identified in different files by FOSSology. Steps towards this direction that will be considered as future work include taking into account the location of the file, where a license was found by FOSSology, in order to conclude whether this refers to a third party library or to the source code of the software package, and examining in more detail the software directory structure as performed in a previous work for binary packages of the Fedora-12 GNU/Linux distribution [6].

6   Related Work

Although the open source phenomenon is relatively new, a wide body of litera-ture exists. Aksulu and Wade identified 618 peer-reviewed papers in published journals and created from those a classification taxonomy [1]. 54 of these arti-cles dealt with FOSS licensing out of which 11 are related to our research. For instance, Madanmohan [11] shows that commercial companies already consider intellectual property and license compatibility issues within their technology adoption procedures. Other scholars, such as Lerner and Tirole [9], and Colazo and Fang [4], obtained quantitative measures on the impact of license selection on project success and contribution rates. License compatibility poses one of the major challenges on the future adoption of FOSS. License compatibility en-forcement is one of the most prevailing, yet, not sufficiently solved challenges in open-source-based and collaborative software development. This is especially intuitive as this type of software development is more and more spread across proprietary software companies such as SAP, IBM, HP and Fujitsu to name a few. However, the vast amount of licenses, license terms and license artifacts in source files renders an automated detection and conflict analysis difficult.

A metamodel on open source licenses in order to address this problem is provided in [2]. The construction of the metamodel was based on an empiri-cal analysis of the license texts in order to extract meaningful terms leading to an informed classification of natural language patterns. As open source licenses usually do not contain extensive compatibility rules, such as ".. *this license is not compatible with...*", and since the metamodel was based on empirical anal-ysis of the existing body of licenses it does not contain compatibility modeling components. The FSF and several other semi-scientific bodies provide license compatibility information based on manual interpretation of the license terms. Wheeler [16] proposed a first compatibility graph that pulls together various information sources. Our work extends prior work with more and recently contributed additional information sources.

Apart from the modeling problem a standardization problem exists. License texts may either form part of the source file or may be missing completely. Even in cases where license information is put at the beginning of a source file, it does not follow a standard or convention. As already mentioned the SPDX format addresses this standardization problem. There are various tools that perform license information extraction from a given source file or repository to address this challenge including OSSLI[4], the Open Source License Checker (OSLC[5]) [17], the Automated Software License Analyzer (ASLA[6]) [14], Ninka [7] and the Nomos project.

Whereas OSSLI is a rather model-centric approach that is implemented as an extension to the Papyrus graphical modeling framework of the Eclipse platform, OSLC, ASLA and Nomos are all standalone tools partly with alternative graphical and command line clients. ASLA was proposed as a result of a feature and performance analysis done on Nomos and OSLC [14]. The authors concluded that ASLA covers all of the 12 elaborated user needs (6 more than FOSSology/Nomos). The authors also claim, that ASLA has several advantages over FOSSology, such as the ability to define license compatibility rules and the identification of licensing problems. This license compatibility map and the ability to maintain those licenses within a graphical user interface are doubtlessly strengths of ALSA. Yet, OSLC provides similar capabilities as it apart from the license texts itself, stores and allows to maintain metadata files that contain compatibility information with other licenses. Ninka has also been exploited in various settings [6].

Nevertheless, only OSSLI and FOSSology+SPDX are using SPDX files. OSSLI does not really do license checking on source code level but only performs compatibility analysis on architectural level. OSSLI can, hence, be better understood as an extension of the UML package model type and a help to construct license compatible architectures than a compatibility analysis tool for a given source code repository or serveral of those repositories. FOSSology through its integration of Nomos and the use of the SPDX standard seems to be the only tool with strong and continuing industry sponsorship and development effort. Most of the other tools are being discontinued for quite some years now.

In the framework of the evaluation of the current work we did not encounter the long runtime of the licenses checker (Nomos) mentioned in [14]. Some of the limitations of FOSSology reported in the same work, such as the manual detection of licenses, have been addressed in the latest version of FOSSology. Furthermore, FOSSology is the only tool that enables the regular scan of repos-

---

[4] http://ossli.cs.tut.fi/
[5] http://sourceforge.net/projects/oslc/
[6] http://sourceforge.net/projects/asla/

itories and source code folders and integrates a web-based dashboard. Overall, FOSSology was the most convincing and better documented basis for our research especially with respect to real scenario applicability.

To the best of our knowledge this is the first work that proposes license violations check in the framework of SPDX. In contrast to existing tools that focus mainly on license information extraction the current work provides the opportunity to standardize license compatibility-relevant activities in a global specifications setting. However, the combination of the automation framework with an augmented license compatibility graph has not yet been covered and is the main direction of our future work.

7 Conclusions

Finding the right licenses associated with a software resource and choosing the appropriate - hence, correct - license for each software product are important issues for any software engineer and organization that employs open source software for various purposes. In this work we have addressed the latter by handling the problem of license compatibilities for open source software packages formatted using the SPDX specification descriptions. Our violation checker is able to identify whether violations exist in the package description and propose corrections on those (if feasible) and suggestions for applicable licenses. These suggestions are based on the constructed license graph that contains compatibility information for commonly used open source licenses.

The initial evaluation performed on the prototype implementation of our approach using existing open source projects showcases that open source license compliance is not treated correctly in many cases. Although there are some disadvantages that make the applied scheme not universally reliable, the implemented tool constitutes important progress towards the automation on license checks and decisions for software systems in the standardized setting of SPDX. Note that whenever it comes to relevant business decisions on licensing issues or detecting flaws, our proposed approach provides guidance but still requires legal expertise to guide a final decision on the licensing matter. As future work we intend to expand the license compatibility graph covering the majority of SPDX supported licenses and considering the complexities of software architectures, make our tool more robust introducing a more detailed software package analysis, and publish it to the community as part of the SPDX tool set. The above will be combined with a more detailed representation of the rights and obligations of the licenses that are now not captured in the license graph.

References

[1] Aksulu, A., Wade, M.: A comprehensive review and synthesis of open source research. Journal of the Association for Information Systems 11(11) (2010)
[2] Alspaugh, T.A., Scacchi, W., Asuncion, H.U.: Software licenses in context: The challenge of heterogeneously-licensed systems. Journal of the Association for Information Systems 11(11) (2010)

[3] Boyle, J.: The public domain: Enclosing the commons of the mind. Yale University Press (2009)

[4] Colazo, J., Fang, Y.: Impact of license choice on open source software development activity. Journal of the American Society for Information Science and Technology 60(5), 997–1011 (2009)

[5] Feller, J., Fitzgerald, B., et al.: Understanding open source software development. Addison-Wesley, London (2002)

[6] German, D.M., Di Penta, M., Davies, J.: Understanding and auditing the licensing of open source software distributions. In: 2010 IEEE 18th International Conference on Program Comprehension (ICPC), pp. 84–93. IEEE (2010)

[7] German, D.M., Manabe, Y., Inoue, K.: A sentence-matching method for automatic license identification of source code files. In: Proceedings of the IEEE/ACM International Conference on Automated Software Engineering, pp. 437–446. ACM (2010)

[8] Gobeille, R.: The fossology project. In: Proceedings of the 2008 International Working Conference on Mining Software Repositories, pp. 47–50. ACM (2008)

[9] Lerner, J., Tirole, J.: The scope of open source licensing. Journal of Law, Economics, and Organization 21(1), 20–56 (2005)

[10] Linux Foundation and its Contributors: A Common Software Package Data Exchange Format, version 1.2 (2013), http://spdx.org/sites/spdx/files/spdx-1

[11] Madanmohan, T., et al.: Notice of violation of IEEE publication principles open source reuse in commercial firms. IEEE Software 21(6), 62–69 (2004)

[12] Mancinelli, F., Boender, J., Di Cosmo, R., Vouillon, J., Durak, B., Leroy, X., Treinen, R.: Managing the complexity of large free and open source package-based software distributions. In: 21st IEEE/ACM International Conference on Automated Software Engineering, ASE 2006, pp. 199–208. IEEE (2006)

[13] Rosen, L.: Open source licensing: Software Freedom and Intellectual Property Law. Prentice Hall PTR (2004)

[14] Tuunanen, T., Koskinen, J., Kärkkäinen, T.: Automated software license analysis. Automated Software Engineering 16(3-4), 455–490 (2009)

[15] Wang, H., He, H., Yang, J., Yu, P.S., Yu, J.X.: Dual labeling: Answering graph reachability queries in constant time. In: Proceedings of the 22nd International Conference on Data Engineering, ICDE 2006, pp. 75–75. IEEE (2006)

[16] Wheeler, D.A.: The free-libre/open source software (floss) license slide (2007), http://www.dwheeler.com/essays/floss-license-slide.pdf

[17] Xu, H., Yang, H., Wan, D., Wan, J.: The design and implement of open source license tracking system. In: 2010 International Conference on Computational Intelligence and Software Engineering (CiSE), pp. 1–4. IEEE (2010)

Automatically Solving Simultaneous Type Equations for Type Difference Transformations That Redesign Code[*]

Ted J. Biggerstaff

Software Generators, LLC, Austin, Texas, USA
dslgen@softwaregenerators.com

Abstract. This paper introduces a generalization of programming data types called *Context Qualified Types* (or *CQ Type*s for short). CQ Types are a superset of programming language data types. They incorporate design features or contexts that fall outside of the programming data type domain (e.g., a planned program scope). CQ Types are functionally related to other CQ Types (and eventually to conventional data types) such that a differencing operation defined on two related types will produce a program transformation that will convert a computational instance (i.e., code) of the first type into a computational instance of the second type. Large grain abstract relationships between design contexts may be expressed as simultaneous type equations. Solving these equations, given some starting code instances, produces transformations that redesign the code from one design context (e.g., a payload context) to a different design context (e.g., a "hole" within a design framework from a reusable library).

Keywords: Type differencing, Context qualified types, CQ Types, Design frameworks, Design features, Functionally related types, Transformations, Domain driven instantiation, Simultaneous type equations.

1 Overview

1.1 The Problem

This paper addresses the problem of automatically integrating two separately derived pieces of code that are potentially compatible but differ in a few design details that will have to be synchronized to achieve compatibility[1]. These design differences arise from slightly differing requirements for the differing specifications. For example, consider a code/design framework (i.e., a combination of skeletal code plus holes designed to accept insertion of foreign, target computation code, e.g., Ref.[2] 1-01) as

---

[*] Patent 8,713,515 [7] and separate patent pending.

[1] This work is a part of the DSLGen™ program generation system, the details of which are beyond the scope of this paper. A more complete discussion of DSLGen™ can be found in [6], as well as other documentation available at www.softwaregenerators.com.

[2] Ref. will be use to designate callouts in figures. Ref. *n-mm* will be the *mm* callout in Fig. *n*.

I. Schaefer and I. Stamelos (Eds.): ICSR 2015, LNCS 8919, pp. 106–121, 2014.

one of those pieces of code. Let's call this framework the "Thread Design Framework" (or TDF for short). The TDF framework example expresses a pattern of parallel computation using threads to implement parallel execution but knows virtually nothing about the code to be executed within those threads (i.e., the code in the "framework holes"). Its design might be constrained by the requirements of the thread package used. For example, a planned user (or generator) written routine for initiating a thread might only allow one user data parameter to be passed to the application programmer's thread routine (along with the thread specific parameters, of course). If that thread routine needs more than a single item of user data to operate (e.g., matrices, the dimensions of the matrices, and perhaps some start and end indexes specific to the algorithm), then the programmer (or generator) may have to formulate some custom "glue" code to connect the target computation data to the holes in TDF. For example, he could setup global variables to communicate that data to the thread routine. Alternatively, the programmer could write some "glue" code to package up the set of needed data into a structure (for example) before calling the thread routine, send a pointer to the structure to the thread routine as the single user argument and then unpack the data items within the application's thread routine. In this latter case, he will also have to adapt (i.e., redesign) elements of his "vanilla" payload computation to fit the details of this glue code.

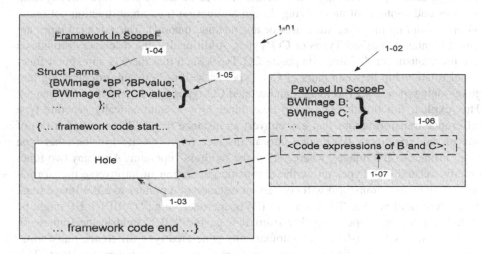

Fig. 1. Skeletal design framework and a code payload

Given those requirements on the thread based code framework (TDF), consider the nature of the target code payload (e.g., Ref. 1-02) that is to be merged into the TDF. That target computation payload might benefit from parallel computation but will require design modifications to execute correctly with the TDF framework (Ref. 1-01). For example, among the modifications that will have to be made to synchronize it with the code in the TDF framework is the redesign of the references to its data (e.g., the matrices, etc.) so that they synchronize with the design implicit in TDF's (skeletally defined) thread routine (Ref. 1-01). As mentioned earlier, direct reference via global variables to the matrices and related data (e.g., indexes) is one possible solution but that may require some scope adaptation to both the payload and the framework to allow sharing of the same scope. However, such changes can be daunting for an automatic generation system because a generator has to first model the global scoping structure, which can be challenging. If the framework design cannot be changed (e.g., it is a reusable library component or it calls unchangeable library routines), then the design of the payload will have to be altered by writing some glue code that packages up references to the payload variables and modifies the payload code to connect through the glue code. The glue code option has the benefit of greater localization of the changes thereby making them easier for an automated generation system. This invention provides an automated method for the class of redesign process that allows the payload code to be redesigned so that it can be relocated into the context of a framework (e.g., TDF). For some background on alternative concepts that are similar to but not exactly the same as design frameworks, see [10, 13].

To create the redesign machinery, this work extends the conventional notion of data types by incorporating into the type specification, design features and contexts (e.g., generator-time design features) that fall outside the domain of programming language data types. Thereby the generator is able to define and work directly with features and contexts of an evolving design abstraction (i.e., an abstraction not based on programming language structures or abstractions thereof). The extended types are called Context Qualified Types or CQ Types. Additionally, the machinery provides a key mechanism for defining composite CQ Types such that there is an explicit functional relationship between pairs of CQ Types as well as between programming language data types (e.g., BWImage) and related CQ types (i.e. a pointer to BWImage). This explicit functional relationship determines how to automatically generate type difference transformations that can convert an instance (e.g., "B" as in Ref. 1-06) of one of the types (e.g., BWImage) into an instance (e.g., "(& B)") of the other type (e.g., Pointer to BWImage), where "&" is the "address" operator. Also, any two functionally related CQ Types allow the automatic generation of an inverse transformation[3]. The inverse transform will convert an instance of a pointer to a BWImage (e.g., a structure field named "BP") into the BWImage itself (e.g., "(* BP)"). BP might be within a different scope altogether from B (e.g., the "*BP" field in the framework scope shown as Ref. 1-05). The automatically generated type difference transformations as a class are called redesign transformations or redesigners for short. This machinery will be used to redesign instances of generated code (e.g., an expression

---

[3] Many difference transformations are not "pure" functions and may therefore introduce existential variables. For example, an instance of a 2D matrix being transformed into a reference to an item in that matrix may introduce one or more programming language index variables such as ?Idx1 and ?Idx2 whose eventual target program identities (e.g., i and j) may not yet be determined. The mechanisms for dealing with such existential variables and their bindings are beyond the scope of this paper but suffice it to say, DSLGen deals with these problems using domain specific knowledge (see the description of the ARPS protocol below) to stand in for those identities until they can be concretely determined later in the generation process.

to compute a convolution of an image) so that they can be used to instantiate a partially complete code framework such as TDF (i.e., a pattern of some code and some receptacles for foreign code). Since the framework may need to use data items that are decorated with design features (e.g., a field containing a pointer to the data) that are not a part of the original data item, the original data item will need to be redesigned to synchronize with the requirements of the framework before it can be used in a context of the framework.

Using code components developed independently in one context (e.g., payload scope) without knowledge of their potential use in and connections to elements of a disparate context (e.g., framework scope) presents a key problem. There is no feasible way to directly connect the elements of the one context (e.g., a payload context) to the conceptually corresponding elements of the other context (e.g., a framework context) without negating the independence of the two contexts and thereby negating the combinatorial reuse value of combining many independent contexts. Identifying the correspondences between disparate code components by explicit names is not feasible because the two contexts are developed independently and likely, at different times. Parameter connections are not feasible because like explicit naming, this would require some *a priori* coordination of the structure of the two disparate code components, which is not desirable. What the two contexts may know about each other is indirect. It is their domain specific entities, features and topology, which opens the door to a reference protocol that is based on one context searching for known or expected domain specific entities, features and relationships within the other context. This is a key mechanism of this invention. It provides the machinery for expressing "anaphoric" references (i.e., references that are implied) in one code entity (e.g., the framework) to data items (e.g., an image data item that is being used as the output data item for a computation) in a separate, disparate and as yet undefined code entity (e.g., a computational payload to be used within the framework). This mechanism is called the *Anaphoric Reference Protocol for Synchronization (ARPS)*. (See [7].) The anaphoric reference mechanism expresses references in terms of semantic (and largely domain specific) abstractions rather than in programming language structural forms or patterns (e.g., loops, code blocks, operators, etc.) or abstractions thereof. For example, a structure field within a framework may need a value from some as yet to be defined computational payload. Semantically, the framework knows only that that value will be an image that is being used as the input image of the payload computation. ARPS provides a domain specific notation whereby that relationship can be expressed in the definition of the field within the framework. ARPS provides machinery such that when a candidate computational payload is eventually identified, that ARPS reference will be used like a search query and will automatically resolve to the specific data item needed by the framework.

Once the ARPS expressions in a framework determine the conceptually corresponding items in the payload, the automated *redesigners* are invoked to redesign those payload items so that they are consistent with the framework design. Then the payload code (suitably redesigned to synchronize with the framework design) can be directly inserted into the holes of the framework.

2   CQ Types, Their Relationships and Type Differencing

2.1   Overview

A CQ type is a programming language type (e.g., a grayscale image matrix type designated as "BWImage") that has additional *Qualifying Properties* specific to another context (e.g., a design feature, such as the payload scope "ScopeP"). CQ Types allow the generator to express concepts that transcend the strictly programming language domain. That is, the CQ type concepts include generation entities, contexts and operations rather than being strictly limited to programming language entities, contexts and operations. Qualifiers can represent design features that do not yet have any program structure manifestation (e.g., an anticipated but not yet created program scope).

A CQ type is designed to have an explicit functional relationship to other CQ types. Fig. 2 shows the conceptual form of relationships between a programming language type (Ref. 2-07) and a number of abstract CQ types (Refs. 2-08a through 2-10), where the CQ property for this example is the name of a payload or framework scope (e.g., ScopeP or ScopeF). In Fig. 2, CQ Types are shown as ovals and instances of those types as boxes. The type to type relationships are implemented via either subtype/supertype relationships (e.g., Refs. 2-08a and 2-09a) or a cross context mapping relationship (Ref. 2-18) that defines some elective transformational mapping between (in the example) an instance of the payload context and a related instance in the framework context. The transformations between instances of CQ subtypes and supertypes (i.e., type differences) are automatically derived from the two CQ types. Cross context mapping transforms (i.e., those between CQ Types that do not have a subtype or supertype interrelationship) are elective and therefore are custom written by a design engineer at the time the related design framework (e.g., TDF) is created. They are designed only once for a specific reusable design framework (e.g., TDF) but will be used/instantiated many times to generate many different concrete, target programs. In the example of this paper, the mapping relationship is computational equivalence between the end points of the type chain (i.e., between instance P2 and instance F2).   That is, execution of the initial computational form (P2) in the payload scope will produce the same result as the execution of a different but operationally equivalent computational form (F2) in the framework scope.

Furthermore, each pair of connected CQ Types (i.e., type/supertype or cross connection) implies two, directionally specific Redesign Transformations that will convert an instance of one of the types into an instance of the other that is one step farther along on the path to computational equivalence. The type/subtype transformations are automatically derivable via so called type differencing operations. The form of the type differencing transformations is deterministically implied by the type constructor operators. By contrast, cross connection transforms are custom created by a domain engineer. Example cross context mappings include, computational equivalence (as in the example presented), data type casts, design translation options, etc. Because all relationships define explicit functional relationships, the generator can use type differencing to harvest a set of Redesign Transformations (i.e., transformations X1 through X5 in Fig. 2) that carry a payload instance P1 of a programming language type used in the payload context into a computationally equivalent instance F1 of a type used in the framework context. X1 and X6 map between the domain of programming language data types and the CQ Types within the design domain.

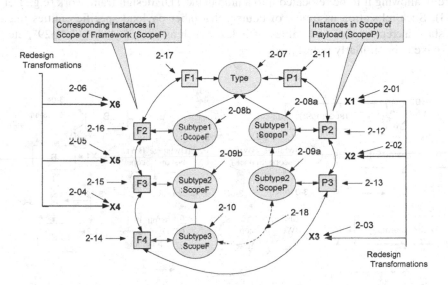

Fig. 2. Chain of CQ Types relating two different design contexts

Fig. 3 provides a concrete example that may be used to solve part of the problem illustrated in Fig. 1. As a debugging aid, CQ Type names are designed to expose both the base programming data type (e.g., "BWImage" or "int") as well as their qualifying property pairs (e.g., ":myscope ScopeF"). The implementation machinery necessitates some special syntax within the type names, specifically, underscores to bind the name parts together and vertical bars to delineate the beginning and ending of the type name. All CQ Types will have "tags" that uniquely identify them (E.g., BWi7, Ptr1 or Field1). These tags may be used in a CQ Type name to reference another CQ Type (e.g., tag "BWi7" in type Ref. 3-02a references its super type Ref. 3-01a).

The instance to instance transformations of Fig. 3 make it clear that subtyping within CQ Types is used to capture subpart/superpart relationships (among others) between design constructs, and thereby it may also imply the construction/deconstruction operations required to achieve transitions between design views and/or design contexts. For example, "B" from the computation specification context (Ref. 3-04) represents the same entity as "B" within the payload scope context (Ref. 3-05) but "(& B)" (Ref. 3-06) is a computational form that represents one step on the pathway to the full computational equivalence finally realized in   Ref. 3-09.

Harvesting the transformations implied in Fig. 3 (i.e., X2 through X5) by differencing the CQ Types and applying those transforms to a payload oriented expression like

$$\text{PartialAns} = (B[idx13+(p29-1)][idx14+(q30-1)] * w[p29][q30]) ; \qquad (1)$$

will convert (1) into a design framework context expression like

$$PartialAns = ((*(rsparms9.BP))[idx13+(p29\ -1)][idx14+(q30\ -1)]$$
$$* \ w[p29]\ [q30]); \hspace{4cm} (2)$$

thereby allowing it to be relocated into a hole in the TDF design framework (e.g., Ref. 1-03). Such relocation assumes, of course, that other payload specific entities (e.g., the start, increment and end values of indexes such as"idx13", "idx14", "p29", etc.) will have to be similarly redesigned.

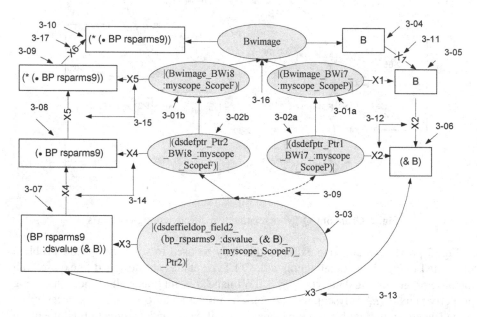

Fig. 3. A concrete example relating framework and payload design contexts

The computational domain of the PartialAns example is the convolution of 2D digital images (where "B" is the image from the example). The deeper programming language design context (i.e., problem specific domain knowledge) for these expressions is as follows: idx13 and idx14 are variables that index over some image matrix B; p29 and p30 are offsets for pixels in a neighborhood around the current pixel "B[idx13, idx14]"; and w is an array of multiplicative coefficients defining the relative contribution of a neighborhood pixel to the overall magnitude of the PartialAns value. In a complete description of the required redesign operations for this example, analogous CQ Type chains would exist for the start, increment and end values of the indexes idx13, idx14, p29, p30, and possibly other needed data entities. And these would engender analogous conversions for these data entities.

While the example in this paper uses the names B, idx13, idx14, p29 and p30 for concreteness, DSLGen uses an abstract domain specific model for the computation it is operating on. That is to say, it models a convolution in terms of image matrix abstractions, matrix index abstractions, neighborhood abstractions and neighborhood loop index abstractions none of which map into concrete programming language names and entities until very late in the generation process. That is, mapping DSLGen's domain abstractions (e.g., neighborhood loop index abstractions) into concrete names like idx13 and idx14 is deferred until the overall design is complete and the design has stopped evolving, because during that evolution process, the associations between domain abstractions and concrete target names will change to accommodate the evolution of the design. That being said, the author believes that the use of concrete names for this description will aid the reader's understanding of the process and therefore, this paper will continue to use concrete names.

Next, we will define the machinery required to construct Fig. 3 and unlimited numbers of similar constructions from (reusable) parameterized type specifications. Then we will use these constructions to redesign code.

2.2   Solving Simultaneous Parameterized Type Equations

The CQ types of Fig. 3 contain design elements that are custom formulated to produce one set of redesign transformations that are specific to the data entity "B" (because of the concrete field names in type 3-03) within a specific target computation that is to be transformed from a specific payload context to a specific framework context. In order to solve the more general problem that is described in Section 1, other analogous QC Type chains and redesign transformations will have to be developed for other specific data entities in that target computation (e.g., other image variables along with loops' start, end and increment values for indexes such as "Idx14"). That is, Fig. 3 must be abstracted and the instantiation of that abstraction automated. It would be a serious impediment to full automation of the generation process to require a human to custom build of each of the individual type structure analogs of Fig. 3 for all of the data entities within a specific computation. Hence, there needs to be a single (reusable) precursor abstraction or abstractions from which all Fig. 3 analogs and the type difference transformation analogs associated with them can be automatically derived for other computations. That single precursor abstraction comprises: 1) a set of parameterized type equations (expressions (3)-(7) below) that capture, in a more abstract and reusable sense, the relationships (i.e., type chains) illustrated in Fig. 3 and 2) two special parameterized type difference transformations specific to the TDF framework that express the cross connection mapping between the two type subtrees. One of these TDF framework supplied difference transformations is shown as expression (9) below. The cross connection transformations are identified in Fig. 3 as Ref. 3-13 (labeled X3). Ref. 3-13 represents both mappings to and from instances of the types 3-02a and 3-03.

The remainder of this section will describe that parameterized precursor specification. It is expressed as a set of simultaneous type equations (expressions (3)-(7) below). This section will further describe the process by which those type equations are incrementally solved to produce concrete CQ Types (Refs. 3-01a & b, 3-02a & b, and 3-03) and simultaneously to produce type difference transformations (Ref. 3-12 through 3-15 in Fig. 3), which are represented more concretely, as expressions (8)-(11) below. In the course of these steps, the type difference transformations are incrementally applied to a starting instance of one of those types (Ref. 3-05) and then to its derivatives (3-06 through 3-08) to derive the correspondence between "B" in scopeP and the equivalent glue code "(* (● BP rsparms9))" in scopeF, which will eventually become the C language code "(*(rsparms9.BP))".

The simultaneous parameterized type equations that will generate Fig. 3 (and all of its analogs for similarly structured problems) are expressions (3)-(7):

(?t1   = (?itype :myscope ?Pscope :Instname   '?StartInst)) ;;spec for type 3-01a   (3)

(?t2   = (DSDefPtr   ?t1 :Instname '?PPtrinst))   ;;spec for type 3-02a   (4)

(?t5   = (?itype :myscope ?Fscope))   ;; spec for type3-01b   (5)

(?t4 =   (DSDefPtr ?t5 :Instname '?FPtrinst))   ;; spec for type 3-02b   (6)

(?t3   = (DSDefFieldOp (?Fldname ?Structname :dsvalue ?PPtrinst
                  :myscope ?Fscope :Instname '?Fldinst)
                  ?t4))   ;; spec for type 3-03   (7)

The *type constructor functions* used in these expressions (i.e., DSDefPtr, DSDef-FieldOp as well as the qualified programming language data types of the form "(<*atype*> <*qualifiers*>...)) will be described here informally. This description in combination with the contextual intuition provided by Fig. 3 and the sampling of formal definitional forms of section 3 of this paper should provide sufficient insight to understand the essence of them and the associated process. However, the full set of type constructors available in DSLGen (e.g., DSDef... constructors for Ptr, Field, Struct, Bit, Enum, Union, Function, Array and qualified programming language data types) is described more completely and formally in [7] (Patent No. 8,713,515). Any additional user defined type constructors will follow the same patterns.

Basically, each equation's right hand side is a type constructor expression of the form *(operator ...arguments ...)*, which specifies a composite CQ Type. Implied functionally related types within these forms are expressed via the variables ?t1, ?t2, etc., and represent recursively related CQ types (often related via type/supertype relationships). For example, the equation (4) of the form "(DSDefPtr ?t1 ...)" is a pointer type (which will eventually become type 3-02a). The referenced supertype is represented by the variable ?t1, which is bound to the "(?itype :myscope ?Pscope :Instname   '?StartInst)" type specification from equation (3). ?t1 will become the type 3-01a in Fig. 3. The "*:name value*" pairs in these expressions (e.g., ":myscope ?Pscope") are qualifying information used to describe generator design contexts or features that fall outside of the strict domain of conventional data types. Explanatory comments appear to the right of the double semicolons. The ":Instname '<?vbl>" pairs (omitted in Fig. 3 to save space) provide (*quoted*) simultaneous variable names to the type differencing routines that harvest the *ReDesign* transformations associated with type pairs. These variables provide global relationships among the individual type equations, the related type difference transformations and the instances upon which those difference transformation operate. For example, difference transformation (9) that relates types 3-01a and 3-02a will bind the instance of type 3-02a (e.g., "(& B)") to the transformation variable name "?PPtrinst." That value of ?PPtrinst is later used in the value slot of the field instance (i.e., 3-07) being constructed for the field type 3-03. Expression (9) also contains some embedded Lisp code that will create a human friendly name for the pointer field thereby making the generated code a bit easier to understand. It concatenates ?Pinst's value (e.g., "B") with the letter "P" resulting in the pointer field being named "BP" in the Fscope context (i.e., "BP" in Fig. 3). It then calls "DSRuntimeDeclare" to declare "BP" to be an instance of type ?t1. The C language code generated to reference the BWimage B within the Fscope will be something like "(rsparms9.BP)" (see expression (2)). The results for other needed variables from Pscope (e.g., "Incr-Idx14) will acquire analogous names (e.g., "Incr-Idx14P").

To solve these type equations, we will need to use the type differencing transforms implied by these type relationships since they express the relationships of these CQ Types to legitimate instances of them and thereby, they recursively constrain subsequent CQ Types and instances. For example, consider the type differencing transformation from ?t1 to ?t2, which is symbolically expressed as "(delta ?t1 ?t2)" and which is nominally defined by the transformation expression to the right of the "=" sign in expression (8) below. Within that transformation expression, the sub-expression to the left of the "=>" is the *pattern* of the (delta ?t1 ?t2) transformation. That pattern is an "*AND*" *pattern* (operationally the Lisp expression "$(PAND ..)"). An AND pattern requires that all of its constituent sub-patterns successfully match some instance of type ?t1. That is, its first pattern element "?inst01" will succeed (because it is initially unbound) by matching an instance of type ?t1 (e.g., "B") and binding that instance to a pattern variable (i.e., "?inst01") where the variable name is uniquely generated by the machinery that generates the type difference transformation. The second pattern element of the AND operator, i.e., "?StartInst", will succeed by binding that same instance to the pattern variable (i.e., "?StartInst"), where "?StartInst" was supplied by the property pair ":Instname '?StartInst" from the specification of type ?t1 shown in expression (3). If the pattern match is successful, then the right hand side of the transformation (i.e., the expression to the right of "=>", which is "(& ?inst01)") will convert ?inst01 to an instance of ?t2 (i.e., "(& B)"). Subsequently, the next type difference (i.e., "(delta ?t2 ?t3)" defined in expression (8)) will bind that newly created instance (i.e., "(& B)") to the variable ?PPtrinst, which will eventually be used in the dsvalue slot of ?t5.

The transformational essences that are the results of differencing the functionally related types in equations (3)-(7) are shown in the expressions (8)-(11). Difference (8) executes the operation that is defined by the DSDefPtr constructor of type equation (4). Similarly, the differences (10) and (11) just express the *implied inverses* of the type constructors DSDefFieldOP and DSDefPtr of type equations (7) and (6). Difference (9) is the cross context mapping relationship and is supplied by the design framework TDF in the generator's library. The TDF framework is built specifically for generating the adaptive "glue code" that we have been discussing up to this point.

((Delta ?t1 ?t2) ~ ($(pand ?inst01 ?StartInst) =>

                (& ?inst01))) ;; ?inst01 is globally unique name   (8)

((Delta ?t2 ?t3) ~ ;; Cross Connection written by a Design Engineer for TDF
    ($(pand ?PPtrInst $(plisp (MakeBinding '?Fldname
                        (DSRuntimeDeclare (quote ?t1) (symb ?StartInst 'P))))))
    => (?Fldname ?Structname :dsvalue ?PPtrInst))) ;;Field Def. form   (9)

((Delta ?t3 ?t4) ~   ;; Field def. form to dot operator
    ($(pand ?Fldinst (?fld ?struct :dsvalue ?PPtrInst)) =>   (● ?fld ?struct)))   (10)

((Delta ?t4 ?t5) ~   ;; Dereference pointer result of dot operation
    ($(pand ?inst02 ?FPtrinst) => (* ?inst02)))   (11)

Operationally, these type Delta transformations are implemented by ReDesign multi-methods[4] that are uniquely determined by the method name ("ReDesign") plus their first two arguments, type1 and type2. ReDesign methods also take additional arguments: 1) an instance of type1, and 2) an initial set of bindings. The initial bindings include bindings determined by the TDF framework context (e.g., the bindings "(?itype bwimage)" and "(?structname rsparms9)") ; bindings that arose during type equation solution process (e.g., "(?t5 |(bwimage_bwi8_:myscope_scopef)|)") ; and bindings created by previously processed ReDesign steps (e.g., "(?startinst   B)").

So, what does a ReDesigner look like? Expression (12) is some CommonLisp like pseudo-code that specifies the essence of a ReDesigner's processing.

```
(ReDesign  type1  type2  instance  bindings) ::=
    (let ((newinstance  nil))
        (multiple-value-bind (success  postmatchbindings )
            (match (LHS (Delta type1 type2))  instance  bindings)
            (if success (setf newinstance
                            (applysubstitution (RHS (Delta type1 type2))
                                                postmatchbindings)))
        (values success postmatchbindings newinstance)))
```
                                                                                (12)

In (12), the CommonLisp *multiple-value-bind* operator defines a scope with two local Lisp variables (i.e., success and postmatchbindings) to receive the multiple values returned from the match routine, which matches the left hand side (LHS) pattern of the specific type Delta transformation against the instance argument. The match starts using the existing bindings in the variable "bindings". If the match is successful (i.e., success equals t on match's exit), then the new instance will be the right hand side (RHS) of the Delta instantiated with the bindings returned from match, i.e.,

---

[4] These multi-methods are expressed in the CLOS (CommonLisp Object System) language embedded in CommonLisp. They are automatically generated during the process that solves the type equations for concrete types. The single exceptions to automatic generation are any cross type differencing methods (e.g., expression (9)), which are written by the Design Engineer at the time the design framework (e.g., TDF) is created and entered into the reusable library of frameworks. They express *elective* design mappings between CQ types.

postmatchbindings, which are the initial bindings extended by any new bindings created by the match routine (e.g., "(?startinst   B)"). The ReDesigner returns three values: 1) the success flag, 2) the postmatchbindings and 3) the newinstance, where the latter two variables will have legitimate values only if success equals t.

Before the type equations are solved, a typical set of initial bindings supplied by the TDF setup code might be:

((?itype bwimage) (?pscope scopep) (?fscope scopef) (?structname rsparms9)) (13)

After the type equations are solved creating a set of types like those shown in Fig. 3, the binding list (13) will be extended with bindings of concrete types for the variables ?t1, ?t2, ?t3,?t4 and ?t5. Following that process, all of the difference expressions (8 11) will be processed, resulting in a set of final bindings, for example:

((?fptrinst (● bp rsparms9)) (?inst02 (● bp rsparms9)) (?fldname bp)
    (?pptrinst (& b)) (?inst01 b) (?startinst b) (?fldinst (bp rsparms9 :dsvalue (& b)))
    (?struct rsparms9)   (?itype bwimage) (?pscope scopep) (?fscope scopef)
    (?structname rsparms9)
    (?t3 |(dsdeffieldop_field1_(?fldname_rsparms9_:dsvalue_ ?pptrinst_:myscope
          scopef:instname_'?fldinst)_ptr2)|)
    (?t4 |(dsdefptr_ptr2_bwi8_:myscope_scopef_:instname_'?fptrinst)|)
    (?t5 |(bwimage_bwi8_:myscope_scopef)|)
    (?t2 |(dsdefptr_ptr1_bwi7_:myscope_scopep_:instname_'?pptrinst)|)
    (?t1 |(bwimage_bwi7_:myscope_scopep_:instname_'?startinst)|)
    …   …)   (14)

The chain of instances produced by this process is shown in expression (15):

  b, (& b), (bp rsparms9 :dsvalue (& b)), (● bp rsparms9), (* (● bp rsparms9))
(15)

Thus, "b" from expression (1) in scopep will map into the expression "(* (● bp rsparms9))" within expression (2), which is in scopef. At code generation time, when the C language surface syntax is added to the internal form, it will be re-expressed as the C language form "(* (rsparms9.bp))".

3   Recursive Type Constructors

The machinery used to synchronize payloads and frameworks uses the CQ Type system to simultaneously define a conventional data type and a design context point of view for that conventional data type. It accomplishes this by defining types as recursive expressions of other types that capture both the data type and the design point of view within some recursive design space. The pattern of types and subtypes will recapitulate the pattern of recursion. That is, a type is some functional composition of its subtypes. For example, a pointer to a BWImage type is a subtype of a BWImage.

Thus, type/subtype structures mimic the specialization and generalization of a design space. However, not all design space relations are specialization or generalizations. Some relations are bridges between design spaces that neither specialize nor generalize design context. They transform design contexts. That is, they establish a transformation or a mapping between design contexts. The cross connection transformation (Ref. 3-09) is just such a bridge. In this case, the design point of view for the BWImage entity has transitioned from a simple design context (i.e., the payload) to a different design context (i.e., the framework context containing the "glue" code manufactured by the generator to synchronize the computational contexts). Within the framework context, the BWImage data entity must have the computational form of a value within a field of the struct manufactured by the generator. That is, in the payload context, the BWImage entity might have the computational form "b" whereas in the related framework context, that data entity might have the related computational form "(*(csparm9.bp))". The computational forms both refer to the same entity but from different design context points of view.

In general, transitions within a design space, be they generalizations, specializations or bridge transformations, represent a transition of design point of view. And this transition may or may not require a transformation of the computational form for a data entity. So, how do we build such a design space?

The system that implements this machinery is defined by a few basic type constructor elements. A sampling of these constructor elements is expressed below in extended BNF, where non-terminals are enclosed in angle brackets and terminals are enclosed in double quotes. Square brackets indicate optionality, braces indicate grouping, and double bars indicate alternation. Parentheses indicate CommonLisp like list and sublist structures that express the form of an instance. Finally, "::=" means "is defined as."

The following sampling of definitions illustrates the form of some typical CQ Type constructor expressions and includes examples, some drawn from expression (14):

<ArrayType>::=("DSDefArray"[<tag>](<D1><D2>...)<atype> <keyword parms>)
Example CQ Type: |(*dsdefarray_array4_(m_n)_colorimage_:instname_'?foo*)|

<FieldType> ::= ("DSDefFieldOP" [<ftag>]
                        (<fieldname>   <structtag> <keyword parms>)
                        <resulttype>)

Example CQ Type: |(*dsdeffieldop_field1_(?fldname_rsparms9_:dsvalue
          _ ?pptrinst_:myscope_scopef_:instname_'?fldinst)_ptr2*)|

<StructType> ::= ("DSDefStruct"   [<stag>]
              ((<ptype1> <name1>   <keyword parms>)
              (<ptype2> <name2>   <keyword parms>)...))

<PointerType> ::= ("DSDefPtr"   [<ptag>] <supertype> <keyword parms>)
Example CQ Type: |(*dsdefptr_ptr1_bwi7_:myscope_scopep_:instname_'?pptrinst*)|

<C-type-specs> ::= { [<storageclass>] || [<typequalifiers>] || [<type-spec>] }
<PLType> ::= (<type> [<ttag>] [<C-type-specs>] [<keyword parms>)])
Example CQ Type: |*(bwimage_bwi7_:myscope_scopep_:instname_'?startinst)*|

Beyond the CommonLisp syntactic framework in which these type specifications
are embedded, these CQ type expressions also borrow from the C programming language, which is the default language emitted by the generation system. As with their
C counterparts, the optional "tag" fields provide a handle for the composite type. The
<keyword parms> (e.g., the keyword ":myscope" paired with the value "ScopeF")
provide the mechanism for qualifying types with design features, design contexts or
other qualifications specific to the generation process. Keyword based qualifications
are "meta-qualifications," which is to say that they are "meta" to data types that are
specific to the *programming language domain*. The list of <ptype *n*> groups within
StructType definition is shorthand for a list of <FieldType> types.

In addition to program generation qualifiers, the qualifiers used in the <PLType>
definition may also include vanilla programming language data types and type qualifiers, e.g., C type qualifiers from <C-type-specs>. For example, <storageclass> may
include auto, extern, register, static and typedef; <typequalifiers> may include const,
restrict, and volatile; and <type-spec> may include short, long, signed, and unsigned.

Declarations are defined using a CQ type specification (e.g., <CQ Type Expres-
sion>) in place of a simple programming language data type, for example:

<Declaration> ::= (DSDeclare <CQ Type Expression> [<Instance>])

4   Related Research

From the most general perspective, the purpose of this research is program generation. For general background, see [1-5] and for the DSLGen umbrella research context of this paper, see [6]. However, the details of the machinery in this paper are
most closely related Programming Data Type research. Therefore, this section will
focus largely on the relationships and differences between the CQ Type research area
the programming date type research area. (See [8-9] and [11-12]). Broadly speaking,
data types have been used in the pursuit of several different but related objectives:

- **Type checking and inference** to reduce errors in the context of strongly
  typed programming languages,
- Program language design for **enhancing reusability of code** (e.g., through
  abstract data types, object oriented programming and polymorphism),
- Program **language design** to simplify programming and enhance the ability
  to write correct programs (e.g., via functional and applicative languages
  where types may play a significant role in specification and compilation),
- **Writing correct programs** from formal specifications (e.g., stepwise
  refinement),

- **Formal specification** of the "meaning" (i.e., semantics) of computer programming elements (e.g., denotational semantics and models like the Z language or the VDM method).

The main difference between the CQ Types research and previous data type research is that CQ Types research is operating in the *design domain space* whereas previous work was to a greater or lesser extent operating in the *programming language domain space*. That is, previous conceptions of types did not provide a way to express design concepts except to the degree that those design concepts were expressible in terms of programming language constructs or abstractions thereof.

To choose a concrete example, consider the Liskov substitution principle. This principle "seems" to bear some cosmetic relationship to CQ Types and their associated operations in the sense that the work is characterizing the situation in which a subtype is computationally substitutable for its super type in a piece of code. That is, the Liskov substitution principle is superficially similar to the CQ Type work in the sense it deals with mapping one form of programming language code to a related form. However, it is different it two obvious and important ways. The Liskov substitution principle works strictly within the domain of programming types and the type/subtype relationship depends on an *implicit* property of both. CQ Types are defined specifically to work within and capture knowledge about the design space (as opposed to the programming language space) and thereby involve entities (e.g., design features and design contexts) that are not explicit elements of the programming language domain. Furthermore, the relationships among CQ Types are *explicit* rather than implicit and they explicitly capture differences in computational structure that are due to implicit relationships within the design and generation domains (i.e., outside of programming language domain).

5   Summary and Conclusions

CQ Types provide a mechanism for expressing abstract relationships between entities within a conceptual design space and thereby for specifying plans for adapting and relocating code from one design context to another. What constitutes a context is completely open. A context might represent a simple design feature, a locale or scope, a set of computational states, an abstract design for code, a computational partition, etc. This expressive freedom allows the generator to evolve logical designs for a computation by adding elective design features (e.g., threaded parallelism) to pedestrian and perhaps inefficient designs of a computation while still having the capability to automatically convert from one design form to another.

Furthermore, CQ Types and their associated type difference transformations can be abstracted to precursor equations that parameterize the concrete entities and relationships, which will become concrete via instantiation from some future concrete code within some future payload instance. This allows design frameworks to factor out and express only those design elements and relationships that are determined by the framework, e.g., the relationship between a yet-to-be-determined variable in a payload and its yet-to-be-determined field representation within a structure that connects the payload data to the framework operations. Once such a concrete future payload has been identified to the generator, the yet-to-be-determined elements can be computed by the generator to complete a fully integrated design for the target program.

References

1. Biggerstaff, T.J.: A perspective of generative reuse. Annals of Software Engineering, 169–226 (1998)
2. Biggerstaff, T.J.: A new architecture of transformation-based generators. IEEE Transactions on Software Engineering 30(12), 1036–1054 (2004)
3. Biggerstaff, T.J.: Automated partitioning of a computation for parallel or other high capability architecture. Patent no. 8,060,857, United States Patent and Trademark Office (2011)
4. Biggerstaff, T.J.: Non-localized constraints for automated program generation. Patent no. 8,225,277, United States Patent and Trademark Office (2012)
5. Biggerstaff, T.J.: Synthetic partitioning for imposing implementation design patterns onto logical architectures of computations. Patent no. 8,327,321, United States Patent and Trademark Office (2012)
6. Biggerstaff, T.J.: Reuse: Right Idea, Wrong Representation? Invited paper. In: DReMeR 2013 – International Workshop on Designing Reusable Components and Measuring Reusability, Pisa, Italy (2013)
7. Biggerstaff, T.J.: Automated Synchronization of Design Features in Disparate Code Components Using Type Differencing. Patent no. 8,713,515, United States Patent and Trademark Office (2014)
8. Cardelli, L., Wegner, P.: On Understanding Types, Data Abstractions, and Polymorphism. ACM Computing Surveys 17(4) (1985)
9. Cardelli, L.: Type Systems. In: CRC Handbook of Computer Science and Engineering, 2nd edn., ch. 97 (2004)
10. Gamma, E., Helm, R., Johnson, R., Vlissides, J.: Design Patterns. Addison-Wesley (1995)
11. Liskov, B., Wing, J.: A Behavioral Notion of Subtyping. ACM Transactions on Programming Languages and Systems (1994)
12. Liskov, B., Wing, J.: A Behavioral Subtyping Using Invariants and Constraints. Carnegie Mellon Report CMU-CS-99-156 (1999)
13. Mattson, T. G., Sanders, B. A., Massingill, B. L.: Patterns for Parallel Programming. Addison Wesley (2008)

Pragmatic Approach to Test Case Reuse - A Case Study in Android OS BiDiTests Library

Suriya Priya R. Asaithambi[1] and Stan Jarzabek[1,2]

[1] School of Computing,
National University, Singapore
suria@nus.edu.sg, stan@comp.nus.edu.sg
[2] Faculty of Computer Science,
Bialystok University of Technology

Abstract. Test libraries explode in size, but both practitioners and researchers report much redundancy among test cases. Similar functions require similar test cases. Redundancy may be particularly overwhelming in test libraries for mobile computing, where we need to test the same functionality implemented on various models/brands of mobile phones. Redundancies create reuse opportunities. We propose a *generic adaptive test template (GATT)* approach to contain explosion of test libraries by reusing common recurring test patterns instead of enumerating the same test case in many variant forms. The objective is to ease the test development and maintenance effort. The process starts with automated detection of test clones. We represent a group of similar test cases by a test template along with specifications for automated generation of test cases in a group. We illustrate GATT with examples from Android OS test libraries, and evaluate its benefits and trade-offs. The approach scales to large test libraries and is oblivious to application domains or programming languages. GATT is practical as it focuses on managing test libraries without affecting the follow up test execution. Therefore, it smoothly blends with any other existing techniques and tools used for testing.

Keywords: Reusability, Test Libraries, Test Clones, Software Testing, Mobile Platform, Android Platform Test Libraries, Test Construction Approach.

1   Introduction

Today mobile devices are important in both personal and enterprise computing. With rapid proliferation of mobile devices comes an expectation of equally rapid rollouts for platform improvements and bug fixes. Android is the largest open source mobile OS platform for creating apps and games, since its inception in 2003. Android thus far has more than ~11,000 device models[1], ~120 unique brands and a total of 19 OS versions. Vendors have to verify (test) Android OS platform compatibility for individual

---

[1] http://opensignal.com/reports/fragmentation-2013/
   Last Retrieved April 2014

I. Schaefer and I. Stamelos (Eds.): ICSR 2015, LNCS 8919, pp. 122–138, 2014.
© Springer International Publishing Switzerland 2014

devices and also systematically incorporate device specific variations into multiple releases of test libraries in order to sustain themselves in the market.

The challenge in testing these releases of Android OS is caused by the complexities of feature variations and device diversity. Platform features include any general computing characteristics such as messaging, web browser, voice based features, multi-touch facilities, application multitasking, screen capture, video calls, multiple language support and other accessibilities. These platform features have slightly different implementation on different mobile phone brands/models. Android OS device diversity is caused by variations among vendor specific hardware, context & location aware features, multiple connectivity protocols, media streaming, handset layouts, storage and sensors (e.g., cameras, gyroscopes, barometers and magnetometers). These two testing challenges create lots of "copy-paste-modify" code among test cases leading to the test libraries explosion, meaning vast increase in the number of test cases needed to verify the correctness of the Android OS platform. Testers must ensure proper functioning of features on various device models, OS versions, and vendor specific firmware versions. Our previous study [1; 2]with Android OS test libraries has confirmed presence of substantial redundancies in Android OS test libraries.

In this paper, we propose the *Generic Adaptive Test Templates (GATT)* approach to tackle the problem of test redundancies and turn them into productivity gains. The approach works as follows: Each group of test clones (redundancies) is represented by a test template written in Adaptive Reuse Technique (ART)[2]. This template embodies what's common to test cases in a group. A template is complemented by specifications of how to generate all test cases in that group from the template. The generation is automated by template processor by using the specifications composed of commonalities and variations based on the test designer's inputs. Further, any development or maintenance to these test libraries take place at the level of non-redundant, smaller and easier to comprehend test templates, while the usual testing execution processes remain unaffected by the GATT method.

We demonstrate GATT approach using BiDiTests test library (BiDiTests can test the bi-directional orientation of any display device) from the Android OS platform. We selected three consecutive versions of the BiDiTests. Then we quantitatively and qualitatively evaluate the results to analyze the benefits in terms testing productivity, as well as trade-offs in integrating the GATT into conventional testing processes. For example, BiDiTests libraries forming three subsequent API versions amounted to ≈18EKLOC (Executable Kilo Lines of Code). With GATT, we were able to reconstruct these test libraries from ≈ 4KLOC of generic test templates. Effectively the process has eliminated more than 77% of the redundancy among the executable test libraries, improving maintainability as well as reduce the efforts needed to develop new test cases.

The paper is organized as following: section 2 presents motivation and brief sketch of the solution, section 3 describes the proposed GATT method, section 4 discusses the case study – BiDiTests test library, section 5 presents various test clones pertinent

---

[2] ART – Adaptive Reuse Technique (`http://art.comp.nus.edu.sg/`)

to BiDiTests, section 6 discusses the test template construction using GATT approach, section 7 presents GATT evaluation and threats to validity, section 8 discusses related work and finally section 9 concludes the paper.

2   Motivation and Sketch of the Solution

A typical test case consists of test inputs, test programs and the assertion of expected results. A common observation is that test cases to test the same feature on different versions of Android OS are similar one to each other. Our analysis also shows that sometimes it is not uncommon to find a fair amount of similarity even among test cases of a single version of test library. To understand the nature of such test clones and visualize how to unify them, consider two fragments from the test files `Bitmap-MeshActivity.java` and `BitmapMeshLayerActivity.java` shown in Fig. 1. As the name suggests these methods test the graphical activity of Bit-Map-Mesh in the Android platform. We see test clone `onCreate()` in the left and the right columns of Fig. 1.

```
package com.android.test.hwui;                package com.android.test.hwui; . . .
. . .                                          public class BitmapMeshLayerActivity
public class BitmapMeshActivity                              extends Activity {
                extends Activity {            protected void onCreate(Bundle
protected void onCreate(Bundle                              savedInstanceState) {
                savedInstanceState) {          super.onCreate(savedInstanceState);
  super.onCreate(savedInstanceState);          final BitmapMeshView view =
  final BitmapMeshView view =                              new BitmapMeshView(this);
                new BitmapMeshView(this);      view.setLayerType(View.LAYER_TYPE, null);
                                               setContentView(view);
  setContentView(view);                        }
}                                              protected void onDraw(Canvas canvas) {
protected void onDraw(Canvas canvas) {          super.onDraw(canvas);
  super.onDraw(canvas);
  canvas.drawARGB(255, 255, 255, 255);         canvas.translate(200, 200);
  canvas.translate(100, 100);                  canvas.drawBitmapMesh(mBitmap1, 9, 9,
  canvas.drawBitmapMesh(mBitmap1, 3, 3,          mVertices, 0, null, 0, null);
    mVertices, 0, null, 0, null);                . . .
    . . .                                      }
}                                              . . .
. . .                                          }
}
```

Normal Text: identical; Underlined Text : Simple Parametric Clones
Bold Text: Complex Non-Parametric Test Clones;

Fig. 1. Similar Test Code Fragments

Common code is shown in regular font in Fig. 1, while variations are either shown as underlined or in bold text. The underlined text indicate parametric variations that can be handled using traditional programming constructs, whereas the bold text indicate complex variations such as different API/method calls, partial names and other gapped test clones whose handling may fall beyond the purview of traditional programming constructs.

Fig. 2 shows how GATT works. T1 refers to the `BitmapMeshActivity` test clone in the left hand side of as Fig. 1, and T2 refers to the `BitmapMeshLayerActivity` test clone in the right hand side of Fig. 1. GATT represents test clones T1 and T2 as a generic test template T. ΔT1 and ΔT2 are specifications of parametric and other variations indicated by the test designer in order to generate T1 and T2 from the template T respectively. Thus when the template T is processed via the Template Processor, it generates test cases (T1 and T2) in their original form. Thus GATT's template constructs promote reuse with only modest extensions to existing test libraries.

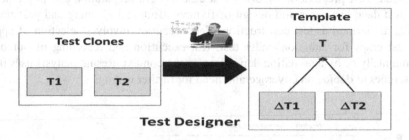

Fig. 2. GATT Template Specification

A sample template for the above test code fragment is shown in Fig. 3**Error! Reference source not found.** (BitMapActivity.art). Both ΔT1 and ΔT2 are in BitMapActivity.spc specification file called SPC for short. Template processor interprets and generates the original test files BitmapMeshActivity.java and BitmapMeshActivity.java.

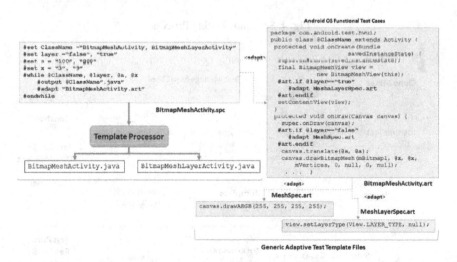

Fig. 3. Representation of motivational example

An ART template is parameterized with ART commands as shown in bold fonts. These parameters are defined in SPC along with their respective values. The template processor propagates the values from template to generate test cases. The motivation of our solution is to simplify testing by promoting reuse and improving abstraction.

3   Overview of Generic Adaptive Test Template (GATT)

Software testing process (shown in Fig. 4) comprises four stages namely, test planning, test preparation, test execution and result analysis. During test planning activities such as identification of tasks, resource estimation, financial and effort budgets
are handled. Test preparation involves test case design, preparation and implementation of test data, test cases and design of fixtures. Both test planning and preparation
activities are termed as test construction. Test execution involves selection of appropriate test cases for situation under test, test execution and recording of outcomes
either manually or by automation depending on the context. Result analysis uses these
test outcomes to decide on coverage and need for further testing.

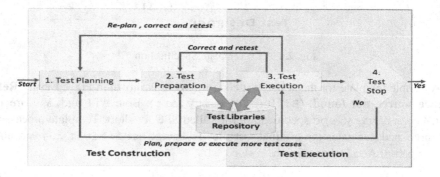

Fig. 4. Software Testing Process

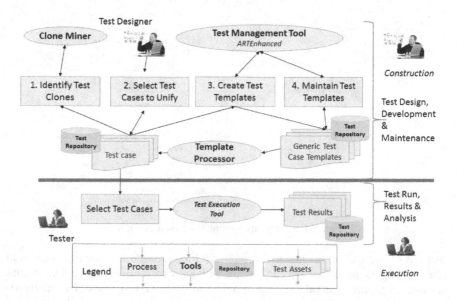

Fig. 5. GATT Approach for Test Libraries

GATT fits into the *Test Preparation* stage and aligns closely with the test library repository. The GATT approach usually starts with identification of test case similarities (clones), selection of test cases for unification, creation of templates and finally maintenance of the same. Fig. 5 illustrates how GATT approach works during *test construction* (planning and design of test cases) and *test execution*. GATT involves two key roles, namely *Test Designer* who is a domain expert contributing towards test case design and development, and *Tester* who executes tests on a targeted system.

As test cases are maintained at template level, testers work with the representation that is smaller in size than the actual test library and may hence find it easier to understand due to non-redundant structure. We build test templates in steps shown in Fig. 5:

1. **Step 1: Identify Test Clones.** Input for this step is the existing test library codes. Using automated clone detection tools followed by manual analysis we zoom into test clones whose elimination is likely to boost testing productivity.
2. **Step 2: Select Test Cases for Unification.** Second step assesses the feasibility of unifying the identified test clone groups. Some of these test clone groups can be handled using either the object oriented programming language constructs or dependency injection constructs. These test clone groups are named as *Reducible* test clones. In spite of such implementation mechanism, we still observe presence of complex test clones. These complex test clone groups that cannot be handled by the traditional testing mechanism and named as *Non-reducible* test clones.
3. **Step 3: Create Test Templates.** Once it has been decided to use template approach, the third step focuses on designing and developing GATT representation for identified test clone groups.
4. **Step 4: Maintain Test Templates.** Maintaining the harvested generic adaptive test templates as a regular configured software artifacts help in sustaining the quality of the test library in the long term.

4   Overview of `BiDiTests`

We demonstrate GATT with test clones found in the `BiDiTests` test library of the Android OS API version 17. `BiDiTests` comprises 5325 ELOC (has 41 Java test files and 37 XML configuration files). We chose `BiDiTests` since it exhibits test clones of different type and granularity which allows us to properly illustrate GATT. The `BiDiTests` test library is a typical example of the traditional graphical interface testing in the Android OS. Additionally, we have used information from the Android developer forum and API documentation to understand the underlying domain and maintenance aspects.

`BiDiTests` is composed of functional test cases designed to test the bidirectional layout of the device's screen orientation. The layout usually defines the visual structure for a user interface as a basis to design further UI components, events, activities and widgets. `BiDiTests` test cases validate UI components of the System API such as `View`, `Widget` and `Canvas`. The `View` is the rectangular canvas component that is responsible for drawing further components and handling its respective events. BiDiTests test cases verifies various layout setting (left-to-right, right-to-left and locale layouts) for the three types of graphical entities namely, View, Layout and Gallery. Each of these entities have unique properties such as size, color, appearance, position, visibility and other associated behavioral properties. Further, the test library verifies different layouts such as LinearLayout, FrameLayout, GridLayout, TableLayout and RelativeLayout. For brevity, Fig. 6 only shows the participating java class names of the BiDiTests test library under the TableLayout.

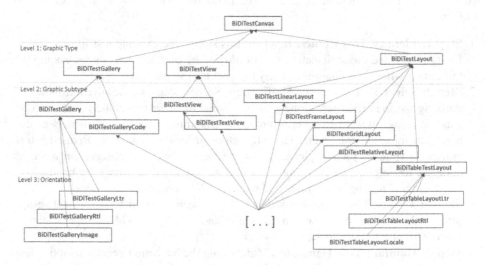

Fig. 6. BiDiTests files for verifying bi-directional layouts

The BiDiTests also allow for declarative definition of layout using XML vocabulary enabling better separation of presentation logic from rest of the platform behavior. Test cases verifying a particular graphical layout exhibit similarity in terms of test fixtures, test data, events tested and action lifecycle. Analyzing from such test variation perspective, BiDiTests classes are organized into three levels (as shown in Fig. 6).

1. At the top level, testing focuses on graphical type Canvas as the basic UI entity. All other graphical components are laid over the canvas component. This apart, Activity, utility and other constants classes forms the top level. The Activity initializes a logical test suite and executes all connected test cases present.
2. In the second level, Canvas is further divided into sub-types (example: various layouts) or specialties (example: text view is a special type of view). For example, let us consider the Layout subtype, this is further divided into five kinds namely, frame, grid, linear, relative and table. Another example is that the View entity is further specialized into sub-class TextView. Thus test attributes related to the View are not sufficient to describe the special attributes for TextView and hence additional tests are designed.

3. In the third level, each graphical entity has to be tested for various orientations namely, left-to-right (ltr), right-to-left (rtl) and locale.

Class naming conventions helps in identifying groups of similar test cases. For example, a graphical entity *Layout* and subtype *Table* with three orientations are named as BiDTestTableLayoutLtr, BiDTestTableLayoutRtl & BiDTest-TableLayoutLocale (as shown in Fig. 6). Similarly, a test file named Bi-DiTestRelativeLayoutRtl.java would verify the graphic canvas for relative layout and right-to-left orientation. BiDiTestTextViewLtr.java would test the graphic canvas for Text View UI and left-to-right orientation. Thus in the BiDi-Tests test files, feature variant layers are explicitly declared in the file names in order.

5   Test Clones in BiDiTests Library

We used Clone Miner and Clone Visualizer [3-5] along with CCFinder to detect test clones in BiDiTests. Subsequently we carried out manual test case analysis to determine the nature of redundancies. We chose a sample of BiDiTests test library with 6733 TLOC (Total Lines of Code) and 5325 ELOC (excluding comments) from a repository of forty over test libraries. The BiDiTests consists of 41 java and 37 XML configuration files (78 files) representing ~53 test cases. These test cases show presence of 83 test clone groups of varying token sizes and types. The summary of the test clone groups are shown in Table 1. TC refers to test clones in short, TCG refers to the test clone groups, each test clone group can have two or more test clone instances (TCI) and LOC refers to the average lines of code for the test clone groups.

Table 1. Summary of test clone groups in BiDiTests

Granularity	Fragments TC			Method Level TC			File Level TC			Total TCG	Reducible TCG	Non-Reducible TCG
Type	TCG	TCI	LOC	TCG	TCI	LOC	TCG	TCI	LOC			
Simple Test Clones	4	8	7	6	12	6	0	0	0	10	2	8
Structural Test Clones	4	10	12	25	50	10	34	87	6	63	4	59
Heterogeneous Test Clones	0	0	0	0	0	0	10	24	35	10	0	10
Total	8			31			44			83	6	77

The *Simple Test Clones* are test code fragments that meet certain (as set by Test Designer) threshold of similarity. Simple test clones are often the result of copying a code fragment and pasting it into another location. This includes identical test code fragments, parametric test code fragments with variations in identifiers, literals, types, parameters and variables and gapped test code fragments that have additional variations in terms of added, modified and removed statements. *Structural Test Clones* are similar program structures such as test classes, files or directories. *Heterogeneous Test Clones* comprise of test code fragments containing multiple programming languages.

Key reasons why test clones appear in `BiDiTests` are due to the similarities among the layouts, event handling, action lifecycle, screen layout configuration and orientation features. By default all events raised by the same component (example button or drop down list) are similar and thus the related test cases have similar codes. In summary, test clones are generally caused by the similarities among graphical components. In this case study, we have managed such non-reducible test clone groups using the proposed GATT approach.

5.1   Test Clone Examples

Consider the following piece of gapped test code fragment extracted from two different java test files namely `BitmapMeshLayerActivity.java` and `BitmapMeshActivity.java` as illustrated in Fig. 7. An analysis of these test clones reveal that the two classes are contiguous segments of redundant test scripts that have intervened code portions that are not parametric.

```
public class BitmapMeshLayerActivity
   extends Activity {
    protected void onCreate(Bundle savedInstanceState) {
        super.onCreate(savedInstanceState);
        final BitmapMeshView view = new BitmapeshView(this);
        view.setLayerType(View.LAYER_TYPE_HARDWARE, null);
        setContentView(view);
    }
    ...
}                                                  Test Clone Fragment 1
public class BitmapMeshActivity
   extends Activity {
    protected void onCreate(Bundle savedInstanceState) {
        super.onCreate(savedInstanceState);
        final BitmapMeshView view = new BitmapeshView(this);
        setContentView(view);
    }
    ...
}                                                  Test Clone Fragment 2
```

Fig. 7. Gapped Test Clone Example

Consider the following piece of test code fragment (Fig. 8) extracted from the `on-CreateView()` method of two different java test files namely `BiDiTestRelativeLayoutLtr.java` and `BiDiTestRelativeLayout2Ltr.java`. The test clones are syntactically identical fragments of test codes or test methods except for non-parametric variations in class names and `inflate()` method calls.

5.2   Non-reducible Test Clone Groups in `BiDiTests`

For the ease of comprehension we grouped the java and xml files as separate templates. GATT approach works equally well when multiple programming language files are combined into same template specification since it works with individual level parsing and not at the programming language syntactical constructs, thus test clone file grouping is purely a test designer's preference. It is easier to logically group the non-reducible test clones based on the test functionality and component under test before translating into test templates. We logically grouped `BiDiTests` into the following constructs:

```
public class BiDiTestRelativeLayout2Ltr extends Fragment {
    @Override
    public View onCreateView(LayoutInflater inflater, ViewGroup
container,
         Bundle savedInstanceState) {
      return inflater.inflate(R.layout.relative_layout_2_ltr,
         container, false);
    }

}
```

```
public class BiDiTestRelativeLayoutLtr extends Fragment {
    @Override
    public View onCreateView(LayoutInflater inflater, ViewGroup
container,
         Bundle savedInstanceState) {
      return inflater.inflate(R.layout.relative_layout_ltr,
         container, false);
    }
    . . .
}
```

Fig. 8. Structural (non-parametric) test clone instances

1. BiDiCanvas[T].java: This group refers to tests that verify proper functioning of display orientation in an embedded graphical canvas. T refers to the canvas instances.
2. BiDiTest[U]Layout[V].java: This group refers to tests that verify the layout graphical entities. U refers to the particular layout under test such as frame, grid, linear, relative and table layouts. V refers to one of the display orientation choices such as Ltr, Rtl and Locale. Similarly, [U]_layout_[V].xml refers to the configuration of the various layout options.
3. BiDiTestGallery[W].java: This group refers to tests that verifies the gallery based graphical entities. W refers to one of display orientation choices such as Ltr, Rtl and Images in gallery. Similarly, Gallery_[W].xml refers to the configuration of the various gallery components.
4. BiDiTestTextView[X][Y].java & BiDiTestTextView[V].java: This group refers to tests that verifies view based graphical entities. X refers to one of display directions or UI component drawn, Y refers to one of display orientation choices such as Ltr or Rtl. V refers to padding, padding mixed, group margin, text and display orientation choices such as Ltr, Rtl and Locale. Test_view_[X]_[Y].xml & Text_view_[V].xml refers to the configuration of the various view options.
5. Rest of the smaller test files (both java and configuration) inclusive can be drafted into miscellaneous templates with test clone groups of lesser granularity.

6   GATT Representation for BiDiTests

In this case study we have built the test templates for an existing test library (maintenance scenario). However, the GATT approach can be applied equally well to test case creation scenarios where new test case are developed with inputs from test designer regarding possible similarities from the test case design. GATT templates contain common parts of test cases in test clone group marked with provision for variation points at which template processor can customize to derive specific variations. The BiDiTests test library is translated into template hierarchy and SPC built using ART. For API version 17 of BiDiTests, we built ~30 templates (details provided later in Table 3). We also built templates for three subsequent versions BiDiTests test cases (namely versions 16, 17 & 18). This case study shows the use of GATT as test libraries evolve together with the Android OS from one release to another. It also provides additional contextual interpretations, refinements related to evolutionary changes, tactics for change propagation visibility and assistance for managing multiple version releases. Finally, versions of Android OS test library can also benefit from the variability management mechanism from a maintenance perspective.

6.1   Selected BiDiTests GATT Examples

In this section we present few representative templates for test clones to showcase our solution. We focus on non-parametric and heterogeneous test clones as they cannot be handled by conventional programming techniques. Consider the first example drawn from BiDiTests to illustrate how GATT handles non-parametric variation amoung test cases (as shown in Fig. 9).

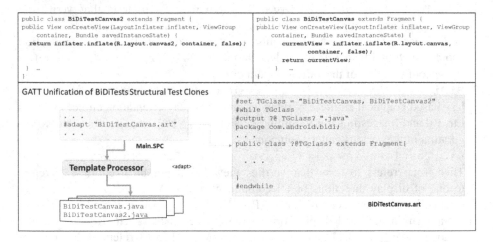

Fig. 9. GATT example for structural test clone group

The variations between the test clones are being highlighted in bold text in the figure. We observe the presence of test clones due to non-parametric variations occur in the form of gapped test codes. Such test clones are reconstructed into templates preserving the common text (in this example BiDiTestCanvas.art). The variations are then managed using adaptation commands. The template processor reads and interprets the art commands and generates the test files BiDiTestCanvas.java and BiDiTestCanvas2.java yielding two different test cases for the canvas component.

Consider the heterogeneous test clone group files (`BiDiTestView` and `Bi-DiTestViewDrawText` java and XML layout files) consisting of test codes written in two programming languages to verify `View` graphic item and its respective layout as shown in Fig. 10. When the graphical entities under test are similar, the test cases contain semantically equivalent constructs. In this example, one tester has chosen to define text size as `int` while another tester chose `float`. In addition, we can also observe that the test codes differ in the way variables are scoped and memory managed (`final` and `static`). In such non-type based variations, java generics `<T>` are inadequate. The GATT solution for this heterogeneous test clone (composed of both xml and java files) example is constructed. Fig. 10 also shows relevant skeletal code fragments for the templates (`BiDiTextView.art` and `XML textview.art`). Also in this case study, we have designed and constructed GATT representation in three iterations. The first iteration named $BiDiTests_{Simple}$ is based on one-to-one translation of test files into templates, with little attention to minimizing redundancies. In the second iteration $BiDiTests_{Optimized}$, redundancies are unified by understanding test smells, refactoring non-parametric and non-type variants. Finally in $BiDiTests_{Unified}$ iteration, we further refined and normalized the test clone group across three subsequent Android OS versions.

Fig. 10. GATT for heterogeneous test clones (Java + XML) files

7 GATT Evaluation

We used the case study `BiDiTests` as a representative slice of Android OS test repository, to demonstrate the GATT representation is feasible and beneficial. We evaluated GATT using measures such as: (1) Lossless-translation of test libraries into templates (2) Quantitative Evaluation (3) Qualitative Analysis (4) Scalability and (5) Assessment of the non-intrusiveness. Finally this section also briefly points threats to validity.

7.1   Lossless Translation of Test Libraries into GATT Representation

It is essential to verify if the templates generate original test libraries without any loss of information. We validated the template construction by generating test cases from templates and comparing them with originals using file and directory comparator tools.

7.2   Quantitative Evaluation

In this case study, we built GATT representation for an existing test library (BiDi-Tests) with an intention of reducing test clones and providing effective reuse solutions. Summary of the GATT representations are shown in Table 2 and Table 3. Table 2 summarizes quantitative statistics of GATT representation across the three test library versions. Table 3 summarizes the improvements achieved through the iterative re-construction process.

Table 2. BiDiTests Project Consecutive Three Version Statistics

Description	API16	API 17	API 18
# of Java Test Files	34	41	39
# of Java Test Methods	61	72	59
# of XML Configuration Files	31	37	36
Total Files	65	78	75
# Files Containing Test clones	46	59	56
% Files Containing Test Clones	71%	76%	74%
File Size (Kbytes)	416	528	512
# Lines Of Code	6556	8422	8102
# of Executable Lines Of Code	4877	6393	6191
# ART Templates	29	29	29
Each Versions (Executable LOC)	3924	4024	4063
ART (%) as compared to Original ELOC	80%	63%	66%
Merged Templates (Executable LOC)			4063
ART(%) compared to Original ELOC			23%

Table 3. Template Files Metrics accross Iterations

Description	BiDiTests$_{Simple}$	BiDiTests$_{Optimized}$	BiDiTests$_{Unified}$
Canvas Related Testing Files	4	2	2
Layout Related Testing Files	37	14	8
Gallery Related Testing Files	5	3	3
View Related Testing Files	26	12	10
Miscellaneous + SPC	6	7	7
Total	78	38	30

As observed from the above data, there is a significant drop in the size of test code to be maintained from original test libraries to BiDiTests$_{Unified}$. Also in the BiDiTest-s$_{Optimized,}$ there is 80%, 63% and 66% reduction in test library size (ELOC) for API 16, 17 and 18 versions respectively. BiDiTests$_{Unified}$ has been compressed to 23% of its original size largely due to unification of three API kernel versions to one. From original code base of approximately 218 files (both Java and XML inclusive), the generic templates where compacted into just 30 template files.

7.3   Qualitative Analysis - Change Propagation

In addition to reducing the size of the test library, GATT also reduces the cognitive complexity, and simplifies test case maintenance. This is due to exposing program relations that matter in maintenance such as change propagation discussed here. We conducted an experiment to verify the hypothesis that test templates improve productivity and reduce update anomalies. We analyzed the impact of change requests, namely Grid Change, Text View Change and Drop Extra Canvas. We compared the number of modifications needed to implement the change requests (in subsequent versions) using the GATT approach to that of the normal approach. From kernel API version 16 to 17 seven files were added to satisfy change requests CR1 & CR2 shown in Table 4. Likewise, from versions API 17 to 18 two files were deleted to satisfy the CR3. #F denotes the number of files affected by the change request while #L denotes the number of modified locations. The number of files affected was further sub-classified as newly added files (#A), Deleted (removed) files (#D) and modified files (#M) as observed from the distribution of impact recorded in Table 5.

Table 4. Change Request List

Grid Change (CR1)	Update BiDiTests app for adding 'Grid Layout' unit tests
Text View Change (CR2)	Add tests to view text alignment
Drop Extra Canvas (CR3)	Clean up code for Test View, 'Canvas Layout' and related code flags

Table 5. Comparison of change propogation

CR	#F	#L	Original Test Library						GATT based Test Library					
			Single Version			Three Versions			Single Version			Three Versions		
			#A	#D	#M	#A	#D	#M	#A	#D	#M	#A	#D	#M
CR1	8	9	7	0	1	21	0	3	2	0	1	1	0	1
CR2	5	5	4	0	1	12	0	3	2	0	1	2	0	1
CR3	4	4	0	3	1	0	9	3	0	2	1	0	2	1

The number of modifications that are needed in order to implement these change requests have decreased from original test library to GATT representation of the same slice of the test library. With reduction of modification points also comes smaller number of change propagation paths which together contribute to ease of navigating in the non-redundant template representation to trace the impact of changes. While we have not conducted yet a controlled experiment to measure the actual impact of GATT on test case maintenance effort, we think the above arguments provide a compelling reasons to think that maintenance effort will be also reduced.

7.4   Scalability

GATT provides a template representation for both test data-structures as well as test case algorithms in its meta-layer. GATT also addresses concept of hierarchy and vertical parameters (i.e. layered components) which are essential ingredients for any scalable test library. The GATT related control constructs work as pre-generators and offers support to building of test library in a hierarchical fashion at the level of meta-layer, thereby guaranteeing scalability.

7.5   Non-intrusiveness

Preliminary evidence presented thus far shows that GATT prototype does not compromise productivity and performance of the generated test libraries. Test designers work with test case code wrapped in ART directives as templates. Template processor then expands these directives to generate the actual test cases from templates in the similar way that the C pre-processor generates code by expanding cpp directives. When the templates are instantiated, the implementation details of the test case are resolved by compile time binding values to the parameters from the template.

7.6   Threats to Validity

There are few threats to validity such as (1) the choice of BiDiTests project over others in repository, (2) the nature of interpretation performed by the tool, and (3) use of text token based comparison. Our work does not claim to have generalized all possible GATT representation. Our estimates on efforts/change metrics for change requests are based on GIT repository information. While we believe that GATT approach can be smoothly accommodated into existing software testing, this hypothesis needs certainly be verified in industrial project settings.

8   Related Work

Antonia Bertolino [7] summarizes the many outstanding research challenges for software testing into a consistent roadmap. From the literature it is observed that in test case construction strategies such as model based testing, combinatorial testing and domain driven tools are popular. Several researchers have proposed different ways of adopting or implementing Model Based Testing (MBT). MBT is extensively discussed in books by Beizer et al [6] and Utting et al [15]. UML diagrams such as state-chart diagrams, use-case diagrams, sequence diagrams, etc. can assist to generate test cases. Research proposals [13; 14] utilize UML profiles and test constraints in form of directives in their generation approach. Combinatorial testing (CT) is another active area of test case generation. Four main groups of methods have been proposed: greedy algorithm, heuristic search, mathematic method and random method [8-10]. Among the different variability management techniques, use of compile-time test case generation is proposed by Mc.Gregor in [12]. Also approaches that work with heterogeneous platforms and polyglot programming languages are sparse. NA Kraft et al [11] describe an approach for cross-language clone detection. The work has been implemented in .Net platform and proved to detect clones from C# and VB codes. While published literature thus far focuses on test generation and selection challenges,

Android being a recent platform, has received less attention particularly in variability management techniques. As long as regular programming language constructs are able to unify the test clones, it remains a traditional solution. But when the complexity of variations cannot be handled, the test designer may resort to the use of GATT approach. As the name suggests, generic adaptive test templates complement than compete with traditional techniques. While the GATT approach proposes that test libraries are handled through reusable and adaptable templates, after generation only test libraries and compiled and executed. Thus at runtime, there is no difference between traditional and GATT generated test libraries.

9   Conclusion

Test libraries of Android OS explode because of the need to test Android OS features on many brands and models of mobile devices. We addressed the problem by representing groups of similar test cases with templates. We demonstrated our template approach with slice of Android OS test library and evaluated engineering merits of the approach. In evaluation, we pointed to reduction of size and cognitive complexity of test library size, and to ease of adoption of our approach due to scamless injection into existing testing processes.   In future work, we will extent the scope of our study covering bigger slice of Android OS test library and will conduct a controlled experiment to assess productivity gains due to adoption of our approach. We also plan to conduct similar studies of Android app test libraries where test clones are expected to be more pervasive.

References

1. Asaithambi, S.P.R., Jarzabek, S.: Generic adaptable test cases for software product line testing: Software product line. In: Proceedings of the 3rd Annual Conference on Systems, Programming, and Applications: Software for Humanity, pp. 33–36. ACM (2012)
2. Asaithambi, S.P.R., Jarzabek, S.: Towards Test Case Reuse: A Study of Redundancies in Android Platform Test Libraries. In: Favaro, J., Morisio, M. (eds.) ICSR 2013. LNCS, vol. 7925, pp. 49–64. Springer, Heidelberg (2013)
3. Basit, H.A., Ali, U., Haque, S., Jarzabek, S.: Things structural clones tell that simple clones don't. In: 28th IEEE International Conference on Software Maintenance (ICSM), pp. 275–284. IEEE (2012)
4. Basit, H.A., Jarzabek, S.: A case for structural clones. In: Proc. Int. Workshop on Software Clones (IWSC 2009) (2009)
5. Basit, H.A., Jarzabek, S.: A data mining approach for detecting higher-level clones in software. IEEE Transactions on Software Engineering 35(4), 497–514 (2009)
6. Beizer, B.: Software testing techniques. Dreamtech Press (2003)
7. Bertolino, A.: Software testing research: Achievements, challenges, dreams. In: 2007 Future of Software Engineering, pp. 85–103. IEEE Computer Society (2007)
8. Cohen, D.M., Dalal, S.R., Fredman, M.L., Patton, G.C.: The AETG system: An approach to testing based on combinatorial design. IEEE Transactions on Software Engineering 23(7), 437–444 (1997)

9. Gnesi, S., Latella, D., Massink, M.: Formal test-case generation for UML statecharts. In: Proceedings of the Ninth IEEE International Conference on Engineering Complex Computer Systems, pp. 75–84 (2004)

10. Hartman, A.: Software and hardware testing using combinatorial covering suites. In: Graph Theory, Combinatorics and Algorithms, pp. 237–266. Springer (2005)

11. Kraft, N., Bonds, B., And Smith, R.: Cross-language clone detection. In: Proceedings of the 20th International Conference on Software Engineering and Knowledge Engineering, SEKE (2008)

12. McGregor, J.D.: Testing a software product line. In: Borba, P., Cavalcanti, A., Sampaio, A., Woodcook, J. (eds.) PSSE 2007. LNCS, vol. 6153, pp. 104–140. Springer, Heidelberg (2010)

13. Offutt, J., Abdurazik, A.: Generating tests from UML specifications. In: France, R.B. (ed.) UML 1999. LNCS, vol. 1723, pp. 416–429. Springer, Heidelberg (1999)

14. Riebisch, M., Philippow, I., Götze, M.: UML-based statistical test case generation. In: Akşit, M., Mezini, M., Unland, R. (eds.) NODe 2002. LNCS, vol. 2591, pp. 394–411. Springer, Heidelberg (2003)

15. Utting, M., Legeard, B.: Practical model-based testing: A tools approach. Morgan Kaufmann (2010) 0080466486

The Supportive Effect of Traceability Links in Change Impact Analysis for Evolving Architectures – Two Controlled Experiments

Muhammad Atif Javed and Uwe Zdun

Software Architecture Research Group
University of Vienna, Austria
{muhammad.atif.javed,uwe.zdun}@univie.ac.at

Abstract. The documentation of software architecture relations as a kind of traceability information is considered important to help people understand the consequences or ripple-effects of architecture evolution. Traceability information provides a basis for analysing and evaluating software evolution, and consequently, it can be used for tasks like reuse evaluation and improvement throughout the evolution of software. To date, however, none of the published empirical studies on software architecture traceability have examined the validity of these propositions. In this paper, we hypothesize that impact analysis of changes in software architecture can be more efficient when supported by traceability links. To test this hypothesis, we designed two controlled experiments that were conducted to investigate the influence of traceability links on the quantity and quality of retrieved assets during architecture evolution analysis. The results provide statistical evidence that a focus on architecture traceability significantly reduces the quantity of missing and incorrect assets, and increases the overall quality of architecture impact analysis for evolution.

Keywords: Software architecture traceability, Architecture evolution, Change impact analysis, Empirical software engineering, Controlled experiment.

1 Introduction

During the last four decades, many investigations on software change impact analysis techniques and its applications have been performed [16][18]. Change impact analysis is about determining the consequences or ripple-effects of proposed changes in the software system. To support software evolution, architectural change impact analysis is considered of great importance as understanding the architecture and its changes is a foundation of software evolution analysis at the architectural level [12]. The architectural level is well suited for software evolution analysis, as the software architecture allows (early) reasoning on the quality attributes of the system [4] and the software architecture not only describes the high-level structure and behaviour of the system, but also incorporates principles and decisions that determine the system's development and its evolution [2].

I. Schaefer and I. Stamelos (Eds.): ICSR 2015, LNCS 8919, pp. 139–155, 2014.
© Springer International Publishing Switzerland 2014

Software change impact analysis techniques and their applications are based on either traceability information or dependence relationships. These techniques do not only provide a basis for analysing and evaluating software evolution, but can also be used for tasks such as reuse evaluation and improvement. For example, the identified impacts of specific software assets from architecture evolution analysis can be used as a basis to examine the level of reuse of those assets throughout a number of evolution steps. It is also pointed out by Selby [13] that, in general, software assets reused without or with limited revisions have fewer faults than software assets reused with major revisions. Hence, understanding change impact provides the means to control reuse and evolution of software assets.

Traceability links between the software architecture and other software assets, such as the source code or the requirements, are considered important to determine the potential evolution impacts at the architectural level [8]. However, none of the published empirical studies on software architecture traceability provide quantitative evidence of the added value of traceability links in the evolution of software architectures. To date, two empirical studies on architecture traceability have been published [7][14]. These studies mainly concern the understanding of architecture designs. The lack of published empirical data on the benefits of architecture traceability is one of the reasons that prevents the wide adoption of traceability approaches in industrial settings [7][14]. It is crucial to conduct more empirical studies on the usefulness of architecture traceability to find out whether the use of architecture traceability can significantly support the development activities in order to justify its costs.

The goal of this paper is to empirically validate whether change impact analysis is more efficient regarding the software architecture evolution activities, if the impact analysis is supported by traceability links. In particular, we intend to answer the following research question: Are the quality and quantity of retrieved assets during software architecture change impact analysis higher for change impact analysis that is supported by traceability links than for change impact analysis without traceability links? Note that the assets to be retrieved during our experiments are source code classes and components in a component model that are affected by a change.

To answer the research question, we conducted two controlled experiments at the University of Vienna, Austria, in May 2014. The first experiment was carried out with 51 students, whereas the other 56 students participated in the second experiment. They were asked to perform seven impact understanding activities that concern the evolution at the architectural level. In both experiments, half of the students were asked to perform the impact analysis of changes in software architecture by using the information from the architectural documentation and the source code of the system, while the other half performed the same tasks with the same provided information and additionally received traceability links between the architectural models and the source code. The former group is referred to as the control group, the latter as the experiment group. The data from the experiments was analysed, and the quantity of missing and erroneous retrieved assets during the architecture evolution analysis and their overall quality were compared. The results of the experiments provide strong evidence for the benefits of using traceability links concerning the quantity and quality of the assets retrieved during change impact analysis activities for evolving software architectures.

The rest of this paper is organized as follows: Section 2 describes the related work. Section 3 discusses the design of the controlled experiments including the introduction of variables and hypotheses, while the subsequent Section 4 explains the details concerning the execution of the experiments. Section 5 presents the hypotheses tested and the analysis of the results of the study. Section 6 contains the interpretation of the findings and a discussion of threats to validity. Section 7 concludes the study and discusses future work.

2   Related Work

As mentioned in the introduction, there exist only two earlier studies, one performed by our research group [7] and one by Shahin et al. [14], that provide quantitative evidence of the added value of traceability links in understanding of architecture designs.

In our own previous study [7] we conducted a controlled experiment and its replication to evaluate the support provided by traceability links between architectural models and the source code. The experiments were conducted with 108 participants. The participants were asked to answer twelve typical questions aimed at gaining an architecture-level understanding of a representative subject system, with and without traceability information. Our findings show that the use of traceability links significantly increases the correctness of the answers of the participants, whereas no conclusive evidence concerning the influence of the experience of the participants are observed.

The work by Shahin et al. [14] analyse the support provided by Compendium tool, a tool to visualize architectural design decisions and their rationale, as a kind of traceability information. The experiment was carried out with 10 participants. The participants were asked to understand the existing design and to make the new design according the new requirement, with and without Compendium tool. The results show that Compendium significantly improves the correctness of understanding architecture design in architecting process, and does not increase the total time for reading software architecture documentations and performing design task.

The contribution of this study is novel for two main reasons. First, there exist no published evidence related to the added value of traceability links in software architecture evolution. Second, most of the earlier works are based on some specific traceability tools, which do not enable a distinction between tool support and the usefulness of traceability links. In our experiments, for practical reasons and to study the foundational concepts rather than a specific tool, the participants were provided with hyperlink-based access of traceability links and the source code, to investigate the support provided by traceability links between architectural models and the source code in evolution of software system architectures, rather than the support provided by a specific tool.

3   Design of the Experiment

For the study design, the guidelines for experiments' conduct by Kitchenham et al. [10] and Wohlin et al. [17], and reporting by Jedlitschka and Pfahl [9] were used. Kitchenham et al. present preliminary guidelines for experimentation in software engineering and give some instructions regarding the context, design, data collection, analysis, presentation, and interpretation of empirical studies without going into detail. Wohlin et al. present the experiment phases in more detail, and also discuss statistical tests and their suitability for different kinds of studies. The former guidelines were primarily used in the planning phase of our experiments, while the latter was used as a reference for the analysis and interpretation of the results. Jedlitschka's and Pfahl's guidelines for reporting controlled experiments are used to describe the experiments in this paper. Please note that the following subsections of the reporting template were omitted, because they were either not applicable, or their content was already mentioned in other sections: Relation to existing evidence is presented in Section 2; inferences and lessons learned are discussed in Section 6; interpretation and general limitations of the study are described in Section 6.2.

3.1 Goal, Hypotheses, Parameters, and Variables

The goal of the experiments is to empirically investigate, if change impact analysis that is based on traceability links significantly reduces the quantity of missing and incorrect retrieved assets, and increases their overall quality during the architecture evolution analysis. The experiments goal led to the following null hypotheses and corresponding alternative hypotheses:

H_{01}: The use of traceability links *does not significantly increase* the quantity of correctly retrieved assets during architecture evolution analysis.

H_1: The use of traceability links *significantly increases* the quantity of correctly retrieved assets during architecture evolution analysis.

H_{02}: The use of traceability links *does not significantly reduce* the quantity of incorrectly retrieved assets during architecture evolution analysis.

H_2: The use of traceability links *significantly reduces* the quantity of incorrectly retrieved assets during architecture evolution analysis.

H_{03}: The use of traceability links *does not significantly increase* the overall quality of retrieved assets during architecture evolution analysis.

H_3: The use of traceability links *significantly increases* the overall quality of retrieved assets during architecture evolution analysis.

Table 1. Dependent Variables

Description	Scale Type	Unit	Range
Quantity of correctly retrieved assets	Interval	Points	[0 - 1]
Quantity of incorrectly retrieved assets	Interval	Points	[0 - 1]
Overall quality of the retrieved assets	Interval	Points	[0 - 1]

Dependent Variables. Three dependent variables were observed during the experiments, as shown in Table 1: the quantity of correctly and incorrectly retrieved assets, and their overall quality, in the architecture evolution analysis. They were accessed by using the standard information retrieval metrics, in particular, recall, precision, and f-measure, respectively [1][6]. Because impact analysis of changes in software architecture consists of a list of system assets, two aspects were specifically taken into consideration to measure the recall and precision of the retrieved assets:

– The set of *correct assets* expected in the solution to *activity a* (C_a).
– The set of *assets retrieved* in the solution to *activity a* by *participant p* ($R_{p,a}$).

$$Recall_{p,a} = \frac{\mid C_a \cap R_{p,a} \mid}{C_a} \qquad Precision_{p,a} = \frac{\mid C_a \cap R_{p,a} \mid}{R_{p,a}}$$

Recall is the percentage of correct matches retrieved by an experiment subject, while precision is the percentage of retrieved matches that are actually correct. Because recall and precision measure two different concepts, it can be difficult to balance between them. Therefore, f-measure, a standard combination of recall and precision, defined as their harmonic mean, is used to measure the overall quality of architecture change impact analysis activities from the experiments' participants.

Table 2. Independent Variables

Description	Scale Type	Unit	Range/Possible Values
Time	Ordinal	Minutes	90 minutes (Max)
Group Affiliation	Nominal	N/A	Control group, Experiment group
Programming experience	Ordinal	Years	4 classes: 0-1, 1-3, 3-7, >8
Architecture experience	Ordinal	Years	4 classes: 0-1, 1-3, 3-7, >8
Affiliation	Nominal	N/A	Academia, Industry, Other

Independent Variables. Five independent variables were observed during the experiments, as shown in Table 2. They relate to the personal information (programming experience, architecture experience, affiliation), group affiliation (control group or experiment group) and time spent in the experiments. These variables could have an influence on the dependent variables, which is eliminated by balancing the characteristics between the control groups and the experiment groups in the same way, in particular, through random assignment to the two groups in both experiments.

3.2   Experiment Design

To test the hypotheses, we conducted two controlled experiments [3] at the University of Vienna, Austria, in May 2014. The experiments were conducted as practical sessions on architecture evolution analysis.

Participants. The participants in the experiments were 107 individual students of the software architecture course held at University of Vienna. The first experiment was conducted with 51 students, while the other 56 students had participated in the second experiment.

Objects. The basis for the architecture impact recovery was UltraESB[1] Version 2.3.0 and PetalsESB[2] Version 4.2.0. Both systems belong to the enterprise service bus (ESB) domain, which provides an connectivity infrastructure to integrate the services within a service-oriented architecture.

Blocking. To be able to explicitly analyse the influence of traceability links in change impact analysis of software architecture evolution, the participants in both experiments were randomly assigned to the two balanced groups. For each experiment, one group of participants was asked to determine the impact of architecture evolution activities by using the information from the architectural documentation and the source code of the system, whereas the other group performed the same tasks, but additionally received the traceability links between architectural models and the source code. The first group is referred to as control group, the latter as experiment group.

Instrumentation. To obtain the necessary data related to the influence of traceability links in architecture evolution analysis, the instruments discussed in the following paragraphs were used to carry out the experiments.

Three pages of architectural documentation about the used objects: The participants in the first experiment were provided with the documentation for UltraESB, while the participants of the second experiment received the documentation for PetalsESB. The documentation describes the conceptual architecture and lists technologies and frameworks used in the implementation. Besides text, a UML component diagram is used to illustrate the components, and their inter-relationships in parts of the architecture.

Web-based access for the source code: The participants in the first and second experiment were provided with the web-based access of syntax-highlighted source code for the UltraESB and PetalsESB, respectively. The cover page alphabetically lists the source code package names and their enclosed code classes, and provides a hyperlink-based support to 'jump' to specific assets (code classes or packages) located in the Git repository[3]. The participants in the experiment groups were also provided with the similar support for traceability links, represented as lists: Each entry in a list contains information about architectural components and their realized code classes, which represent individual traceability link.

A questionnaire to be filled-in by the experiments' participants: At the first page of the questionnaire, the participants had to rate their programming experience, architecture experience and affiliation, while the subsequent pages contains the seven architecture impact analysis activities, as shown in Table 3. In the context of these activities, two important criteria are applied: (i) the activities should be representative for key architecture impact analysis and evolution contexts for both UltraESB and PetalsESB, and

---

[1] http://adroitlogic.org/products/ultraesb.html
[2] http://petals.ow2.org
[3] http://git-scm.com

(ii) they should be imaginatively constructed to measure the deeper impact understanding from participant groups. Note that the same impact evaluation activities listed in Table 3 were used for both UltraESB and PetalsESB, which was possible as different ESBs share many similar architectural concerns. The results expected from participants for each activity were sets of retrieved asset names (i.e., names of source code classes and components from the provided component models).

Table 3. Impact evaluation activities at the architectural-level (used for both UltraESB and PetalsESB)

ID	Description
A1	Investigate the impact of extensions in the transport senders and listeners
A2	Investigate the consequences of extensions in the traffic monitoring
A3	Determine the ripple-effects of changes in the ESB configuration
A4	Investigate the impact of changes in the message interception
A5	Evaluate the effects of high availability and capacity of ESB server
A6	Investigate the consequences of new message endpoints
A7	Determine the impact of new deployment aspect implementation

Blinding. To eliminate subjective bias on the part of both experiments' participants and the experimenters, double blinding was applied in the experiments. Although, participants perceived that there are two different groups for each experiment, they were not aware about the purpose of group division and their group affiliation.

The results of the experiments were handed over to two independent researchers who did not know the real identity of the participants. This was done to prevent the experiments from being biased. To be able to compute the results of the change impact analysis of retrieved assets, the researchers were asked to compute the information retrieval statistics by matching the participants' answers with the original solution model. This allows us to objectively evaluate the quantity and quality of the retrieved assets rather than by intuitive or ad-hoc human measures.

Data Collection Procedure. After introduction and grouping, the participants received the instruments, mentioned in Section 3.2. The provided instruments had to be used to perform the impact analysis of architecture evolution activities. The participants were distributed over separate rooms according to their group membership. At least one experimenter was present in each room to answer the questions related to the instructions and to restrict the participants from consulting others and using forbidden material. The participants were given 90 minutes to determine the ripple effects of architecture evolution activities. After completion of the session, the filled-in questionnaires were collected by the experimenters and finally a discussion in the wrap-up phase was arranged to gather further information from the participant groups. All the participants were present during the discussion.

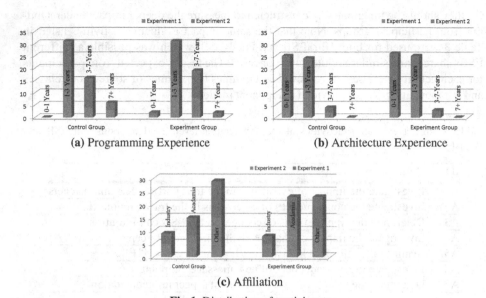

(a) Programming Experience   (b) Architecture Experience

(c) Affiliation

Fig. 1. Distribution of participants

4   Execution

4.1   Sample and Preparation

As described in Section 3.2, the experiments were conducted in two practical sessions on architecture evolution analysis at the University of Vienna, Austria. The first experiment took place with 51 students of the software architecture course; the second experiment was conducted with another 56 students of the same course.

Figure 1 shows the distribution of the participants based on their previous experience and affiliation, as assigned to the control group and the experiment group. The data presented in the figures was accumulated from all the participants in the two experiments, but also shows the separate data of the experiments. The Sub-figures (a) and (b) show the previous experience of the participants concerning programming and software architecture, while Sub-figure (c) shows the affiliation of the participants. Note that the previous experiences in the control groups is slightly better both regarding programming and architecture. In the experiment groups slightly more people with an academic affiliation and slightly less with an industry affiliation are present. However, overall the experiences and affiliations are rather well balanced in the two experiments.

4.2   Data Collection Performed

The data collection procedure was performed as planned in the study design. There were no participants who dropped out and no deviations from the study design occurred.

4.3   Validity Procedure

The experiments were conducted in a controlled environment. The participants in both experiments were assigned to different rooms according to their group membership (control group or experiment group). The participants in each rooms were supervised by at least one experimenter during the whole duration, enabling them to ask clarification questions and restrict them from talking to each other or using forbidden material. All the participants had to return the questionnaire before leaving the room. The filled-in questionnaire were collected from the remaining participants after completion of experiments' sessions. No unexpected situation occurred during the experiments.

5 Analysis

5.1 Descriptive Statistics

The descriptive statistics shows the results of the experiments as a first step in the analysis. The first two subsections concern the quantity of correctly and incorrectly retrieved assets respectively. The last subsection presents an analysis of the overall quality of retrieved assets during architecture evolution analysis.

Quantity of Correctly Retrieved Assets. The descriptive statistics for the quantity of correctly retrieved assets for the control groups and the experiment groups from the two experiments are shown in Table 4 and Figure 2. The data in the table is based on the sum of the recall of the experiments' activities for each participant, while the figure concerns the recall for each experiment activity.

Table 4. Descriptive analysis of the quantity of correct retrieved assets

Execution	Group Affiliation	Mean	Median	Std. Dev.
Experiment 1	Control Group	2.701009 (0.3858584 %)	2.565584 (0.3665121 %)	1.808094 (0.2582992 %)
	Experiment Group	4.439981 (0.634283 %)	4.868956 (0.6955651 %)	1.708463 (0.2440661 %)
Experiment 2	Control Group	2.04751 (0.2925014 %)	1.908818 (0.2726883 %)	1.023914 (0.1462735 %)
	Experiment Group	4.114883 (0.5878404 %)	4.491484 (0.6416406 %)	1.421371 (0.203053 %)

As we see from Table 4, the total quantity of correctly retrieved assets is higher in the experiment groups than in the control groups. The results in Figure 2 show that the participants of the experiment group belonging to the first experiment have a higher number of correctly retrieved assets for all impact analysis activities than the control group. However, the participants of the control group of the second experiment have outperformed the participants of the experiment group in Activity 4.

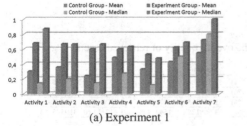
(a) Experiment 1

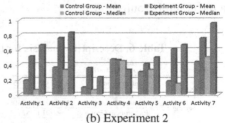
(b) Experiment 2

Fig. 2. Quantity of correctly retrieved assets for each experiment activity

Quantity of Incorrectly Retrieved Assets. Table 5 and Figure 3 show the comparisons for the quantity of retrieved assets that are actually correct for the control groups and the experiment groups in the two experiments. The data in the table is based on the sum of the precision values of the experiments' activities for each participant. In total, the quantity of retrieved assets that are actually correct is higher in the experiment groups than the control groups. As a consequence, this means that the quantity of incorrectly retrieved assets is lower in the experiment groups compared to control groups.

Table 5. Descriptive analysis of the quantity of actually correctly retrieved assets

Execution	Group Affiliation	Mean	Median	Std. Dev.
Experiment 1	Control Group	3.774333 (0.5391905 %)	3.208333 (0.4583333 %)	1.779565 (0.2542236 %)
	Experiment Group	4.826603 (0.6895147 %)	4.6875 (0.6696429 %)	1.865917 (0.2665595 %)
Experiment 2	Control Group	2.278481 (0.3254973 %)	2.242929 (0.3204185 %)	1.191005 (0.1701435 %)
	Experiment Group	4.454726 (0.6363894 %)	4.523485 (0.6462121 %)	1.593693 (0.2276704 %)

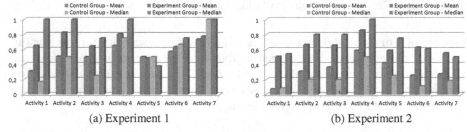

(a) Experiment 1   (b) Experiment 2

Fig. 3. Quantity of actually correctly retrieved assets for each experiment activity

The results in the Figure 3 concern the precision for each experiment activity, in which the participants of the control group only outperformed the participants of the experiment group in Activity 5 of the first experiment.

Overall Quality of Retrieved Assets. The descriptive statistics for the overall quality of retrieved assets for the control groups and the experiment groups from the two experiments is shown in Table 6 and Figure 4. The results in the table are based on the sum of the overall quality of retrieved assets (i.e., the f-measure) of the experiments' activities for each participant, while the figure shows the f-measure results for each experiment activity. The data in the table and figure show that the average quality of retrieved assets in the experiment groups seems to be higher than the average quality of retrieved assets in the control groups.

Table 6. Descriptive analysis for the overall quality of retrieved assets

Execution	Group Affiliation	Mean	Median	Std. Dev.
Experiment 1	Control Group	2.767399 (0.3953427 %)	2.516986 (0.3595694 %)	1.624837 (0.2321195 %)
	Experiment Group	4.377607 (0.6253725 %)	4.275092 (0.6107274 %)	1.722879 (0.2461256 %)
Experiment 2	Control Group	1.755936 (0.2508479 %)	1.769355 (0.252765 %)	0.7923499 (0.1131928 %)
	Experiment Group	3.66901 (0.5241442 %)	3.608125 (0.5154464 %)	1.617311 (0.2310445 %)

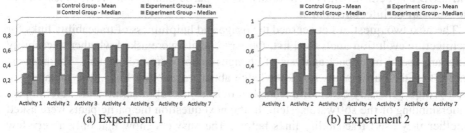

Fig. 4. Overall quality of retrieved assets for each experiment activity

Dataset Reduction. Outliers in the dataset, i.e., data points that are either much lower or much higher than other data points, are potential candidates for dataset reduction. Thirteen of the participants from the two experiments did not perform all the activities. This results in nineteen missing data points in the experiments. As it seems that these participants have spend sufficiently longer time in exploring the source code, we have not excluded these data points from the study.

To find potential outliers, we also calculated the quantity and quality of the architecture evolution activities for each participant. Note that four of the participants from the experiment groups reached a considerable lower quantity and quality of architecture evolution analysis activities than the other members of these groups. A closer analysis showed that they could not properly make use of traceability links to perform the architecture impact understanding activities. However, their results were not excluded as outliers, because the difference to the other participants is not strong enough. Excluding these data points would have introduced a potential vulnerability of the study results.

5.2 Analysis of the Opinion of Participants

This subsection summarizes the results of the wrap-up discussion phase which was arranged after each experiment session to gather further information from the participant groups.

The participants in the experiment groups from the two experiments and the control group of the first experiment have acknowledged that they had enough time to perform the architecture evolution analysis activities. However, the participants in the control group of the second experiment showed concerns related to the provided time for performing the activities. This is probably because the second experiment was conducted with a rather large system (PetalsESB) compared to first experiment (UltraESB). The same happened also for the experience and difficulties of the participants: The participants of the control groups experienced more difficulties in performing the activities than the participants of the experiment groups, in addition, the participants with '0-1 years' of experience encountered more difficulties than the participants with '1-8+ years' of experience.

The participants were also asked about their familiarity with the application domain. The answers imply that enterprise service bus, which is the application domain of the

UltraESB and PetalsESB, is well-known to the participants from previous lectures of the software architecture course.

The next two questions concerned the usage and helpfulness of traceability links for architecture evolution analysis. First, the participants were asked whether traceability links are useful in impact analysis of changes in software architecture. The answers reflect that the participants had knowledge about traceability links. The members of both groups generally consider traceability links as useful in architecture-level impact understanding of the software system. In the next question the participants were asked whether they used traceability links before. The answers show that only a very few participants have previously used traceability links for understanding of software assets outside of the lecture in which the experiments took place.

Finally, the participants were asked to briefly describe how the architecture evolution analysis was performed. This was primarily done to confirm that the experiment groups used the traceability links and to find out if the control groups used any other systematic way to perform architecture evolution analysis. The answers of the control groups reveal a focus on an intuitive approach, which was mainly driven by personal experience or judgements. The respondents stated that they performed the activities by reading the textual description in the architecture document and intuitively exploring the code classes. They acknowledged that it is hard to find the correct links between architecture and implementation artefacts. This might stem from the fact that software architecture is not explicitly represented in the code classes, e.g. as packages and classes or similar code-level abstractions. The answers of the experiment groups show a focus on the traceability links. The respondents of experiment groups stated that they used traceability links to identify the ripple-effects of architecture artefacts in the code classes and vice versa. They confirmed that they primarily used this additional knowledge for performing architecture impact analysis for evolution.

5.3   Hypothesis Testing and Results

Quantity of Correctly Retrieved Assets. To be able to test the first null hypothesis H_{o1}, the influence of traceability links on the quantity of correctly retrieved assets is measured. In the analysis of the experiments, the Shapiro-Wilk normality test [15] and Wilcoxon Rank-Sum test [11] are used. First, the Shapiro-Wilk normality test is used to find out whether equal variances of the level of correctness can be assumed. Second, as a consequence of non-normal distributions, the corresponding non-parametric statistical test, Wilcoxon Rank-Sum test, is used to test the significance of the found results. Note that the results of tests were interpreted as statistically significant at $\alpha = 0.05$ (i.e., the level of confidence is 95%).

Table 7. Wilcoxon-test for quantity of correct retrieved assets

Execution	Factor	Wilcoxon Rank-Sum Test
Experiment1	Control Group vs. Experiment Group	W = 492, **p-value = 0.001332**
Experiment 2	Control Group vs. Experiment Group	W = 686.5, **p-value = 0.000001451**

Table 7 shows the results of the Wilcoxon rank-sum test for the control groups and the experiment groups. The table shows that both experiments (Experiment 1 and Experiment 2) provide strong evidence that H_{o1} can be rejected. This means that in our two experiments the use of traceability links significantly improved the quantity of correctly retrieved assets during the architecture evolution analysis.

Quantity of Incorrectly Retrieved Assets. Hypothesis H_{o2} was also evaluated with a Wilcoxon rank-sum test. The results are shown in Table 8. The table shows that the both experiments (Experiment 1 and Experiment 2) provide strong evidence that H_{o2} can be rejected. This means that in our two experiments the use of traceability links significantly reduces the quantity of incorrectly retrieved assets in the architecture impact analysis for evolution. Note that there is a noticeable difference in the p-values between the two experiments. The main reason behind this difference probably is the varying sizes and complexity of the objects (software systems) in the first and second experiment.

Table 8. Wilcoxon-test for quantity of incorrect retrieved assets

Execution	Factor	Wilcoxon Rank-Sum Test
Experiment 1	Control Group vs. Experiment Group	W = 437.5, **p-value = 0.03446**
Experiment 2	Control Group vs. Experiment Group	W = 661, **p-value = 0.00001083**

Overall Quality of Retrieved Assets. The Wilcoxon rank-sum test is also used to evaluate the Hypothesis H_{o3}. The results are shown in Table 9. The table shows that the both experiments provide strong evidence that H_{o3} can be rejected. This means that in our two experiments the use of traceability links significantly improved the overall quality of the retrieved assets for architecture evolution analysis.

Table 9. Wilcoxon-test for overall quality of retrieved assets

Execution	Factor	Wilcoxon Rank-Sum Test
Execution 1	Control Group vs. Experiment Group	W = 497, **p-value = 0.0009243**
Execution 2	Control Group vs. Experiment Group	W = 659, **p-value = 0.000004097**

6   Interpretation

6.1   Evaluation of Results and Implications

As discussed in the previous section, all three null hypotheses can be rejected and hence we can deduce the following implications:

- As H_{o1} can be rejected, according to our experiments, there is evidence that the quantity of correctly retrieved assets during the architecture evolution analysis is higher if traceability links are used.

- As H_{o2} can be rejected, according to our experiments, there is evidence that the quantity of incorrectly retrieved assets during the architecture evolution analysis is lower if traceability links are used.
- As H_{o3} can be rejected, according to our experiments, there is evidence that the quality of retrieved assets for architecture evolution analysis is higher if traceability links are used.

6.2 Threads to Validity and Limitations of the Study

Multiple levels of validity threats have to be considered in the experiments. We have considered the classification scheme for validity in experiments by Cook and Campbell [5]. The internal validity concerns the cause effect inferences between the treatment and the dependent variables measured in the experiments. External validity refers to the generalizability of the results for a larger population. Construct validity is about the suitability of the study design for the theory behind the experiments. Finally, conclusion validity focuses on the relationship between treatment and outcome and on the ability to draw conclusions from this relationship. All validity threats in the experiments are categorized based on this classification.

Internal Validity

- The architecture evolution analysis activities could have been biased towards the experiment groups. The threat, however, is mitigated by considering many characteristics of software architecture evolution. As a result, the change impact analysis activities concerned both architecture recovery and evolution contexts. Therefore, we do not consider it a highly relevant threat to validity.
- The analysts in the experiments could have graded the retrieved assets incorrectly. We tried to mitigate this risk by providing the original solution model to the analysts. The analysts were asked to apply the solution model to the recovered participants' solutions. The solution model clearly states the correct assets for each architecture evolution analysis activity. Furthermore, the results have also been verified by the authors of this paper.
- Finally, the analysts could have been biased towards the experiment groups. We tried to exclude this threat to validity by not revealing the identity of the participants or in which of the two groups they have participated to the analysts. Hence, it is rather unlikely that this threat occurred.

External Validity

- As discussed in Section 3.2, the experiments were conducted with rather inexperienced participants, the students of a software architecture course. Nevertheless, the results of our previous study, where we compared the results from two controlled experiments with students and professionals, imply that the participants' experience does not have a significant influence on the external validity of results [7]. Therefore, we conclude that it is likely the limited level of experience of the participants in the two experiments does not distort the study results.

– The instrumentation in the experiments might have been unrealistic or old-fashioned. In this case, the architecture evolution analysis was based on the hyperlinks. In practice, different tools would be used to support evolution analysis. These tools are primarily used to formulate and maintain the traceability or dependence relationships between the related software assets. In our experiments, for practical reasons and to study the foundational concepts rather than a specific tool, the source code of the software systems and traceability links were readily provided in a web-based format. We assume that the measured effect of the experiment groups during traceability recovery is independent of the way in which a tool would visualize the traceability links, but a threat to validity remains that our results cannot be 1:1 translated to all existing tools and visualizations.

Construct Validity

– The use of one object in the experiment introduces the risk that the cause construct is under-represented. In this case, the experiments were conducted with different objects, in particular, the UltraESB and PetalsESB, although the objects belong to the same domain but represent software systems, of significantly different size (in terms of number of source code classes). The threat, however, cannot totally be ignored.
– Another potential threat to validity is the number of measures used to evaluate the quantity and quality of retrieved assets. In our case we only used standard information retrieval metrics, in particular, recall, precision, and f-measure, to measure the quantity of correctly and incorrectly retrieved assets, and their overall quality, respectively. This does not allow for cross-checking the results with different measures.

Conclusion Validity

– A threat to validity might result from the interpretation of the architecture evolution analysis activities because impact of these activities consists of a list of system assets (e.g., architectural components, source code classes). We mitigated this risk by calculating the standard information retrieval metrics for retrieved assets from all architecture evolution analysis activities. We argue that information retrieval measures allow analysts to objectively evaluate the correctness of architecture evolution analysis activities rather than intuitive or ad-hoc human measures. We conclude that this potential threat is mitigated to large degree.
– Finally, the violation of assumptions made by statistical tests could distort the results of the experiments. In the analysis of the experiments, the Shapiro-Wilk normality test and Wilcoxon Rank-Sum test are used. First, Shapiro-Wilk normality test is used to find out whether equal variances of the level of correctness can be assumed. Second, as a consequence of non-normal distributions, the corresponding non-parametric statistical test, the Wilcoxon Rank-Sum test, is used to test the significance of the found results. Note that the results of the tests were interpreted as statistically significant at $\alpha = 0.05$ (i.e., the level of confidence is 95%). Thus, this factor is not seen as a threat to validity.

7   Conclusions and Future Work

In this paper, we describe the results of two controlled experiments that were conducted to find out if traceability links are beneficial for change impact analysis of evolving architectures. Three aspects were specifically taken into consideration: the quantity of correctly and incorrectly retrieved assets, and their overall quality. The evaluation of the experiments shows that using traceability links leads to significantly lower quantity of missing and incorrect assets, and overall, a higher quality of architecture evolution analysis. Because the calculation procedure for architecture-centric reuse evaluation, with the focus on traceability links, is carried out in a similar manner to the calculation of the architecture evolution analysis, it is likely that the results can be generally applicable for architecture-centric reuse of the software systems making use of traceability links.

As it is usual for empirical studies, replications in different contexts, with different objects and participants, are good ways to corroborate our findings. Comparing the results of the different objects (software systems) in terms of their sizes and complexity is part of our future work agenda. Another direction for future work is to replicate the experiments with our evoluation and reusability evaluation tool that is currently under development.

Acknowledgements. This work is supported by the Austrian Science Fund (FWF), under project P24345-N23. We also thank to all the participants for taking part in the experiments.

References

[1] Baeza-Yates, R.A., Ribeiro-Neto, B.: Modern Information Retrieval. Addison-Wesley Longman Publishing Co., Inc., Boston (1999)

[2] Bengtsson, P., Lassing, N., Bosch, J., van Vliet, H.: Architecture-level modifiability analysis (alma). J. Syst. Softw. 69(1-2), 129–147 (2004)

[3] Boehm, B., Rombach, H.D., Zelkowitz, M.V.: Foundations of Empirical Software Engineering: The Legacy of Victor R. Basili. Springer-Verlag New York, Inc., Secaucus (2005)

[4] Clements, P., Kazman, R., Klein, M.: Evaluating Software Architectures: Methods and Case Studies. Addison-Wesley Longman Publishing Co., Inc., Boston (2002)

[5] Cook, T.D., Campbell, D.T.: Quasi-experimentation: Design & analysis issues for field settings. Houghton Mifflin Harcourt, Boston (1979)

[6] Harman, D.: Ranking algorithms. In: Frakes, W.B., Baeza-Yates, R. (eds.) Information Retrieval: Data Structures & Algorithms, pp. 363–392. Prentice-Hall, Inc., Upper Saddle River (1992)

[7] Javed, M.A., Zdun, U.: The supportive effect of traceability links in architecture-level software understanding: Two controlled experiments. In: Proceedings of the 11th Working IEEE/IFIP Conference on Software Architecture, WICSA 2014, pp. 215–224. IEEE (2014)

[8] Javed, M.A., Zdun, U.: A systematic literature review of traceability approaches between software architecture and source code. In: Proceedings of the 18th International Conference on Evaluation and Assessment in Software Engineering, EASE 2014, pp. 16:1–16:10. ACM (2014)

[9] Jedlitschka, A., Pfahl, D.: Reporting guidelines for controlled experiments in software engineering. In: 2005 International Symposium on Empirical Software Engineering, ISESE 2005, pp. 95–104. IEEE (2005)

[10] Kitchenham, B.A., Pfleeger, S.L., Pickard, L.M., Jones, P.W., Hoaglin, D.C., El Emam, K., Rosenberg, J.: Preliminary guidelines for empirical research in software engineering. IEEE Transactions on Software Engineering 28(8), 721–734 (2002)

[11] Mann, H., Whitney, D.: On a test of whether one of two random variables is stochastically larger than the other, vol. 18, pp. 50–60. Institute of Mathematical Statistics (1947)

[12] Mens, T., Magee, J., Rumpe, B.: Evolving software architecture descriptions of critical systems. IEEE Computer 43(5), 42–48 (2010)

[13] Selby, R.W.: Enabling reuse-based software development of large-scale systems. IEEE Transactions on Software Engineering 31(6), 495–510 (2005)

[14] Shahin, M., Liang, P., Li, Z.: Architectural design decision visualization for architecture design: Preliminary results of a controlled experiment. In: Proceedings of the 5th European Conference on Software Architecture: Companion Volume, ECSA 2011, pp. 2:1–2:8. ACM (2011)

[15] Shapiro, S.S., Wilk, M.B.: An analysis of variance test for normality (complete samples). Biometrika 52(3/4), 591–611 (1965)

[16] Stevens, W.P., Myers, G.J., Constantine, L.L.: Structured design. IBM Syst. J. 13(2), 115–139 (1974)

[17] Wohlin, C., Runeson, P., Höst, M., Ohlsson, M.C., Regnell, B., Wesslén, A.: Experimentation in Software Engineering: An Introduction. Kluwer Academic Publishers, Norwell (2000)

[18] Yau, S., Collofello, J., MacGregor, T.: Ripple effect analysis of software maintenance. In: The IEEE Computer Society's Second International on Computer Software and Applications Conference, COMPSAC 1978, pp. 60–65. IEEE (1978)

How Often Is Necessary Code Missing?
— A Controlled Experiment —

Tomoya Ishihara, Yoshiki Higo, and Shinji Kusumoto

Graduate School of Information Science and Technology, Osaka University,
1-5, Yamadaoka, Suita, Osaka, Japan
{t-ishihr,higo,kusumoto}@ist.osaka-u.ac.jp

Abstract. Code completion is one of the techniques used for realizing efficient code implementations. Code completion means adding the lacking code required for finishing a given task. Recently, some researchers have proposed code completion techniques that are intended to support code reuse. However, these existing techniques are designed to support the following programming steps. They cannot add necessary code in already-implemented code lines. In this research, we first investigate how often developers forget to write the necessary code in their programming tasks. We also investigate the extent to which opportunities of code reuse are increased by considering middle code completion. To investigate middle code completion, we propose a new technique that leverages type-3 clone detection techniques. We conducted a controlled experiment with nine research participants. As a result, we found that the participants had forgotten to write the necessary code in 41 of 51 (80%) programming tasks. We also found that the proposed technique was able to suggest useful code by middle code completion in 10 of 41 (24%) programming tasks for which the participants had forgotten to write the necessary code.

Keywords: Code completion, Clone detection, Static analysis.

1 Introduction

Code completion is one of the techniques that promote efficient code implementation. Code completion adds the code that developers are going to implement by acting on their triggers. Developers do not need to write all the code they need if they use the code completion functions in their integrated development environments (IDEs). Consequently, the cost of code implementation can be reduced by using code completion appropriately. Currently, IDEs generally have their own code completion functions [1,2,3]. Many developers actually use code completion functions in software development [13].

Recently, several techniques have shown that code completion is useful for promoting code reuse [7,8,14]. If we use existing code completion techniques for code reuse, we can obtain code following the half-written code that we have. However, existing techniques do not consider complementing already-implemented code lines with the necessary code. It often happens that developers forget to

I. Schaefer and I. Stamelos (Eds.): ICSR 2015, LNCS 8919, pp. 156–163, 2014.

```
private String getRectCoords(Rectangle2D rectangle){
    int x1=(int)rectangle.getX();
    int y1=(int)rectangle.getY();
}
```

(a) Half-written method

```
private String getRectCoords(Rectangle2D rectangle){
    int x1=(int)rectangle.getX();
    int y1=(int)rectangle.getY();
        int x2=x1 + (int)rectangle.getWidth();
        int y2=y1 + (int)rectangle.getHeight();
        return x1 + "," + y1+ ","+ x2+ ","+ y2;
}
```

(b) Code completion for following code

```
private String getRectCoords(Rectangle2D rectangle){
        if(rectangle == null) { }
        throw new IllegalArgumentException(
            "Null 'rectangle' argument.");
    int x1=(int)rectangle.getX();
    int y1=(int)rectangle.getY();
        int x2=x1 + (int)rectangle.getWidth();
        int y2=y1 + (int)rectangle.getHeight();
        return x1 + "," + y1+ ","+ x2+ ","+ y2;
}
```

(c) Code completion for middle and following code

```
1  private String getRectCoords(Rectangle2D rectangle){
2    if(rectangle == null) {
3      throw new IllegalArgumentException(
                "Null 'rectangle' argument.");
     }
4    int x1=(int)rectangle.getX();
5    int y1=(int)rectangle.getY();
6    int x2=x1 + (int)rectangle.getWidth();
7    int y2=y1 + (int)rectangle.getHeight();
8    return x1 + "," + y1+ ","+ x2+ ","+ y2;
   }
```

(d) Base method for suggesting candidate statements to the method

Fig. 1. Examples of code completion

write the necessary code in their tasks. Consequently, if we consider the middle code in code completion, the opportunities of code completion should be increased and developers can implement more reliable code more efficiently.

In this research, we examine how often developers forget to write the necessary code in their implementations. We also investigate the extent that complementing with middle code increases code reuse. Then, we propose a new code completion technique, which can add both the middle and the following code. The proposed technique leverages type-3 clone detection techniques to identify code to be used to complement.

The aforementioned items were investigated by conducting a controlled experiment with research participants. In the experiment, all the participants were given tasks of code implementations, and their PC screens were captured as video. By using the videos, we found that the developers had forgotten to write the necessary code in 80% (41/51) tasks. We also found that the proposed technique was able to suggest reusable code in 63% (32/51) tasks and 31% (10/32) of them were for the middle code.

The remainder of this paper is organized as follows. Section 2 shows a motivating example of this research, introduces two research questions (RQs) for investigation, and explains some terms used in this paper. Section 3 explains our proposed technique. Section 4 describes the experiment conducted for answering the RQs. Lastly, Section 5 concludes this paper.

2 Preliminaries

This section plays a preliminary role in this paper. First, we explain the motivation of this research. Then, we introduce some terms used in this paper.

2.1 Motivating Example

Figure 1(a) shows a half-written method. In this case, the developer is writing code to obtain the X-Y coordinates of the upper left and lower right corners of a given rectangle and to return them in the determined form. If she/he uses existing code completion techniques (e.g., [15]), the code following the half-written code complements it as shown in Fig. 1(b). As a result, she/he can obtain two program statements that retrieve the lower right corner and another statement that translates the coordinates into the *String* form. She/he can avoid writing all the statements in the method by applying the code completion technique.

However, complementing with code following the half-written code is not sufficient to implement reliable code efficiently because it is possible that developers occasionally forget to write some necessary code. For example, developers often notice that they forgot to write error-checking code for the formal parameters of methods when they see *NullPointerException*. If code completion techniques consider not only the code following the half-written code but also the middle code in the half-written code, developers can implement more reliable code more efficiently. Figure 1(c) shows an example. If code completion techniques consider the middle code, too, we obtain null checking code for the formal parameter.

In this research, we investigate the following research questions related to code completion for the middle code.

RQ1. How often do developers forget to write the necessary code?
RQ2. To what extent is code reuse promoted by middle code completion?

2.2   Terms

In this paper, a half-written method where code completion is performed is called a **target method**, program statements suggested as completion candidates are called **candidate statements** and methods used to identify candidate statements are called **base methods**.

If we apply the definitions to Fig. 1, the method `getRectCoords` is a target method. In Figs. 1(b) and 1(c), some program statements, which are in the balloons, are suggested to the developers. These are called candidate statements. To suggest candidate statements to the developers, the proposed technique leverages the information of the other methods. In the example, the method shown in Fig. 1(d) was used. Thus, this method is called a base method.

As shown in Figs. 1(a) and 1(d), base methods include all the program statements in the half-written method. In other words, half-written code is a type-3 clone[1] of the base methods and some extra statements are in the base methods. In this research, base methods are called the **super-clones** of the target method. The proposed technique complements half-written code with both the middle and following code by detecting its super-clones.

3   Code Completion for Middle Code

In this research, we propose a new code completion technique that complements with both the middle and the following code. Figure 2 shows an overview of

---

[1] Bellon et al. defined type-3 clones as follows: *"type-3 is a copy with further modifications; statements were changed, added, or removed."* [4]

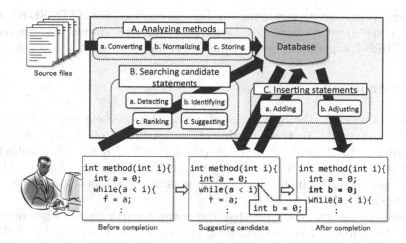

Fig. 2. Overview of the proposed technique

the proposed technique. The proposed technique extracts methods from given source files and the information obtained by analyzing the methods is stored in a database. Once the database is created, the proposed technique can suggest candidate statements for every completion position in a given half-written method. When a developer chooses a candidate statement, the statement is added at the suggested position in the half-written method. The proposed technique continues to suggest candidate statements as long as not all of the candidate statements are chosen by the developer.

As shown in Fig. 2, the proposed technique consists of the following three procedures. PROCEDURE-A extracts methods from a target set of source files and converts each of the methods into a list of statements. Next, it generates information such as a hash value from each statement and stores the information in a database. The information is used to detect super-clones.

PROCEDURE-B first obtains the information of statements included in a given target method by analyzing it. Second, it detects super-clones from the database. Third, it finds candidate statements in the super-clones (base methods). Statements of a base method are classified into two types: one is a set of statements that are common to the statements in the target method; the other is a set of statements that do not correspond to any statement in the target method. The latter statements are regarded as candidate statements. Finally, these candidate statements are ranked and suggested to the developers in the order of their rank.

PROCEDURE-C inserts a candidate statement selected by the developer. After inserting the statement, the proposed technique continues to suggest other candidate statements in the target methods. This allows developers to continue to insert multiple candidate statements as long as they want. If they do operations other than selecting suggested candidate statements, the proposed technique stops suggesting candidate statements.

To perform PROCEDURE-B based on the developer's demands, the database needs to be created by performing PROCEDURE-A in advance. PROCEDURE-A is performed only once to create the database. In contrast, PROCEDURE-B is performed every time a developer looks for candidate statements. Similarly, PROCEDURE-C is performed every time a candidate statement is selected.

4   Experiment

To provide answers to the RQs, we conducted a controlled experiment with nine research participants. In this experiment, we used *UCI source code data set*[2] for creating a database for code completion. The *UCI* dataset is a collection of open source software that is open to the public on the Web. The size of the *UCI* dataset is huge: it includes 13,192 projects, 2,127,877 Java source files, and 20,449,896 methods.

We need to identify the code that the research participants forgot to write to answer the RQs. In this experiment, forgotten code was defined as follows: a chunk of program statements written into the front or the middle of already-written program statements.

Research participants were one research associate, two PhD candidates, and six master's course students. All of them belonged to the same department as the authors. All of them had at least a half-year experience in Java programming. Their Java experiences were gained from their classes and research activities.

Each research participant was provided six tasks and she/he implemented a Java method to meet the specification. For each task, the participants were given a method signature and Javadoc comments. The method signature consisted of modifiers, a return type, a method name, parameters, and a throws clause. The Javadoc comments contained descriptions on the specification of the method.

4.1   Procedure

Firstly, the authors performed PROCEDURE-A of the proposed technique to create a database for code completion. It took approximately 2 hours to complete these operations.

Secondly, the research participants implemented Java methods according to the specifications of given tasks. They used a workstation equipped with an environment for recording motion captures. We used *CamStudio*[3] for recording the participants' screens. Windows Server 2008 R2 was installed in the workstation, and each participant logged in by using the *Remote Desktop* function.

We imposed no restrictions for the participants' implementations. They implemented Java methods as always. Some test cases had been prepared for each task. If a participant's implementation passed all the test cases, we judged that the implementation met the specification.

Thirdly, we investigated the motion pictures. In the investigation for RQ1, we watched all of each motion picture to check the order of program statement implementations. In the investigation of RQ2, we obtained the half-written code

---

[2] http://www.ics.uci.edu/~lopes/datasets/
[3] http://camstudio.org

from the motion pictures. Then, we input the obtained half-written code into our tool for checking whether the tool was able to suggest any code for completion and compared the suggested code and the participants' full-written code. In the investigation, half-written code was obtained every time that a new program statement was implemented.

4.2 Investigation for RQ1

Table 1 shows the participants who forgot to write the necessary code on their tasks. Each circle ("o") means there were one or more program statements that the participant forgot to write, and a hyphen ("-") means the recording of the motion picture failed for that the participant's task. The number of total tasks was 54 (6 tasks × 9 participants) but the recording motion pictures of three participant's tasks failed. We were not able to obtain any data from the failed tasks.

Table 1 shows that the participants forgot to write the necessary code in 41 out of 51 tasks. Such tasks are approximately 80% of the total number of tasks. In addition, we found the following phenomena.

- All the participants forgot to write the necessary code on at least two tasks.
- At least four participants forgot to write the necessary code on all the tasks.

Consequently, our answer to RQ1 is as follows: research participants forgot to write the necessary code in approximately 80% of the implemented methods.

4.3 Investigation for RQ2

Table 2 shows the participants and tasks for which the proposed technique was able to suggest code equal to each participant's final implementations. We judged

Table 1. Tasks and participants having forgotten code ("o" means one or more program statements were forgotten, and "-" means recording of the motion picture failed)

	T1	T2	T3	T4	T5	T6	Total
P1	-	o		o		o	3
P2	o	o	o	o	o	o	6
P3	-	o	o	o		o	4
P4	o	o	o	o	o	o	6
P5	-	o	o	o		o	4
P6	o	o	o	o	o	o	6
P7	o	o	o	o	o	o	6
P8	o	o	o	o			4
P9				o		o	2
Total	5	8	7	9	4	8	41

Table 2. Tasks and participants for which the tool was able to suggest correct candidates ("o" and "•" mean correct following code and correct middle code were suggested, respectively.)

	T1	T2	T3	T4	T5	T6	Total
P1	-		o	o	o	•o	4
P2	•o		•o	•o	o	•o	5
P3	-				o	•	2
P4	o	o		•o		•o	4
P5	-	o				o	2
P6	o					o	2
P7	•o	•o	o	o	o	o	6
P8	o					o	2
P9	o	o	o	o		o	5
Total	6	4	4	5	4	9	32

the semantically equal code to also be correct. *"Semantically equal"* means suggested code that has different syntax from the participant's final code but has the same semantics. For example, if the tool suggests "if(i - 1 > j)" and the participant's final code is "if(i > j + 1)", their semantics are the same. White circles ("∘") and black circles ("•") mean the tool was able to suggest correct code following the half-written code or correct code in the middle of the half-written code, respectively.

The table shows that the tool was able to suggest correct code for 32 tasks. Those tasks are 63% (32/51) of all the participants' tasks. In addition, the tool was able to suggest correct code in the middle of the half-written code for 10 participants' tasks, which are 24% (10/41) of the tasks where participants forgot to write the necessary code. The tasks where the tool suggested the correct middle code are 31% (10/32) of the tasks where the tool suggested the correct code.

We can see that the tool was able to suggest the correct code for at least two tasks for all of the participants. Especially, for participant P7, correct candidates were suggested for all tasks. Also, for task T6, the tool was able to suggest the correct code for all of the participants.

Our answer to RQ2 is as follows: for 24% (10/41) of the users' tasks, the proposed method was able to suggest correct code for the forgotten code.

4.4 Discussion

The proposed technique suggests code included in the database, which means that code completion by the proposed technique makes code clones between the code in the database and the user's development system. The presence of code clones is said to be one of the factors that makes software maintenance more difficult. Some research studies have shown that code clones are harmless [6,10,12]. On the other hand, other studies report that only a small part of code clones are harmful to software maintenance [5,9,11]. In the proposed technique, the source code used for creating the database is very important. If we make reliable code that is well tested or executed for a long time for creating the database, the proposed technique can suggest code based on such reliable code. Clones of reliable code are not harmful because clones only become harmful when they require simultaneous modifications. Identifying all the code fragments to be modified simultaneously is a costly and error-prone task, and unintentional inconsistencies occur if we forget to modify some of these code fragments [6].

Consequently, we can say that the proposed technique promotes the generation of code clones without problems if we use reliable code for creating the database.

5   Conclusion

In this paper, we investigated the following: *(RQ1) How often developers forget to write the necessary code in their implementation tasks* and *(RQ2) To what extent code completion for such forgotten code is useful.* To conduct the investigation, we developed a new technique that can complement half-written code with the following code and the middle code. The investigation was conducted with nine research participants. Each participant performed six implementation tasks and their PC screens were recorded as motion pictures. By using the motion pictures, we investigated the RQs. As a result, we provided these answers: participants forgot to write the necessary code in 80% (41/51) of their tasks and the proposed technique was able to suggest correct statements in 24% (10/41) of such tasks.

Acknowledgments. This work was supported by JSPS KAKENHI Grant Numbers 25220003, 24650011, and 24680002.

References

1. Eclipse, http://www.eclipse.org
2. Intellij idea, http://www.jetbrains.com/idea/
3. Intellisense, http://msdn.microsoft.com/en-us/library/hcw1s69b.aspx
4. Bellon, S., Koschke, R., Antoniol, G., Krinke, J., Merlo, E.: Comparison and Evaluation of Clone Detection Tools. IEEE TSE 33(9), 577–591 (2007)
5. Göde, N., Koschke, R.: Frequency and risks of changes to clones. In: Proc. of ICSE, pp. 311–320 (2011)
6. Higo, Y., Kusumoto, S.: How Often Do Unintended Inconsistencies Happened? – Deriving Modification Patterns and Detecting Overlooked Code Fragments–. In: Proc. of ICSM, pp. 222–231 (2012)
7. Hill, R., Rideout, J.: Automatic method completion. In: Proc. of ASE, pp. 228–235 (2004)
8. Holmes, R., Walker, R.J.: Systematizing pragmatic software reuse. ACM TOSEM 21(4), 1–44 (2012)
9. Hotta, K., Sano, Y., Higo, Y., Kusumoto, S.: Is duplicate code more frequently modified than non-duplicate code in software evolution?: An empirical study on open source software. In: Proc. of ERCIM/IWPSE, pp. 73–82 (2010)
10. Inoue, K., Higo, Y., Yoshida, N., Choi, E., Kusumoto, S., Kim, K., Park, W., Lee, E.: Experience of finding inconsistently-changed bugs in code clones of mobile software. In: Proc. of IWSC, pp. 94–95 (2012)
11. Kapser, C.J., Godfrey, M.W.: "cloning considered harmful" considered harmful: Patterns of cloning in software. ESE 13(6), 645–692 (2008)
12. Li, Z., Lu, S., Myagmar, S., Zhou, Y.: CP-Miner: Finding Copy-Paste and Related Bugs in Large-Scale Software Code. IEEE TSE, 176–192 (2006)
13. Murphy, G.C., Kersten, M., Findlater, L.: How Are Java Software Developers Using the Eclipse IDE? IEEE Software 23(4), 76–83 (2006)
14. Nguyen, A.T., Nguyen, T.T., Nguyen, H.A., Tamrawi, A., Nguyen, H.V., Al-Kofahi, J., Nguyen, T.N.: Graph-based pattern-oriented, context-sensitive source code completion. In: Proc. of ICSE, pp. 69–79 (2012)
15. Yamamoto, T., Yoshida, N., Higo, Y.: Seamless Code Reuse Using Source Code Corpus. In: Proc. of IWESEP, pp. 31–36 (2013)

An Analysis of a Project Reuse Approach in an Industrial Setting

Marko Gasparic, Andrea Janes, Alberto Sillitti, and Giancarlo Succi

Center for Applied Software Engineering
Free University of Bolzano-Bozen
Piazza Domenicani, 3
I-39100 Bolzano-Bozen, Bolzano-Bozen, Italy
marko.gasparic@stud-inf.unibz.it,
{andrea.janes,alberto.sillitti,giancarlo.succi}@unibz.it

Abstract. We performed an industrial exploratory case study to analyze the software reuse process of a medium size company which is a technology leader in a niche market. Two unstructured interviews and code duplication analyses of four SVN dumps report about a development practice that resulted in more efficient maintenance, due to archiving complete versions of every shipped software, and more efficient development, due to duplication and modification of the most similar program, instead of implementing a new program from scratch.

Keywords: reuse, case study, software product line.

1 Introduction

Software engineering research often aims to investigate how development, operation, and maintenance are conducted by software engineers and other stakeholders under different conditions [26]. That is why collaboration between industry and academia is an important part of scientific research.

In the last two years we have collaborated with a medium size company that aims to improve the development process and the quality of its high cost products, which consist of proprietary hardware and software. The company has more than 20 years of experience and is a technology leader in a niche market. The entire company has more than 100 employees, and more than 20 engineers are working in research and development.

Hardware evolution triggers new software projects, while customer requirements trigger maintenance and customization of already installed software products. The development team has created its own (undocumented) process and good practice.

We started to work with the team to help them to improve the maintainability of their code base. The project started in June 2012 and ended in June 2014, as planned. During the project we realized that the development team is following a (for us) unusual software development process, which could be described as *ad-hoc* software product line development or "copy-paste and modify",

I. Schaefer and I. Stamelos (Eds.): ICSR 2015, LNCS 8919, pp. 164–171, 2014.
© Springer International Publishing Switzerland 2014

a practice usually considered harmful by the software development community. Nevertheless, in this specific context, the team was assuring us that it supported reuse.

The contribution of this paper is to report about this practice in this particular case and to describe the motivations of the team to choose this development method.

The paper is structured as follows: section 2 presents related work on software reuse, software product lines, and source code libraries; section 3 presents used methodology; section 4 contains results of the interviews and the analysis; in section 5 validity threats are discussed; and in the last section the conclusions are presented together with future plans.

2   Related Work

The process of creating new software products from existing products was introduced in 1968, at the NATO Software Engineering Conference, where McIlroy proposed the usage of standard catalogues of routines that can be applied to any of large classes of different machines, without extensive effort [14].

Industrial studies have shown that more reuse results in a better quality [8] and in higher customer satisfaction [25]. Common advantages of software reuse are: reduced time and effort to build new software systems, higher quality of the system, when high quality software artifacts are reused, and reduced time and effort to maintain an existing system. However, concise and expressive abstractions are essential for development of reusable software artifacts, and useful abstractions of large and complex artifacts are complex as well. Software developers have to be familiar with abstractions or they have to study and understand them, if they want to successfully reuse such artifacts. In some cases this can defeat the gains of reuse [11].

The ultimate goal of systematic software reuse is to maximize profit, but it requires initial investment. Proactive investment, reactive investment, and extractive model are three reuse approaches in a corporate environment [7]: the most costly and risky is proactive investment, since it requires a large investment at the beginning for analyses and planning, but the returns can be seen only when products are developed. Reactive approach is more incremental; reusable assets are developed when they are identified during project development [7]. The extractive model is effective in quick transitions from conventional engineering to product line development; an initial baseline are existing products that do not require substantial re-engineering effort to be reused [13].

A software product line is a set of software systems that have a managed set of features in common. These features are developed in a prescribed way from a common core assets. Successfully implemented software product lines improve productivity, increase quality, decrease costs and labor needs, and decrease time to market [24]. The majority of the engineering effort in the life of a single software system and in the life of a software product line in practice is spent at the source code level. Success of a software product line deployment is therefore dependent on the quality of support of implementation activities [12].

Another common reuse approach is to save reusable components into a source code library. The probability of reusing a component increases if the component was already reused many times [18]. Obstacles to reuse libraries are poor documentation associated with them [1] and lack of component libraries [20].

Dunn and Knight [5] performed an industrial case study to analyze the problems that limit reuse; they built two subsystems from a reusable library. Domain analysis to design blocks for large-scale reuse from which new products are composed with minimum effort was found beneficial in an industrial setting by Ramachandrm and Fleischer [17]. Baldassarre et. al. [2] showed that reuse oriented development lead to higher quality of the developed software and improved effectiveness of the development process in two industrial projects. In the following sections we present an industrial case study of an *ad-hoc* software product line development.

3　Research Methodology

As said already above, the goal of this project was to improve the maintainability of the source code developed by the company. We operationalized this goal using three questions:

– How much code is repeated from one project to another?
– How reusable is the code?
– What are the changed parts between the most similar classes?

We had regular meetings with the chief technology officer (CTO), where we defined these questions, presented intermediate results, collected feedback, and defined goals for next iteration. During the project we realized that the development team is following a (for us) uncommon software development process. We decided to perform a case study to explore the process more in detail with the goal to understand how the company is developing (and reusing) software.

3.1　Case and Subject Selection

Our *case* was the company's software development process followed during the development of new software, during the maintenance of old software, and during the adaptation of old software to a new hardware. We included four software projects in our study because these projects were the ones currently under development and therefore representing the projects of most relevance for the company.

3.2　Data Collection Procedure

The company gave us access to their SVN[1] dumps of four projects. Each project is structured according to a predefined folder structure. The source code of a

---

[1] https://subversion.apache.org

product is stored in a *project*. A project consists of several solutions. Solutions are special versions of a product that have similar or the same functionality, but are customized for a specific customer to better meet his or her requirements. Solution specific source code files are placed in a folder named *src*. Source code that is common for all solutions is stored in a folder named *Common*, which also contains a folder named *classlib*. *Classlib* contains libraries that are shared between projects.

In February and March 2014 we also conducted two unstructured interviews in which we interviewed the CTO. We presented the results of our analyses and discussed the correctness and relevancy of our findings with him. We also encouraged him to present more details about the software development process and we took notes of the presented information. We focused on discussing our findings that were based on SVN analyses.

3.3   Analysis Procedure

To analyze a software development process, one can collect [6]: process, product, or resource metrics. To collect these metrics we used PROM [4, 9, 10, 15, 16, 19, 21–23], a measurement framework, developed in our department. All the source code we received was written in C++, that is why we used the Eclipse CDT library to extract the source code into an abstract syntax tree (AST). We analyzed the ASTs and calculated the similarity levels of clone pairs with our implementation of Baxter's clone detection algorithm [3].

$$Similarity = 2 \times S \div (2 \times S + L + R) \tag{1}$$

where:
S = number of shared nodes
L = number of different nodes in method 1
R = number of different nodes in method 2

We agreed with the company that it is not reasonable to count method pairs which have similarity lower than 70%, since it is more likely that they are different methods with different functionality than true code clones. We counted different methods that were cloned, and we calculated a custom metric, which we named *uniqueness*, to estimate whether methods were duplicated once or several times. If the uniqueness value is 1, it means that every method is duplicated exactly once; the closer the value is to 0, the more methods are duplicated several times. The formula of uniqueness is:

$$Uniqueness = 2 \times number\ of\ clones \div number\ of\ different\ methods \tag{2}$$

Additionally, we counted the logical lines of code (LLOC)[2] of the four projects. We used the existing plugins of the PROM framework to perform the calculations.

---

[2] The number of lines from the beginning to the end of a certain artifact, e.g., project, file, class, method, excluding commentary lines and whitespaces.

4   Results

The projects' revisions date between September 16th 2009 and February 20th 2014. All first revisions are very large: between 19,000 and 46,000 LLOCs. It is hard to assess the size of project specific source code in Project 1, because the structure of Project 1 does not meet current company's standards and there are no folders that can be recognized as *Common* or *classlib*. Projects 2, 3, and 4 all contain common libraries, which constitute the major part of the source code; however, all three projects also contain substantial amount of project specific source code.

Projects 1, 2, and 3 contain also branches. When we observed the difference in numbers of clones between the first trunk revision and the first branch revision, we noticed that the majority of methods stayed the same, but also more than 100 methods changed in every project. We classified methods with less than 6 statements as short[3]; if we exclude them, the uniqueness values become high (between 0.8 and 1), which implies that cloned methods from the trunk have only one match in a branch, and vice-versa. Comparison of first and last revision of trunk showed that the initial code was modified even further in projects 1, 2, and 3, and that Project 4 is implemented according to the same pattern as other three.

The majority of the clones in the last revisions originate from methods implemented in different folders. However, the differences between projects are large, e.g., even though the Project 1 branch has a similar size as the Project 3 trunk, according to LLOCs, between folders the Project 1 branch contains 969 code clones with 100% similarity and 2539 code clones with similarity higher than 70%, while the Project 3 trunk does not contain clones. Low uniqueness values (less than 0.4) at Project 1 suggest that the same methods were duplicated several times. The inspection of a file hierarchy showed that the Project 1 branch contains several solutions, in this case there are five. We detected much less code clones inside folders than between folders, e.g., on a folder level the Project 1 branch and the Project 3 trunk are very similar.

Interviews with the CTO provided the reasoning behind the process identified by SVN analyses. When creating a new version for a product for a specific customer, the folders *Common* and *classlib* are always fully copied into the new solution (the only exception is Project 1, which is the oldest of all four projects and is implemented according to deprecated practice). Neither *Common* nor *classlib* folders are maintained in a centralized way. The latest version of the folder is reused in a new project or solution, and older versions are not updated even if the libraries evolve; the only exception is bug fixing. The CTO is aware that bug fixing tasks are very costly due to this approach, but, based on the past experience, the company decided to use it because they are shipping their software together with their hardware and they have to be able to maintain software that is older than a decade. Newer versions of *Common* and *classlib*

---

[3] A *statement* is either a variable or an execution command, e.g., "return 0;" consists of two statements: "return" and "0".

libraries would not work on old hardware anymore, that is why they have to package and permanently store each solution that was ever shipped to a customer. The practice was developed before the company started to use revision control system, and even though the company is using SVN now, they decided to keep this kind of configuration management.

The company is using this "copy-paste and modify" approach also for the development of a new product. Instead of implementing products from scratch, they modify a duplicate of the most similar project. The CTO claims that code duplication and project reuse have improved development team's productivity.

In summary, the study of the observed practice to branch projects to develop a customer specific version, results in the following findings:

- Archiving complete versions of every shipped software improves maintenance efficiency, and it seems that it outweighs benefits of centralized maintenance of common system libraries, e.g., easier debugging,
- Regardless of the previous finding, it is beneficial to treat and mark solution specific, project specific, and universal source code blocks differently, i.e., the creation of common libraries is advantageous even if they are always "copy-pasted" between projects and solutions,
- In specific settings, it can be more efficient to always duplicate and modify the most similar program than to implement a new program from scratch.

5   Validity Threats

Validity of a case study consists of four aspects: construct, internal, and external validity and reliability [26]. Construct validity reflects how well studied operational measures represent an investigated research question. Internal validity of a case study is of concern when causal relations are examined. External validity deals with possibility of generalizations of findings and how interesting are findings to people outside investigated case. Reliability of a case study is high if the data and the analyses are independent on a specific researcher.

The performed interviews and the SVN analyses are exposed to construct validity and reliability threats. It is possible that an interviewee does not know all the data or that he provided wrong information. We interviewed the CTO, who is also actively participating in development, and knows the software development process best; however, the reliability is lower, since we were not able to interview other developers, due to access restrictions. Construct validity and reliability can also be lowered by inaccurate collection and interpretation of the data collected during interviews or by bugs in implementation of Baxter's algorithm. We addressed these threats with triangulation of interviews and SVN analyses; we used them both to answer the same research question.

6   Conclusions and Future Work

This paper reports about a development practice in medium size company that resulted in more efficient maintenance, due to archiving complete versions of every shipped software, and more efficient development, due to duplication and modification of the most similar program, instead of implementing a new program from scratch.

Two unstructured interviews and analyses of four SVN dumps show that the company initiates a new project with duplication of the most similar project; first revisions, which already contain between 19,000 and 46,000 LLOCs, clearly show that. Many methods stayed the same and around hundred were modified; high uniqueness values and many close-duplicates indicate that methods were reused on a large scale, but they had to be adopted, since they were not implemented to be reused.

The company has built one library on a company level. Its policies require the storage of methods that are common for different project solutions inside a separate folder. SVN analyses showed that common libraries are "copy-pasted" between solutions, while source code duplication inside folders is uncommon.

The company has developed an *ad-hoc* software product line development process mixed with a use of component libraries. They want to achieve the same goals as are achieved by successful implementation of software product lines: improved quality and reduced costs. The company implemented a set of software systems with common features, however, they were not developed in a prescribed way from common core assets. The approach is similar to the extractive model; the baseline are projects that are reused without extensive re-engineering effort.

Nevertheless, source code duplications are breaking software engineering principle of encapsulation, lowering reusability of components, and increasing maintenance costs. We would strongly advise the company to improve their development process with documenting it and enforcing process rules to all projects.

The CTO claims that code duplication and project reuse have already improved development team's productivity, and they want to improve it further. Unfortunately, the company is not in favour of big process changes, which is paradoxical, since they are all aware that their development process is not optimal. If the company decides to change some practices, we would like to analyze whether the shift was beneficial or not. We will further analyze the data collected during the project and report other findings. We also plan to compare the effectiveness of this company's development team with the effectiveness of other teams we are collaborating with.

References

1. Alnusair, A., Zhao, T., Bodden, E.: Effective api navigation and reuse. In: IEEE International Conference on Information Reuse and Integration (2010)
2. Baldassarre, M.T., Bianchi, A., Caivano, D., Visaggio, G.: An industrial case study on reuse oriented development. In: IEEE International Conference on Software Maintenance (2005)
3. Baxter, I., Yahin, A., Moura, L., Sant'Anna, M., Bier, L.: Clone detection using abstract syntax trees. In: IEEE International Conference on Software Maintenance (1998)
4. Coman, I., Sillitti, A., Succi, G.: A case-study on using an automated in-process software engineering measurement and analysis system in an industrial environment. In: IEEE International Conference on Software Engineering (2009)

5. Dunn, M., Knight, J.: Software reuse in an industrial setting: A case study. In: IEEE International Conference on Software Engineering (1991)
6. Fenton, N.E., Pfleeger, S.L.: Software Metrics: A Rigorous and Practical Approach, 2nd edn. Course Technology (1998)
7. Frakes, W., Kang, K.: Software reuse research: Status and future. IEEE Transactions on Software Engineering, 529–536 (2005)
8. Frakes, W.B., Succi, G.: An industrial study of reuse, quality, and productivity. The Journal of Systems and Software, 99–106 (2001)
9. Janes, A., Piatov, D., Sillitti, A., Succi, G.: How to calculate software metrics for multiple languages using open source parsers. In: Petrinja, E., Succi, G., El Ioini, N., Sillitti, A. (eds.) OSS 2013. IFIP AICT, vol. 404, pp. 264–270. Springer, Heidelberg (2013)
10. Janes, A., Sillitti, A., Succi, G.: Non-invasive software process data collection for expert identification. In: International Conference on Software Engineering and Knowledge Engineering (2008)
11. Krueger, C.: Software reuse. ACM Computing Surveys, 131–183 (1992)
12. Krueger, C.: Software product line reuse in practice. In: IEEE Symposium on Application-Specific Systems and Software Engineering Technology (2000)
13. Krueger, C.: Eliminating the adoption barrier. IEEE Software, 29–31 (2002)
14. McIlroy, D.: Mass-produced software components. In: NATO Software Engineering Conference (1968)
15. Moser, R., Janes, A., Russo, B., Sillitti, A., Succi, G.: Prom: taking an echography· of your software process. In: Congresso Annuale AICA. AGILE Publications (2005)
16. Piatov, D., Janes, A., Sillitti, A., Succi, G.: Using the eclipse C/C++ development tooling as a robust, fully functional, actively maintained, open source C++ parser. In: Hammouda, I., Lundell, B., Mikkonen, T., Scacchi, W. (eds.) OSS 2012. IFIP AICT, vol. 378, pp. 399–399. Springer, Heidelberg (2012)
17. Ramachandran, M., Fleischer, W.: Design for large scale software reuse: An industrial case study. In: International Conference on Software Reuse (1996)
18. Sametinger, J.: Software Engineering with Reusable Components. Springer (1997)
19. Scotto, M., Sillitti, A., Succi, G., Vernazza, T.: A non-invasive approach to product metrics collection. Journal of Systems Architecture, 668–675 (2006)
20. Shatnawi, A., Seriai, A.D.: Mining reusable software components from object-oriented source code of a set of similar software. In: IEEE International Conference on Information Reuse and Integration (2013)
21. Sillitti, A., Janes, A., Succi, G., Vernazza, T.: Collecting, integrating and analyzing software metrics and personal software process data. In: Euromicro Conference (2003)
22. Sillitti, A., Janes, A., Succi, G., Vernazza, T.: Non-invasive Measurement of the Software Development Process. In: International Workshop on Remote Analysis and Measurement of Software Systems (2003)
23. Sillitti, A., Succi, G., Panfilis, S.D.: Managing non-invasive measurement tools. Journal of Systems Architecture, 676–683 (2006)
24. Software Engineering Institute, Carnegie Mellon University: Software product lines overview, http://www.sei.cmu.edu/productlines/
25. Succi, G., Benedicenti, L., Vernazza, T.: Analysis of the effects of software reuse on customer satisfaction in an rpg environment. IEEE Transactions on Software Engineering, 473–479 (2001)
26. Wohlin, C., Runeson, P., Höst, M., Ohlsson, M.C., Regnell, B.: Experimentation in Software Engineering. Springer (2012)

HadoopMutator: A Cloud-Based Mutation Testing Framework

Iman Saleh[1] and Khaled Nagi[2]

[1] Graduate School, University of Miami, Coral Gables, Florida
[2] Dept. of Computer and Systems Engineering, Faculty of Engineering,
Alexandria University, Egypt
iman@miami.edu, khaled.nagi@alexu.edu.eg

Abstract. Mutation testing is a software engineering methodology where code mutation is used to assess the quality of a testing technique. Mutation testing is carried out by injecting errors in the code and measuring the ability of a testing tool to detect these errors. However, it is a time-consuming process, as tests need to be run on many variants of the code, called *mutants*. Each mutant represents a version of the code under test, with an injected error. In this paper, we propose HadoopMutator; a cloud-based mutation testing framework that reuses the MapReduce programming model in order to speed up the generation and testing of mutants. We show, through experimentation, that we can significantly enhance the performance of automated mutation testing and provide a scalable solution that is applicable for large-scale software projects. Based on two use cases, we show that the performance can be enhanced 10 folds, on average, using our proposed framework. By treating source code as data, our work paves the way for new reuse opportunities of the novel data-centric frameworks.

Keywords: Hadoop, MapReduce, Mutation Testing, Experimentation.

1   Introduction

Mutation testing [25][27] is a software engineering methodology where code mutation is used to assess the quality of a testing technique. It is carried out by injecting errors in the code and measuring the ability of a testing tool to detect these errors. The main assumption with this methodology is that the number of mutation errors detected by a tool is an indication of number of errors that this tool can detect in the future when unknown bugs are present in the code. However, mutation testing is a time-consuming process as tests need to be run on many mutants of the code. Each mutant represents a version of the code under test, with an injected error. A recent study [16] concludes that mutation testing is not suitable for real-world software projects. The problems mostly encountered with this technique are the complexity to derive the process as the higher the number of generated mutants, the higher the computation time [16].

We believe that low-cost parallel computing is an ideal candidate to execute unit tests on the different mutants during nightly builds as part of the regression testing

I. Schaefer and I. Stamelos (Eds.): ICSR 2015, LNCS 8919, pp. 172–187, 2014.

within common Continuous Integration frameworks [12]; such as Jenkins [32], CruiseControl [30], and Bamboo [29]. In this paper, we propose HadoopMutator; a cloud-based mutation testing framework that reuses the MapReduce programming model [2] in order to speed up the *generation* and *testing* of software mutants. Our experimentation shows that we can significantly enhance the performance of automated mutation testing by implementing it as a cloud-based service. We use Hadoop® [22][26] in our experimentation as the de-facto standard implementation of the MapReduce model. The Hadoop® project is part of the open-source Apache™ foundation [35]. Hadoop® is designed to scale up from a single server to thousands of nodes. Each node offers local computation and storage and relies on the Hadoop® Java libraries to deliver high-availability. Hadoop® detects and handles failures at the application layer thus delivering a highly-available services on top of a cluster of low-cost commodity machines.

The typical usage for Hadoop® and other MapReduce frameworks is to employ the cluster to run the same code on several nodes in parallel with different data sets and then aggregate the results. However, the novelty of our framework is that we use the cluster to run mutants (i.e., same code but with different injected defects), each on a separate node and use the same data set - the input data to the tests – across all nodes. During the reduce phase, the report on success or failure of the tests is aggregated. Two arguments support our theses:

- While dealing with mutants, it is reasonable to assume that their execution time would be similar, thus making them a perfect candidate for running them in parallel and optimally consuming the available computation resources.
- Running unit-tests in general is a typical batch operation, which fits the offline batch nature of the MapReduce paradigm.

The rest of the paper is organized as follows. Section 2 contains a brief overview about Mutation testing, the tool we employ in our proposed system and the typical operators supported in our implementation. In Section 3, the MapReduce paradigm together with Hadoop® are explained. In Section 4, the architecture of our proposed HadoopMutator is explained. Additionally, the steps to run test suites on our framework are briefly stated. Section 5 contains the results of our experimentation on the new framework highlighting the gain in speed. We present a brief overview on related work done on testing using Hadoop in Section 6 before concluding the paper in Section 7.

2 Mutation Testing

Since its introduction in the 70's, mutation testing has been extensively studied as an effective technique to enhance software quality. A comprehensive survey of mutation testing research can be found in [27]. One of the earliest set of mutation operators are defined by the Mothra mutation testing system [3]. Mothra defines a set of operators derived from studies of programmers' errors and correspond to mistakes that programmers typically make. This set of operators represents more than ten years of refinement through several mutation systems. The authors of [4] further extend these operators to support C# object orientation and syntax. They also present in [5] an empirical study that evaluates the quality of these mutation operators and establish their relationship to actual programmers' errors.

Using mutation testing, a test suite is evaluated by calculating its *mutation score*. The mutation score is a ratio value capturing the percentage of errors detected to the total number of errors injected into the code. i.e.,

$$Mutation\ Score = \frac{Number\ of\ detected\ errors}{Total\ number\ of\ errors}$$

Table 1. Mutation Operators Supported by HadoopMutator

Mutator	Description and Example
Conditionals Boundary	Replacing the relational operators <, <=, >, >= with their boundary counterpart. For example: `if (a < b)` is mutated to `if (a <= b)`
Negate Conditionals	Replacing a condition by its negation. For example: `if (a == b)` is mutated to `if (a != b)`
Math	Replacing binary arithmetic operations with another operation. For example: `a = b + c` is mutated to `a = b - c`
Increments	Replacing increments with decrements and vice versa. For example: `i++` is mutated to `i--`

Return Values	Mutating the return values of method calls. For example:
	`public Object foo(){`
	`   return new Object();`
	`}`
	is mutated to
	`public Object foo(){`
	`   new Object();`
	`   return null;`
	`}`

Void Method Calls	Removing method calls to void methods. For example:
	`public int foo(){`
	`   int i = 5;`
	`   doSomething(i);`
	`   return i;`
	`}`
	is mutated to
	`public int foo(){`
	`   int i = 5;`
	`   return i;}`

The main assumption of mutation testing is that the number of mutation errors detected by a tool is an indication of number of errors that this tool can detect in the future when unknown bugs are present in the code [25]. In our implementation of HadoopMutator, we employed the *Pitest* mutation framework [34]. *Pitest* is an open-source mutation testing tool for Java that supports a range of frequently-used mutation operators. Pitest seems to be the most active open-source mutation testing tool. Other research effort, e.g., µJava [13] and Javalanche [21][20][6] seem to be present but do not enjoy a large user base. For demonstration, some of the mutation operators used by the Pitest tool are listed in Table 1. The complete list of mutators can be found under [33].

By using Pitest, mutations are automatically induced into the Java Virtual Machine (JVM) byte-code. If a single test fails upon execution of the test suite, the mutation is said to be *KILLED*. If all tests succeed then the mutation is called to be *SURVIVED*. Other outcomes include *TIME OUT* if the mutant causes an infinite loop, such as the case of removing the increment from a counter in a `for-loop`; or runtime errors such as mutant leading to the consumption of memory heap. Generally, if the unit test does not fail on the mutant, this usually indicates an issue with the test suite. By running tests on mutant, the quality of the tests can be enhanced since traditional test coverage (e.g., line, and code blocks) only measures which code is executed by the tests. It does not check that the tests are able to detect faults in the executed code. The downside of using Pitest is the tremendous increase in the execution time taken for running the same test suite on the different variants of the code.

```
821        private void markTheLastButOneChildDirty(TreeItem parent, TreeItem child)
822        {
823   1        if (parent.getChildren().indexOf(child) == parent.getChildren().size() - 1)
824            {
825                // go through the children backwards, start at the last but one
826                // item
827   1            for (int i = parent.getChildren().size() - 2; i >= 0; --i)
828                {
829                    TreeItem item = parent.getChildren().get(i);
830
831                    // invalidate the node and it's children, so that they are
832                    // redrawn
833                    invalidateNodeWithChildren(item.getModelObject());
834
835                }
836            }
837        }
838
839        /**
840         * @see javax.swing.event.TreeModelListener#treeNodesInserted(javax.swing.event.TreeModelEvent)
841         */
842        @Override
843        public final void treeNodesInserted(TreeModelEvent e)
844        {
845            if (dirtyAll)
846            {
847                return;
848            }
```

Fig. 1. Example snippet taken from coverage report of Wicket Core

Fig. 1 illustrates the reports produced by Pitest. It combines line coverage and mutation coverage information. Light green highlights in lines 829, 833 and 845 show line test coverage. Dark green highlight in line 827 shows a mutation coverage in which a Math mutator is applied where the integer subtraction is replaced by addition and the mutation was killed by at least one test case. The light pink of line 847 shows lack of line coverage, whereas dark pink highlighting line 823 shows a lack of mutation coverage for another Math mutation similar to the one at line 827.

3   The Map/Reduce Programming Model

MapReduce is a programming model used for batch processing of large amounts of data and solving large-scale computing problems. The MapReduce abstraction is inspired by the Map and Reduce functions, which are commonly used in functional languages such as Lisp. The MapReduce system allows users to easily express their computation as map and reduce functions. The following discussion of MapReduce model is based on [2] This paper describes how Google split, processed, and aggregated their humongous data set. The reader can also refer to [1] and [14] for more details.

The map function, written by the user, processes a key/value pair to generate a set of intermediate key/value pairs:

<code>map (key1, value1) → list (key2, value2)</code>

The reduce function, also written by the user, merges all intermediate values associated with the same intermediate key:

<code>reduce (key2, list (value2)) → list (value2)</code>

The simplest and most common example for MapReduce is the problem of counting the number of occurrences of each word in a large collection of documents [31].

```
map(String key, String value){
  // key: document name
  // value: document contents
  for each word w in value{
    EmitIntermediate(w, "1");
  }
}

reduce(String key, Iterator values){
  // key: a word
  // values: a list of counts
  int result = 0;
  for each v in values{
    result += ParseInt(v);
  }
  Emit(AsString(result));
}
```

The user writes code to fill in a mapreduce specification object with the names of the input and output files, and optional tuning parameters. The user then invokes the MapReduce function, passing it the specification object.

More examples include a *distributed Grep* function, a *count of URL access frequency*, a *reverse web-link graph*, and several other examples found in literature. The rapid emergence of MapReduce implementation for parallelizable batch-oriented programs motivated the authors of [15] to group them in reusable MapReduce software design patterns.

After the release of [2], Doug Cutting worked on a Java-based MapReduce implementation to solve scalability issues on Nutch [8]; which is the core of an open source search engine based on Lucene [7]. This was the base for the Hadoop® open source project; which became a top-level Apache Foundation project. Several complementary open source projects have been built with Hadoop at their core. Some of the more popular ones include Pig, Hive, HBase, Mahout, and ZooKeeper. Currently, the project includes these modules:

- Hadoop Common: The common utilities that support the other Hadoop modules.
- Hadoop Distributed File System (HDFS™): A distributed file system that provides high-throughput access to application data.
- Hadoop YARN: A framework for job scheduling and cluster resource management.
- Hadoop MapReduce: A YARN-based system for parallel processing of large data sets.

Each Hadoop® (Map or Reduce) task works on the small subset of the data it has been assigned so that the load is spread across the cluster. The map tasks generally load, parse, transform, and filter data. Each reduce task is responsible for handling a subset of the map task output. Intermediate data is then copied from mapper tasks by the reducer tasks in order to group and aggregate the data. The input to a MapReduce job is a set of files in the data store that are spread out over the Hadoop Distributed File System (HDFS). In Hadoop, these files are split with an input format, which defines how to separate a file into input splits. Each map task in Hadoop is broken into the following phases: *record reader, mapper, combiner,* and *partitioner*. The *record reader* parses the data into records and passes them to the *mapper* in the form of a key/value pair. The *mapper*, in-turn, executes user-provided code on each key/value pair to produce zero or more new key/value pairs, called the *intermediate pairs*. Typically, the key is what the data is grouped on and the value is the information to be analyzed later on by the reducer. The *combiner* is an optional localized reducer. It groups data during the mapping phase. In many situations, this optional step significantly reduces the amount of data that has to be transferred over the network. The *partitioner* splits the key/value pairs into shards, one shard per reducer. By default, the reducer uses the hash code of the intermediate object to randomly distribute the shards evenly over the available reducers.

During the *Reduce* phase, the task starts with the *shuffle* and *sort*. Here, the output files are transferred to the local machine that runs the reducer. The data is sorted by key into one large data list. The purpose of this sort is to group equivalent keys together so that their values can be iterated over easily in the reduce task. The *reducer* task then runs a user-provided reduce function once for each key grouping. Here, data is typically filtered and aggregated. The output of the reduce function is sent to the *output format* that translates the final key/value pair from the reduce function and writes it out to a file by a record writer. In the end, the data is written out to HDFS.

4   HadoopMutator

Our HadoopMutator logically consists of two parts: the *generation* parts of mutants and the *testing* part of the mutants. While the generation part heavily depends on Pitest testing framework, the testing part is totally built on top of Hadoop®.

The generation part consists of the following four steps:

- Mutant generation: in which the classes are analyzed and the mutants are created.
- Test selection: in which tests are selected to run against the mutants.
- Mutant insertion: in which mutants are loaded into a JVM.
- Mutant detection: in which the selected tests are run against the loaded mutant.

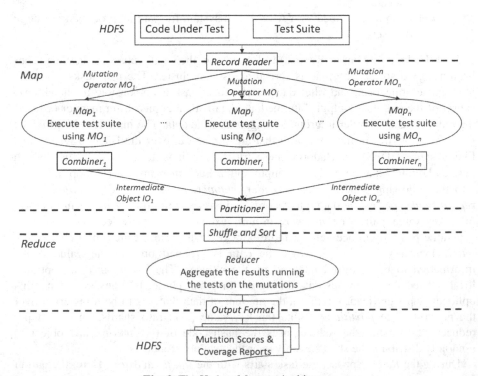

Fig. 2. The HadoopMutator Architecture

All these four steps are done within the Map phase in Hadoop, while the Reduce phase aggregates the results. Each Map node is assigned to a mutation operator. This way, we can assume that:

- the jobs are distributed evenly over the nodes,
- the variance between the execution times of the jobs would be small, and
- the number of nodes can be fixed a-priori.

The processing steps within HadoopMutator are illustrated in Fig. 2.

The *record reader* of the Map phase uses the Enumerator of the mutation operator as the key and the byte-code of the code under test to the mapper. Each *map* node uses the Hadoop® streaming utility that allows the creation and execution of Map jobs with any executable or script as the mapper. The HadoopMutator utility is invoked from a command line as follows:

> *HadoopMutator <code under test> <Hadoop master node path>*

The utility code is shown in Listing 1.

```bash
#!/bin/bash

#Read code directory name
tested_code="$1"
Hadoop_path="$2"

#Create path to the code under test
code_path=$Hadoop_path
code_path+=$tested_code
code_path+=".jar#inputdirs1"

#Print out a timestamp
echo "***** HadoopMutator started for $tested_code *****"
date

hadoop jar /usr/lib/hadoop-0.20-
mapreduce/contrib/streaming/hadoop-streaming.jar \
-input hminput \
-output hmoutput \
-mapper hmmap.sh \
-reducer hmreduce.sh \
-file hmmap.sh \
-file hmreduce.sh \
-cmdenv CODE_UNDER_TEST="$tested_code" \
-cacheArchive $code_path \
-cacheArchive '$Hadoop_path/apache-maven-3.2.1.jar#mvndirs1' \
-verbose

date
echo "***** HadoopMutator ended *****"
```

Listing 1. The HadoopMutator Script

The mapper executes the complete test suite on all the packages of the code under test using Pitest and applying the mutation operator assigned to that mapper node. The results of the Pitest are transformed into the intermediate pair objects. The *intermediate object* has as key the fully qualified classname concatenated to the line number for each line. The value is an ordered list containing the outcome of the Pitest on this operation. Possible items of the list are `KILLED`, `SURVIVED`, `NO_COVERAGE` or `TIMED_OUT`. The `KILLED` and `NO_COVERAGE` outcomes are logically the same as they both represent a surviving mutant. `NO_COVERAGE` status is however used to identify mutants that have no test coverage. In HadoopMutator, we use local *combiner* step since one line of code can be replaced by several mutations as in line 63; as illustrated in Fig. 3. Finally, the Hadoop® default *partitioner* would direct the intermediate key/value pairs to the reducer.

CDFPiecewiseLinearRandomGenerator.java

...

63 4   long result = (long) ((probability - segmentProbMin) / segmentProbRange * segmentDatumRange)

...

Mutations

...

63
1. Replaced double subtraction with addition → KILLED
2. Replaced double division with multiplication → KILLED
3. Replaced double multiplication with division → KILLED
4. Replaced long addition with subtraction → KILLED

Fig. 3. Example of a line resulting in four mutations of the same type, drawn from a Java class of the Hadoop® source code

Since we use only one reducer, the *shuffle and sort* step is relatively simple, the output files are collected from the map nodes and sent to the reducer node. The *reducer* has now a list of execution outcomes `KILLED`, `NO_COVERAGE`, `SURVIVED`, `ERROR` for each single line of the source code under test. The reducer's sorting phase results in grouping the mutation testing results for each line of code. The final state of a line of code is then decided according to state transition table listed in Table 2. Light green highlights normal non-mutated line coverage. Dark green highlights a successful mutation coverage of that line. The light pink shows lack of line coverage; whereas dark pink shows lack of mutation coverage. Grey indicates an internal error such as memory error or timeout. Line numbers missing from the key of the intermediate object point to non-executed code such as comments, variable declarations, method and class names, etc. Additionally, the reducer updates statistical counters for the number of `KILLED`, `NO_COVERAGE`, `SURVIVED`, `ERRORS` together with the total number of injected errors through mutations in order to calculate the *Mutation Score* for each Java package and for the whole code under test. Therefore, the output of the reducer is logically another key/value pair in the form of:

```
Key:  fully qualified classname + line number
Value:Object consisting of {
          Boolean isEmpty;
          List<Comments> commentsForKilled;
          List<Comments> commentsForNoCoverage;
          List<Comments> commentsForSurvived;
          List<Comments> commentsForError;
          Statistics mutationScore
      }
```

Table 2. State transition for each mutated line while iterating over its comments

	KILLED	SURVIVED	NO_COVERAGE	ERROR
KILLED	KILLED	SURVIVED	NO_COVERAGE	KILLED
SURVIVED	SURVIVED	SURVIVED	SURVIVED	SURVIVED
NO_COVERAGE	NO_COVERAGE	SURVIVED	NO_COVERAGE	ERROR
ERROR	KILLED	SURVIVED	ERROR	ERROR

These key/value pairs are sent to the final step, which is the output format, to produce a package report as illustrated in Fig. 4 and a report for each class as illustrated in Fig. 5.

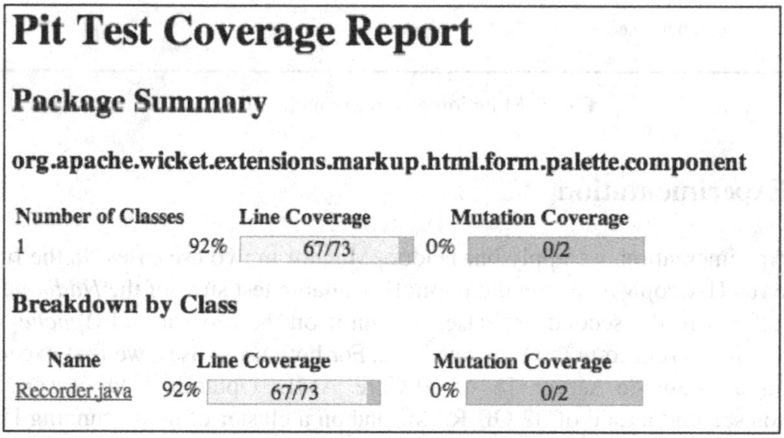

Pit Test Coverage Report

Package Summary

org.apache.wicket.extensions.markup.html.form.palette.component

Number of Classes	Line Coverage		Mutation Coverage	
1	92%	67/73	0%	0/2

Breakdown by Class

Name	Line Coverage		Mutation Coverage	
Recorder.java	92%	67/73	0%	0/2

Fig. 4. Mutation coverage on package level

As can be seen from Fig. 4, the Recorder.java class has a relatively high code coverage (92%). However, the tests fail to detect the injected errors leading to a mutation coverage of 0%. Fig 5. Shows an example where at lines 201 and 207, two Math mutations that replace the subtraction with addition survive the tests despite the fact that these lines are covered by at least one test case. This example illustrates the role of mutation testing in assessing the effectiveness of the implemented tests and the inadequacy of depending solely on code coverage in that assessment.

```
194     /**
195      * @return list over unselected choices
196      */
197     protected List<T> getUnselectedList()
198     {
199         final Collection<? extends T> choices = getPalette().getChoices();
200
201 1     if (choices.size() - getSelectedIds().size() == 0)
202         {
203             return Collections.<T> emptyList();
204         }
205
206         final IChoiceRenderer<T> renderer = getPalette().getChoiceRenderer();
207 1     final List<T> unselected = new ArrayList<T>(Math.max(1, choices.size() -
208             getSelectedIds().size()));
209
210         for (final T choice : choices)
211         {
212             final String choiceId = renderer.getIdValue(choice, 0);
213
214             if (getSelectedIds().contains(choiceId) == false)
215             {
216                 unselected.add(choice);
217             }
218         }
219         return unselected;
220     }
```

Fig. 5. Mutation coverage on class level

5   Experimentation

In our experimentation, we apply our HadoopMutator in two use cases: In the first use case, we run HadoopMutator on the publicly available test suite of the *Hadoop® code base* itself and in the second use case, we run it on the test suite of *Apache Wicket* [28] which is referenced in the Pitest website. For both uses cases, we first execute the Pitest on a one-node server [8 Quad-Core AMD Opteron^{TM} Processor, 64-bit instruction set, and a total of 32 GB RAM] and on a cluster of nodes running Hadoop using our HadoopMutator framework. The cluster used in our experimentation is comprised of 13 nodes where each node is an IBM System x3550, with 32GB of memory, 1.8TB of storage, CPU Intel Xeon, 2.33GHz, 8 cores and running Centos 6.3 64-bit operating system. Our current implementation of the reducer does not generate the mutation score field as it can be easily calculated offline from the aggregated results.

During our validation experiments, we measure the execution time of running Pitest tool both in serial mode and using our HadoopMutator scripts. Fig. 6 and 7 display boxplots of the execution time for our two use cases: the Apache Wicket and the Hadoop code, respectively. A boxplot [24] is a graphical way for depicting a set of data values. The bottom of the box is the 25th percentile and the top of the box the 75th percentile. The line across the middle of the box is the median or 50th percentile. The plot also displays outliers, which is a value that is significantly distant from the rest of the data. The plot is used to visualize the differences/similarities between data sets.

As shown in Fig. 6, the running time for the Wicket code ranges from 1.161 to 1.637 sec/mutation in the serial case, with mean value equal to 1.374 sec/mutation. Using HadoopMutator, the running time ranges from 0.075 to 0.211 sec/mutation with mean equal to 0.13 sec/mutation.

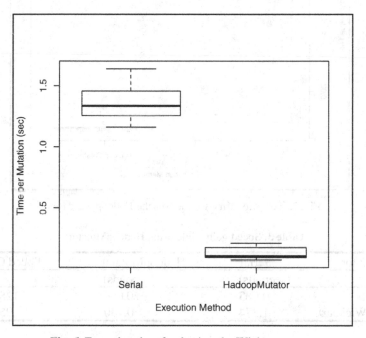

Fig. 6. Execution time for the Apache Wicket use case

In case of the Apache Hadoop use case, shown in Fig. 7, the running time ranges from 0.07 to 0.09 sec/mutation in the serial case, with mean value equal to 0.08 sec/mutation. Using HadoopMutator, the running time ranges from 0.004 to 0.013 sec/mutation with mean equal to 0.006 sec/mutation.

Table 3 summarizes the average gain in speed. The first column contains the execution time in seconds while running in a serial mode on a server. The second column lists the execution time and the increase in percentage when using HadoopMutator. The speed is largely increased more than 12 and 9 times for the Hadoop® and the Apache Wicket® code bases, respectively, when we use HadoopMutator on our Hadoop cluster.

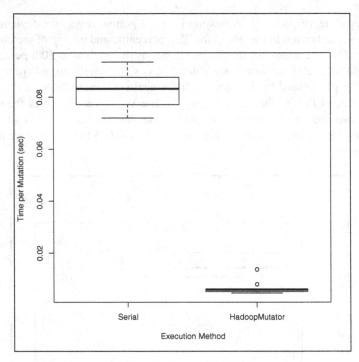

Fig. 7. Execution time for the Apache Hadoop use case

Table 3. Speed gain while using HadoopMutator

Test suite for	Serial	HadoopMutator	Speed Gain
	(seconds)	(seconds)	(%)
Hadoop®	0.083	0.006	1283%
Apache Wicket®	1.374	0.130	957%

It is worth noting here that the expected performance gain is around 13 times as HadoopMutator distributes the generation of mutants and the execution of tests over 13 nodes. The results demonstrate that we get closer to the expected performance gain as the size of the code and tests increases. This can be seen with the Apache Hadoop use case for which the Pitest tool generates over 300K different mutants.

For a relatively smaller code base such as the Apache Wicket, the tool generates around 32K mutants. In that case, the overhead of running Hadoop on the compute nodes becomes significant relative to the time needed to generate and executes the tests and hence the optimal performance gain is not attained. While the gain in speed is still significant in both cases, our approach is most useful with large projects that exhibit a significant code testing time. HadoopMutator can significantly decrease the running time from the order of hours to minutes and hence enabling mutation testing to be efficiently applied to projects in industrial settings as part of the continuous integration tests.

6   Related Work

The literature is scarce about research using the MapReduce programming model to perform tests. HadoopTest [9] is a test harness solution for MapReduce-based systems. It is based on the control of distributed workers to coordinate the execution of test case actions on different workers in parallel. HadoopTest allows the combination of fault injection and functional tests to build complex test cases. Test cases are written in Java and annotations are used to mark test action methods. Similar to our approach, the authors in [9] validate their solution and measure the overhead of the HadoopTest. Nevertheless, their system is used to test MapReduce-based systems against bugs, hardware problems, and outages. They inject the failures typical to the cluster operation and define them to be their mutant. In our HadoopMutator, we use mutation testing on normal code and do not restrict ourselves to MapReduce-based systems. We use the cloud-based Hadoop MapReduce to execute in parallel the test suite on the different mutants, which are variations of the original code under test.

HadoopUnit [17] and [23] is a distributed execution framework for JUnit test cases that is developed as a Hadoop MapReduce job. A tester uploads the production code and the test code and any other libraries that are needed for test cases to execute. An Ant task generates the Java commands to execute all the test cases. It writes the commands in a text file in the form: *<testcase name><java, TestRunner, classpath, libraries, testcase name, testcase properties>*. The Hadoop framework splits this text file and sends each line of text to each mapper. On each node, the command gets executed as a process. At the end of the map task, the intermediate values are generated on the form of *<key, value> -> <test name, test result>*. The Reducer combines all these *<test name, test result>* pairs and outputs them to a file. The primary motivation behind developing HadoopUnit is to test the Hadoop production code using the Hadoop platform itself. Similar to our HadoopMutator, the authors validate their approach by testing the Hadoop production code. Nevertheless, they use the normal JUnit test suite and their approach does not support mutation testing. Furthermore, HadoopTest does not produce coverage reports.

Furthermore, research has recognized the importance of parallelizing mutation testing to overcome the performance barrier. The work recently presented in [10][11] is an example of a Java mutation testing framework that supports parallel execution. In contrast, we propose reusing existing technologies, specifically Big Data frameworks, to achieve the same goal. Finally, in previous work, mutation testing has been used to evaluate the effectiveness of formal code specification [19][18].

7   Conclusion and Future Work

In this paper, we provided a scalable solution for applying mutation testing on real-life software projects. We reuse the MapReduce programming model to efficiently generate and test mutants of large-scale software projects. We hence provide a useful tool to enhance the quality of software in real-life settings using the mutation testing technique. We also encourage research in reusing the state-of-the-art data-centric architectures to speed up the software engineering processes by treating source code as data. Using two use cases, we show the huge increase in speed when executing tests on mutants using our HadoopMutator framework.

In the sequel of this paper, we plan to apply the MapReduce programming model to different code profiling functions and to use the same model to formally specify and verify code correctness. Formal code verification remains largely another impractical technique due to its complexity and the large space that a code verifier needs to examine to prove correctness. By implementing verifiers as cloud-based services, we anticipate a significant enhancement in performance. On the implementation level, we plan to integrate HadoopMutator with the common Continuous Integration environments such as Jenkins [32].

References

1. Buyya, R., et al.: Cloud computing: Principles and paradigms. John Wiley & Sons (2010)
2. Dean, J., Ghemawat, S.: MapReduce: Simplified Data Processing on Large Clusters. Communications of the ACM, 51(1), 107–113 (2008)
3. DeMillo, R.A., et al.: An extended overview of the Mothra software testing environment. Presented at the Proceedings of the Second Workshop on Software Testing, Verification, and Analysis (1988)
4. Derezińska, A.: Advanced Mutation Operators Applicable in C# Programs. In: Sacha, K. (ed.) Software Engineering Techniques: Design for Quality. IFIP, vol. 227, pp. 283–288. Springer, Boston (2007)
5. Derezinska, A., Szustek, A.: Tool-Supported Advanced Mutation Approach for Verification of C# Programs. In: 3rd International Conference on Dependability of Computer Systems (2008)
6. Fraser, G., Zeller, A.: Mutation-Driven Generation of Unit Tests and Oracles. IEEE Transactions on Software Engineering 38(2), 278–292 (2012)
7. Gospodnetic, O., Hatcher, E.: Lucene. Manning (2005)
8. Khare, R., et al.: Nutch: A flexible and scalable open-source web search engine. Oregon State University 1, 32 (2004)
9. Marynowski, J.E., et al.: Testing MapReduce-Based Systems. arXiv preprint arXiv:1209.6580 (2012)
10. Mateo, P.R., Usaola, M.P.: Bacterio: Java Mutation Testing Tool: A Framework to Evaluate Quality of Tests Cases. In: 28th IEEE International Conference on Software Maintenance (ICSM). IEEE (2012)
11. Mateo, P.R., Usaola, M.P.: Parallel Mutation Testing. Software Testing, Verification and Reliability 23(4), 315–350 (2013)
12. Matyas, S., et al.: Continuous Integration: Improving Software Quality and Reducing Risk. Addison-Wesley (2007)
13. Ma, Y.-S., et al.: MuJava: An Automated Class Mutation System. Software Testing, Verification and Reliability 15(2), 97–133 (2005)
14. Miller, M.: Cloud Computing: Web-Based Applications that Change the Way you Work and Collaborate Online. Que Publishing (2008)
15. Miner, D., Shook, A.: MapReduce Design Patterns: Building Effective Algorithms and Analytics for Hadoop and Other Systems. O'Reilly Media, Inc. (2012)

16. Nica, S., et al.: Is Mutation Testing Scalable for Real-World Software Projects?. In: The 3rd International Conference on Advances in System Testing and Validation Lifecycle, VALID 2011, pp. 40–45 (2011)
17. Parveen, T., et al.: Towards a Distributed Execution Framework for JUnit Test Cases. In: IEEE International Conference on Software Maintenance (ICSM 2009), pp. 425–428. IEEE (2009)
18. Saleh, I., et al.: Formal Methods for Data-Centric Web Services: From Model to Implementation. In: Proceedings of the IEEE International Conference on Web Services (ICWS 2013), pp. 332–339 (2013)
19. Saleh, I.: Formal Specification and Verification of Data-Centric Web Services. Virginia Polytechnic Institute and State University (2012)
20. Schuler, D., et al.: Efficient Mutation Testing by Checking Invariant Violations. In: Proceedings of the Eighteenth International Symposium on Software Testing and Analysis, pp. 69–80. ACM (2009)
21. Schuler, D., Zeller, A.: Javalanche: Efficient Mutation Testing for Java. In: Proceedings of the 7th Joint Meeting of the European Software Engineering Conference and the ACM SIGSOFT Symposium on The Foundations of Software Engineering, pp. 297–298. ACM (2009)
22. Shvachko, K., et al.: The Hadoop Distributed File System. In: 26th IEEE Symposium on Mass Storage Systems and Technologies (MSST 2010), pp. 1–10. IEEE (2010)
23. Tilley, S., Parveen, T.: HadoopUnit: Test Execution in the Cloud. In: Software Testing in the Cloud, 37–53. Springer (2012)
24. Tukey, J.W.: Exploratory Data Analysis. Addison Wesley (1977)
25. Voas, J.M., McGraw, G.: Software Fault Injection: Inoculating Programs Against Errors. John Wiley & Sons (1998)
26. White, T.: Hadoop: The definitive guide: The definitive guide. O'Reilly Media, Inc. (2009)
27. Jia, Y., Harman, M.: An Analysis and Survey of the Development of Mutation Testing. IEEE Transactions on Software Engineering 37(5), 649–678 (2011)
28. Apache Wicket, http://wicket.apache.org
29. Bamboo, https://www.atlassian.com/software/bamboo
30. CruiseControl, http://cruisecontrol.sourceforge.net/
31. Hadoop Word Count Problem, http://wiki.apache.org/hadoop/WordCount
32. Jenkins, http://jenkins-ci.org/
33. Pitest Mutation Operators, http://Pitest.org/quickstart/mutators/
34. Pitest Mutation Testing Framework, http://pitest.org/
35. The Apache Software Foundation, http://www.apache.org/

Template-Based Generation of Semantic Services

Felix Mohr and Sven Walther

Department of Computer Science
University of Paderborn, Germany
{felix.mohr,sven.walther}@upb.de

Abstract. There are many technologies for the automation of processes that deal with services; examples are service discovery and composition. Automation of these processes requires that the services are described semantically. However, semantically described services are currently not or only rarely available, which limits the applicability of discovery and composition approaches. The systematic support for creating new semantic services usable by automated technologies is an open problem.

We tackle this problem with a template based approach: *Domain independent* templates are instantiated with domain specific services and boolean expressions. This process yields both the description and the implementation of new services whose correctness directly follows from the correctness of the template. Besides the theory, we present a preliminary evaluation for service repositories in which 85% of the services were generated automatically in efficient time and explain why these are indeed useful.

Keywords: services, templates, correctness, semantic descriptions, automation, composition.

1   Introduction

We are currently witnessing an enormous interest in technologies that deal with semantic services; that is, services with machine readable descriptions of the task they carry out. Two examples are the *discovery* [6,7,13] and the *composition* [2, 3,9,14] of semantic services. The semantic service descriptions, which are usually given by logical preconditions and effects with vocabulary from an ontology, are necessary for the automation of these technologies.

Unfortunately, it is not only laborious but also error-prone to develop semantic services by hand, and there are very few such services available today. The descriptions must be coherent with the used ontology, and proving correctness is often omitted. The absence of semantically described services, which is also documented in [8], is a strong concern for the above mentioned techniques.

To the best of our knowledge, there are no approaches that support the development process in this regard through automation. There are, of course, code generators, but these do not support semantic descriptions of the generated code. Automated service composition itself addresses this problem but is limited in two ways. First, classical composition solves particular tasks, so we can

I. Schaefer and I. Stamelos (Eds.): ICSR 2015, LNCS 8919, pp. 188–203, 2014.

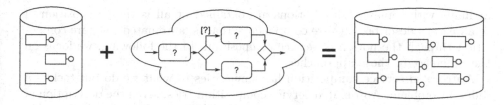

Fig. 1. Template-Based Generation of Semantic Software Services

only use it if we have a specification for a concrete required service. However, it would be helpful to compose services in advance that solve problems that can be reasonably expected to occur. Second, service composition is either based on highly domain specific templates [14] or is limited to sequential compositions. We are not aware of any approach that can compose a service with conditional statements and loops without the help of a template that is specific for the task.

This paper shows how semantically described services can be generated by automatically instantiating *domain independent* templates. The idea is captured in Fig. 1. Our templates are workflows that are semantically described through preconditions and effects and that contain placeholders for service calls and logical expressions. The instantiation of a template replaces its placeholders with existing services and logical expressions from a domain specific ontology. Instantiation produces both the implementation of the new services and their domain specific semantic description whose *correctness* directly follows from the correctness of the template. Hence, exploiting the semantic description of existing services enables us to generate new semantic, correct, and useful services.

Our evaluation shows that the presented approach can significantly increase reuse and that it is technically efficient. We conducted an evaluation for different repository sizes with two templates. The ratio of automatically created services to the number of all services in our scenario is over 85%, while the generation process is efficient and the artificially derived services can be considered useful. In other words, for every service written by the developer, our approach generates 6 new and presumably useful semantically described services.

Summarizing, the contribution is that we *significantly increase* the number of *useful, semantically described*, and *correct* services in an *efficient* way.

The rest of this paper is structured as follows. Section 2 discusses related work. Section 3 introduces templates and their syntax, and Section 4 explains how their correctness can be shown. The instantiation mechanism is described in Section 5, and Section 6 shows the validation of our approach.

2   Related Work

The approach in this paper is different from what is usually understood by code generation in that the generated software has semantic descriptions. Classical code generation as known from model driven development does not exhibit this kind of performance. To the best of our knowledge, the only field where software artifacts with semantic descriptions are obtained at all is the composition of semantically describe software components; that is, automated software composition through the notion of service composition. In the following, we focus on the difference to those approaches.

Automated service composition has similarities to what we do but tackles a different problem. Automated service composition tries, given the description of a desired service as a state transition system [3], preconditions and effects [2], or a workflow [14], to find a correct implementation. That is, automated service composition asks whether a goal can be achieved with a given set of services. In contrast, we address the question of what can be achieved with a given set of services. This is somewhat analogous to backward chaining and forward chaining in logic. The trade-off is in the complexity of the composed artifacts; service composition aims for composing complex services, while we aim at composing rather simple services that are expected to have high reuse potential.

In our previous work [10], we combined these two ideas of composition to overcome the limitation to sequential compositions. For example, none of the above mentioned approaches supports compositions with loops. In [10], code blocks are computed in a preprocessing step and are then arranged by a composition algorithm. The approach presented in this paper differs from the previous work in that templates are now specified explicitly and not, as in the above work, hidden in generator implementations.

A similar concept of composing template instances is persued in PROPHETS [12]. The basis for the composition are so called *service independent building blocks* (SIBs), which are templates. Likewise as in our paper, templates can be equipped with logical expressions in order to constrain their instantiation. However, templates in PROPHETS are different in that they are domain specific. Even though they are not bound to specific services, templates are not independent as opposed to the ones in this paper; their semantics is fixed a priori.

Program synthesis based on preconditions and effects generates algorithms to solve a domain specific task [15]. It does not allow for complex, domain independent algorithmic descriptions that have to be instantiated in different domains.

Compositional verification is part of the large field of program verification. Automatic composition and verification of services is proposed, e.g., in [4], where it relies on linear programming, but service specifications are very simple and not based on ontologies. [11] analyzes (Web) service compositions using Petri nets; [14] automatically creates compositions, but does not focus on verification. ESC/Java2 checks pre-/postconditions of Java methods annotated in JML [5], utilizing a theorem prover, but without relation to ontological knowledge.

3   The Service and Template Model

This section formally defines services and templates. Services are described through inputs, outputs, preconditions, and effects. Templates are workflows with placeholders, a black box description, and instantiation constraints.

3.1   Service and Knowledge Model

We describe services like atomic services in OWL-S as black boxes through inputs, outputs, precondition, and effect. We do not treat stateful services as used in [3] specially, because these can be also encoded through IOPE if necessary.[1]

Definition 1. *A **service description** is a tuple (I, O, P, E). I and O are disjoint sets of input and output variables. P and E describe the precondition and effect of the service in first-order logic formulas without existence quantifiers or functions. Free variables in P must be in I; free variables in E must be in $I \cup O$.*

Consider our exemplary service *getAvailability*, which determines the availability of a book. The service has one input b for the ISBN of a book and one output a for the availability info; we have $I=\{b\}$ and $O=\{a\}$. The precondition is $P = Book(b)$ and requires that the object passed to the input b is known to belong to the ontological concept *Book* (which is the same as requiring b to have the type *Book*). The effect is $E = HasAvInfo(b, a)$ and assures that the object where the output a is stored contains the info whether b is available. An exemplary rule of Ω would be $HasAvInfo(x, y) \wedge y = \text{'}yes\text{'} \Rightarrow isAvailable(x)$.

A knowledge base Ω captures relations among the predicates that are used in the service descriptions. Ω is an ontology (e.g. OWL) together with a set of implications (rules) of the form $a_1 \wedge \ldots \wedge a_n \Rightarrow a_{n+1}$ where $a_1, \ldots, a_{n+1}$ are predicates whose arguments are universally quantified variables. A set of such rules is called *Horn formula*. For simplicity, we assume the ontological part of Ω, which could be expressed e.g. in description logic, to be axiomatized through implications such that we simply consider Ω as a set of logical implications. Note that the satisfiability problem is guaranteed to be decidable for Ω unless the ontological part contains existential quantifiers.

3.2   The Template Model

A template is a *generic workflow* together with a *generic black box description* and *constraints* for instantiation. The generic workflow describes a control and data flow between service calls and serves as a blueprint for the implementation of the derived services. The black box description of the template is a blueprint for the description of the derived services and is expressed according to Def. 1. Constraints define conditions that template instantiation must satisfy to be considered valid and are encoded as a first-order logic Horn formula.

There is one placeholder type for service calls, boolean expressions, and helper predicates respectively. The syntax of placeholders for service calls is explained in Def. 2; we refer to these placeholders as *generic service calls*. Placeholders for boolean expressions and helper predicates are predicates themselves. While placeholders for boolean expression occur in the workflow, the description, or the constraints of a template, the helper predicates only occur in its description and the constraints.

---

[1] This is easily achieved by using fluents to capture the state of the session.

Predicates in a template description must be disjoint with predicates in the knowledge base Ω by convention. For example, we specify a placeholder for a boolean expression in the control flow through $F(x)$ instead of $IsAvailable(x)$. To distinguish the two predicate types, we call the predicates of Ω the *domain specific predicates* and all others the *abstract predicates*. Template descriptions contain only abstract predicates. The abstract predicates P_s and E_s are reserved and represent the precondition and effect of the service that will replace the generic service call with the name s.

In this paper, we write the generic workflow of a template in a simple imperative language (Def. 2)[2]. We allow *variables* to be of either some scalar type (like Boolean, integer, custom data types), or a (finite) set type; the types correspond to concepts of the ontology encoded in Ω. We allow the basic set operations union, intersection, and difference.

Definition 2. *Assuming the usual semantics of these programs, a **generic workflow** can be written as a product of these rules:*

$$W ::= \text{skip} \mid u := t \mid W; W \mid (u_1, \ldots, u_n) := s(i_1, \ldots, i_m) \tag{1}$$

$$\mid \textbf{if } B \textbf{ then } W \textbf{ else } W \textbf{ end} \tag{2}$$

$$\mid \textbf{while } B \textbf{ do } W \textbf{ end} \mid \textbf{foreach } a \in A \textbf{ do } W \textbf{ end} \tag{3}$$

where $u, u_1, \ldots, u_n, i_1, \ldots, i_m$ with $m, n \geq 0$ are variables, t is a basic workflow term (variable or arithmetic/set expression), $(u_1, \ldots, u_n) := s(i, \ldots, i_m)$ is a generic service call, B is an abstract predicate, and A is a set.

We can then formally define a template as follows:

Definition 3. *A **template** is a tuple $t = (D, W, C)$ where D is a description as in Def. 1, W is a workflow as in Def. 2, and C are constraints as a Horn formula. This specification implicitly defines a set G_t of generic service calls, a set B_t of generic boolean expressions, and a set H_t of abstract helper predicates.*

As an example, consider the FILTER template in Fig. 2. This template describes workflows that compute a subset $A' \subseteq A$. For every $a \in A$, the (still undetermined) service s is invoked and determines the value of some (still undetermined) property of a. The obtained value is compared to some value or constant using the (still undetermined) filter predicate F. The item a is added to A' if this comparison has a positive result. Placeholders are the service placeholder s, the abstract predicate F for the boolean expression, and the abstract helper predicate R. The constraint requires that the predicate that replaces R must logically follow from the effect of the service used for s and the positive test of the predicate that replaces F.

Note that, although we call the predicates in the template description "abstract", the approach is completely based on first-order logic. The distinction between abstract (domain-independent) and domain specific predicate is only relevant for the design task; to our verification (Section 4) and instantiation (Section 5), they both are standard first-order logic predicates.

---

[2] This language captures core concepts of workflow descriptions. For real-world applications, it has to be mapped to desired languages like OWL-S or BPEL.

Name   : FILTER
Inputs   : A
Outputs   : A'
Precondition: $\{\forall a \in A : P_s(a)\}$
Effect   : $\{\forall a \in A' : R(a)\}$
Constraints : $\{\forall a, y : E_s(a, y) \land F(y) \Rightarrow R(a)\}$

1 $A' := \emptyset$
2 **foreach** $a \in A$ **do**
3     $(y) := s(a)$
4   **if** $F(y)$ **then** $A' := A' \cup \{a\}$ **end**
5 **end**

Fig. 2. Generic list filter template

3.3   Template Instantiation

A template instantiation substitutes the placeholders of the templates by concrete service calls, boolean expressions and domain specific predicates. Generic service calls are substituted by existing services and a binding between the inputs and outputs of the services and the variables in the service calls. Boolean expressions are substituted by *evaluable* domain specific predicates; that is, predicates for which a programmatic implementation is known, such as the predicate $\leq$ over the domain of integers. Helper predicates in the precondition, effect, or constraints are substituted by a domain specific predicate from Ω. A set of placeholder substitutions is a *template instantiation* or simply instantiation.

Definition 4. *Let* $t = (D, W, C)$ *be a template with* G_t, B_t, *and* H_t *as in Def. 3; S be a set of services;* $P(\Omega)$ *be the domain specific predicates; and* $P_{eval}(\Omega) \subseteq P(\Omega)$ *be the evaluable predicates. An* **instantiation** $\sigma = m_G \cup m_B \cup m_H$ *is the union of (partial) mappings* $m_G : G_t \rightsquigarrow S$, $m_B : B_t \rightsquigarrow P_{eval}(\Omega)$, *and* $m_H : H_t \rightsquigarrow P(\Omega)$ *from placeholders to the respective domain specific elements.*

A *complete* instantiation yields a new service (composition) with semantic descriptions. A template instantiation is complete if each of the three mappings is complete; that is, if there is a substitution for every placeholder in the template. Fig. 3 is an example for a complete instantiation. The result is a new service with its description and its implementation, and the implementation can be considered a service composition.

Note that Def. 4 is somewhat sloppy in that the real mappings also cover a data flow mapping. That is, we not only map an abstract helper predicate R to a domain specific predicate *isAvailable*, but also define the mapping between the arguments of those predicates. In the case of generic service calls, the mapping m_G also defines which inputs and outputs of the placeholder correspond to which input and output of the concrete service. However, such a specification would add an unnecessary level of detail at this point, which is why we neglected this aspect in the formal definition.

Based on the idea of a template and its instantiation given in this section, we now explain how we prove the correctness of the services obtained by template instantiation.

4   Correctness of Services by Correctness of Templates

The eventual goal of verification here is to show that the *template instantiations* are correct. A service, a template, or a template instantiation is correct, if the following property holds: Under the assumption that its *precondition* is true for its input data, its *effect* is also guaranteed for its output data after calling it. The generated service compositions are the result of template instantiation, so verifying these compositions means to verify template instantiations.

The advantage of our approach is that we can show that a template instantiation is correct *by construction* if the constraints of the template are implied by the domain knowledge for the particular instantiation. In the following, we give a high level sketch of this idea. We already elaborated the technical aspect of the mechanism in our previous work [17], so we refer to that work for details.

Every substitution of placeholders defines a logical relationship between abstract predicates of the template on one side and domain specific predicates on the other side. For example, the effect of the template in Fig. 2 contains an abstract helper predicate R. Replacing R with a domain specific predicate, say *IsAvailable*, means to define the equivalence of the predicates, that is $\forall x : R(x) \Leftrightarrow IsAvailable(x)$. The same holds for generic service calls and generic boolean expressions. In this way, every template instantiation i defines a set of such equivalences between abstract and domain specific predicates, which we denote as Ψ_i.

We use these relationships to check whether the domain knowledge Ω entails the constraints of a template for a particular instantiation. The equivalences Ψ_i defined by an instantiation i connect the domain specific predicates, which only occur in Ω, and the abstract predicates, which only occur in the constraints C of template. One could say that the instantiation knowledge Ψ_i *grounds* the predicates in C to the domain specific predicates in Ω. Hence, this grounding enables the check of the validity of the constraints, which implies the correctness of the service defined by the instantiation. We say that an instantiation is *valid* if this condition holds.

Definition 5. *Let Ω be the domain knowledge, inst be a template instantiation, C be the constraints of that template, and Ψ_{inst} be the equivalences defined by inst. inst is a **valid instantiation** if the formula $\Omega \wedge \Psi_{inst} \Rightarrow C$ is always true.*

A template instantiation is correct if it is valid and if the template and the services used for instantiations are correct. Since the existing services are black boxes, we *must* assume them to be correct. Verifying the correctness of the template must be performed by an expert and can be achieved in different ways, e.g., manually using proof outlines [1], or encoding correctness as satisfiability problem based on the control flow [16]. In our implementation, we used the latter one. This yields the following theorem, which we proved in [17].

Name   : FILTERBOOKS
Inputs   : A
Outputs   : A'
Precondition: $\{\forall a \in A : Book(a)\}$
Effect   : $\{\forall a \in A' : IsAvailable(a)\}$
Constraints   : $\{\forall a, y : HasAvInfo(a, y) \wedge y =\text{'}yes\text{'} \Rightarrow IsAvailable(a)\}$

1 $A' := \emptyset$
2 **foreach** $a \in A$ **do**
3 $\quad$ $(y) := getAvailabilty(a)$
4 $\quad$ **if** $y = \text{'}yes\text{'}$ **then** $A' := A' \cup \{a\}$ **end**
5 **end**

Fig. 3. Instantiation of the filter template that filters available books

Theorem 1. *Let* t *be a correct template,* S *be a set of correct services over domain knowledge* Ω, *and* i *be a valid instantiation of* t *using only services from* S. *Then* i *is correct with respect to the preconditions and effects of* t *where predicates have been mapped to the predicates in* Ω *according to* Ψ_i.

In the following, we assume that both *templates* and *existing services* are correct. The correctness of the instantiations then follows by Theorem 1 and the check on validity of instantiations.

5   Systematic Template Instantiation

This section describes how new services are generated through the systematic instantiation of templates. A possible template instantiation for the above filter template is depicted in Fig. 3. We present a basic instantiation mechanism to explain the rough idea and an enhanced instantiation mechanism that tackles complexity issues.

5.1   The Basic Instantiation Mechanism

Our instantiation mechanism replaces placeholders in three steps, which correspond to the placeholder types. First, the generic service calls are replaced by basic service calls. We obtain one new template instantiation for every substitution of a service placeholder by a basic service for every possible mapping between the input and output variables of the basic service and the placeholder service call. Second, the boolean expression placeholders are mapped to domain specific evaluable predicates. As explained above, we only allow for substitutions to predicates that have an implementation such as $\leq$ over the domain of integers. Third, the instantiation mechanism replaces the abstract helper predicates. Fig. 4 depicts the idea of the instantiation mechanism.

After each substitution of a placeholder, the validity of the resulting instantiation i is checked. That is, the algorithm checks the validity of the formula

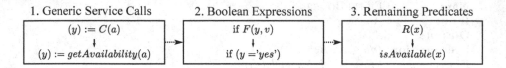

Fig. 4. The Basic Instantiation Mechanism

$\Omega \wedge \Psi_i \Rightarrow C$. Depending on the structure of the domain knowledge, this is step must be performed by an SMT solver. This step can be guaranteed to be decidable unless the ontological part of the domain knowledge contains existential quantifiers. If the check is positive, the instantiation is valid and is added to the set of solutions. Note that, theoretically, also incomplete instantiations can be valid; in this case, every further instantiation is a valid and, hence, correct instantiation.

Since the set of possible instantiations is finite, the routine eventually terminates. However, this number may be very high, so we examine the complexity of the set of possible instantiations in more detail.

5.2   No Serious Combinatorial Explosion

In general, the number of possible instantiations of a template is notoriously high; in fact, it grows exponentially in several parameters. The number of possible instantiations depends on the number of generic service calls of the template (u) and their maximum number of inputs (i_1) and outputs (o_1); the number of basic services (n) and their maximum number of inputs (i_2) and outputs (o_2); and the number of abstract predicates (v), the maximum arity among the abstract predicates (a_1), the number of domain specific predicates (m), and the maximum arity of the domain specific predicates (a_2). It can be easily checked that the number of possible instantiations is then limited in $\mathcal{O}((i_1{}^{i_2} \cdot o_2{}^{o_1} \cdot n)^u \cdot (a_1{}^{a_2} \cdot m)^v)$.

In common settings, however, the exponents in this term are relatively small constants. In fact, we may reasonably require that the number of placeholders, the arity of abstract predicates, and the maximum number of inputs and outputs of both generic service calls and services can be bound to a small constant, say $i_1, i_2, o_2, o_1, u, v, a_1 \leq 5$ (according to our observations). Equally, we have $a_2 = 2$ because common ontologies, e.g. ontologies based on description logics, only allow binary predicates [3]. This polynomially limits the number of possible instantiations in $\mathcal{O}(n^5 \cdot m^5)$; in fact, the above filter template imposes a bound in $\mathcal{O}(n \cdot m^2)$.

Of course, the possible instantiations are, even within this bound, still numerous. Therefore, we enhanced the basic instantiation mechanism as described in Section 5.1 in order to cope with a relatively high number of concrete services and predicates.

---

[3] It is possible to simulate predicates with higher arity by introducing supporting concepts, but the concrete predicates that are encoded in an ontology are only binary.

5.3   An Enhanced Instantiation Mechanism

We increase the efficiency of the instantiation mechanism in three steps.

First, we reduce the effort for the validity check of instantiations. To this end, the instantiation mechanism maintains a *reduced* list of constraints C' for every template instantiation. For every such instantiation σ, the instantiation mechanism stores a set of *remaining* constraints C'_σ. Whenever the mechanism replaces a placeholder in σ, it computes the reduced constraint set $C'_{\sigma'}$ of the resulting instantiation σ' as follows: The knowledge that was added to $\Psi_{\sigma'}$ by the instantiation step is used to eliminate those constraints in C'_σ whose conclusion can be shown; that is, a constraint $a_1 \wedge \cdots \wedge a_n \to b$ is in $C'_{\sigma'}$ if it is in C'_σ and if $\Psi_{\sigma'} \wedge \Omega \wedge a_1 \wedge \ldots a_n \models b$ is not true. We can then say that an instantiation σ is valid if C'_σ is *empty*.

Second, we prune instantiations for which we can prove that the validity check must fail. This is the case whenever there is an constraint where all placeholders have been replaced but where the conclusion of the constraint cannot be shown. In accordance with the first optimization, this happens if there is a constraint in C' that has no more placeholders to be substituted.

Third, we limit the substitutions for abstract predicates in the third phase of the instantiation mechanism. When replacing the abstract predicates of the template, the generic service calls and the boolean expressions have already been replaced. By these replacements, the constraints have been partially connected to the domain specific level through the respective instantiation knowledge Ψ. For each partially mapped constraint that has only one placeholder open, we determine the concrete predicates that may be candidates to replace the abstract ones. The concrete predicates are determined either through forward chaining (if the placeholder is in the conclusion of the constraint) or backward chaining (if it is in the premise of the constraint). Other predicates are not considered, because they would fail on this constraint.

6   Preliminary Practical Evaluation

This paper addresses the question if we can efficiently generate semantically described and correct components that can be considered useful. The correctness and the theoretical efficiency were discussed in Section 4 and Section 5. This section analyzes the remaining questions of practical *efficiency* of the instantiation mechanism and *usefulness* of the obtained services. We used two templates and instantiated them for different service repository and knowledge base sizes. On one hand, we see that the presented approach can be also applied for rather large service repositories. On the other hand, the usefulness of the obtained services directly follows from the usefulness of the services used for instantiation themselves.

6.1   Evaluation Setting

Our evaluation is based on two templates. The first template is the filter that is depicted in Fig. 2, which we used as a running example of this paper. The second

Name   : PEAKFINDER
Inputs   : A
Outputs   : a^*
Precondition: $\{\forall a \in A : P_C(a)\}$
Effect   : $\{\forall a \in A : R(a^*, a)\}$
Constraints : $\{\forall a, y, a', y' : E_C(a, y) \land E_C(a', y') \land F(y, y') \Rightarrow R(a, a'),$
$\qquad\qquad \forall x, y, z : F(x, y) \land F(y, z) \Rightarrow F(x, z)\}$

```
1  begin
2  |   a* := nil
3  |   tmp := nil
4  |   for a ∈ A do
5  |   |   (y) := C(a)
6  |   |   if F(y, tmp) then
7  |   |   |   a* := a
8  |   |   |   tmp := y
9  |   |   end
10 |   end
11 |   return a*
12 end
```

Fig. 5. Template for finding the item of a set that is maximal or minimal with respect to a property. The constraints define that the test must be transitive.

template is shown in Fig. 5 and is blueprint for workflows that determine, for a given set A, the element a^* that has the maximum (or minimum) value of a particular property among all the elements of the set. This property is determined by a generic service call and compared in a generic boolean expression, which is usually resolved to $\leq$. For example, it determines the object with the maximum (or minimum) price in a given set. The correctness of both templates has been proven with the methodology described in Section 4.

The services and boolean expressions that we use to replace the placeholders stem from an environment of reading comparable *object properties*. Similar to getter methods in object oriented languages, our basic services determine properties of objects. For example, one service determines the price of a flight ticket, another service determines the time within which a book will be available, and a third one may determine the revenue of a client. The property values can be compared to other values through the four operators $=, \neq, \leq$, and $<$, which are the concrete boolean expressions; note that these operators are transitive except $\neq$, which is important for the second template.

For each property, we introduce a predicate to declare the relation between a variable that holds an object and a variable that holds the value of the property of the object. Formally, we use the predicate $P^i(x, y)$ to denote that the variable y *contains* the value for property i of the object represented by variable x; that is, $P^{price}(x, y)$ means that y holds the value of the price of x. There is one service for each property i with one input x and output y and with $P^i(x, y)$ as effect.

In order to express relations of property values, we introduce four more predicates for each property. Formally, we use $Q^i_=(x,v)$, $Q^i_{\neq}(x,v)$, $Q^i_<(x,v)$, and $Q^i_{\leq}(x,v)$ to express how the value of property i of object x relates to some value v. For example, $Q^{price}_{\leq}(x,v)$ means that the price of object x is lower than v. In the knowledge base Ω, we define the rules that associate the P predicate of a property and the operators with the respective Q properties. For example, $P^{price}(x,y) \wedge y \leq z \Rightarrow Q^{price}_{\leq}(x,z)$ contains the knowledge that, if the price of x is y and y is at most z, than the price of x is at most z. The special case that z is a constant, like yes in Fig. 3, is not treated specially in the evaluation. This knowledge enables instantiations of the filter template.

Finally, we add a predicate that compares two objects according to a property value. That is, for every property i, we use the predicate $R^i(x,y)$ to express that the object x can be (totally) ordered before object y *according to* property i. For example, $R^{price}(x,y)$ means that x is *at least as cheap* as y. In the knowledge base Ω, we add the respective rule that allows us to determine this predicate. For property i, this rule is $P^i(x_1,y_1) \wedge P^i(x_2,y_2) \wedge y_1 \leq y_2 \Rightarrow R^i(x_1,x_2)$. These rules intuitively satisfy the constraints of the second template depicted in Fig. 5 and, in this way, enables its instantiation.

The knowledge base contains no more rules than the mentioned ones. In particular, there is no knowledge about relationships between different properties.

We measured the time that was required to find all valid instantiations for different numbers of properties. In accordance with the above explanations, we used one service, six predicates, and five rules for each of i properties to instantiate the two templates. The instantiation was performed as described in Section 5. Our algorithm is implemented in Java and was performed on an Intel(R) Core(TM) i7-2600 with 3.4 GHz CPU and 8.0 GB memory in a 64 bit environment.

6.2 Quantitative Evaluation: The Efficiency of the Approach

Table 1 summarizes the results of the efficiency evaluation. The actual results are the number of effectively found valid instantiations and the runtime; the other columns are merely additional information to get a rough idea of the conditions in the respective scenario. The first four columns contain the number of properties (problem size), services, predicates, and rules respectively. The columns "Tree Size", "Explored", and "% Pruned" reflect the number of possible (complete) substitutions of the placeholders, the number of actually considered instantiations that were visited during the run, and the corresponding prune rate respectively. Note that all valid instantiations were found; there were no valid instantiations that could not be found e.g. due to memory overflow.

The synthetic design of the service repository and the knowledge base of course directly implies that the number of valid instantiations is 6 times the number of properties. The first template can be used to derive four new services for every basic service. The second template can be used to derive two new services; one determines the element with the maximum value and one the element with the minimum value for the property that is computed by the basic service.

Table 1. Runtime for template instantiation when maximal knowledge is available

#	Services	Predicates	Rules	Tree Size	Explored	% Pruned	Valid	Time(s)
100	100	600	500	2.902k	16.802	0,9884	600	30
200	200	1.200	1.000	11.563k	33.602	0,9942	1.200	109
500	500	3.000	2.500	72.108k	84.002	0,9977	3.000	874
1000	1000	6.000	5.000	288.216k	168.002	0,9988	6.000	3378
1500	1500	9.000	7.500	648.324k	252.002	0,9992	9.000	7801
2000	2000	12.000	10.000	1.152.432k	336.002	0,9994	12.000	14623

The pruning techniques explained in Section 5.3 help solve also relatively large problems. The number of possible instantiations increases very fast even though only quadratically (Section 5.2). The critical part is the instantiation of helper predicates, because there are so many possibilities to replace them. The pruning techniques allow us to avoid the great majority of the invalid instantiations. In fact, we can prune up to over 99% of the possible instantiations.

Summarizing, the results show us that we can efficiently generate a large number of semantically described services on the basis of templates. If we use the two templates as presented in this paper in an arbitrary domain, we can efficiently increase the repository size such that up to more than 85% of its services have been implemented and proven to be correct by the fully automatized instantiation algorithm. Of course, this requires that the respective knowledge has been formalized.

6.3   Qualitative Evaluation: Usefulnes of Generated Services

When software is written automatically, it is paramount to discuss the usefulness of the obtained artifacts. For example, we could think of a generated service that always returns the boolean value `false`. Even if we have a correct description for this service, it would never be used in practice. In contrast to efficiency, the usefulness of the obtained artifacts cannot be quantified with a metric, so we argue verbally why the generated services are useful in our setting.

In the case of the two evaluated templates, all produced services can be considered useful in the sense that there may be a situation in which they will be needed. We discuss each of the templates separately.

Services created with the first template compute subsets of the form $A' = \{a \mid a \in A \land P(a)\}$, where P models some property that objects in A may or may not have. Such a service is only created through instantiation if there already exists a (basic) service s that determines whether $P(a)$ holds for a single object a[4]. Therefore, this property must be of some interest; otherwise s would not exist. There is no reason to assume that computing a subset of items that have property P is irrelevant if determining P for a single object is relevant enough to have a service for it.

---

[4] It is not the basic service itself that determines the truth of $P(a)$ but an if-statement that tests the result of the service.

A variant of this argument also works for the second template. If we know that the values of a particular property can be compared, it is reasonable to assume that there could be a situation where we want to determine the object with the minimum or maximum value of that property among a set of objects. Consequently, for every service produced by the instantiation of one of the templates, we can easily give a reasonable task where this service would be used.

6.4 Discussion

On one hand, this paper presents a sufficient technical evaluation of the approach introduced. That is, the technical evaluation consists of the theoretical part on one hand and the practical part on the other hand. The theoretical part, which addresses the correctness of templates and the services obtained by instantiation (Section 4 and Section 5), can be considered complete. The practical part, which addresses the efficiency and the (expected) usefulness of generated services, has just been shown and discussed (Section 6). Hence, we consider the technical evaluation of our approach sufficient.

On the other hand, we acknowledge that our evaluation *only* demonstrates that the presented approach technically works, and that its *practically utility* has not been analyzed at all. Due to the synthetic character of the services used in our evaluation, the results presented here are only a proof of concept. Also, writing domain independent templates is a demanding intellectual task, and it is not completely clear how many of such templates can be found.

However, we think that the evaluation given is the most reasonable one at this point of time. The interesting question is, of course, how strong the impact of the approach on every day development is. But establishing an evaluation for practical utility is not at all a trivial issue; in particular, it would not be sufficient to address this question by a small case study. We do not claim that such an evaluation cannot be performed but certainly not as a side product of presenting the approach itself. In other words, we conducted the evaluation that was important for this stage of research, and the evaluation of the practical utility remains future work.

7 Conclusion and Future Work

This paper describes an approach that allows to automatically produce services consisting of a semantic description and an implementation that is correct with respect to the description. Templates as language and domain independent control and data flow specifications with placeholders are verified on a generic level and then automatically instantiated with basic services from a domain. The correctness of the generated services directly follows from the correctness of the template and the adherence of the instantiation process to the template constraints. Our experimental evaluation supports the theoretical elaboration and shows that over 85% of the services in the final repository are produced automatically and efficiently; all of them can be considered useful. The presented mechanism is flexible in that it can be applied to all programming or workflow languages that have the semantics like the language used in this paper.

As a final remark, we would like to add that the presented approach is also relevant for development environments that do not visibly rely on semantic descriptions. For example, one could see the getter methods of classes in Java or .Net as services for getting the properties whose semantic descriptions are automatically derived by naming conventions. The generation of new methods can then be performed on the basis of the techniques shown in this paper. The fact that the obtained code is also semantically described adds significant automatization power to the development environment, even though the (common) developer does not even know that there are semantics involved.

A great deal of possible future work remains in finding more templates, refining the verification technique, improving the instantiation mechanism, and creating tool support. Currently, we use three templates, two of which were explained in this paper. The approach strongly benefits from the number of templates, so it is a natural interest to identify more of them and make them available. The verification technique can be refined by attempts to (semi-) *automatically* find the constraints for a template. The instantiation mechanism can still be improved by more sophisticated pruning techniques or a generally different instantiation strategy. Also, due to the fact that the tools that were used to obtain the results in this paper are isolated, we are planning to provide a tool that supports the development, verification, and instantiation of semantic templates in an integrated application.

Acknowledgments. This work was partially supported by the German Research Foundation (DFG) within the Collaborative Research Centre "On-The-Fly Computing" (SFB 901).

References

1. Apt, K., de Boer, F., Olderog, E.R.: Verification of sequential and concurrent programs. Springer (2009)
2. Bartalos, P., Bieliková, M.: Automatic dynamic web service composition: A survey and problem formalization. Computing and Informatics 30(4), 793–827 (2012)
3. Bertoli, P., Pistore, M., Traverso, P.: Automated composition of web services via planning in asynchronous domains. Artificial Intelligence 174(3), 316–361 (2010)
4. Cavallaro, L., Nitto, E.D., Furia, C.A., Pradella, M.: A tile-based approach for self-assembling service compositions. In: Proceedings of 15th International Conference on Engineering of Complex Computer Systems, pp. 43–52 (2010)
5. Cok, D.R., Kiniry, J.R.: ESC/Java2: Uniting ESC/Java and JML. In: Barthe, G., Burdy, L., Huisman, M., Lanet, J.-L., Muntean, T. (eds.) CASSIS 2004. LNCS, vol. 3362, pp. 108–128. Springer, Heidelberg (2005)
6. Junghans, M., Agarwal, S., Studer, R.: Towards practical semantic web service discovery. In: Aroyo, L., Antoniou, G., Hyvönen, E., ten Teije, A., Stuckenschmidt, H., Cabral, L., Tudorache, T. (eds.) ESWC 2010, Part II. LNCS, vol. 6089, pp. 15–29. Springer, Heidelberg (2010)
7. Klusch, M., Kaufer, F.: WSMO-MX: A hybrid semantic web service matchmaker. Web Intelligence and Agent Systems 7(1), 23–42 (2009)

8. Klusch, M., Zhing, X.: Deployed semantic services for the common user of the web: A reality check. In: Proceedings of the 2nd IEEE International Conference on Semantic Computing. pp. 347–353. IEEE (2008)
9. Lécué, F., Silva, E., Pires, L.F.: A framework for dynamic web services composition. In: Emerging Web Services Technology, vol. II, pp. 59–75. Springer (2008)
10. Mohr, F., Kleine Büning, H.: Semi-automated software composition through generated components. In: Proceedings of the 15th International Conference on Information Integration and Web-based Applications & Services. ACM (2013)
11. Narayanan, S., McIlraith, S.: Simulation, verification and automated composition of web services. In: Proceedings of the 11th International World Wide Web Conference (WWW 2011), pp. 77–88. ACM (2002)
12. Naujokat, S., Lamprecht, A.-L., Steffen, B.: Loose programming with PROPHETS. In: de Lara, J., Zisman, A. (eds.) FASE 2012. LNCS, vol. 7212, pp. 94–98. Springer, Heidelberg (2012)
13. Schulte, S., Lampe, U., Eckert, J., Steinmetz, R.: LOG4SWS. KOM: self-adapting semantic web service discovery for SAWSDL. In: Proceedings of the 6th World Congress on Services, pp. 511–518. IEEE (2010)
14. Sohrabi, S., McIlraith, S.A.: Preference-based web service composition: A middle ground between execution and search. In: Patel-Schneider, P.F., Pan, Y., Hitzler, P., Mika, P., Zhang, L., Pan, J.Z., Horrocks, I., Glimm, B. (eds.) ISWC 2010, Part I. LNCS, vol. 6496, pp. 713–729. Springer, Heidelberg (2010)
15. Srivastava, S., Gulwani, S., Foster, J.S.: From program verification to program synthesis. In: Proceedings of the 37th Annual ACM SIGPLAN-SIGACT Symposium on Principles of Programming Languages, POPL 2010, pp. 313–326. ACM, New York (2010)
16. Walther, S., Wehrheim, H.: Knowledge-based verification of service compositions – An SMT approach. In: Proceedings of the 18th International Conference on Engineering of Complex Computer Systems, pp. 24–32 (2013)
17. Walther, S., Wehrheim, H.: Verified service compositions by template-based construction. In: Formal Aspects of Component Software. LNCS. Springer, Heidelberg (2014)

Automatic Color Modification for Web Page Based on Partitional Color Transfer

Xiangping Chen[1,3], Yonghao Long[2,3], and Xiaonan Luo[2,3]

[1] Institute of Advanced Technology, Sun Yat-sen University, Guangzhou, China
[2] School of Information Science and Technology, Sun Yat-sen University, Guangzhou, China
[3] Research Institute of Sun Yat-sen University in Shenzhen, Shenzhen, China
{Chenxp8,lnslxn}@mail.sysu.edu.cn, longyh3@mail2.sysu.edu.cn

Abstract. Designing or modifying the color of a website is a time-consuming and difficult task for most software engineers. The idea of this paper is inspired by the color transfer methods proposed for automatically alter an image's color during image processing. The color of a web page can be modified by reusing color characteristic of a reference page. However, a web page cannot be simply viewed as an image because it has structure and constraints for color modifying. In this paper, we propose an approach for automatic color modification of web page based on partitional color transfer. Our approach starts from the clustering of visible UI elements for page partition. And then, elements in the source page are color transferred with their matched elements in the reference page. Our approach automatically modifies the color of web pages based on the color transfer result. We generate 72 modified web pages to evaluate the page structure preserving and color characteristic transformation result of our approach.

Keywords: color modification, user interface design, color transfer.

1   Introduction

In a website, color is one of the most notable features to invoke an emotional reaction [12]. Color has been shown to influence perceived trustworthiness, users' loyalty, purchase intention [12, 14] and also the energy cost in the research field of web engineering. The choice of color is important for a website.

For most low-cost web applications developed for small companies or intuitions, the applications are developed without an UI design expert. Designing or modifying the color of a website is a time-consuming and difficult task for most software engineers, even with lots of websites in the internet. The hardest part of the task is to decide which colors the elements should be changed to. However, directly reusing the colors from a good looking reference webpage rarely works out well because features of the page beyond color (e.g., physical structure, grouping and intra-page relationships) may affect the overall result and can lead to problems such as color distortion. (See the discussion of Fig.1 below).

This paper describes an approach based on reusing domain specific knowledge, abstractions and methods from the color transfer domain[1,2,3,4,5] to automatically

I. Schaefer and I. Stamelos (Eds.): ICSR 2015, LNCS 8919, pp. 204–220, 2014.
© Springer International Publishing Switzerland 2014

build an abstract model of one image's features that are critical to successful color transfer and then use that model to automatically revise the color characteristics of a different page.

Figure 1 illustrates the problems of direct transfer. In Figure 1, (a) is the source page; (b) is the reference page. We apply statistical transfer method [1] in the source page using the reference page. (c) is the resulting page. We can see that: (1) the colors of the header and footer in the reference page are not transferred to the resulting page; (2) the colors of an image are changed; (3) some texts in the result page seem unclear.

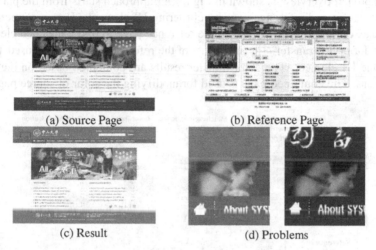

(a) Source Page   (b) Reference Page

(c) Result   (d) Problems

Fig. 1. An Example of Color Transfer

The color distortion problem occurs because a web page cannot be simply viewed as an image. A web page can be divided into several sub-parts. Each sub-part can be viewed as a standalone image. Modification of its color should be guided by the color characteristics of a corresponding sub-part in the reference page. Second, the content, both image and text in the web page is not clear in the output page. Colors are transferred without consideration for user interaction. Because the color contrast ratio between text and its background colors is relatively low, the text seems unclear.

In this paper, we propose an approach for automatic color modification of web page based on partitional color transfer. Our approach starts from the clustering of visible UI elements for page partition. And then, elements in the source page are color transferred with their matched elements in the reference page. Our approach automatically modifies the color of web pages based on the color transfer results. We generate 72 modified web pages to evaluate the page structure preserving and color characteristic transformation result of our approach.

The remainder of the paper is organized as follows: Section 2 gives an overview of our approach; Section 3 introduces how to segment page according the page structure and matching each sub-part for color transfer; Section 4 introduce how to modify color based on color transfer result. Section 5 presents the experiments for evaluating the web structure and color characteristic change during color transfer. Finally, Section 6 discusses some related works before Section 7 concludes our work.

2   Approach Overview

The structure of a web page affects the color characteristic of different parts of the page. A web page can be divided into several sub-parts according to its structure. And two sub-parts with different color characteristic should be color transferred with different reference images. As a result, our approach applies color transfer in different parts of a web page and combines the results for modifying the color of web pages.

The approach overview is shown in Fig 2. Our approach starts from the partition of both source page and reference page by clustering UI elements. For an element of the source page, our approach searches in the reference page to find a matched element as candidate for color transfer. The snapshots of the reference element are used to color transfer the UI element. The color transfer results are combined based on their original positions. The combined page is used for modifying the color of source page.

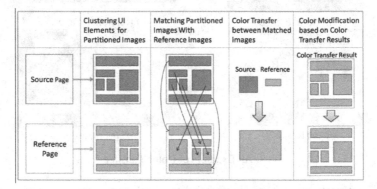

Fig. 2. Approach Overview

In order for the automatic color modification, the main problems are:

(1) How to divide a page into sub-parts? From the source code of a web page, we can find out all the UI elements and their relationships. Which criterions are important to decide whether two elements belong to the same cluster?

(2) How to match elements in different pages for color transfer? The web pages may be of different programming styles. The matching of elements should consider more about the appearance, and less about the implementation detail.

(3) How to modify the color of a web page based on an image? The color transfer result is an image. The color of an image may be very complex and hard to be implemented by revising CSS definition in the page.

3   Partitional Color Transfer

Regardless of the granularity for divided a web page into sub-part, the requirement for partitional color transfer includes two aspects: (1) for a visible UI element in the source page, it can be matched to another element in the reference page. (2) for two visible UI elements, if they are supposed to be transferred to the same color characteristic, their reference elements are supposed to be of the same color characteristic.

Our approach first clusters the UI element in both source page and reference page. Elements in the same cluster are required to be transferred with the same color characteristic. And then, we propose an algorithm to search a reference element for each UI element in the source page.

3.1 Dimensions for UI Element Comparison

A UI element e can be abstracted as *<type, size, position, color, structure>*. We evaluate how similar two UI elements are considering following dimensions:

(1) Types: For the elements of different types, they are considered to be of different color characteristic. An element type can be implemented using different tag in HTML. We group the visible element types. The definition of element type is related to granularity for divided a web page into sub-part. We choose 15 HTML tags used for implementing visible UI elements. These tags are *<button>*, *<link>*, *<div>*, *<span>*, *<nav>*, *<section>*, *<aside>*, *<list>*, *<ul>*, *<ol>*, *<form>*, *<table>*, *<header>*, *<footer>*, *<img>*. If an element defined using one of these tags and its inner structure does not include any of these tags, it is an atom element. Atom element is considered as basic unit during element clustering and matching.

(2) Size: A UI element is a rectangle in the web page. Its size is decided by the width and height of the rectangle. If the sizes of two elements are the same, the possibility that they are related is higher.

(3) Position: The coordinates of a UI element is the coordinates of the upper left pixels of the UI element. The position is decided by its coordinates. If the X-coordinates or Y-coordinates of two elements are the same, they are in the same vertical axis or horizontal axis.

(4) Color: A UI element can be viewed as an image. The colors characteristic of an UI element is decided by the number of color types and distribution of colors.

(5) Structure: In the DOM tree, a UI element is a node. The distance between two nodes indicates possible relationship between two elements. For example, two nodes with the same parent are possibly very similar elements.

3.2 Web Page Partition Based on Cluster of UI Elements

Our approach first partitions web page into parts. The division considers the UI elements which are visible in the user interface. It first filters the elements which are not suitable to be changed. Images used to provide content are required to preserve its original color. When we screen capture an UI element, its background image are also included in the image. As a result, our approach do not consider image.

And then, our approach clusters elements. The color of the elements in the same cluster should be changed in the same way. The rules are defined according to the dimensions for the comparison of UI element. The rules for clustering and filtering are used to decide whether two elements are in the same cluster or not. The rules for comparison are used to evaluate the relationship between two elements.

Table 1. Rules for Clustering of UI Elements

	Rules	Description	Usage
1	CSS	Elements share the same CSS class are belong to the same cluster	Clustering
2	Type	Elements of different types are belonging to different clusters.	Filtering
3	Color	1. How similar the background colors of two elements are?	Comparison
		2. The difference between numbers of colors in two elements	
4	Size	How similar the width and height of two elements are?	Comparison
5	Position	1. Whether two elements are neighbors?	Comparison
		2. Whether two elements are in the same vertical or horizontal axis?	
6	Structure	The relationship between the nodes of two elements?	Comparison
7	Neighbor	Whether there are neighbors of these two elements are in the cluster?	Comparison

The distance between two element e_i and e_j in a web page is defined as:

$$dist(e_i, e_j) = \begin{cases} 1 & \text{if rule 1 is fulfilled} \\ 0 & \text{if rule 2 is fulfilled and rule 1 is not fulfilled} \\ \lambda_1 c_{color}(e_i, e_j) + \lambda_2 c_{size}(e_i, e_j) + \lambda_3 c_{position}(e_i, e_j) \\ + \lambda_4 c_{structure}(e_i, e_j) + \lambda_5 c_{neighbor}(e_i, e_j) & \text{other} \end{cases} \quad (1)$$

(1) Color: We generate the number of colors and the RGB of the background color. The description for the color of an element is defined as $e.color = (number, RGB)$. The RGB color model is an additive color model in which red, green, and blue light are added together in various ways to reproduce a broad array of colors. We compare the RGB values of their background colors using Euclidean distance.

$$c_{color}(e_i, e_j) = \frac{1}{1 + \sqrt{(r_i - r_j)^2 + (g_i - g_j)^2 + (b_i - b_j)^2}} \times 50\%$$
$$+ \frac{|e_i.number + e_j.number| - |e_i.number - e_j.number|}{|e_i.number + e_j.number|} \times 50\% \quad (2)$$

(2) Size: In a list or a table, related elements are usually of the same size. In some condition, these elements may be of different width/ height with the same height /width because of space limit. We define a threshold α to determine whether the two elements' sizes are the same: if the difference of the two elements' widths or heights is higher than α pixels, we think their sizes are not the same. Usually we assign α as 3. For two element e_i and e_j, $e_i.size = (w_i, h_i)$, $e_j.size = (w_j, h_j)$,

$$c_{size}(e_i, e_j) = \begin{cases} \max(\dfrac{\alpha - |w_i - w_j|}{\alpha}, \dfrac{\alpha - |h_i - h_j|}{\alpha}) & ((0 \leq |w_i - w_j| \leq \alpha) \wedge (0 \leq |h_i - h_j| \leq \alpha)) \\ 0 & \text{other} \end{cases} \quad (3)$$

(3) Position: Two types of relationship are defined based on the positions of elements: neighbor and in the same axis. Similarly, we define a threshold β to avoid the deviation produced in the designing phase, in this paper, we assign β as 3. For two element e_i and e_j, $e_i.position = (x_i, y_i)$, $e_j.position = (x_j, y_j)$.

The neighbor relationship is defined as:

$$(((x_i = x_j) \vee (y_i = y_j)) \wedge \{e \mid (y_i < e.position.y < y_j) \vee (y_j < e.position.y < y_i)\} = \phi)$$
$$\wedge \{e \mid (x_i < e.position.x < x_j) \vee (x_j < e.position.x < x_i)\} = \phi)) \rightarrow neighbor(e_i, e_j) \quad (4)$$

Then we can calculate the similarity of the two elements' positions:

$$c_{position}(e_i, e_j) = \begin{cases} 1 & neighbor(e_i, e_j) \\ \max(\dfrac{\beta - |x_i - x_j|}{\beta}, \dfrac{\beta - |y_i - y_j|}{\beta}) \times 90\% & \\ ((0 \leq x_i - x_j \leq \beta) \vee (0 \leq y_i - y_j \leq \beta)) \wedge (!neighbor(e_i, e_j)) \\ 0 & other \end{cases} \quad (5)$$

(4) Structure: the structure of an element e is defined as $e_{structure}$=<p, n, $hasTxt$, $hasImg$>, where p is the parent of e, n is the number of the element's children, the $hasTxt$ and $hasImg$ are Boolean parameters which describe whether the element has txt children or image children.

The similarity of the two element's structures can be described as:

$$C_{structure}(e_i, e_j) = \begin{cases} 1, & parent_i = parent_j \\ \lambda_1 comp(p) + \lambda_2 + \lambda_3(hasTxt_i \wedge hasTxt_j) + \lambda_4(hasImg_i \wedge hasImg_j), & |n_i - n_j| \leq 3 \\ \lambda_1 comp(p) + \lambda_3(hasTxt_i \wedge hasTxt_j) + \lambda_4(hasImg_i \wedge hasImg_j), & other \end{cases} \quad (6)$$

(5) Neighbor: an element has four neighbors at most: the left neighbor, the right neighbor, the upper neighbor, the bottom neighbor. If the neighbors of two elements e_i and e_j exist, we compare their neighbors' distance; if one of the neighbors of the same kind does not exist, the distance between these two neighbors is 0.

$$dist_{neighbor}(neighbor_i, neighbor_j) = (\lambda_1 c_{color}(neighbor_i, neighbor_j) + \lambda_2 c_{size}(neighbor_i, neighbor_j)$$
$$+ \lambda_3 c_{position}(neighbor_i, neighbor_j) + \lambda_4 c_{structure}(neighbor_i, neighbor_j))/(\lambda_1 + \lambda_2 + \lambda_3 + \lambda_4) \quad (7)$$

$$c_{neighbor}(e_i, e_j) = \max(dist_{neighbor}(leftneighbor_i, leftneighbor_j),$$
$$dist_{neighbor}(rightneighbor_i, rightneighbor_j), dist_{neighbor}(upperneighbor_i, upperneighbor_j), \quad (8)$$
$$dist_{neighbor}(bottomneighbor_i, bottomneighbor_j))$$

We use an open source tool CSSBox to generate the information of color, size, position, and HTML node for each UI element. Fig 3 shows the results of clustering UI elements using the setting of λ_1=0.2, λ_2=0.3, λ_3=0.3, λ_4 =0.1, λ_5=0.1. The elements with black frame are images which are filtered. Elements with the same color of frame are in the same cluster.

Fig. 3. Example of Clustering Results

3.3 Matching UI Elements

The matching can be viewed as the comparison between an element e_{source} in the source page P_{source} to all the elements e_i in the reference page P_{ref} to find out an element e_{ref}. The distance between the elements e_{source} and e_{ref} is the minimum.

$$dist(e_{source}, e_{ref}) = \min_{e_i \in P_{ref}} (dist(e_{source}, e_i)) \tag{9}$$

The calculation of distance between two elements is similar to the method we propose in 3.2. However, there are differences between method for calculating the distance between elements in the same page and method for calculating the distance between elements in different pages. The relation of CSS definition and color are not required to be the same for elements belonging to different pages. In addition, the possibility for the elements have similar neighbors is very low. As a result, the rules related to CSS definition, the color and the neighbor of element are not considered.

Table 2. Rules for Matching UI Elements

	Rules	Description	Usage
1	Type	How similarity of the two elements' types	Comparison
2	Size	How similar the shapes of two elements are?	Comparison
3	Position	How similar the positions of two elements in their page?	Comparison
4	Html Structure	How similar the structures of the nodes of two elements are?	Comparison

During matching, all the rules listed in Table 2 are used to evaluate the relationship between two elements. Based on these rules, the distance between two element e_i and e_j, e_i in the source page P_{source}, e_j in the reference page P_{ref}, is defined as:

$$dist(e_i, e_j) = \lambda_1 c_{type}(e_i, e_j) + \lambda_2 c_{size}(e_i, e_j) + \lambda_3 c_{position}(e_i, e_j) + \lambda_4 c_{structure}(e_i, e_j) \tag{10}$$

(1) Type: In HTML, different tags of HTML can be used to implement UI elements which are similar in the user interface. Since the pages implemented by different developers may have different programming styles. We group the tags into

different types in Table 3 based on our implementation experiments. If two elements are implemented using the same tag or tags of the same type, their types are the same. $C_{type}(e_i, e_j)$ is 1 when e_i and e_j are of the same type.

Table 3. Types of UI Elements

Cluster Types	TAG
Function	<button>,<link>
Container	<div>,<span>,<nav>, <section>,<aside>
List	<list>,<ul>,<ol>
Table	<form>,<table>
Other	<header>,<footer>

(2)   Size: it is hard to find two elements belonging to different pages with the same size. As a result, we do not compare the size using the evaluation method in clustering stage. We use the quotients of element's width and height to see whether two elements' sizes are match with each other. If there is more than one element which has the same quotient with the element in the target page, we choose the one which have the minimum deviation of widths and heights. For two element e_i and e_j, $e_i.size = (w_i, h_i)$, $e_j.size = (w_j, h_j)$.

$$C_{size} = \begin{cases} \frac{w_i/h_i}{w_j/h_j} \times 80\% + 20\% - |\frac{w_i - w_j}{w_j}| \times 10\% - |\frac{h_i - h_j}{h_j}| \times 10\% & w_j/h_j \geq w_i/h_i \\ \frac{w_j/h_j}{w_i/h_i} \times 80\% + 20\% - |\frac{w_i - w_j}{w_j}| \times 10\% - |\frac{h_i - h_j}{h_j}| \times 10\% & w_j/h_j < w_i/h_i \end{cases} \tag{11}$$

(3)   Position: Because users' reading habits are considered by developers when implementing the web page, elements of the same kinds are usually placed in similar relative positions. For two element e_i and e_j, $e_i.position = (x_i, y_i)$, $e_j.position = (x_j, y_j)$ and the two pages' widths and heights are w_i, w_j, h_i, h_j.

$$C_{position} = \begin{cases} \frac{1}{1 + \sqrt{(\frac{x_i}{w_i} - \frac{x_j}{w_j})^2 + (\frac{y_i}{h_i} - \frac{y_j}{h_j})^2}} & (\frac{x_i}{w_i} - \frac{x_j}{w_j})^2 + (\frac{y_i}{h_i} - \frac{y_j}{h_j})^2 < 1). \\ 0 & others \end{cases} \tag{12}$$

(4)   Unlike the judgment in clustering step, it's hard to find two elements from different pages which have same number of children or siblings. Instead we just see whether the two elements contain same types of children: we think the two elements' structure are same if half of the children's types in the source page are same as the children's types in the reference page, otherwise they're not same.

Figure 4 shows the results of matching UI elements from source page to reference page using the setting of $\lambda_1 = 0.1$, $\lambda_2 = 0.5$, $\lambda_3 = 0.3$, $\lambda_4 = 0.1$.

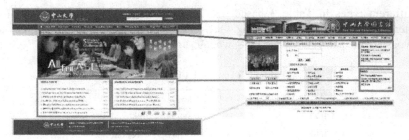

Fig. 4. Example of Matching UI Elements

3.4   Color Transfer between UI Elements

Web page partition results are clusters of elements which should be transferred with the same color characteristic. All the visible UI elements in a web page are clustered. For a web page P, it contains one or more clusters of UI elements. The results of matching UI elements from source page to reference page are the matching relationship between elements. For each element in the source page, there exist a matching element e_j in the reference page:

$$\forall e_i \in P_{source}, \exists e_j, \; s.t. \; e_j \in P_{reference} \wedge matchEleme\,nt(e_i) = e_j \tag{14}$$

Our algorithm takes the matching element as candidate element for color transfer. For a cluster $cluster_i$ in P_{source}, all the elements in the cluster should be matched with the elements belong to the same cluster in the reference page:

$$\exists cluster_j \in P_{reference}, \{matchEleme\,nt(e) \mid e \in cluster_i\} \subseteq cluster_j \tag{15}$$

In this case, $$refElement(e_i) = matchElement(e_i) \tag{16}$$

If the matched elements do not belong to the same cluster in the reference page, our algorithm searches all the clusters in the reference page to find a cluster which contains the most matched elements of elements in $cluster_i$. If there is more than one cluster in which the numbers of matched elements are the same, we randomly select one cluster. In this case, if a matched element of an element does not belong to $cluster_j$, we randomly choose an element in the $cluster_j$ as its reference element.

$$refElement(e_i) = \begin{cases} matchEleme\,nt(e_i) & matchEleme\,nt(e_i) \in cluster_j \\ random \; e \in cluster_j & matchEleme\,nt(e_i) \notin cluster_j \end{cases} \tag{17}$$

The color transfer is carried out between two images: two snapshots containing e_i and e_j. The choice of color transfer method is based on the following considerations.

(1) Color distortion: In some cases, the elements expected to be of the same colors become not uniform; in some cases, the element is changed to colors which are not similar to reference colors or original colors. We consider color distortion problem when choosing the to-be colors. Color transfer method with less color distortion can improve our approach.

(2) Grain effect: The grain effect is a phenomenon appears due to enhancing the noise level of the picture under the stretched mapping. Commonly, it looks like some noises or irregular blocks [15]. The grain effect influences the user experience by decreasing readability of text or making image unclear.

(3) Time cost: Since the webpage contains a great number of elements, the color transfer algorithm should run quickly and effectively. Some color transfer algorithms include a lot of iterations to generate result; they are not suitable to our method.

(a) Color Transfer Result Color   **(b) Modification Result**

Fig. 5. Color Transfer and Modification Result

With these considerations, we choose Reinhard et al.'s color transfer algorithm [1]. This algorithm runs very quickly and its results satisfy our requirement. After color transfering every UI element of source page, the color transfer results are combined based on their original positions in the source page. Figure 5(a) shows the resulting page based on the clustering result in Fig.3 and the matching result in Fig 4.

4   Color Modification Based on Color Transfer Result

After color transfer, an image is generated to guide the modification of color of the source page. Since the result of color transfer may have color distortion, the color modification considers the colors in both reference page and color transfer result.

For an element e_i in the source page, if its reference element e_j has a CSS color definition, this CSS definition is preferred to be used to change e_i's color. If there is no CSS definition for the reference element e_j, our algorithm extracts e_j's color of background and text by random sampling. The colors of randomly selected pixels in the color transfer result are used to extract an average color as the to-be color.

In the implementation, all the information of UI elements is saved in the data base. The to-be changed color of each element is recorded. The color modification is done by revising the CSS color definition for each element. We use jQuery in the implementation. Because the CSS selector names of elements are saved in the data base, the modification of color is done using the following methods:

```
// for class selector
$(".className").css("background-color","resultColor");
// for id selector
$("#idName").css("background-color","resultColor");
// for special elements (e.g. words)
$(".className a").css("color","resultColor")
```

Figure 5(b) shows the web page generated after color modification. Some colors used during color modification are colors used in the reference pages. As a result, there is less color distortion. In addition, we can see that the colors of the logos of Sun Yat-sen University are not changed because images are not color transferred.

5   Experiments

The goal of our approach is to modify the color of a web page based on a reference page automatically. The requirements of the color transfer are:

(1) The structure of a web page can be kept. In a web page, the structure of a web page is expressed as different color characteristic of different sub-part of the page. In order to keep the page structure, the number of color types and the distribution of colors of both source page and resulting page should be similar.
(2) The color characteristic of the reference page and the resulting page are similar.

We choose 9 web pages, as list in Table 4. We use our tool to automatically modify the color of each web page using the other 8 web pages as reference pages. The evaluation considers the keeping of structure and color characteristic.

Table 4. Web Pages

ID	Address	Number of element	Number of cluster
Page1	http://www.sysu.edu.cn/2012/en/index.htm	166	11
Page2	http://library.sysu.edu.cn/web/guest/index	108	12
Page3	http://www.ccf.org.cn/sites/ccf/paiming.jsp	21	4
Page4	http://www.yale.edu/	75	7
Page5	http://www.xmu.edu.cn/	125	8
Page6	http://www.alexa.com/tools	62	19
Page7	http://www.ask.com/answers/browse?qsrc=321&qo=channelNavigation&o=0&l=dir	73	9
Page8	http://www.bojistudio.org/	172	12
Page9	http://academic.research.microsoft.com/	53	6

5.1   Web Structure Preserving

In order to evaluate whether the structure of a web page is preserving during color modification, we compare the change of color types and the distribution of colors between source page and the resulting page.

In order to compare the change of color types for each page, we evaluate the change of numbers of color as $\frac{|\text{resulting page's color types}|}{|\text{source page's color types}|}$. Figure 6(a) shows how the numbers of color changed in the resulting pages with different source page and reference page. We can see that the numbers of added/reduced colors in most pages are less than 20%. Because the structure of page3 is relatively simple, the choice of reference page has little effect on the numbers of color.

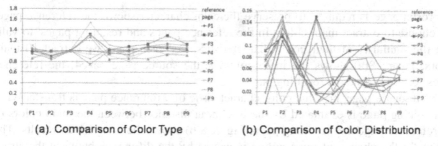

(a). Comparison of Color Type   (b) Comparison of Color Distribution

Fig. 6. Comparison Results

For each page, we extract its color distribution status using color histograms. We traverse all the pixels to count the pixel number of for each color. When comparing the source page and resulting page, the distribution of the same color are not required to be similar in these two pages. Instead, a color in the source page is expected to be changed to another color in the resulting page. As a result, we group the color according to its distribution descending. Figure 7 shows the color histograms for the page4 and its resulting pages.

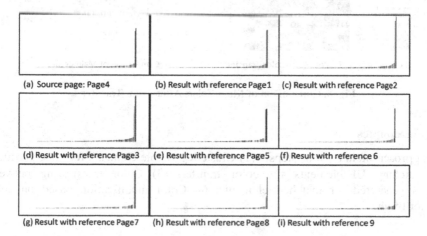

(a) Source page: Page4   (b) Result with reference Page1   (c) Result with reference Page2

(d) Result with reference Page3   (e) Result with reference Page5   (f) Result with reference 6

(g) Result with reference Page7   (h) Result with reference Page8   (i) Result with reference 9

Fig. 7. Color Histograms of Page 4 and Its Color Transfer Results

The similarity between the source page and the resulting page are evaluated using the Euclidean distance between their color distributions. Fig 6(b) shows the Euclidean distances between source pages and the result generated with different reference pages. All the distances are less than 0.15. We can see that the change of color distributions of page 2 with any reference page is more than change in average. In Fig 10, we can see that page2 is different from other pages. In page2, a color is usually distributed in scattered sub-parts. In addition, the pages generated using page2 as reference page also suffer from a relatively high value of change in the color distribution.

5.2   Color Characteristic Preserving

The result page is required to preserve the color characteristic of the reference page. We choose to extract main colors in the reference pages and resulting pages, to validate the similarity of their color characteristics. For each page, we extract 10 main colors. Figure 8(a) shows the main colors in the source page page4, the reference pages for page4, and the resulting pages.

For a source page, how the color characteristic of a reference page is transferred to the resulting page is evaluated by the Euclidean distance between the main colors of the reference page and resulting page. Figure 8(b) shows the comparison results. The reason for the change of main colors is caused by the difference between the structures of reference page and result page.

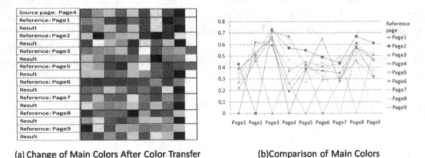

(a) Change of Main Colors After Color Transfer   (b)Comparison of Main Colors

Fig. 8. Comparison of Main Colors After Color Transfer

5.3   Examples

Our approach includes four steps: (1) Clustering visible elements for page partition; (2) matching UI elements for color transfer; (3) Color transferring between images generated for matched elements; (4) Color modification based on color transfer result.

Table 5. Experiment Settings

	Element clustering	Element matching	Color transfer	Color Modification
Setting 1	×	×	×	×
Setting 2	×	√	√	√
Setting 3	√	√	√	×
Setting 4	√	√	√	√

We use different settings in Table 5 to see how each step improves the result using the web pages we used as examples in this paper. In each setting, we modify the color of web page using a sub-set of our approach.

Fig. 9. Color Transfer Result with Different Settings

The result is shown in Figure 9. We can see that clustering and matching elements improve the preserving of page structure. The revision of color in the color modification stage reduces color distortion.

Figure 10 shows the results generated using Page4 as source page, and other pages as reference page. For the resulting page generated using page8 as reference, its structure preserving feature evaluated in 5.1 is the worst. We can see that the page structure is changed. In the resulting page generated using page6 as reference page, we can see that the color characteristic of the resulting page is completely different from the color characteristic of the reference page. In Figure 6(a), the distance between the resulting page and the reference page page6 is 0.67, which is the max value among the values of distances between reference pages and their results in this example.

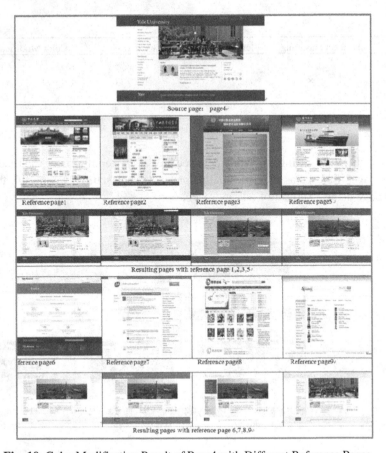

Fig. 10. Color Modification Result of Page4 with Different Reference Pages

6   Related Work

Color Transfer

Color transfer is a way to make the target image have the color appearance from the given "example" image. This method can help artists do less manually adjust color appearance in the image editing. In the last decade, rapid development has been witnessed in the field of color transfer. Representative approaches include classical histogram matching, statistical transfer [1], N-dimensional probability density function transfer [2], gradient-preserving transfer [3], non-rigid dense correspondence transfer [4], progressive transfer [5] and so on.

The statistical transfer method proposed by Reinhard et al. just needs to subtract the mean from the data points, and scale the data points comprising the synthetic image by factors determined by the respective standard deviations, and we can get the result page by adding the averages computed for the photograph. This method is quite efficient when the target image and the reference image are quite similar and simple.

The N-dimensional probability density function transfer can be regarded as finding a one-to-one color mapping that transfers the palette of a target picture to the reference picture, but it will cost a lot of time when the two images are very big, and the grain effect is very seriously. The histogram matching is able to specify the shape of the referred histogram that we expect the target image to have, but the grain effect or the color distortion is very serious.

Web Page Refactoring

With the development of Internet, traditional web pages on the computer monitors are moved to numbers of screens with different sizes, such as the mobile display, the touch screen etc. One of the important questions is making a plan about how the traditional designed web page should be re-designed in order to suit the current display's size. An intuitive method is cutting the page into many pieces, and each piece is suitable to the display [6]. The touch screen is different from the traditional mobile screen [7]; it's bigger and more flexible for interacting [8, 9]. The method proposed in [9] developed a plug-in which can do the page segmentation; it collects user performance data for different device characteristics in order to help them identify potential design problems for touch interaction.

Flatla et al. proposed a webpage's color refactoring method for CVD users [10, 11], they have developed a new simulation approach that is based on a specific empirical model of the actual color perception abilities of a person with CVD. They subtract the colors defined in the CSS files, and find a replacement color on the dichromat Trichromat equivalency plane (DTEP) to replace it, and then optimize the result and rewrite the CSS files to finish the refactoring. The resulting simulation is therefore a more exact representation of what a particular person with CVD actually sees.

Some works focus on the color refactoring of the smartphones' web pages in order to save the cell phones' energy. Ding et al. [16] proposed a technique for automatically transforming the color scheme of a mobile web application. Their method replaced the large, light colored background areas with dark colors to reduce the energy consumed by OLED screens. Mian et al. [17] also proposed a similar web pages' color refactoring method, they kept the difference of transformed colors by keeping the Euclidean distance in CIELAB color space of each related colors.

7   Conclusion

In this paper, we propose an approach for automatically generating color modification solution with different color characteristic. Software developers just need to choose some reference pages they like and they can get numerous refactoring pages generating by our methods. This method can be used for reusing existing web pages' color schemes in order to shorten the development cycle especially the developers are not familiar with color designing.

Acknowledgments. This research is supported by the National Natural Science Foundation of China (61100002), NSFC-Guangdong Joint Fund (No. U1201252), the Fundamental Research Funds for the Central Universities and the Projects for International Cooperation of Guangzhou (No. 2013J4500004).

References

1. Reinhard, E., Ashikhmin, M., Gooch, B., Shirley, P.: Color Transfer Between Images. IEEE Computer Graphics and Applications 21, 34–41 (2001)
2. Pitié, F., Kokaram, A.C., Dahyot, R.: N-dimensional Probability Density Function Transfer and Its Application to Colour Transfer. In: 10th IEEE International Conference on Computer Vision, pp. 1434–1439. IEEE Press, New York (2005)
3. Xiao, X., Ma, L.: Gradient-Preserving Color Transfer. Computer Graphics Forum 28, 1879–1886 (2009)
4. HaCohen, Y., Shechtman, E., Goldman, D.B., Lischinski, D.: Non-rigid Dense Correspondence With Applications for Image Enhancement. ACM Transactions on Graphics 30, 70:1–70:10 (2011)
5. Pouli, T., Reinhard, E.: Progressive Color Transfer for Images of Arbitrary Dynamic Range. Computers & Graphics 35, 67–80 (2011)
6. Furche, T., Grasso, G., Kravchenko, A., Schallhart, C.: Turn the Page: Automated Traversal of Paginated Websites. In: Brambilla, M., Tokuda, T., Tolksdorf, R. (eds.) ICWE 2012. LNCS, vol. 7387, pp. 332–346. Springer, Heidelberg (2012)
7. Dubroy, P., Balakrishnan, R.: A Study of Tabbed Browsing Among Mozilla Firefox Users. In: Proc. CHI 2010, pp. 673–682. ACM Press, New York (2010)
8. Holz, C., Baudisch, P.: Understanding Touch. In: Proc. CHI 2011, pp. 2501–2510. ACM Press, New York (2011)
9. Warr, A., Chi, E.H.: Swipe vs. Scroll: Web Page Switching On Mobile Browsers. In: Proc. CHI 2013, pp. 2171–2174. ACM Press, New York (2013)
10. Flatla, D.R., Reinecke, K., Gutwin, C., Gajos, K.Z.: SPRWeb: Preserving Subjective Responses to Website Colour Schemes through Automatic Recolouring. In: Proc. CHI 2013, pp. 2069–2078. ACM Press, New York (2013)
11. Flatla, D.R., Gutwin, C.: "So that's what you see": Building Understanding With Personalized Simulations of Colour Vision Deficiency. In: 14th International ACM SIGACCESS Conference on Computers and Accessibility, pp. 167–174. ACM Press, New York (2012)
12. Cyr, D., Head, M., Larios, H.: Colour Appeal in Website Design within and Across Cultures: A Multi-method Evaluation. International Journal of Human-Computer Studies 68, 1–21 (2010)
13. Lavie, T., Tractinsky, N.: Assessing Dimensions of Perceived Visual Aesthetics of Web Sites. International Journal of Human-Computer Studies 60, 269–298 (2004)
14. Cyr, D.: Modeling Website Design across Cultures: Relationships to Trust, Satisfaction and E-loyalty. Journal of Management Information Systems 24, 47–72 (2008)
15. Su, Z., Zeng, K., Liu, L., Li, B., Luo, X.: Corruptive Artifacts Suppression for Example-based Color Transfer. IEEE Transactions on Multimedia 11, 1–12 (2013)
16. Ding, L., Tran, A.H., Halfond, W.G.J.: Making Web Applications More Energy Efficient for OLED Smartphones. In: 36th International Conference on Software Engineering, pp. 527–538. ACM Press, New York (2014)
17. Mian, D., Zhong, L.: Chameleon: A Color-Adaptive Web Browser for Mobile OLED Displays. IEEE Transactions on Mobile Computing 11, 724–738 (2012)

Software Development Support
for Shared Sensing Infrastructures:
A Generative and Dynamic Approach

Cyril Cecchinel[1,2], Sébastien Mosser[1,2], and Philippe Collet[1,2]

[1]Université Nice Sophia Antipolis, I3S, UMR 7271, 06900 Sophia Antipolis, France
[2]CNRS, I3S, UMR 7271, 06900 Sophia Antipolis, France
{cecchine,mosser,collet}@i3s.unice.fr

Abstract. Sensors networks are the backbone of large sensing infrastructures such as *Smart Cities* or *Smart Buildings*. Classical approaches suffer from several limitations hampering developers' work (*e.g.*, lack of sensor sharing, lack of dynamicity in data collection policies, need to dig inside big data sets, absence of reuse between implementation platforms). This paper presents a tooled approach that tackles these issues. It couples *(i)* an abstract model of developers' requirements in a given infrastructure to *(ii)* timed automata and code generation techniques, to support the efficient deployment of reusable data collection policies on different infrastructures. The approach has been validated on several real-world scenarios and is currently experimented on an academic campus.

Keywords: Sensor Network, Software Composition, Modeling.

1 Introduction

The *Internet of Things* [13] relies on physical objects interconnected between each others, creating a mesh of devices producing information flow. The Gartner group predicts up to 26 billions of things connected to the Internet by 2020. These *things* are organized into sensor networks deployed in *Large-scale Sensing Infrastructures* (LSIs), *e.g.*, *Smart Cities* or *Smart Buildings*, which continuously collect data about our environment. These LSIs implement *Cyber Physical Systems* (CPSs) that monitor ambiant environments.

Facing the problem of managing tremendous amounts of data, a commonly used approach is to rely on sensor pooling [9], [19] and to push data collected by sensors in a central cloud-based platform [15]. Consequently, sensors cannot be exploited at the same time and one needs to rely on data mining solutions to extract and exploit relevant data according to usage scenarios [1], [17]. This approach is adapted for many scenarios where data mining techniques are required, and has the advantage of separating concerns of data collection from data exploitation. Nevertheless, there are many real-life case studies and scenarios where developers need to exploit shared LSIs and implement a diversity of applications that do not need data mining expertise [4]. In this context, the cloud servers create *de facto* silos that isolate datasets from each others and

I. Schaefer and I. Stamelos (Eds.): ICSR 2015, LNCS 8919, pp. 221–236, 2014.
© Springer International Publishing Switzerland 2014

act as a centralized bottleneck. In addition, the computation capabilities of the other layers of the LSI (*e.g.*, the micro-controllers used to pilot the sensors at the hardware level, or the nano-computers acting as network bridges to connect a local sensor infrastructure to the Internet) are under-exploited [10].

To develop software that fully exploits a LSI, the infrastructure must be considered as a white box. But the developer tasks is then more complex as they have to deal with tedious low-level details of implementation out of their main business concerns. This assumes a deep knowledge of micro-controller (sensor platforms) and nano-computer (bridges) programming [4], while a diversity of technological platforms must be handled. In such a situation, programming at the higher level of abstraction and reusing as much code as possible between scenarios and LSIs is of crucial importance. Moreover developers also have to deal with the sharing aspects. It is hard for them as new requirements must be enacted on the LSI and may easily interfere with the other ones.

In this paper, we propose a tooled approach that tackles all these problems and aims at improving reuse, supporting sharing and dynamic data collection policies. A software framework enables developers to specify and program at an appropriate level their sensor exploitation code. It relies on an abstract model of developers' requirements in a given infrastructure so that timed automata and code generation techniques can be combined to support the efficient deployment of data collection policies into a LSI. As a result, several applications can rely on the same sensors, and thus share them. A given code can be reused, translated and deployed on different infrastructures. The framework also ensures that multiple policies can be dynamically composed, so that the generated code automatically handle all requirements and get only relevant data to each consumer.

The remainder of this paper is organized as follows. In SEC. 2, we describe the motivations of our work by introducing a real-life case study and organizing requirements. We present in SEC. 3 the foundations of our framework. In SEC. 4 we assess our approach, providing an illustration, discussing current applications and validating the identified requirements. SEC. 5 discusses related work while SEC. 6 concludes this paper and describes future work.

2   Motivations

In this section, we motivate our work by first introducing the SMARTCAMPUS project, then by defining requirements for a development support for shared LSIs. SMARTCAMPUS has been deployed on the SophiaTech campus[1] of the University of Nice, located in the Sophia Antipolis technology park. We also introduce a running example extracted from SMARTCAMPUS.

2.1   The SmartCampus Project

The SMARTCAMPUS project is a prototypical example of an LSI [4]. It acts as an open platform to enable final users (*i.e.*, students, teaching and administrative staff) to build their own innovative services on top of the collected (open) data.

---

[1] http://campus.sophiatech.fr/en/index.php

This project is exactly the class of LSI this work is addressing as it faces the following issues : *(i)* it is not possible to store all the collected data in a big data approach and *(ii)* even if one can afford to store all these data, the targeted developers do not master data mining techniques to properly exploit it. Typically, pieces of software deployed in SMARTCAMPUS are driven by functional requirements (*e.g.*, "where to park my car?") and leverage a subset of the available sensors (here the parking lot occupation sensors) to address these requirements. Contrarily to classical systems that use sensor pooling [9,19], different applications, such as the parking place locator and an emergency system assessing the availability of fire brigade access in the parking lots, rely on the same set of sensors at the very same time. Moreover, developers do not know the kind of hardware deployed physically in the buildings. To support software reuse across different architectures, there is a need to abstract the complexity of using such heterogeneous sensor networks at the proper level of abstraction.

2.2   Supporting Shared Sensing Infrastructure

From the functional analysis of the SMARTCAMPUS project (ended in December 2013), we highlighted four requirements with respect to software reuse [4]. These requirements are not only project specific, but also do apply to any IoT-based platform needing to share its sensors on a large scale, *e.g.*, LSIs. This class of system include upcoming smart-building or smart cities wishing to aggregate communities of users to leverage sensors-based system and produce innovative services based on citizen needs.

Pooling and Sharing (R_1). Classical systems rely on sensor polling, with corresponding booking policies. Typical examples of such systems are, for example, the IoT lab platform in France, containing 2,700 sensors deployed in 5 research centers across the country for experiments [9], or the Santander smart city with a closed set of IoT based scenarios [19]. Users book a subset of sensors, work with it and release it afterwards. This setup does not match what is expected in the SMARTCAMPUS context. Moreover sensors available in an LSI are classically available through pooling mechanisms [12], [21]. On the one hand, this mechanism is useful when sensors are installed to match a particular setup and deliver a single service. But on the other hand, it is completely irrelevant to the set of scenarios defined by our class of application. Providing a system that only support sharing is also irrelevant, as one needs to deploy critical pieces of software to sensors and be assured that such a critical process will be isolated from other processes (this is similar to the virtual machine isolation requirement in cloud computing).

Yield only relevant data (R_2). To support sharing, classical architectures actually collect data at the minimal available frequency, and store the complete dataset in a cloud-based system, like in Xively [15]. Then, data mining techniques are used to recompute the relevant data from this complete dataset [1], [17]. This faked sharing leads to two type of issues: *(i)* application developers must be aware of the data mining paradigm instead of focusing on their system and *(ii)* as their is no model of what data was expected by the application, it is impossible to reuse the code written for a given LSI into another one. It is worth to note that by yielding only relevant data, developers who want to express mining scenarios will simply define as relevant a wider set of data than classical developers, making the two approaches non-exclusive.

Dynamically support data collection policies (R_3). There is a need to model what kind of data are expected by a given application, in a data collection policy. From a developer perspective, this requirement is critical as it is not reasonable to program specifically for each LSI addressed by the same application, utterly preventing software reuse. In addition applications exploiting the sensors require to change their policies, for example by temporarily increasing some collection frequency during a short period of time. These policies must be enacted dynamically on the LSI to support such changes. Working with a formal definition of what data are expected by the different consumers is the entry point to apply verification and validation techniques on LSIs.

Handling the infrastructure diversity (R_4). As the state of the art relies on artifacts defined at the code level, it is difficult if not impossible to support software reuse across different LSIs. Several approaches leverage operating systems techniques to provide a standard way to program sensors (*e.g.*, TinyOS [14], Contiki [8]). However, these operating systems must be supported by the available sensors. If not, it is up to the developer to manually translate the code from one system to another. In addition, even in the same LSI, hardware obsolescence requires to replace old sensors by new one, often with new hardware due to sensor production life cycle [3]. Thus, it is critical to operate at a code-independent level to express data collection policies.

Summary. Classical approaches are deporting all the sensing intelligence to a cloud-based solution, under-exploiting the computation capabilities of the other layers of the LSI [10]. This also floods the cloud storage with irrelevant data. Even with the help of data mining solutions, the resulting architectures are either centralized with important overhead, or distributed, but still based on an inflexible mining pipeline with identified bottlenecks [17]. Thus, based on the analysis made in the SMARTCAMPUS, there is no solution covering all the four requirements expressed by the project. To some extent, this is not surprising. These approaches rely on a strong hypothesis of single consumer and very limited access to the sensors. Thus, only half of R_1 (*i.e.*, pooling) and half of R_2 (*i.e.*, mining) are covered. The two last requirements R_3 & R_4 are covered at the code level, preventing reuse and making maintenance and evolution complex. Considering the emerging class of system that targets communities of developers such as the FIREBALL project[2], the previous assumptions does not hold anymore.

2.3   Running Example

We introduce here a running example to illustrate the approach. It is a simplification of the use cases identified in the SMARTCAMPUS's experimental LSI [4].

---

[2] http://www.fireball4smartcities.eu/

The SMARTCAMPUS implementation defines a CPS based on two layers: micro-controllers (sensors and sensor boards) and nano-computer (bridging the sensor network and the Internet). Sensor measurements are sent to a sensor board, which aggregates sensors physically connected to it. The board is usually implemented by a micro-controller that collects data and send them to its associated bridge. A bridge aggregates data coming from multiple sensor boards (thanks to radio or wire-based protocols) and broadcasts on the Internet the received streams to a data collection API, using classical Ethernet connection.

In our example we consider two users, Alice and Bob, who need to use the same sensors to build their own application. Alice develops an application exploiting the associated LSI by collecting data from a temperature sensor every couple of second. Without any specific support, she has to write *(i)* code to be enacted on the different micro-controllers linked to temperature sensors (an infinite loop measuring the temperature every 2 seconds), *(ii)* code to aggregates these data at the bridge level (reading the data sent by the micro-controllers in proprietary representations, and sending it to the cloud-based collector, after having performed data translation from micro-controller format to the collector one), and finally *(iii)* the code that exploits the collected data to implement her application. We claim here that only the latter should be Alice's concern. On his side, Bob develops an application exploiting a temperature sensor each second and a humidity sensor every three seconds. He needs to perform the same kinds of actions as Alice : *(i)* writing the code that reads temperature sensors each second and humidity sensors every 3 seconds, *(ii)* aggregating these data at the bridge level and *(iii)* implementing his application exploiting the collected data.

As simple as this example is, it illustrates the identified requirements. Both users will need to use the same temperature sensor (R_1), and as they have different usages of this sensor, we do not want them to be flooded with non-desirable data (R_2). As the sensor network evolves and has to support new users (*i.e.*, the arrival of Bob), it needs to dynamically adapt the data collection policies (R_3). Finally, as the sensor networks is going to be heterogeneous and composed of different layers (*i.e.*, collection and network), the produced code must automatically fit the infrastructure (R_4).

3   Contribution: The COSmIC Framework

To address the four identified requirements, we propose the *COSmIC* framework, a set of *Composition Operators for Sensing InfrastruCtures*. This section describes the foundations underlying the framework.

3.1   Data Collection Policies as Timed Automata

In sensor networks, automata are commonly used for protocol modeling, and component model approaches [23] are used to develop embedded applications, focusing on the definition of *Interface Automaton* between each components. These automaton-based interfaces enable the different components. We propose to leverage this representation to *(i)* model the data collection policy expressed by the developer, implementing what she expects from an LSI through code generation *(ii)* compose and decompose (dynamically) these policies to handle sharing and infrastructure diversity.

We define a data collection policy $p = \langle Q, \delta, q_0 \rangle$ as a simplification of a classical timed automaton. Q is the set of states defined by the automaton, $\delta : Q \to Q$, its (deterministic) transition function from a given state to another one and finally q_0 its initial state. In real LSIs, tick period is rarely lesser than one second, thus our model assumes a single logical clock that triggers a transition each second. As a policy aims to be indefinitely executed on an LSI, it must be cyclic, and the length of the cycle represents the period of p, denoted as P_p. A given state $q \in Q$ contains an ordered set of actions A implementing the way the developer interacts with the LSI.

In our example, the corresponding policy for Alice p_a is represented by an automaton (depicted in FIG. 1) with two states $\{a_1, a_2\}$.

As a policy needs to be enacted on different platforms, user requirements are translated into a set of basic operations:

– *read*: Read the value of a *sensor*, e.g., for actions used in our temperature and humidity example.
– *emit*: Send a value to an external *endpoint*, which is usually implemented as a Web service exposing a destination URL for the collected data.

According to this representation and the associated actions, a software developer is able to model what she expects from the LSI for her given use case. The key point is that the developer is completely unaware of the internal implementation of the LSI, and only focuses on reading sensor values and sending data over communication interfaces.

3.2   The Generator Operator (γ)

The designed models are useless if not coupled to code generation algorithms that transform these logical representations into executable code. One of the main issues to tackle here is the variability existing between the different hardware elements that compose an LSI (R_4). For example, at the micro-controller level, a plain Arduino board does not support the *emit* action, whereas an Arduino coupled to an Ethernet communication shield supports it.

We thus define a code generator γ as a couple of functions (pre, do), each consuming as input a policy p. The *pre* function checks a set of preconditions on

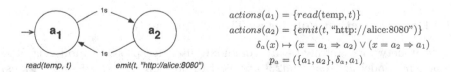

$$actions(a_1) = \{read(\text{temp}, t)\}$$
$$actions(a_2) = \{emit(t, \text{"http://alice:8080"})\}$$
$$\delta_a(x) \mapsto (x = a_1 \Rightarrow a_2) \vee (x = a_2 \Rightarrow a_1)$$
$$p_a = (\{a_1, a_2\}, \delta_a, a_1)$$

Fig. 1. Excerpt of a data collection policy

p to ensure that this policy can be projected to the hardware platform targeted by p. The *do* function takes as input the policy to transform, as well as additional parameters given by the environment. These parameters map logical names to physical elements when relevant (*e.g.*, sensors on an Arduino platform are only identified by the pin number they are plugged in). In a production environment, the generators are not executed by the developer herself. She will only express her needs, and will enact them on the LSI which actually knows its internal infrastructure.

For example, we consider here the policy p_a defined in the previous section, and an Arduino platform as generation target. The corresponding precondition checker assesses the absence of *emit* actions in the following way:

$$pred_{ard}(p) \mapsto \forall q \in Q_b, \nexists emit(\_, \_) \in actions(q) \tag{1}$$

In this case, the checker detects that this policy cannot be deployed on an infrastructure based solely on Arduino, as this hardware does not match the requirements expressed in the policy, *i.e.*, emiting a data to the Internet.

Considering a policy p valid for the Arduino platform (the decomposition operator described in the next section shows how to make p_a valid), the do_{ard} function then visits p to produce the code to be executed on the board, using the Wiring[3] language as target. It also takes as input a *map* acting as a registry (stored in the LSI environment) binding a sensor name to the physical pin that connects it to the board. LST. 1.1 shows the resulting code for a board coupled to temperature sensor *temp* on pin 9 and an humidity one *hum* on pin 10. The generator maps actions such as $read(temp, t)$ into Wiring code like v_t = analogRead(9).

```
1  void setup() { // Initialization
2    pinMode(9,INPUT); pinMode(10,INPUT);
3  }
4  void a1() {
5    v_t = analogRead(9); v_h = analogRead(10);
6    delay(1000); return a2();
7  }
8  void a2() {
9    v_t = analogRead(9);
10   delay(1000); return a1();
11 }
12 void loop() { return a1(); } // Entry point
```

Listing 1.1. Generated code example: $do_{ard}(p)$

Code generators also allow users to reuse their policy for different sensing infrastructures as a given COSmIC policy can be translated to many targets.

3.3   The Decomposition Operator (δ)

Considering a given policy, it has to be decomposed into software artifacts that make sense on the different layers of the LSI, *i.e.*, the micro-controller and bridge layers. For each layer, there may be actions that are incompatible with the hardware. Consequently, a given policy p must be decomposed into n layer-specific sub-policies p'_{layer} (where n is the number of layers) that communicate together

---

[3] Wiring is an open-source framework for micro-controllers (http://wiring.org.co/).

and where incompatible actions are substituted by internal communication [20]. This decomposition is performed thanks to a compatibility table T. A function $f_T(a, P)$ applied on this table returns a boolean value reflecting the compatibility of an action a on the platform P^4. This decomposition process is defined as follows:

$$\delta(p) \equiv \forall a \in p, \forall P \in layers, f_T(a, P) \Rightarrow a \in p'_a \tag{2}$$

If we consider micro-controllers implemented by Arduino boards and bridges implemented by Raspberry nano-computers, the micro-controller level will not support the emission of data to external endpoints, due to a lack of proper communication interface. In our example, Alice's policy will be decomposed by the operator into two sub-policies: $\delta(p_a) = \{p'_{mic}, p'_{bri}\}$. Consequently, the p_{mic} will read the sensor value and send it to an internal endpoint (substitution of the *emit* action) thanks to the serial communication that links the sensor board to its bridge. This policy is accepted by the $pred_{ard}$ function defined in the Arduino code generator, meaning that p_{mic} can be deployed on such hardware. The p_{bri} policy is executed on the bridge to read the internal communication port and emit the received data to the external endpoint.

3.4   The Composition Operator ($\oplus$)

On a shared LSI, policies designed by different developers will be executed on the very same piece of hardware COSmIC provides a composition operator denoted as $\oplus$ at the automaton level. It composes two given policies and produces a single policy containing an automaton corresponding strictly to the parallel composition of the two inputs.

The $\oplus$-operator assimilates a timed automaton implementing a policy p with a period P_p as a periodic function. The composition of two periodic functions f_1 and f_2 is a periodic function $f = f_1 \circ f_2$ where its period P_f is the least common multiple of P_{f_1} and P_{f_2}. Applied to policies, this means that the composition of two policies p_1 and p_2, denoted as $p = p_1 \oplus p_2$ is a policy with a period $P_p = lcm(P_{p_1}, P_{p_2})$, where each actions of p_1 (respectively p_2) are executed according to P_{p_1} (respectively P_{p_2}). As this $\oplus$-operator is endogenous, it allows a software developer to dynamically reuse a policy by composing it with new incoming policies.

In our example, the policies defined by Alice in p_a and Bob in p_b will exploit the same temperature sensor on the same micro-controller and use the same bridge to emit their values. More details on the composition and decomposition processes are given in SEC. 4.2.

4   Assessment

In this section, we describe the current implementation and its application to our prototypical LSI. Then, we show how COSmIC can be used to model and deploy the running example. We validate our identified requirements through some acceptance criteria and finally discuss threats to validity.

---

[4] An example of such a table is given in SEC. 4.2.

4.1   Implementation and Application

The initial prototype of the COSmIC framework is available on GitHub[5]. It is implemented with the Scala language ($\sim$ 3500 lines of code) and covers all the concepts presented in SEC. 3. We are currently experimenting COSmIC on Arduino, Raspberry Pi and Cubieboard platforms as part of the SMARTCAMPUS project. We also used the FIT IoT-lab platform[6], featuring a pool of over 2700 sensors nodes spread across France, to experiment on the ARM Cortex M3 platform.

To experiment and demonstrate the abstraction of platforms, code generation capabilities, sharing and reuse, we have modeled four identified SMARTCAMPUS scenarios and then generated code for each platform type we experiment with:

- *S1 - Late worker detection*: at night, occupied offices are detected by checking if the light is on (*light sensor*) and if there is someone in the office (*presence sensor*);
- *S2 - Fire prevention*: a warning signal on a temperature threshold (*temperature sensor*);
- *S3 - Heat monitoring*: air-conditioning and heating are controlled by checking the ambient air in buildings (*temperature sensor*);
- *S4 - Energy wasting*: To comply with environmental standards, the quality manager wants to monitor light kept on when the building is empty (*light sensor* and *presence sensor*).

Table 1 presents the number of lines of code (LoC) generated for each platform. Every code generator includes a static overhead (template code), specific to the targeted platform. This template provides the implementation of methods called by the COSmIC code generation. The corresponding LoC (italic row on TAB. 1) vary between platforms as some of them are providing more features. The Raspberry Pi template contains only 85 LoC, corresponding to serial reading and value emission on the Internet (a Raspberry Pi cannot read values directly from sensors in the SMARTCAMPUS infrastructure). On the other hand, the ARM Cortex M3 template comprises 169 LoC to handle its sensor and network interface. Using a template is efficient as we target low-level platforms, and those functions encapsulate a part of their complexity. For example, a method provided in the ARM Cortex M3 template handles the IPv6 retrieval of sensor measures from a border-router.

We can first observe that without considering the boilerplate code defined in the templates, there is no real difference in terms of LoC between COSmIC and the underlying programming languages. This is not surprising as the design choice of using templates hides low-level details to raise the level of abstraction of each platform. But the key point is that the code written with the COSmIC framework is not a single-target code but actually a model, which can be verified, composed automatically and projected to multiple platforms. Another interesting property is that users do not need to know the underlying platform. For example, if a policy relies only on digital sensors, one can use the Contiki operating system [8] to use a thread-based implementation of this policy. If a new

---

[5] http://ace-design.github.io/cosmic/
[6] https://www.iot-lab.info/

Table 1. LoC resulting from scenario generation

	Arduino native	Arduino contiki	Raspberry / Python	ARM Cortex M3 / Python	COSmIC source
Template	*13*	*22*	*85*	*169*	*0*
S_1	6	14	13	11	7
S_2	5	13	11	10	5
S_3	5	13	11	10	7
S_4	6	14	13	11	7
$S = S_1 \oplus S_2 \oplus S_3 \oplus S_4$	63	51	45	39	27
Deployed: S + *Template*	76	73	160	208	N/A

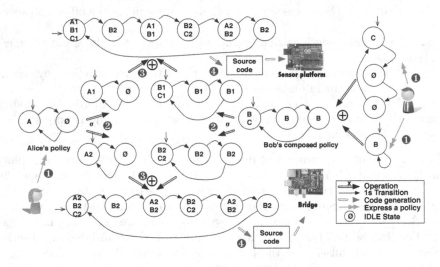

Fig. 2. COSmIC processes on the running example

requirement including values coming from analog sensors needs to be enacted on the same board, Contiki cannot be used anymore and the implementation must be completely rebuilt using only native operations. This is not the case with COSmIC: the two policies will be automatically composed, and it simply implies to change the call to the code generator as the Contiki one will reject the composed policy.

4.2 Illustration

We illustrate the application of the COSmIC operators from policy definition to code generation on the Alice and Bob example (see SEC. 2.3), on the top of the SMARTCAMPUS infrastructure[7]. FIG. 2 gives an overview of the different activities.

---

[7] More details can be found on a companion web page:
https://github.com/ace-design/cosmic/blob/master/publications/ICSR15.md

❶ *Policies definition.* In a first step, both users have to define their data collection policies in terms of timed automaton. The Alice's timed automaton p_a is already presented in SEC. 3.1. Bob has to express two policies: *(i)* temperature collection policy (p_{bt}) and *(ii)* humidity collection policy (p_{bh}). Bob uses the $\oplus$-operator to build a single policy p_b containing both temperature collection and humidity collection policies.

❷ *Decomposition process.* The next step is related to the decomposition process thanks to the δ-operator. Policies p_a and p_b are global policies that contain incompatible actions for the Arduino micro-controller (e.g. the *emit* action) platform and for the Raspberry nano-computer (e.g. the *read sensor* action). The appropriate compatibility table (TAB. 2) drives the decomposition process, reifying the compatibility of actions per platform.

As presented in SEC. 3.3, incompatible actions are substituted by internal communications. After this decomposition process, four layer specific sub-policies are obtained:

$$\delta(p_a) = \{p_{amic}; p_{abri}\} \qquad \delta(p_b) = \{p_{bmic}; p_{bbri}\} \tag{3}$$

❸ *Composition process.* These four sub-policies will be then deployed on the shared infrastructure. The $\oplus$-operator will compose those policies and allow Alice and Bob to exploit the same piece of hardware. p_{amic} is composed with p_{bmic}, and p_{abri} is composed with p_{bbri}:

$$p_{amic} \oplus p_{bmic} = p_{\text{Sensor platform}} \qquad p_{abri} \oplus p_{bbri} = p_{\text{Bridge}} \tag{4}$$

The composition process is an endogenous operation returning a policy that can be reused to be composed, possibly in a dynamic way, with future policies. $p_{\text{Sensor platform}}$ and p_{Bridge} are the policies that will be instantiated on the infrastructure.

❹ *Code generation.* The final step of the deployment process is handled by code generators working directly on the two latter policies. The generated codes are then flashed on the appropriate micro-controllers and bridges using classical LSI deployment tools. At runtime, Alice and Bob will receive sensor values for their application according to their respective needs, although the same sensor is used for both of them.

4.3   Validation

To validate the four requirements presented in SEC. 2, we define an acceptance criterion for each of them and discuss how they are met.

Table 2. Excerpt of the COSmIC compatibility table

	Arduino Uno	Raspberry Pi	ARM Cortex M3
read	✓	✗	✓
emit	✗	✓	✓

R_1: *Pooling and Sharing - More than one application can rely on a given sensor.* The illustration in SEC. 4.2 shows that different policies can be enacted on the sensing infrastructure to feed different applications. We performed also this validation on the SMARTCAMPUS infrastructure with four scenarios (cf. SEC. 4.1). In this context Table 3 illustrates that the same sensor will be used for different scenarios, validating requirement R_1.

R_2: *Yield only relevant data - A given application is only fed with what it expects.* As shown in our illustration (SEC. 4.2), a COSmIC user models her data collection policies with timed automaton and triggering of *emit* actions with requested data periodically. The composition operator also maintains this property by construction. It handles two policies p_1 and p_2 respectively T_1 and T_2 periodic, and produces a new lcm(T_1,T_2)-periodic policy. This process is transparent for COSmIC users as her expressed policy will not be modified while she will only receive data as specified in her initial policy. This validates requirement R_2.

R_3: *Dynamically support data collection policies - Multiple policies can be dynamically composed.* The ⊕-operator allows the composition of data collection policies on a sensor network. In the illustration (SEC. 4.2), Bob's policies have been composed into a single one using the ⊕-operator. The resulting policy can be used by other operators. Therefore, when a new policy needs to be added to the sensor network, one has just to compose it with the already deployed policy. This endogenous property validates requirement R_3.

R_4: *Handling the infrastructure diversity - A given code can be deployed on more than one infrastructure.* The infrastructure hardware variability is handled with code generators. These code generators handle a COSmIC DSL input code and produce the code for a given platform. We have successfully modeled and deployed the SMARTCAMPUS scenarios on Arduino, Raspberry Pi and ARM Cortex M3 platforms, validating requirement R_4.

4.4   Threats to Validity

Scenarios. Our approach is only applied to the SMARTCAMPUS context. Even if the corresponding scenarios have been validated through questionnaires and are close to other case studies such as SmartSantander [19], we are aware that we

Table 3. Sensor sharing

	Light	Temperature	Presence
Scenario 1 - Late worker detection	✓		✓
Scenario 2 - Fire prevention		✓	
Scenario 3 - Heat monitoring		✓	
Scenario 4 - Energy wasting	✓		✓

need to step back and introduce more complex scenarios to benchmark COSmIC on a larger scale.

Timed automata. Our data collection policies are represented by timed automata. If this approach fits the SMARTCAMPUS use case, the combination of different scenarios can lead to a combinatorial explosion, (*e.g.*, collections on a shared sensor at frequencies of one second and one hour would lead to a 3600 states automaton with only two relevant states). The code generation process is impacted by such automata. We currently reduce the size of such automata thanks to a factorization process, but this optimization does not scale with a large number of concurrent scenarios. The use of such automata also impacts the resources. Platforms have to be always powered on, to the detriment of the battery autonomy, to maintain a running clock delivering periodic clock tick. Devising better techniques to handle such cases and providing resource management is part of our future work.

Action execution duration. Our automata represent clocks with a 1 Hz frequency. If the execution of an action is longer than one second, it might be overlapped and aborted by the state transition leading the policy into an inconsistent state. In the future, we plan to use languages based on the formal Clock Constraint Specification Language (CCSL) [6] to determine the duration of action execution and to ensure the temporal correctness of policies.

Deployment of new policies. Our approach handles the dynamic composition of data collection policies and code generation for a given platform. However, we do not support dynamic deployment as some sensor platforms need to be reflashed with a new firmware. When the platform support it, we rely on operating systems (*e.g.*, Contiki) to support this feature.

5   Related Work

Programming sensor networks with specific OS. Several operating systems have been specifically designed for sensing infrastructures, *e.g.*, TinyOS [14] or Contiki [8]. TinyOS is based on a component architecture and comes with its programming language NesC. A developer can create new components or reuse components from the TinyOS's component library to build her own application. Contiki is adapted for networked and resource-constrained devices. Contiki applications can be written and compiled using a specific C compiler. Those OS abstract some complexities of application development, such as memory or energy optimization, but the developer has to be aware of what kind of sensor platforms she is using, directly dealing with their implementation details at a lower level. This leads to a lack of reusability, whereas our approach introduces a generic way to program sensor network. The COSmIC code is written independently from a sensing infrastructure and code generators handle the transformation to a targeted platform.

Sensor network as a database. On top of operating systems deployed on sensing infrastructure, several approaches consider the sensor network itself as a database [7]. Storing the data as close as possible to the sensor producing it instead of pushing everything to the Cloud was demonstrated as cost-efficient and energy saving [22]. The TinyDB system [16] (not maintained since 2005) provides processing mechanisms for sensor querying and data retrieval. It considers a sensor as a micro-database storing their collected data, and allows developers to query sensors according to different criteria (*e.g.*, location). The Cougar system [24] also considers data collected by sensors, and supports users by only expressing queries that are automatically propagated to the sensors. This system does not support sharing (as queries cannot be composed easily), and relies on a centralized engine that computes a collection planning and collects data. On the contrary, COSmIC fully distributes the policies to the different sensors and the infrastructure layers, and supports multiple endpoints for each application.

Model-driven and generative approaches. The model-driven development paradigm has been notably used to design dynamically adaptive systems and to evolve them at runtime [18]. In this approach, the current context model is analyzed at runtime and, if an adaptation needs to be performed, a suitable configuration is built thanks to reference models. The approach can fit lightweight nodes in a sensor network [11]. Our work differs as we do not perform adaptiveness according to the context but design sensor network applications with policies based on a composition equation that can be reused for other compositions or for verification purposes. Exploiting runtime composition is a perspective of our work. The way we generate code is close to the Scalaness approach [5]. It is a type-safe language used to wirelessly program embedded networks running under TinyOS. Two stages are required to program these networks: (*i*) one writes a Scalaness program, which is then (*ii*) translated into Java bytecode. We differ from this approach as we use behavior models to generate code and we do not always have the same destination platforms as we target heterogeneous sensor networks.

6   Conclusions and Perspectives

In this paper we have presented the *COSmIC* Framework used for supporting different developers' collect policies on a shared LSI, generating code deployed at the approriate layer of the LSI. It addresses several limitations of classical approaches, focusing on the sharing of the infrastructure and the production of relevant-only datasets, and allowing software developers to focus on their concerns instead of LSI implementation details. The framework is implemented using the Scala language and preliminary experiments have been conducted on top of the SMARTCAMPUS platform [4]. The *COSmIC* framework is a first step for composing policies on an LSI, with a focus on policy definition and composition operators.

Future work aims at extending the approach and making it scale to very large LSIs. First, we will extend this set of operators to build a complete composition algebra, with a formal definition of operator properties (*e.g.*, commutativity, associativity, idempotency), conflict detection mechanisms to prevent inconsistent states (*i.e.*, sending a value before reading it) and a formal support to attach constraints to actions. We also plan to extend these constraints to timed ones, using the TimeSquare toolkit [6] to specify and analyze constraints based on its logical time model and to check them also at runtime. We also plan to en-large the set of interactions with the LSI by introducing new actions allowing a developer to perform some data computation within the sensor network (*e.g.*, Compute the average value of data coming from different sensors.

For those developers, we will improve the available abstractions by providing a higher level DSL. It will notably hide the creation and management of states and transitions, providing a real focus on what data are collected, processed and used in applications.

The decomposition operator also triggers interesting challenges with respect to the variability of hardware (*i.e.*, Arduino, Phidgets platforms) and facilities (*i.e.*, Supported programming language, resources available) available in the context of LSIs. We plan to use a feature modeling [2] approach to capture this variability, and to bind these models to the generation mechanisms, providing a variable code generation according to the available hardware in a given LSI. Finally, we also plan to support policy composition and variability reasoning at runtime to handle dynamic adaptiveness. We expect the resulting tooled approach to provide an end-to-end support for developers of the massively under-deployment sensing infrastructures.

References

1. Aggarwal, C.C. (ed.): Managing and Mining Sensor Data. Springer (2013)
2. Apel, S., Batory, D.S., Kästner, C., Saake, G.: Feature-Oriented Software Product Lines - Concepts and Implementation. Springer (2013)
3. Buratti, C., Conti, A., Dardari, D., Verdone, R.: An overview on wireless sensor networks technology and evolution. Sensors 9(9), 6869–6896 (2009), http://www.mdpi.com/1424-8220/9/9/6869
4. Cecchinel, C., Jimenez, M., Mosser, S., Riveill, M.: An Architecture to Support the Collection of Big Data in the Internet of Things. In: International Workshop on Ubiquitous Mobile Cloud (UMC 2014, Co-located with SERVICES 2014), pp. 1–8. IEEE, Anchorage (2014)
5. Chapin, P.C., Skalka, C., Smith, S.F., Watson, M.: Scalaness/nesT: Type Special-ized Staged Programming for Sensor Networks. In: Järvi, J., Kästner, C. (eds.) GPCE, pp. 135–144. ACM (2013)
6. DeAntoni, J., Mallet, F.: TimeSquare: Treat your Models with Logical Time. In: Furia, C.A., Nanz, S. (eds.) TOOLS Europe 2012. LNCS, vol. 7304, pp. 34–41. Springer, Heidelberg (2012)
7. Diao, Y., Ganesan, D., Mathur, G., Shenoy, P.J.: Rethinking data management for storage-centric sensor networks. In: Third Biennial Conference on Innovative Data Systems Research, CIDR 2007, Asilomar, CA, USA, January 7-10, pp. 22–31 (2007)
8. Dunkels, A., Gronvall, B., Voigt, T.: Contiki - A lightweight and flexible operating system for tiny networked sensors. In: 29th Annual IEEE International Conference on Local Computer Networks, pp. 455–462 (November 2004)
9. Fambon, O., Fleury, E., Harter, G., Pissard-Gibollet, R., Saint-Marcel, F.: Fit iot-lab tutorial: Hands-on practice with a very large scale testbed tool for the internet of things. In: 10èmes Journées Francophones Mobilité et Ubiquité (UbiMob), pp. 1–5 (June 2014)

10. Fleurey, F., Morin, B., Solberg, A.: A Model-Driven Approach to Develop Adaptive Firmwares. In: Giese, H., Cheng, B.H.C. (eds.) SEAMS, pp. 168–177. ACM (2011)
11. Fouquet, F., Morin, B., Fleurey, F., Barais, O., Plouzeau, N., Jezequel, J.M.: A Dynamic Component Model for Cyber Physical Systems. In: Proceedings of the 15th ACM SIGSOFT Symposium on Component Based Software Engineering, CBSE 2012, pp. 135–144. ACM, New York (2012)
12. Gluhak, A., Krco, S., Nati, M., Pfisterer, D., Mitton, N., Razafindralambo, T.: A Survey on Facilities for Experimental Internet of Things Research. IEEE Communications Magazine 49(11), 58–67 (2011), http://hal.inria.fr/inria-00630092
13. Gubbi, J., Buyya, R., Marusic, S., Palaniswami, M.: Internet of Things (IoT): A Vision, Architectural Elements, and Future Directions. Future Generation Comp. Syst. 29(7), 1645–1660 (2013)
14. Levis, P., Madden, S., Polastre, J., Szewczyk, R., Woo, A., Gay, D., Hill, J., Welsh, M., Brewer, E., Culler, D.: Tinyos: An operating system for sensor networks. In: Ambient Intelligence. Springer (2004)
15. LogMeIn: Xively (May 2014), http://xively.com/
16. Madden, S.R., Franklin, M.J., Hellerstein, J.M., Hong, W.: Tinydb: An acquisitional query processing system for sensor networks. ACM Trans. Database Syst. 30(1), 122–173 (2005), http://doi.acm.org/10.1145/1061318.1061322
17. Mahmood, A., Ke, S., Khatoon, S., Xiao, M.: Data mining techniques for wireless sensor networks: A survey. IJDSN 2013 (2013)
18. Morin, B., Barais, O., Jezequel, J., Fleurey, F., Solberg, A.: Models@run.time to Support Dynamic Adaptation. Computer 42(10), 44–51 (2009)
19. Sanchez, L., Galache, J., Gutierrez, V., Hernandez, J., Bernat, J., Gluhak, A., Garcia, T.: Smartsantander: The meeting point between future internet research and experimentation and the smart cities. In: Future Network Mobile Summit (FutureNetw), pp. 1–8 (June 2011)
20. Stickel, M.E.: A Unification Algorithm for Associative-Commutative Functions. J. ACM 28(3), 423–434 (1981)
21. Tonneau, A.S., Mitton, N., Vandaele, J.: A Survey on (mobile) wireless sensor network experimentation testbeds. In: DCOSS - IEEE International Conference on Distributed Computing in Sensor Systems, Marina Del Rey, California, États-Unis (May 2014), http://hal.inria.fr/hal-00988776
22. Tsiftes, N., Dunkels, A.: A database in every sensor. In: Proceedings of the 9th ACM Conference on Embedded Networked Sensor Systems, SenSys 2011, pp. 316–332. ACM, New York (2011), http://doi.acm.org/10.1145/2070942.2070974
23. Völgyesi, P., Maróti, M., Dóra, S., Osses, E., Lédeczi, Á.: Software Composition and Verification for Sensor Networks. Sci. Comput. Program. 56(1-2), 191–210 (2005)
24. Yao, Y., Gehrke, J.: The cougar approach to in-network query processing in sensor networks. SIGMOD Rec. 31(3), 9–18 (2002), http://doi.acm.org/10.1145/601858.601861

Flexible and Efficient Reuse of Multi-mode Components for Building Multi-mode Systems

Hang Yin and Hans Hansson

Mälardalen Real-Time Research Centre,
Mälardalen University, Västerås, Sweden
{young.hang.yin,hans.hansson}@mdh.se

Abstract. Software component reuse is deemed as an effective technique for managing the growing software complexity of large systems. Software complexity can also be reduced by partitioning the system behavior into different modes. Such a multi-mode system can change behavior by switching between modes under certain circumstances. Integrating component reuse and the multi-mode approach, we have developed the Mode Switch Logic (MSL), a framework dedicated to the development of multi-mode systems composed by reusable multi-mode components, i.e. components which can run in different modes. The mode switch handling of MSL is based on a fully distributed architecture in the sense that a system mode switch is achieved by the joint mode switches of different independently developed components. In this paper, we propose a mode transformation technique as a supplement to MSL for converting the distributed mode switch handling of MSL to a centralized mode switch handling. The goal is to enhance the run-time mode switch efficiency when components are deployed on a single hardware platform and global mode information is available. We demonstrate this technique by an example and reveal its potential industrial value.

Keywords: component reuse, mode switch, mode transformation.

1 Introduction

The growing software complexity is posing a challenge to the software development of complex systems. Component-Based Software Engineering (CBSE) [4] is a promising design paradigm for managing software complexity at design time, characterized by the reuse of independently developed software components. The success of CBSE has been evidenced by a number of component models [5,19]. As a complementary approach, software complexity can be reduced at both design time and runtime by partitioning the system behavior into different operational modes. Such a multi-mode system is able to change its run-time behavior by switching modes under certain conditions. For instance, the control software of an airplane could run in the modes *taxi*, *taking off*, *flight* and *landing*.

Building on the advantages of both CBSE and multi-mode systems, we aim at exploring theoretical foundations for developing multi-mode systems by reusing

I. Schaefer and I. Stamelos (Eds.): ICSR 2015, LNCS 8919, pp. 237–252, 2014.

multi-mode components, i.e. components which can run in different modes. Figure 1 illustrates the component hierarchy of a component-based system. The system, i.e. Component a, consists of components b, c and d. Component c is composed by e and f, while d is composed by g and h. Among these components, b, e, f, g, and h are *primitive components* which are directly implemented by code, while a, c, and d are *composite components* composed by other components. The tree structure of the component hierarchy implies a parent-and-children relationship between each composite component and the components directly composing it. For instance, a is the parent of b, c, d which in turn are the subcomponents or children of a. What makes this system distinctive compared with traditional component-based systems is that some of its components may run in multiple modes. For example, depicted in Fig. 1, a is a multi-mode component which can run in two modes: m_a^1 and m_a^2, with each mode being represented by a unique local configuration. When a runs in mode m_a^1, d is deactivated (represented by the dimmed color); when a runs in m_a^2, d becomes activated and extra connections are established within a. In addition, b exhibits different mode-specific behaviors (distinguished by black and grey colors) when a is running in different modes. Similar to a, the other components may also support multiple modes. All the components in Fig. 1 can be reused together with their supported modes.

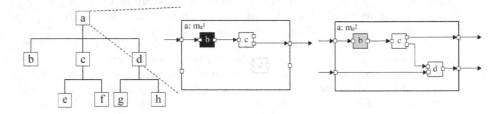

Fig. 1. A multi-mode system built by reusable multi-mode components

The key challenges of reusing multi-mode components are the seamless composition of multi-mode components and mode switch handling. To overcome these challenges, we have developed a framework—the Mode Switch Logic (MSL) [7]. In MSL, each component has its own mode switch run-time mechanism (MSRM) controlling its behavior and how it communicates with other components during a mode switch at runtime. Since we only allow a component to exchange mode information with its parent and subcomponents, a mode switch can be jointly handled by a number of components without any component knowing the global information.

A practical issue that MSL has not addressed is mode switch run-time efficiency. For a system where all the components are deployed onto the same physical hardware platform and the mode information of all components is globally accessible, it is more efficient to use a global mode switch manager to handle mode switch. Then there will be no need for each component to run its own MSRM and communicate with other components, thus reducing mode switch time and run-time mode switch overhead. As the contribution of this paper, we provide a mode transformation technique that improves the run-time mode switch efficiency of MSL by transforming component modes to system modes to be handled by the global mode switch manager. After mode transformation, a mode switch process is facilitated as the system can directly switch from one mode to another mode without intercommunication between components.

The remainder of the paper is organized as follows: Section 2 gives a brief introduction of MSL. Section 3 presents our mode transformation technique which is further demonstrated in Section 4. Section 5 discusses the industrial value and verification of our approach, as well as some other practical issues. Related work is reviewed in Section 6. Finally, Section 7 concludes the paper and envisions some future work.

2   The Mode Switch Logic (MSL)

MSL includes three major elements: a mode-aware component model, a mode mapping mechanism, and a mode switch run-time mechanism (MSRM).

The mode-aware component model is not a full-fledged component model. Instead it captures the essential elements of any component model compatible with MSL, i.e. it specifies the fundamental features of a multi-mode component. Illustrated in Fig. 2, a multi-mode component can support multiple modes, with each mode being associated with a unique configuration. A mode switch is performed by reconfiguration, i.e. by changing its configuration in the current mode to another configuration in the new mode. The mode switch behavior of a multi-mode component is controlled by its MSRM. Each multi-mode component can exchange mode-related information with its parent and subcomponents via dedicated mode switch ports (marked in solid squares in Fig. 2).

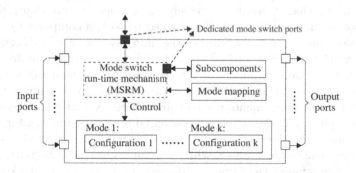

Fig. 2. A multi-mode component

Shown in Fig. 2, each composite multi-mode component has a mode mapping mechanism that interacts with its MSRM. This mechanism maps its modes to the modes of its subcomponents. Given the mode mapping, a composite component should know the current modes of its subcomponents for each of its current mode. Figure 3 lists the mode mappings of a, c, and d of the system in Fig. 1. Modes of the same column in the same table are mapped. For instance, indicated in Fig. 3(a), when a runs in mode m_a^1, b must run in m_b^1, c may run in either m_c^1 or m_c^3, and d is deactivated (denoted as D). Besides, if a composite component or one of its subcomponents switches mode, the composite component should know how this mode switch affects the modes of the other components among them. This is beyond the expression of the tables in Fig. 3, yet can be described by Mode Mapping Automata (MMAs) [7].

Component	Modes	
a	m_a^1	m_a^2
b	m_b^1	m_b^2
c	m_c^1 m_c^2	m_c^2
d	D	m_d^1

(a)

Component	Modes		
c	m_c^1	m_c^2	m_c^3
e	m_e^1 m_e^2	m_e^3	D
f	m_f^1		

(b)

Component	Modes	
d	m_d^1	
g	m_g^1	m_g^2
h	m_h^1	m_h^2

(c)

Fig. 3. The mode mappings of a, c, and d

In general, a mode switch can be either event-triggered or time-triggered. MSL considers event-triggered mode switch, where a mode switch is triggered by a mode switch event (e.g. when a sensor value reaches a pre-defined threshold). Time-triggered mode switch can be considered as a special case of event-triggered mode switch since timeouts resulting from the advancement of time are events. A mode switch event can be detected by any component (primitive or composite), called the *Mode Switch Source (MSS)*. An MSS may initiate a mode switch by triggering a *mode switch scenario*, or simply *scenario*, denoted as $c_i : m_{c_i}^1 \rightarrow m_{c_i}^2$, where c_i is the MSS, $m_{c_i}^1$ is the mode of c_i when it triggers the scenario, and $m_{c_i}^2$ is the mode that c_i wants to switch to. A scenario may imply the mode switch of some other components. For each scenario k, a component c_j is called a *Type A component* for k if k implies the mode switch of c_j. Otherwise, c_j is called a *Type B component* for k. Type A and Type B components for k can be identified by the mode mappings of the composite components of a system. It is the responsibility of the MSRM of each component to coordinate the mode switches of Type A components without disturbing Type B components.

Figure 4 depicts a mode switch process based on the example in Fig. 1. Component e is the MSS which triggers a scenario k, implying the mode switches of Type A components a, b, c, and f, while d, g, and h are Type B components for k. All components follow the same MSRM. Scenario k is propagated stepwise by a primitive msr^k (mode switch request) from e to Type A components. Upon receiving the msr^k, each component starts its reconfiguration, represented by the black bars in Fig. 4. After reconfiguration, each component except a sends another primitive msc^k (mode switch completion) to its parent. As composite components, a and c complete their mode switches only when their reconfigurations are completed and they have received all the expected msc^k primitives from their subcomponents. This explains the white bar in Fig. 4 which implies that a is still waiting for the msc^k from b and c after its reconfiguration.

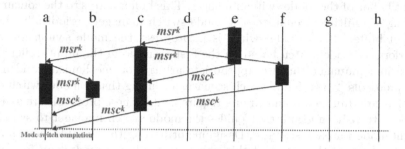

Fig. 4. A mode switch process following the MSRM

In Fig. 4, each component runs a simple MSRM, however, different MSRMs may be required depending on the system requirement. For instance, sometimes a mode switch may be taken only when all Type A components are ready to switch mode [9], or the MSRM may need to consider the concurrent triggering of different scenarios from different MSSs [8].

3   Mode Transformation

The value of MSL is mostly attributed to its support for the reuse of multi-mode components as it brings more flexible design choices for the software development of multi-mode components while preserving the benefits of CBSE. The distributed nature of the mode switch handling of MSL makes it possible to replace/add/remove components on the fly without reconfiguring the entire system. However, the mode switch process in Fig. 4 implies that the mode switch time could be rather long due to inter-component communication. This motivated us to develop the mode transformation technique, the main contribution of this paper, for transforming a system built by multi-mode components into a monolithic system. Given a system, the mode mappings of all its composite components, and the specification of all scenarios, the mode transformation technique is able to derive a *mode transition graph* of the entire system, including all the possible system modes and mode switches between them. Then the stepwise communication between components as illustrated in Fig. 4 will no longer be needed. Instead, a mode switch can be completed by a single transition between system modes, thereby enhancing run-time mode switch efficiency.

3.1   Overview

The purpose of mode transformation is to replace the distributed mode switch handling of MSL with a centralized solution which yields better run-time performance. Illustrated in Fig. 5, mode transformation transfers the responsibility of mode switch handling from the MSRM of each component to a single mode switch manager for the system. Figure 5 also showcases the internal overall structure of the mode switch manager. When a scenario is triggered, it is first stored in an input buffer of the mode switch manager. This buffer caters to the concurrent triggering of multiple scenarios. The mode switch manager periodically checks the input buffer. If no mode switch is in progress, the mode switch manager will perform a mode switch based on the first scenario in the input buffer. The mode switch manager can use appropriate arbitration mechanisms and mode switch protocols [21] to handle each scenario, ensuring that a mode switch does not violate any functional and timing requirements. These protocols are assisted by a mode transition graph that guides the mode switch manager to switch to the right mode for each scenario. Designing or finding the suitable mode switch protocols is out of the scope of this paper. Instead, our mode transformation technique focuses on the construction of the mode transition graph.

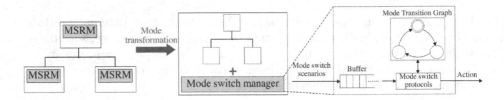

Fig. 5. Overview of the mode switch manager after mode transformation

Figure 6 presents the mode transformation process, including two sequential steps. First, given the mode mappings of all composite components, we construct an intermediate representation, a *Mode Combination Tree (MCT)* where all the possible system modes are identified. In the second step, the mode transition graph is constructed by adding all the possible transitions between the identified system modes according to the scenario specification. Next we shed light on the two transformation steps separately.

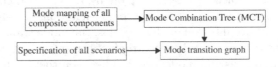

Fig. 6. The mode transformation process

3.2   Construction of the Mode Combination Tree

The purpose of constructing the MCT is to identify all the system modes:

Definition 1. *For a system composed by a set of components* $C = \{c_1, c_2, \cdots, c_n\}$ *($n \in \mathbb{N}$), a system mode* $m = \{(c_i, m_{c_i}) | i = [1, n]\}$ *is the mode combination of all components.*

Let *Top* be the component at the top of the component hierarchy. Let d_{c_i} denote the *depth level* of c_i in the component hierarchy, with $d_{Top} = 0$. Let $\mathcal{M}_{c_i}$ denote the set of supported modes of c_i. Moreover, let D denote the current mode of a deactivated component. Then the MCT is defined as follows:

Definition 2. *A Mode Combination Tree (MCT) is a tree with a set of nodes $\mathcal{N} = \{\mathcal{N}_0, \mathcal{N}_1, \cdots, \mathcal{N}_n\}$ ($n \in \mathbb{N}$), where $\mathcal{N}_0 = \varnothing$ is the root node, and each other node $\mathcal{N}_i = \{(c_j, m_{c_j}) | j = [1, k], k \in \mathbb{N}\}$, where for all j, $m_{c_j} \in \mathcal{M}_{c_j} \cup \{D\}$ and all c_j have the same depth level.*

Definition 2 implies that each node of an MCT, except for the root node, provides a mode combination of components with the same depth level. For instance, Fig. 7 shows an MCT based on the example in Fig. 1. Section 4 will demonstrate how this MCT is constructed.

To formally present the construction of the MCT, we need to introduce a number of additional notations and concepts. Let $\mathcal{PC}$ and $\mathcal{CC}$ be the set of primitive components and composite components of a system, respectively. Let $\mathcal{SC}_{c_i}$ be the set of subcomponents of c_i. For $c_i \in \mathcal{CC}$, a *valid local mode combination (LMC)* is defined as follows:

Definition 3. *For $c_i \in \mathcal{CC}$ with $\mathcal{SC}_{c_i} = \{c_j^1, \cdots, c_j^n\}$ ($n \in \mathbb{N}$), we call the set $\mathcal{V}_{c_i} = \{(c_i, m_{c_i}), (c_j^1, m_{c_j^1}), \cdots, (c_j^n, m_{c_j^n})\}$ a valid local mode combination (LMC) of c_i, if (1) $m_{c_i} \in \mathcal{M}_{c_i} \cup \{D\}$ and $\forall k = [1, n]$, $m_{c_j}^k \in \mathcal{M}_{c_j^k} \cup \{D\}$; and (2) m_{c_i} and all $m_{c_j^k}$ ($k = [1, n]$) can be simultaneously executed by the corresponding components, i.e. conforming to the mode mapping of c_i.*

When c_i is running in m_{c_i}, if $\forall c_j^k \in \mathcal{SC}_{c_i}$ ($k = [1, n]$), $\exists m_{c_j^k}$ s.t. $\{(c_i, m_{c_i}), (c_j^1, m_{c_j^1}), \cdots, (c_j^n, m_{c_j^n})\}$ is a valid LMC of c_i, then the set $\mathcal{V}_{c_i, m_{c_i}} = \{(c_j^1, m_{c_j^1}), \cdots, (c_j^n, m_{c_j^n})\}$ is a valid LMC of c_i for m_{c_i}.

Note that each element in $\mathcal{V}_{c_i}$ or $\mathcal{V}_{c_i, m_{c_i}}$ is a pair (x, y) where $x \in \mathcal{SC}_{c_i} \cup \{c_i\}$ for $\mathcal{V}_{c_i}$ and $x \in \mathcal{SC}_{c_i}$ for $\mathcal{V}_{c_i, m_{c_i}}$, and $y \in \mathcal{M}_x \cup \{D\}$. A better illustration can be found in Fig. 3(c) where both $\{(d, m_d^1), (g, m_g^1), (h, m_h^1)\}$ and $\{(d, m_d^1), (g, m_g^2), (h, m_h^2)\}$ are valid LMCs of d. Additionally, $\{(g, m_g^1), (h, m_h^1)\}$ and $\{(g, m_g^2), (h, m_h^2)\}$ are the valid LMCs of d for m_d^1.

Depending on the mode mapping of c_i, multiple valid LMCs of c_i may exist for m_{c_i}. Let $\mathcal{W}_{c_i, m_{c_i}}$ be the set of all valid LMCs of $c_i \in \mathcal{CC}$ for m_{c_i}. Each element in $\mathcal{W}_{c_i, m_{c_i}}$ is a set $\mathcal{V}_{c_i, m_{c_i}}$. The total number of all valid LMCs of c_i for m_{c_i} is $|\mathcal{W}_{c_i, m_{c_i}}|$. For instance, according to Fig. 3(b), $\mathcal{W}_{c, m_c^2} = \{\mathcal{V}_{c, m_c^2}^1, \mathcal{V}_{c, m_c^2}^1\}$, where $\mathcal{V}_{c, m_c^2}^1 = \{(e, m_e^2), (f, m_f^1)\}$ and $\mathcal{V}_{c, m_c^2}^2 = \{(e, m_e^3), (f, m_f^1)\}$. It is easy to automatically generate $\mathcal{W}_{c_i, m_{c_i}}$ based on the mode mapping of c_i.

Note that when a composite component c_i with $\mathcal{SC}_{c_i} = \{c_j^1, \cdots, c_j^n\}$ ($n \in \mathbb{N}$) is deactivated, all its enclosed components must also be deactivated. Hence $\mathcal{V}_{c_i, D} \equiv \{(c_j^1, D), \cdots, (c_j^n, D)\}$ and $|\mathcal{W}_{c_i, D}| = 1$.

Next we introduce an important operator for combining different valid LMCs:

Definition 4. *Let* $\mathcal{W}_1 = \{\mathcal{V}_1, \mathcal{V}_2, \cdots, \mathcal{V}_m\}$ *and* $\mathcal{W}_2 = \{\mathcal{V}_{k+1}, \mathcal{V}_{k+2}, \cdots, \mathcal{V}_{k+n}\}$, *where* $m, n, k \in \mathbb{N}$. *Then let* $\oplus$ *be an operator s.t.* $\mathcal{W}_1 \oplus \mathcal{W}_2 = \{\mathcal{V}_i \cup \mathcal{V}_{k+j} | i = [1, m], j = [1, n]\}$. *In addition, for each* $l \in \mathbb{N}$, $\mathcal{W}_1 \oplus \mathcal{W}_2 \oplus \cdots \oplus \mathcal{W}_l$ *can be represented as* $\bigoplus_{o=[1,l]} \mathcal{W}_o$.

Given the component hierarchy and the mode mappings of all composite components in the component hierarchy, the MCT of the system can be constructed by creating nodes top-down from the root node. For each node $\mathcal{N}$ of an MCT, let $d_\mathcal{N}$ be its depth level, and $\lambda_\mathcal{N}$ be the number of new nodes created from this node. We use $\mathcal{N}_i \succ \mathcal{N}_j$ to denote that a new node $\mathcal{N}_i$ is created from an old node $\mathcal{N}_j$. Moreover, let $\mathcal{M}_{Top} = \{m_T^1, m_T^2, \cdots, m_T^{|\mathcal{M}_{Top}|}\}$ be the set of supported modes of *Top*. The MCT is constructed by the following steps:

1. From $\mathcal{N}_0$, create $\lambda_{\mathcal{N}_0} = |\mathcal{M}_{Top}|$ new nodes, s.t. for each new node $\mathcal{N}_i \succ \mathcal{N}_0$, $\mathcal{N}_i = \{(Top, m_T^i)\}$ $(i = [1, |\mathcal{M}_{Top}|])$.
2. From each $\mathcal{N}_i = \{(Top, m_T^i)\}$ $(i = [1, |\mathcal{M}_{Top}|])$, create $\lambda_{\mathcal{N}_i} = |\mathcal{W}_{Top, m_T^i}|$ new nodes, s.t. for each $\mathcal{N}' \succ \mathcal{N}_i$, $\mathcal{N}' \in \mathcal{W}_{Top, m_T^i}$. Moreover, if $\lambda_{\mathcal{N}_i} > 1$, then for each $\mathcal{N}', \mathcal{N}'' \succ \mathcal{N}_i$, $\mathcal{N}' \neq \mathcal{N}''$.
3. From each node $\mathcal{N} = \{(c_1, m_{c_1}), (c_2, m_{c_2}), \cdots, (c_n, m_{c_n})\}$ $(n \in \mathbb{N})$ with $d_\mathcal{N} \geq 2$, if $\forall i = [1, n]$, $c_i \in \mathcal{PC}$, then $\mathcal{N}$ is marked as a leaf node and no new node is created from $\mathcal{N}$. Otherwise, if $\exists i = [1, n]$ s.t. $c_i \in \mathcal{CC}$, then create
$$\lambda_\mathcal{N} = \prod_{\substack{i=[1,n], \\ c_i \in \mathcal{CC}}} |\mathcal{W}_{c_i, m_{c_i}}| \text{ new nodes, s.t. for each } \mathcal{N}' \succ \mathcal{N}, \mathcal{N}' \in \bigoplus_{\substack{i=[1,n], \\ c_i \in \mathcal{CC}}} \mathcal{W}_{c_i, m_{c_i}}.$$
Moreover, if $\lambda_\mathcal{N} > 1$, then for each $\mathcal{N}', \mathcal{N}'' \succ \mathcal{N}$, $\mathcal{N}' \neq \mathcal{N}''$.
4. Repeat Step 3 until all branches of the MCT have reached the leaf node.

A remarkable property of an MCT is that all leaf nodes have the same depth level. Once the MCT is constructed, the system modes can be derived as a path from the root node to a leaf node of the MCT. Let $\mathcal{N}^k$ be the set of nodes of an MCT with depth level k. Then,

Theorem 1. *Given an MCT, a system mode is represented by a valid mode combination* $\bigcup_{i=0}^{\delta} \mathcal{N}_i$ *where* $\mathcal{N}_i \in \mathcal{N}^i$, *and* δ *is the maximum depth level of the MCT, i.e.* $\mathcal{N}_\delta$ *is a leaf node. The total number of system modes is equal to the total number of leaf nodes of the MCT.*

The proof of Theorem 1 can be found in [10]. Among the system modes, the initial system mode can be recognized based on the specification of the initial modes of all components.

3.3 Deriving the Mode Transition Graph

Let $\mathcal{M} = \{m_1, m_2, \cdots, m_n\}$ $(n \in \mathbb{N})$ be the set of identified system modes. The next step is to derive the (system) mode transition graph. A mode switch is a transition from m_{old} to m_{new}, where $m_{old}, m_{new} \in \mathcal{M}$ and $m_{old} \neq m_{new}$.

A mode transition graph contains all the possible transitions between these system modes and associates each transition with the corresponding scenario. Here we provide the formal definition of a mode transition graph:

Definition 5. *A mode transition graph is a tuple:*

$$< \mathcal{S}, s^0, \mathcal{K}, \mathcal{T} >$$

where $\mathcal{S}$ is a set of states, with each state $s \in \mathcal{S}$ corresponding to a system mode; $s^0 \in \mathcal{S}$ is the initial state, corresponding to the initial system mode; $\mathcal{K}$ is a set of scenarios specified for the system; $\mathcal{T} = \mathcal{S} \times \mathcal{K} \times \mathcal{S}$ is a set of state transitions, each state transition representing a system mode switch.

Each state of a mode transition graph is graphically represented as a location with a circle, with the initial state being marked by a double circle. Each state transition with scenario $k \in \mathcal{K}$ from s_1 to s_2 ($s_1, s_2 \in \mathcal{S}$) is denoted as $s_1 \xrightarrow{k} s_2$ and graphically represented by an arrow starting from s_1 to s_2 with the label k. Figure 9 illustrates the mode transition graph of the example in Fig. 1.

The key issue of deriving the mode transition graph is to identify the system modes m_{old} and m_{new} for each scenario k such that $m_{old} \xrightarrow{k} m_{new}$ is possible. Mentioned in Section 2, a scenario k can be represented as $c : m_c^1 \to m_c^2$. Hence the only condition satisfying the triggering of k is that the MSS c is currently running in m_c^1. For each k, m_{old} can be easily identified as long as $(c, m_c^1) \in m_{old}$. Note that more than one system modes could be identified as m_{old}, i.e. the same scenario may enable different transitions depending on the current system mode.

Unlike m_{old}, only one system mode can be the m_{new} for each scenario k. The identification of m_{new} for k is more difficult because it depends not only on m_c^2, but also on the target modes of the other components. We identify the m_{new} for each scenario by a Component Target Mode (CTM) table which tells the target modes of all Type A components for all scenarios. Figure 9 also includes the CTM table for the same example. For example, it tells that the target mode of a for k_1 is m_u^2. In contrast, since f is a Type B component for k_1, its target mode is independent of k_1, denoted as X in Fig. 9. A CTM table can be automatically constructed offline based on the scenario specification and the mode mapping of each composite component. Let $m_{c_i}^k$ be the target mode of c_i for k, then with the assistance of the CTM table, the m_{new} for each scenario k can be identified as follows: For each system mode $m = \{(c_i, m_{c_i}) | i = [1, n], n \in \mathbb{N}\}$, if $\forall i$ where $m_{c_i}^k \neq X$, we have $m_{c_i} = m_{c_i}^k$, then m is the m_{new} for k.

The mode transition graph is stored in a global mode switch manager (Fig. 5 in Section 3.1) which keeps track of the current system mode and makes the system switches to the right target mode upon the triggering of a scenario.

We have developed algorithms implementing our mode transformation technique that can be found in the technical report [10].

4   An Example Illustrating the Transformation

To ease the apprehension of our mode transformation technique, we demonstrate mode transformation by the example in Fig. 1 together with the mode mappings in Fig. 3. The construction of the MCT exactly follows the procedures in Section 3.2:

1. From the root node $\mathcal{N}_0 = \varnothing$, create $\lambda_{\mathcal{N}_0} = |\mathcal{M}_a| = 2$ nodes: $\mathcal{N}_1 = \{(a, m_a^1)\}$ and $\mathcal{N}_2 = \{(a, m_a^2)\}$.
2. From $\mathcal{N}_1$, create $\lambda_{\mathcal{N}_1} = |\mathcal{W}_{a,m_a^1}|$ nodes. According to Fig. 3(a), there are in total two valid LMCs of a for m_a^1: $\mathcal{N}_3 = \{(b, m_b^1), (c, m_c^1), (d, D)\}$ and $\mathcal{N}_4 = \{(b, m_b^1), (c, m_c^3), (d, D)\}$. Hence, $\lambda_{\mathcal{N}_1} = 2$. The same procedure is applied to $\mathcal{N}_2$, i.e. by creating $\lambda_{\mathcal{N}_2} = |\mathcal{W}_{a,m_a^2}|$ nodes from $\mathcal{N}_2$. Figure 3(a) indicates that there is only one valid LMC of a for m_a^2. Therefore, $\lambda_{\mathcal{N}_2} = 1$ and the new node $\mathcal{N}_5 = \{(b, m_b^2), (c, m_c^2), (d, m_d^1)\}$.
3. Now there are three nodes with depth level 2: $\mathcal{N}_3$, $\mathcal{N}_4$, and $\mathcal{N}_5$. Let's first look at $\mathcal{N}_3 = \{(b, m_b^1), (c, m_c^1), (d, D)\}$. Among b, c and d, there are two composite components: c and d. Hence $\mathcal{N}_3$ is not a leaf node and $\lambda_{\mathcal{N}_3} = |\mathcal{W}_{c,m_c^1}| * |\mathcal{W}_{d,D}|$ new nodes are supposed to be created. Figure 3(b) implies that $|\mathcal{W}_{c,m_c^1}| = 1$ and $\mathcal{W}_{c,m_c^1} = \{\{(e, m_e^1), (f, m_f^1)\}\}$. Meanwhile, $|\mathcal{W}_{d,D} = 1|$ and $\mathcal{W}_{d,D} = \{\{(g, D), (h, D)\}\}$. Hence, $\lambda_{\mathcal{N}_3} = 1$. In addition, $\mathcal{W}_{c,m_c^1} \oplus \mathcal{W}_{d,D} = \{\{(e, m_e^1), (f, m_f^1), (g, D), (h, D)\}\}$. Let $\mathcal{N}_6$ be the new node created from $\mathcal{N}_3$. Since $\mathcal{N}_6 \in \mathcal{W}_{c,m_c^1} \oplus \mathcal{W}_{d,D}$, $\mathcal{N}_6 = \{(e, m_e^1), (f, m_f^1), (g, D), (h, D)\}$.
4. Repeat Step 3 for $\mathcal{N}_4$. Create $\lambda_{\mathcal{N}_4}$ nodes from $\mathcal{N}_4$. Since $\lambda_{\mathcal{N}_4} = 1$, let $\mathcal{N}_7$ be the new node created from $\mathcal{N}_4$, and $\mathcal{N}_7 = \{(e, D), (f, m_f^1), (g, D), (h, D)\}$.
5. Repeat Step 3 for $\mathcal{N}_5$. We need to create $\lambda_{\mathcal{N}_5} = |\mathcal{W}_{c,m_c^2}| * |\mathcal{W}_{d,m_d^1}|$ new nodes from $\mathcal{N}_5$. Figure 3(b) implies that $|\mathcal{W}_{c,m_c^2}| = 2$ and $\mathcal{W}_{c,m_c^2} = \{\{(e, m_e^2), (f, m_f^1)\}, \{(e, m_e^3), (f, m_f^1)\}\}$. Figure 3(c) implies that $|\mathcal{W}_{d,m_d^1}| = 2$ and $\mathcal{W}_{d,m_d^1} = \{\{(g, m_g^1), (h, m_h^1)\}, \{(g, m_g^2), (h, m_h^2)\}\}$. Hence, $\lambda_{\mathcal{N}_5} = 4$ and

$$
\begin{aligned}
\mathcal{W}_{c,m_c^2} \oplus \mathcal{W}_{d,m_d^1} = \{ & \{(e, m_e^2), (f, m_f^1), (g, m_g^1), (h, m_h^1)\}, \\
& \{(e, m_e^3), (f, m_f^1), (g, m_g^1), (h, m_h^1)\}, \\
& \{(e, m_e^2), (f, m_f^1), (g, m_g^2), (h, m_h^2)\}, \\
& \{(e, m_e^3), (f, m_f^1), (g, m_g^2), (h, m_h^2)\}\}
\end{aligned}
$$

   where each element of this set is a new node created from $\mathcal{N}_5$. This corresponds to $\mathcal{N}_8$, $\mathcal{N}_9$, $\mathcal{N}_{10}$, and $\mathcal{N}_{11}$ in Fig. 7.
6. The nodes with depth level 3 are $\mathcal{N}_6$–$\mathcal{N}_{11}$. Since all these nodes are associated with e, f, g, and h, all of which are primitive components, $\mathcal{N}_6$–$\mathcal{N}_{11}$ are all identified as leaf nodes, thus terminating the construction of the MCT.

The constructed MCT is presented in Fig. 7. The MCT consists of 12 nodes, including one root node $\mathcal{N}_0$, two nodes with depth level 1, three nodes with depth level 2, and 6 nodes with depth level 3.

By Theorem 1, six system modes m_1–m_6 are identified. For instance, m_1 corresponds to the leftmost path of the MCT in Fig. 7, i.e. $m_1 = \mathcal{N}_0 \cup \mathcal{N}_1 \cup \mathcal{N}_3 \cup \mathcal{N}_6 =$

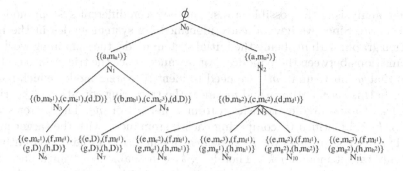

Fig. 7. Demonstration of the Mode Combination Tree

$\{(a, m_a^1), (b, m_b^1), (c, m_c^1), (d, D), (e, m_e^1), (f, m_f^1), (g, D), (h, D)\}$. The other five modes can be identified in the same way. Here we assume that the initial mode of a is m_a^1 and the initial modes of the other components can be derived accordingly. Then m_1 will be the initial system mode. Each system mode has a unique global configuration that is characterized by factors such as activated components and their connections at all nested levels, or the mode-specific behaviors of certain primitive components. Figure 8 illustrates a possible set of global configurations for the six system modes. To simplify the view, composite components c and d are removed in Fig. 8. Similar to Fig. 1, deactivated components are dimmed while black and grey colors represent different mode-specific behaviors.

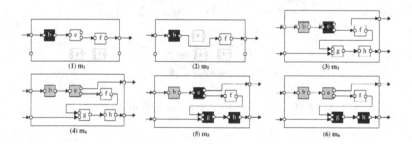

Fig. 8. The global configurations of different system modes

After the identification of system modes, the next step is to derive the mode transition graph. A key intermediate step is to construct the CTM table. This requires the complete mode mappings of all composite components represented by Mode Mapping Automata (MMAs) [7]. Due to limited space, we shall not present the MMAs here which yet can be found in [10]. Shown by Fig. 9, this example consists of six scenarios. The mode mapping and scenario specification enable the construction of the CTM table presented in Fig. 9.

Finally, using the CTM table, the mode transition graph (depicted in Fig. 9) can be either manually derived or automatically generated by means of a thorough analysis of the possible transitions between different system modes for each scenario. Since we have already identified six system modes in the mode transition graph, with m_1 being the initial system mode, the remaining work is to add transitions between these modes. For instance, since the triggering condition of k_1 is that a must run in m_a^1, we need to identify system modes which include (a, m_a^1). In this case, both m_1 and m_2 meet the triggering condition of k_1. Hence k_1 can lead to an outgoing transition from either m_1 or m_2. The target system mode for k_1 is identified by comparing each system mode with the target modes of all Type A components for k_1 provided by the CTM table. Apparently, m_3 is the only target mode for k_1. Therefore, k_1 can enable two transitions, either from m_1 to m_3 or from m_2 to m_3. The mode transition graph is completed by repeating the same logic for all scenarios.

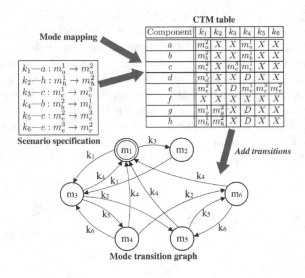

Fig. 9. Deriving the mode transition graph

In [10] we compared the mode switch time for k_1 before and after mode transformation, showing that the mode switch time was significantly reduced by mode transformation. This improvement will become even more conspicuous when the depth level of the component hierarchy is increased, or when each component runs a more complex MSRM.

5   Discussion

This section begins with a discussion on the industrial value and verification of our mode transformation technique, followed by some practical issues which need to be considered during mode transformation.

5.1 Industrial Value

Our mode transformation technique adds significant potential industrial value to MSL since it allows more efficient reuse of multi-mode components. The applicability of MSL has been initially evaluated by a proof-of-concept implementation—an Adaptive Cruise Control system [9]. Our ongoing work is to investigate the usability of MSL for Rubus [12], an industrial component model developed by Arcticus[1] for the software development of ground vehicles. In Rubus, a system running on an ECU (Electronic Control Unit) can support multiple modes while each mode is associated with a unique global configuration represented by factors such as activated components and activated component connections. Mode switch is guided by a transition diagram similar to our mode transition graph. Therefore, mode in Rubus is treated in the same way as our mode switch handling after mode transformation.

Rubus does not support multi-mode components, however, MSL is able to improve the design time flexibility by allowing Rubus to reuse multi-mode components. For each ECU, mode transformation can derive the system modes, the global configurations for each mode, and the mode transition graph, all of which are consistent with the original mode switch handling of Rubus.

Apart from Rubus, we have previously established the theoretical foundation [11] for integrating MSL in the ProCom component model [22]. In addition, we believe that MSL also conduces to some other component-based frameworks with mode switch support such as AUTOSAR [23].

5.2 Verification

Figure 6 indicates that our mode transformation is conducted in two sequential steps: the construction of the MCT and then the derivation of the mode transition graph. The correctness of these two steps can be verified separately. First, we should ensure that the correct set of system modes is identified based on the constructed MCT. Then in the subsequent step, it should be proved that the correct set of transitions is added between the system modes. We refer to [10] for the details on the verification of our mode transformation technique that are omitted here due to lack of space.

5.3 Merging System Modes

Using mode transformation, the number of identified system modes is sensitive to the number of modes of each single component and the mode mapping of each composite component. Consequently, our mode transformation may end up with a huge number of system modes. Nonetheless, it only makes sense to distinguish one mode from another mode when the system behaviors are noticeably different in these modes. Depending on the application, it is more efficient to merge several modes with similar global configurations into one mode. For

---

[1] http://www.arcticus-systems.com/

instance, in Fig. 8, m_5 and m_6 can be merged since the only difference between their global configurations is the behaviors of Component e, which can be simply distinguished by an "IF...ELSE..." expression. Following this principle, the number of system modes will be dramatically reduced. The criteria for merging system modes are application-dependent and out of the scope of this paper.

5.4   Partial Mode Transformation

Mode transformation does not have to be applied to an entire system. Sometimes it might be recommended or necessary to conduct mode transformation partially, i.e. on a composite component instead of the top component. There are at least two motivating reasons for partial mode transformation. Firstly, when a system consists of a third-party composite component whose internal information is unavailable, it will be impossible to derive the system modes represented by the modes of all components. Secondly, for a distributed system, separate mode transformation for each node would be preferred. For instance, suppose the example in Fig. 1 is a distributed system with three nodes b, c, and d. Then mode transformation can be locally performed on c and d.

6   Related Work

The most closely related work is the Oracle-based approach [20] which abstracts component behaviors into a global property network. The value change of a property of one component can potentially change the values of some properties of the other components. Mode switch is handled by a global manager called Oracle which can derive different architecture variants that resemble our system mode. The Oracle-based approach differs from our mode transformation technique in that a component mode in [20] depends on the property network, while we explicitly map component modes by the mode mapping mechanism. Since the construction of the property network highly relies on the specification of application-specific properties, our approach is less application-dependent. Moreover, the Oracle-based approach does not have any local mode switch manager in each component that can be compared with our MSRM, thus unable to support distributed mode switch handling.

Another interesting work related to MSL is the extended MechatronicUML (EUML) [14] that supports the reconfiguration of hierarchical components. Reconfiguration requests can be triggered by an EUML component and propagated to other relevant components via the reconfiguration ports of each component akin to the dedicated mode switch ports of our multi-mode component. Each composite EUML component executes its reconfiguration by two dedicated subcomponents which play the same role as the MSRM of MSL. EUML assumes a fully distributed execution of reconfiguration. No works of EUML have been reported on improving run-time reconfiguration efficiency.

Apart from Rubus (Section 5.1), mode switch has also been addressed in a number of other component models, e.g. SaveCCM [13], Koala [18], and

MyCCM-HI [3]. In Koala and SaveCCM, a special *switch* connector is introduced to achieve the structural diversity of a component. Depending on the input data, *switch* can select one of multiple outgoing connections. In MyCCM-HI, each component is associated with a mode automaton which implements its mode switch mechanism. In addition, Fractal [2] is a component model supporting component reconfiguration. Each Fractal component has a membrane (a container for local controllers) that is able to control the reconfiguration of the component. There are also numerous existing languages taking mode into account. For instance, AADL [6] uses a state machine to represent the mode switch behavior of a component. An internal/external event may trigger the state transitions (i.e. mode switch) of the state machine. Mode is also supported by some other languages such as Giotto [15], and mode automata [17] used in SCADE [16]. However, they only treat mode as a system-wide property without considering components. Unfortunately, none of the aforementioned component models and languages provides any systematic strategy to coordinate the mode switches of different components.

More generally, mode switch can be considered as a specific software variability technique [1]. Compared with most other existing software variability techniques, MSL is the only work supporting the reuse of multi-mode components and providing mode switch handling at both component and system levels.

7 Conclusion

In this paper we have presented a mode transformation technique for more efficient reuse of multi-mode components. This technique is based on our previous work, the Mode Switch Logic (MSL), which provides the seamless composition of multi-mode components with a fully distributed mode switch handling mechanism. The mode transformation technique is able to replace the distributed mechanism of MSL with a centralized mechanism by transforming component modes to system modes. After mode transformation, a mode switch is performed directly between system modes without inter-component communication, thus enhancing its efficiency at runtime [10]. We have demonstrated our approach by an example and revealed its potential industrial value.

Concerning the future work, we intend to integrate our mode transformation technique and MSL into the Rubus component model [12]. It is also our ambition to evaluate MSL in a real-world system.

Acknowledgment. This work is supported by the Swedish Research Council via the ARROWS project at Mälardalen University.

References

1. Bachmann, F., Bass, L.: Managing variability in software architectures. In: Proceedings of SSR, pp. 126–132 (2001)
2. Bennour, B., Henrio, L., Rivera, M.: A reconfiguration framework for distributed components. In: Proceedings of SINTER, pp. 49–56 (2009)

3. Borde, E., Haïk, G., Pautet, L.: Mode-based reconfiguration of critical software component architectures. In: Proc. DATE (2009)
4. Crnković, I., Larsson, M.: Building reliable component-based software systems. Artech House (2002)
5. Crnković, I., Sentilles, S., Vulgarakis, A., Chaudron, M.R.V.: A classification framework for software component models. IEEE Transactions on Software Engineering 37(5) (2011)
6. Feiler, P.H., Gluch, D.P., Hudak, J.J.: The architecture analysis & design language (AADL): An introduction. Tech. Rep. CMU/SEI-2006-TN-011, Software engineering institute, MA (February 2006)
7. Hang, Y.: Mode switch for component-based multi-mode systems. Licentiate thesis, Mälardalen University, Sweden (December 2012)
8. Hang, Y., Hansson, H.: Handling multiple mode switch scenarios in component-based multi-mode systems. In: Proc. APSEC (2013)
9. Hang, Y., Hansson, H.: Mode switch timing analysis for component-based multi-mode systems. Journal of Systems Architecture 59(10, Part D), 1299–1318 (2013)
10. Hang, Y., Hansson, H.: Flexible and efficient reuse of multi-mode components for building multi-mode systems—An extended report. Tech. Rep. MDH-MRTC-288/2014-1-SE, Mälardalen University (August 2014)
11. Hang, Y., Qin, H., Carlson, J., Hansson, H.: Mode switch handling for the ProCom component model. In: Proc. CBSE (2013)
12. Hänninen, K., Mäki-Turja, J., Nolin, M., Lindberg, M., Lundbäck, J., Lundbäck, K.: The Rubus component model for resource constrained real-time systems. In: Proc. SIES (2008)
13. Hansson, H., Åkerholm, M., Crnković, I., Törngren, M.: SaveCCM - A component model for safety-critical real-time systems. In: Proc. Euromicro Conference (2004)
14. Heinzemann, C., Becker, S.: Executing reconfigurations in hierarchical component architectures. In: Proc. CBSE (2013)
15. Henzinger, T.A., Horowitz, B., Kirsch, C.M.: Giotto: A time-triggered language for embedded programming. In: Henzinger, T.A., Kirsch, C.M. (eds.) EMSOFT 2001. LNCS, vol. 2211, pp. 166–184. Springer, Heidelberg (2001)
16. Labbani, O., Dekeyser, J.-L., Boulet, P.: Mode-automata based methodology for Scade. In: Morari, M., Thiele, L. (eds.) HSCC 2005. LNCS, vol. 3414, pp. 386–401. Springer, Heidelberg (2005)
17. Maraninchi, F., Rémond, Y.: Mode-automata: About modes and states for reactive systems. In: Hankin, C. (ed.) ESOP 1998. LNCS, vol. 1381, p. 185. Springer, Heidelberg (1998)
18. Ommering, R.V., Linden, F.V.D., Kramer, J., Magee, J.: The Koala component model for consumer electronics software. Computer 33(3) (2000)
19. Pop, T., Hnětynka, P., Hošek, P., Malohlava, M., Bureš, T.: Comparison of component frameworks for real-time embedded systems. Knowledge and Information Systems, 1–44 (2013)
20. Pop, T., Plasil, F., Outly, M., Malohlava, M.: Bureš, T.: Property networks allowing oracle-based mode-change propagation in hierarchical components. In: Proc. CBSE (2012)
21. Real, J., Crespo, A.: Mode change protocols for real-time systems: A survey and a new proposal. Real-Time Systems 26(2), 161–197 (2004)
22. Sentilles, S., Vulgarakis, A., Bures, T., Carlson, J., Crnkovic, I.: A component model for control-intensive distributed embedded systems. In: Proc. CBSE (2008)
23. Warschofsky, R.: AUTOSAR software architecture. Tech. rep., Hasso-Plattner-Institute for IT-Systems Engineering (2009)

A Method to Generate Reusable Safety Case Fragments from Compositional Safety Analysis

Irfan Sljivo[1], Barbara Gallina[1], Jan Carlson[1],
Hans Hansson[1], and Stefano Puri[2]

[1] Mälardalen Real-Time Research Centre, Mälardalen University,
Västerås, Sweden
{irfan.sljivo,barbara.gallina,jan.carlson,hans.hansson}@mdh.se
[2] Intecs, SpA,
Pisa, Italy
stefano.puri@intecs.it

Abstract. Safety-critical systems usually need to be accompanied by an explained and well-founded body of evidence to show that the system is acceptably safe. While reuse within such systems covers mainly code, reusing accompanying safety artefacts is limited due to a wide range of context dependencies that need to be satisfied for safety evidence to be valid in a different context. Currently the most commonly used approaches that facilitate reuse lack support for reuse of safety artefacts.

To facilitate reuse of safety artefacts we provide a method to generate reusable safety case argument-fragments that include supporting evidence related to safety analysis. The generation is performed from safety contracts that capture safety-relevant behaviour of components within assumption/guarantee pairs backed up by the supporting evidence. We illustrate our approach by applying it to an airplane wheel braking system example.

Keywords: Component- and contract-based architectures, Compositional safety analysis and argumentation, Safety argumentation reuse.

1 Introduction

A recent study within the US Aerospace Industry shows that reuse is more present when developing embedded systems than non-embedded systems [16]. The study reports that code is reused most of the time, followed by requirements and architectures in significantly smaller scale than code. Aerospace industry, as most other safety-critical industries, needs to follow a domain specific safety standard that requires additional artefacts to be provided alongside the code to show that the code is acceptably safe to operate in a given context. The costs of producing the verification artefacts are estimated at more than 100 USD per code line, while for highly critical applications the costs can reach up to 1000 USD [4]. In most cases, as part of the certification efforts an additional time-consuming and expensive task of providing a safety case is required. A safety case

I. Schaefer and I. Stamelos (Eds.): ICSR 2015, LNCS 8919, pp. 253–268, 2014.
© Springer International Publishing Switzerland 2014

is documented in form of an explained and well-founded structured argument to clearly communicate that the system is acceptably safe to operate in a given context [13].

Most safety standards are starting to acknowledge the need for reuse, hence the latest versions of both aerospace (DO178-C) and automotive (ISO 26262) industry standards explicitly support techniques for reuse, e.g., the notion of Safety Element out of Context (SEooC) within automotive [12] and Reusable Software Components (RSC) within aerospace industry [1]. This allows for easier integration of reusable components, such as Commercial of the shelf (COTS), but it also means that some safety artefacts of the reused components should be reused as well if we are to fully benefit from the reuse and safely integrate the reused component into the new system. The difficulty that hinders reuse is that safety is a system property. This means that hazard analysis and risk assessment used to analyse what can go wrong at system level, as required by the standards, can only be performed in a context of the specific system. To overcome this difficulty compositional approaches are needed. CHESS-FLA [7] is a plugin within the CHESS toolset [6] that supports execution of Failure Logic Analysis (FLA) such as Fault Propagation and Transformation Calculus (FPTC). FPTC allows us to calculate system level behaviour given the behaviour of the individual components established in isolation. Such compositional failure analyses enable reuse of safety artefacts within safety-critical systems.

Component-based Development (CBD) is the most commonly used approach to achieve reuse within embedded systems of the aerospace industry [16]. While CBD is successfully used to support reuse of software components, it lacks means to support reuse of additional artefacts, alongside the software components, in form of argument-fragments and supporting evidence. As a part of an overall system safety argument, argument-fragments for software components present safety reasoning used to develop a particular component and its safety-relevant behaviour, e.g., failure behaviour.

In our previous work we developed the notion of safety contracts related to software components to promote reuse of the components together with their certification data and we have proposed a (semi)automatic method to generate argument-fragments for the software components from their associated safety contracts [14]. In this work we propose a method called FLAR2SAF that uses failure logic analysis results (FLAR) to generate safety case argument-fragments (SAF). More specifically, we derive safety contracts for a component from FLAR. Then, we adapt our method for generation of argument-fragments to provide better support for reuse of the argument-fragments and the evidence they contain.

In particular, the input/output behaviour of a component developed out-of-context can be specified by FPTC rules. For example, in case of omission failure on the input I1 of the component, the component can have a safety mechanism to still provide the output O1 but with additional delay. In that case FPTC rule describing such behaviour can be specified as: $I1.omission \rightarrow O1.late$. We can use these behaviours obtained by FPTC analysis to derive safety contracts that can be further supported by evidence and used to form clear and comprehensive argument-fragments. For example, if the late failure on the output of the component can cause a hazardous event, then the corresponding argument-fragment should argue that the late failure is sufficiently handled in the context of the particular system and attach supporting evidence for that claim. For generating argument-fragments associated to the failure behaviour of the components we use an established argument pattern [18].

The main contribution of this paper is a method for the design and preparation for certification of reusable COTS-based safety-critical architectures. More specifically, we provide a conceptual mapping of FPTC rules to safety contracts. Moreover, we extend the argument-fragment generation method to generate reusable argument-fragments based on an existing argumentation pattern.

The rest of the paper is organised as follows: In Section 2 we provide background information. In Section 3 we present the rationale behind our approach and methods to derive safety contracts from FPTC analysis and generate corresponding argument-fragments. In Section 4 we illustrate our approach by applying it to a wheel-braking system. We present the related work in Section 5, and conclusions and future work in Section 6.

2   Background

In this section we briefly provide some background information on COTS-based safety-critical architectures and safety contracts. Furthermore, we recall essential information concerning the CHESS-FLA plugin within the CHESS toolset. Finally, we provide brief information on safety cases and safety case modelling.

2.1   COTS-Based Safety-Critical Architectures

In the context of safety critical systems, COTS-driven development is becoming more and more appealing. The typical V model that constitutes the reference model for various safety standards is being combined with the typical component-based development. As Fig.1 depicts, the top-down and bottom-up approach meet in the gray zone. Initially a top-down approach is carried out. The typical safety process starts with hazards identification which is conducted by analysing (brainstorming on) failure propagation, based on an initial description of the system and its possible functional architecture. If a failure at system level may lead to intolerable hazards, safety requirements are formulated, decomposed onto the architectural components, and mitigation means have to be designed. Safety requirements are assigned with Safety Integrity Levels (SILs) as a measure of quantifying risk reduction. Iteratively and incrementally the system architecture is changed until a satisfying result is achieved (i.e. no intolerable behaviour at system level). More specifically, once the safety requirements are decomposed onto components (hardware/software), COTS (developed via a bottom-up approach) can be selected to meet those requirements. If the selected components do not fully meet the requirements, some adaptations can be introduced.

To ease the selection of components, contracts play a crucial role. In our previous work, we have proposed a contract-based formalism with strong $\langle A, G \rangle$

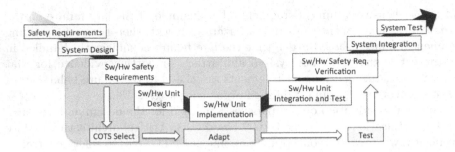

Fig. 1. Safety-critical system development/COTS-driven development

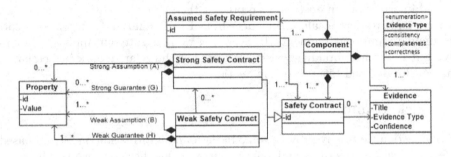

Fig. 2. Component and safety contract meta-model [14]

and weak $\langle B, H \rangle$ contracts to distinguish between context-specific properties and those that must hold for all contexts [15]. A traditional component contract $C = \langle A, G \rangle$ is composed of assumptions (A) on the environment of the component and guarantees (G) that are offered by the component if the assumptions are met. The strong contract assumptions (A) are required to be satisfied in all contexts in which the component is used, hence the corresponding strong guarantees (G) are offered in all contexts in which the component can be used. For example, a strong assumption could be minimum amount of memory a component requires to operate. The weak contract guarantees (H) are offered only in those contexts where besides the strong assumptions, the corresponding weak assumptions (B) are satisfied as well. This makes the weak contracts context specific, e.g., a timing behaviour of a component on a specific platform is captured by a weak contract.

We denote a contract capturing safety-relevant behaviour as a safety contract. In [14] we introduced a component meta-model (Fig. 2) that connects safety contracts with supporting evidence, which provides a base for evidence artefact reuse together with the contracts. The component meta-model specifies a component in an out-of-context setting composed of safety-contracts, evidence and the assumed safety requirements. Each safety requirement is satisfied by at least one safety contract, and each contract can be supported by one or more evidence. For example, if we assume that late output failure of the component can be hazardous, then we define an assumed safety requirement that specifies that late failure should be appropriately handled. This requirement is addressed by a contract that captures in its assumptions the identified properties that need to hold for the component to guarantee that the late failure is appropriately handled. The evidence that supports the contract includes contract consistency report and analyses results used to derive the contract.

2.2 CHESS-FLA within the CHESS Toolset

CHESS-FLA [7] is a plugin within the CHESS toolset [6] that includes two FLA techniques: (1) FPTC [17] - a compositional technique to qualitatively assess the dependability of component-based systems, and (2) FI^{4}FA [9] - FPTC extension that allows for analysis of mitigation behaviour. In this paper we limit our attention to FPTC that allows users to calculate the behaviour at system-level, based on the specification of the behaviour of individual components. In the CHESS toolset components can be modelled as component types or component implementations. Component types are more abstract and can be realised by system-specific component implementations. Component implementations inherit all behaviours of the corresponding component type.

The behaviour of the individual components is established by studying the components in isolation. This behaviour is expressed by a set of logical expressions (FPTC rules) that relate output failures (occurring on output ports) to combinations of input failures (occurring on input ports). These behaviours can be classified as: (1) a source (e.g., a component generates a failure due to internal faults), (2) a sink (e.g., a component is capable to detect and correct a failure received on the input), (3) propagational (e.g., a component propagates a failure it received on the input), and (4) transformational (e.g., a component generates a different type of failure from the input failure). Input failures are assumed to be propagated or transformed deterministically, i.e., for a combination of failures on the input, there can be only one combination of failures on the output.

The syntax supported in CHESS-FLA to specify the FPTC rules is shown in Fig. 3. An example of a compliant expression that demonstrates the transformational behaviour of a component is "$R1.late \rightarrow P1.valueCoarse$", which should be read as follows: if the component receives on its port R1 a late failure, it generates on its output port P1 a coarse (i.e. clearly detectable) value failure (a failure that manifests itself as a failure mode by exceeding the allowed range).

---

behaviour = expression + expression = LHS '→' RHS
LHS = portname'.' bL | portname '.' bL (',' portname '.' bL) +
RHS = portname'.' bR | portname '.' bR (',' portname '.' bR) +
failure = 'early' | 'late' | 'commission' | 'omission' | 'valueSubtle' | 'valueCoarse'
bL = 'wildcard' | bR
bR = 'noFailure' | failure

Fig. 3. FPTC syntax supported in CHESS-FLA

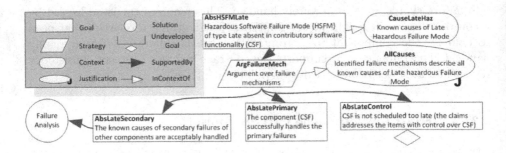

Fig. 4. Hazardous Software Failure Mode absence pattern for type late failure

2.3 Safety Cases and Safety Case Modelling

A Safety case in form of an explained (argued about) and well-founded (evidence-based) structured argument is often required to show that the system is acceptably safe to operate in a given context [13]. Goal Structuring Notation (GSN) is a graphical argumentation notation for documenting the safety case [10]. GSN can be used to represent the individual elements of any safety argument and the relationships between these elements. The argument usually starts with a top-level claim/goal stating absence of a failure, as in Fig. 4 the argument starts with a goal that has *AbsHSFMLate* identifier. The goals can be further decomposed to sub-goals with *supportedBy* relations denoting inference between goals or connecting supporting evidence with a goal. The decomposition can be described using strategy elements e.g., *ArgFailureMech* in Fig. 4. To define the scope and context of a goal or provide its rationale, elements such as context and justification are attached to a goal with *inContextOf* relations. For example, context *CauseLateHaz* is used to clarify the *AbsHSFMLate* goal by providing the list of known causes of the late failure mode. The undeveloped element symbol indicates elements that need further development. For more details on GSN see [10].

GSN was initially used to communicate a specific argument for a particular system. Since similar rationale exists behind specific argument-fragments in different contexts, argument patterns of reusable reasoning are defined by generalising the specific details of a specific argument [10]. In this work we use the argument pattern for Handling of Software Failure Modes (HSFM) [18], a portion of which is shown in Fig. 4, to structure the generated argument-fragments related to late timing failure modes. To build an argument, HSFM pattern requires information about known causes of the failure mode and failure mechanisms that address those causes. Moreover, the failure mechanisms can be classified into three categories: (1) Primary failures within Contributory Software Functionality (CSF) that can cause the failure; (2) Secondary failures relating to other components within the system on which CSF is dependent; and (3) Failures caused by items controlling CSF e.g., in case of late hazardous failure mode the controlling item is the scheduling policy.

3   FLAR2SAF

In this section we present FLAR2SAF, a method to generate reusable safety case argument-fragments. We first provide the rationale of the approach in Section 3.1. We provide a method to translate FPTC rules into safety contracts in Section 3.2, and we adapt and extend the method for semi-automatic generation of argument-fragments from safety contracts in Section 3.3.

3.1   Rationale

In our work we use safety contracts to facilitate reuse of safety-relevant software components. The method to semi-automatically generate argument-fragments from safety contracts, mentioned in Section 2.1, can be used to support the reuse of certification-relevant artefacts from previously specified contracts. Just as evidence needs to be provided with a reusable component to increase confidence in the component itself, similarly in some cases the trustworthiness of the evidence should be backed up as well [11]. To reuse evidence-related artefacts together with the argument fragments, additional information about the rationale linking the artefacts and the safety contracts they support should be provided. Furthermore, the issue of trustworthiness of such evidence needs to be addressed. For example, we might need to describe the competence of the engineers that performed a particular analysis or even qualification of the analysis tool.

To capture the additional information related to evidence we enrich the component meta-model presented in Section 2.1. We enrich the connection between a contract and evidence by adding optional descriptive attribute capturing the rationale for how the particular evidence, or set of evidence, supports the goal. This information is used to provide additional clarification on the connection between the evidence and the claims made by the contract. Clarification of confidence in the evidence itself can be made in two different ways: either by directly including or referencing supporting information in the context of the evidence (e.g., competence of person performing the failure analysis can be found in document x); or to point to an already developed goal, called an *away goal* [10], presenting the supporting information (we could have a repository of generic argument-fragments related to staff competence and tool-qualification [8]). In the presented component meta-model we append attributes to the evidence to capture supporting information related to the evidence, including a set of references to the supporting away goals.

FLAR2SAF based on FPTC analysis can be performed by the following steps:

- Model the component architecture in CHESS-FLA;
- Specify failure behaviour of a component in isolation using FPTC rules;
- Translate the FPTC rules into corresponding safety contracts and attach FPTC analysis results as initial evidence;
- Support the contracts with additional V&V evidence and enrich the contract assumptions accordingly;
- Upon component selection, depicted in Fig. 1 in Section 2.1:

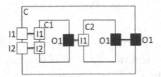

C1.R1: I1.late,I2.late -> O1.late;
C1.R2: I1.coarse,I2.coarse -> O1.coarse;
C2.R1: I1.late -> O1.noFailure;
C2.R2: I1.coarse -> O1.late;
C.R1: I1.late,I2.late -> O1.noFailure;
C.R2: I1.coarse,I2.coarse -> O1.late;

Fig. 5. Composite component example with FPTC rules

- Perform FPTC analysis and calculate system-level failure behaviour;
- Translate the results of FPTC analysis to system-level safety contracts;
- Support and enrich the contracts with additional V&V evidence;
- Use the approach to semi-automatically generate an argument-fragment based on the argument pattern presented in Section 2.3.

The generated argument-fragment is tailored for the specific system so that only contracts satisfied in the particular system are used to form the argument, and accordingly only evidence associated to such contracts is reused to support confidence in the contracts. Particular evidence can only be reused if all the captured assumptions within the associated contract are met by the system.

3.2 Contractual Interpretation of FPTC Rules

In this section we focus on the step of translating the FPTC rules to safety contracts. We use the simple example in Fig. 5 to explain the translation process and provide a set of steps that can be used to perform the translation

In Fig. 5 we have FPTC rules specified for a composite component C and its subcomponents C1 and C2. When both inputs I1 and I2 exhibit late or coarse failure, component C1 acts as a propagator and outputs late/coarse failure on O1 output. Component C2 acts as a sink in case of a late failure and transforms it to no failure (e.g., a watchdog timer expires and triggers a satisfactory response), while it transforms coarse to late failure (e.g., due to additional filtering).

Safety contracts for these components can be made based on the FPTC rules. When translating the rules into contracts we consider two types of rules with respect to each failure mode: rules that describe when a failure happens (e.g., C1.R1) and rules that describe behaviours that mitigate a failure (e.g., C2.R1). We translate the first type of rules by guaranteeing with the contract that the failure described by the rule will not happen, under assumptions that the behaviour that causes the failure does not happen. The contract $\langle B, H \rangle_{C1}$ for component C1, shown in Table 1, guarantees that O1 will not be late if both inputs I1 and I2 never fail at the same time with late failure. This type of contracts is specified as weak since, unlike for strong contracts, their satisfaction in every context should not be mandatory. For example, in some contexts late timing failure is not hazardous, hence it is not required to be ensured.

We translate the second type of rules differently as they do not identify causes of failures, but they specify behaviours that help mitigate failures in certain cases.

Table 1. Contracts for components C1 and C

$\mathbf{B}_{C1}$: (not (I1.late and I2.late)); $\mathbf{H}_{C1}$: not O1.late;
$\mathbf{A}_{C-1}$: -; $\mathbf{G}_{C-1}$: I1.late, I2.late → noFailure;
$\mathbf{B}_{C-2}$: (not (I1.coarse and I2.coarse)); $\mathbf{H}_{C-2}$: not O1.late;

Since these contracts specify safety behaviour of components that should be satisfied in every context, without imposing assumptions on the environment, we denote these contracts as strong contracts. The corresponding contracts state in which cases the component guarantees that it will not exhibit any failures. We do this by guaranteeing the rule that describes this behaviour, as shown in Table 1 for the $\langle A, G \rangle_{C-1}$ contract for component C.

As shown on an example of translating FPTC rules from the example in Fig. 5 to contracts in Table 1, the translation can be performed in the following way for each failure:

- Identify FPTC rules that are directly related to the failure mode (either describing when it happens or describing behaviour that prevents it);
- For the rules describing when the failure mode happens:
  - Add the negation of the combination of the input failures to the contract assumptions. Connect with other assumptions with AND operator;
  - Use the absence of the failure mode as the contract guarantee;
- For the rules that describe behaviours that prevent the failure mode:
  - Use the rule within the contract guarantee to state that the component guarantees the behaviour described by the rule;

The abstract behaviour specified within the FPTC rules can be further refined so that more concrete behaviours of the component are described. For example, a refined contract related to timing failures would include concrete timing behaviour of the component in a particular context and additional assumptions related to the timing properties of the concrete system should be made.

3.3 Argument-Fragment Generation

As mentioned in Section 2, safety relevant components usually need to provide argument and associated evidence regarding absence of particular failures. We generate the required argument-fragment based on previously established argument pattern HSFM for presenting absence of late failure mode, briefly recalled in Section 2.3. By providing means to generate context-specific argument-fragments, i.e., argument-fragments that include only information related to those contracts satisfied in the particular context, we allow for reuse of certain evidence related to the satisfied contracts.

To build an argument based on the HSFM pattern, we identify the known causes of primary and secondary failures from the corresponding FPTC rules.

We identify the primary failures from the contracts translated from FPTC rules that describe behaviours that mitigate a failure mode. The secondary failures are captured within the contracts translated from FPTC rules that describe when a failure mode happens. All causes and assumptions not captured by the corresponding FPTC rules should be additionally added to the safety contracts, e.g., scheduler policy constraints. We construct the argument-fragment by using the reasoning from the HSFM pattern. The top-most goal claiming absence of the failure mode is decomposed into three sub-goals focusing on primary, secondary and controlling failures as described in Section 2.3. We adapt the contract-satisfaction fragment from [14] to further develop the sub-goals.

We use the safety contracts to generate the supporting sub-arguments for the primary and secondary failures and leave the goal related to controlling failures undeveloped. Supporting sub-arguments for both primary and secondary failures are generated to argue that the corresponding safety contracts are satisfied with sufficient confidence. The sufficient confidence is determined based on the specific SIL of the requirements allocated on the component and may require additional evidence in case of higher SILs. We argue the satisfaction of contracts as in [14] where we make a claim that the contract is satisfied with sufficient confidence, i.e., that the guarantee of the contract is offered. We further decompose the claim into two supporting goals: (1) an argument providing the supporting evidence for confidence in the claim in terms of completeness of the contract, and (2) an argument showing that the assumptions stated in the contract are met by the contracts of other components. We further focus on the first sub-goal related to evidence and adapt the rules related to generating the evidence sub-argument to include additionally specified information about the evidence artefacts.

For every evidence attached to a safety contract we create a sub-goal to support confidence in the corresponding safety contract. At this point we can use the additional information about the rationale connecting evidence and the safety contract and present it in form of a context statement to clarify how this particular evidence contributes to increasing confidence in the corresponding safety contract. The evidence can be further backed up by the related trustworthiness arguments that can be attached directly to a particular evidence. If the evidence trustworthiness information is provided in a descriptive form then additional context statements are added to the solutions, otherwise an away goal is created to point to the argument about the trustworthiness of the evidence, e.g., an argument presenting competence of a person that conducted the analysis which resulted in the corresponding evidence.

To achieve the argument-fragment generation we extended the approach for generation of argument-fragments from safety contracts [14] to allow for argument-fragment generation in the specific form of the selected pattern. The approach is adapted to generate an argument-fragment that clearly separates and argues over primary, secondary and controlling failures as described above, and to include additional information related to the evidence.

While the benefits of reusing evidence are great, a big risk can be falsely reusing evidence which may result in false confidence and potentially unsafe system.

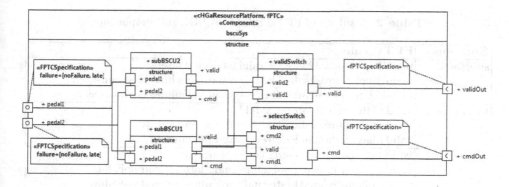

Fig. 6. BSCU model in CHESS

It must be noted that deriving safety contracts from safety analyses does not necessarily result in complete contracts. To increase confidence in reuse of safety artefacts, additional assumptions should be captured within the safety contracts to guarantee the specified behaviour with sufficient confidence. While this will limit reuse of the particular contract and the associated evidence, the weak safety contracts notion allows us to specify a number of alternative contracts describing particular behaviour in different contexts.

4   Application Example

In this section we demonstrate FLAR2SAF by applying it to a Wheel-Braking System (WBS). We first briefly introduce the WBS in Section 4.1. In Section 4.2 we apply CHESS-FLA/FPTC analysis on WBS. We use the translation steps from Section 3.2 to translate the contracts from the FPTC analysis results in Section 4.3. We present the generated argument-fragment in Section 4.4.

4.1   Wheel Braking System (WBS)

In this section we recall WBS, which was originally presented in ARP4761 [2]. We use a simplified version of WBS to illustrate the use of FLAR2SAF.

WBS is a part of an airplane braking system. It takes two input brake pedal signals that are used by the Brake System Control Unit (BSCU) to calculate the braking force. The software architecture of BSCU modelled in CHESS is shown in Fig. 6. Based on the preliminary safety analysis performed on the system, the BSCU is designed with two redundant dual channel systems to meet the availability and integrity requirements. Each of the two subBSCU systems, namely subBSCU1 and subBSCU2, provide a calculated command value and a valid signal that indicates the validity of the corresponding command value. The selectSwitch forwards by default the command value from subBSCU1 if the corresponding valid signal is true, otherwise the command value from subBSCU2 is forwarded. The validSwitch component returns true if any of the signals is true,

Table 2. A subset of FPTC rules for BSCU subcomponents

Component	FPTC rule
subBSCU	pedal1.late, pedal2.late → valid.late, cmd.late;
	pedal1.noFailure, pedal2.late → valid.noFailure, cmd.omission;
	pedal1.late, pedal2.noFailure → valid.noFailure, cmd.omission;
validSwitch	valid1.late, valid2.late → valid.late;
	valid1.noFailure, valid2.late → valid.noFailure;
	valid1.late, valid2.noFailure → valid.noFailure;
selectSwitch	valid.late, cmd1.late,cmd2.late → cmd.late
	valid.noFailure, cmd1.noFailure,cmd2.late → cmd.noFailure
	valid.noFailure, cmd1.late,cmd2.noFailure → cmd.noFailure
	valid.omission, cmd1.omission,cmd2.omission → cmd.omission

otherwise it returns false indicating that an alternate braking mode should be used, as the braking command calculated by BSCU cannot be trusted.

4.2   FPTC Analysis

To perform the FPTC analysis we first model the system architecture in the CHESS-toolset (Fig. 6) and then define FPTC rules for the modelled components. The architecture and the corresponding failure behaviour of the components are defined based on the system description in Section 4.1.

The specified FPTC rules are shown in Table 2. As mentioned in Section 2.2, the FPTC rules specified for components are inherited by all the instances, hence the FPTC rules for the two subBSCU component implementations are the same as they are instances of the same component. The validSwitch component requires at least one valid signal present in order to forward the correct response, i.e., at least to signal that there is a problem within BSCU. Similarly, the selectSwitch component output depends both on valid and cmd signals.

As shown in Fig. 6 in the FPTC specifications on the input ports, we run the analysis for noFailure and late failure behaviours on the inputs. The FPTC analysis then computes the possible failures on the output ports of BSCU based on the FPTC rules for the BSCU subcomponents. The results show that the validOut port can either not fail or propagate late failures, while the cmdOut port in addition to noFailure and late failure can exhibit omission failure as well.

Table 3. The results of the FPTC analysis for bscuSys component

Port type	Port label	Port values
input	pedal1	noFailure, late
input	pedal2	noFailure, late
output	cmdOut	noFailure, omission, late
output	validOut	noFailure, late

Table 4. The translated BSCU contracts and associated evidence information

$\mathbf{B}_{BSCU-1}$:	not (pedal1.late and pedal2.late);
$\mathbf{H}_{BSCU-1}$:	not validOut.late and not cmdOut.late;
$\mathbf{C}_{BSCU-1}$:	The contract is derived from the FPTC analysis results for the bscuSys component;
$\mathbf{E}_{BSCU-1}$:	*name*: bscuSys FPTC analysis report *description*: FPTC analysis is performed in CHESS-toolset. *supporting argument*: FPTC_analysis_conf;
$\mathbf{A}_{BSCU-2}$:	-;
$\mathbf{G}_{BSCU-2}$:	pedal1.noFailure, pedal2.late → validOut.noFailure,cmdOut.omission;
$\mathbf{C}_{BSCU-2}$:	The contract is derived from the FPTC analysis results for the bscuSys component; Unit testing is used to validate that the contracts are sufficiently complete with respect to the implementation;
$\mathbf{E}_{BSCU-2}$:	*name*: bscuSys FPTC analysis report *description*: FPTC analysis is performed in CHESS-toolset. *supporting argument*: FPTC_analysis_conf; *name*: Unit testing results *description*: - *supporting argument*: Unit_test_conf;

4.3   The Translated Contracts

The results of the FPTC analysis can be interpreted in the form of FPTC rules for the system component *bscuSys*. The resulting FPTC rule "pedal1.late, pedal2.late → validOut.late, cmdOut.late" for *bscuSys* can be translated to the contract $\langle B, H \rangle_{BSCU-1}$ shown in Table 4. The contract specifies that the outputs of BSCU will not be late if both input pedals are not late. The contract is supported by the FPTC analysis report from which the contract is derived.

The second translated contract $\langle A, G \rangle_{BSCU-2}$ describes the behaviour when only the second pedal is faulty. In that case the failure is detected by the BSCU component and reported through the validOut port, hence the validOut port reports no failure, while the cmdOut signal is omitted. The additional information related to the supporting evidence includes context statements C_{BSCU-1} and C_{BSCU-2} and a set of evidence (E_{BSCU-1} and E_{BSCU-2}). Each evidence can be further described by a context statement and supported by a set of arguments.

4.4   The Resulting Argument-Fragment

A part of the resulting argument-fragment is shown in Fig. 7. In this argument snippet we focus only on the identified causes of primary failures (*AbsLatePrimary* goal), while the other goals shown in Fig. 4 remain undeveloped. We identified the BSCU-2 contract shown in Table 4 as the one related to primary failures as it describes behaviour of the component that mitigates a possible failure. By applying the rules to generate the contract satisfaction argument (goal *BSCU-2_sat*), we divide the argument to argue over the satisfaction of the supporting contracts (*BSCU-2_supp_sat*) and supporting evidence in contract completeness

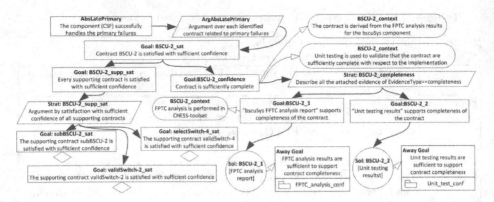

Fig. 7. Argument-fragment based on the HSFM pattern

(*BSCU-2_confidence*). While the argument for the *BSCU-2_supp_sat* goal follows the same pattern as for goal *BSCU-2_sat*, we focus on the argument related to the *BSCU-2_confidence* goal.

The goal *BSCU-2_confidence* is clarified by the two context statements stating that the contract has been derived from the FPTC analysis and that unit testing has been performed to validate that the contracts are sufficiently complete. In the rest of the argument we create a goal for each of the attached artefacts and enrich them with additional evidence information. The goal *BSCU-2_1* presents the confidence in the FPTC analysis. Since we do not have an argument supporting qualification of the tool used to perform the analysis we attach context statement clarifying that the FPTC analysis is performed in the CHESS-toolset. We provide an away goal related to the evidence to support trustworthiness in the analysis by arguing confidence in the FPTC analysis. Further evidence might be provided to present competences of the engineers that formed the FPTC rules and performed the analysis.

5   Related Work

The use of model-based development in safety-critical systems to support the development of the system safety case has been the focus of much research during the past years. Integration of model-based engineering with safety analysis to ease the development of safety cases is presented in [5]. The work presents how the architecture description language EAST-ADL2 can be used to support the development of safety-critical systems. Similarly, an approach to handling safety concerns and constructing safety arguments within a system architectural design process is presented in [19]. The work presents a set of argument patterns and a supporting method for producing architectural safety arguments. The focus of these works is usually on extending the modelling approaches to support the safety case development process and provide guidelines on how to produce the corresponding safety arguments. Unlike in these approaches, in our work we provide a method for generating safety-arguments from the safety contracts that are based on and supported by the safety analysis performed on the system.

Deriving a safety argument from the actual source code is presented in [3]. The work focuses on constructing an argument for how the actual code complies with specific safety requirements based on the V&V artefacts. The argument skeleton is generated from a formal analysis of automatically generated code and integrates different information from heterogeneous sources into a single safety case. The skeleton argument is extended by separately specified additional information enriching the argument with explanatory elements such as contexts, assumptions, justifications etc. In contrast, in this work we generate an argument-fragment from safety contracts obtained from and supported by FPTC analysis. We utilise the contracts to specify the additional information regarding the context and additional assumptions and generate an argument-fragment for a specific failure mode covered by the FPTC analysis.

6   Conclusion and Future Work

Reuse within safety-critical systems is not complete without reuse of safety artefacts such as argument-fragments and the supporting evidence, since they are the key aspects of safety-critical systems development that require significant efforts. In this work we have presented a method called FLAR2SAF for generating reusable argument-fragments. This method first derives safety contracts from failure logic analysis results and then uses the contracts supported by evidence to generate reusable pattern-based argument-fragments. By an illustrative example we have shown how an argument-fragment could be generated and supporting evidence reused. The application of FLAR2SAF gives a clear indication that safety contracts can be derived from failure logic analyses. Moreover, accompanying COTS with a set of such safety contracts supported by safety evidence artefacts allows us to generate context-specific argument-fragments based on the satisfied contracts.

As our future work we are planning an evaluation of FLAR2SAF on an industrial case study. Moreover, we plan to extend the CHESS toolset to include our methods for derivation of contracts and generation of argument-fragments. We plan to explore how different types of safety analyses can be used to derive and support contracts, hence how different types of evidence could be easily reused. Another interesting future direction would be to explore how this approach can help us with change management and reuse of safety artefacts in case of changes in the system.

Acknowledgements. This work is supported by the Swedish Foundation for Strategic Research (SSF) via project SYNOPSIS as well as EU and Vinnova via the Artemis JTI project SafeCer.

References

1. AC 20-148: Reusable Software Components. FAA (2004)
2. ARP4761: Guidelines and Methods for Conducting the Safety Assessment Process on Civil Airborne Systems and Equipment. Society of Automotive Engineers (1996)
3. Basir, N., Denney, E., Fischer, B.: Building heterogeneous safety cases for automatically generated code. In: Infotech@ Aerospace Conference. AIAA (2011)
4. Bloomfield, R., Cazin, J., Craigen, D., Juristo, N., Kesseler, E., et al.: Validation, Verification and Certification of Embedded Systems. Tech. rep., NATO (2005)
5. Chen, D., Johansson, R., Lönn, H., Papadopoulos, Y., Sandberg, A., Törner, F., Törngren, M.: Modelling support for design of safety-critical automotive embedded systems. In: Harrison, M.D., Sujan, M.-A. (eds.) SAFECOMP 2008. LNCS, vol. 5219, pp. 72–85. Springer, Heidelberg (2008)
6. CHESS-toolset, http://www.chess-project.org/page/download
7. Gallina, B., Javed, M.A., Muram, F.U., Punnekkat, S.: Model-driven Dependability Analysis Method for Component-based Architectures. In: Euromicro-SEAA Conference. IEEE Computer Society Press (2012)
8. Gallina, B., Kashiyarandi, S., Zugsbratl, K., Geven, A.: Enabling cross-domain reuse of tool qualification certification artefacts. In: Bondavalli, A., Ceccarelli, A., Ortmeier, F. (eds.) SAFECOMP 2014 Workshop. LNCS, vol. 8696, pp. 255–266. Springer, Heidelberg (2014)
9. Gallina, B., Punnekkat, S.: FI^{4}FA: A Formalism for Incompletion, Inconsistency, Interference and Impermanence Failures Analysis. In: International Workshop on Distributed Architecture Modeling for Novel Component Based Embedded Systems. IEEE Computer Society (2011)
10. GSN Community Standard Version 1. Origin Consulting (York) Limited (2011)
11. Hawkins, R., Habli, I., Kelly, T., McDermid, J.: Assurance cases and prescriptive software safety certification: A comparative study. Safety Science 59, 55–71 (2013)
12. ISO 26262:2011: Road vehicles — Functional safety. International Organization for Standardization (2011)
13. Kelly, T.P.: Arguing Safety — A Systematic Approach to Managing Safety Cases. Ph.D. thesis, University of York, York, UK (1998)
14. Sljivo, I., Gallina, B., Carlson, J., Hansson, H.: Generation of Safety Case Argument-Fragments from Safety Contracts. In: Bondavalli, A., Di Giandomenico, F. (eds.) SAFECOMP 2014. LNCS, vol. 8666, pp. 170–185. Springer, Heidelberg (2014)
15. Sljivo, I., Gallina, B., Carlson, J., Hansson, H.: Strong and weak contract formalism for third-party component reuse. In: International Workshop on Software Certification. IEEE Computer Society (2013)
16. Varnell-Sarjeant, J., Andrews, A.A., Stefik, A.: Comparing Reuse Strategies: An Empirical Evaluation of Developer Views. In: International Workshop on Quality Oriented Reuse of Software. IEEE Computer Society (2014)
17. Wallace, M.: Modular architectural representation and analysis of fault propagation and transformation. In: International Workshop on Formal Foundations of Embedded Software and Component-Based Software Architectures. Elsevier (2005)
18. Weaver, R., McDermid, J., Kelly, T.: Absence of Late Hazardous Failure Mode, http://www.goalstructuringnotation.info/archives/218
19. Wu, W.: Architectural Reasoning for Safety — Critical Software Applications. Ph.D. thesis, University of York, York, UK (2007)

A Comparison of Methods for Automatic Term Extraction for Domain Analysis

William B. Frakes, Gregory Kulczycki, and Jason Tilley

Software Reuse Laboratory
Virginia Tech
Falls Church, VA USA
{wfrakes,gregwk}@vt.edu, tilley_jason@hotmail.com

Abstract. Fourteen word frequency metrics were tested to evaluate their effectiveness in identifying vocabulary in a domain. Fifteen domain-engineering projects were examined to measure how closely the vocabularies selected by the fourteen word frequency metrics were to the vocabularies produced by domain engineers. Stemming and stopword removal were also evaluated to measure their impact on selecting proper vocabulary terms. The results of the experiment show that stemming and stopword removal do improve performance and that term frequency is a valuable contributor to performance. Most word frequency metrics gave similar results. A few of the metrics did poorly compared to the others.

Keywords: domain engineering, vocabulary extraction, stemming, stoplists, word frequency metrics, software reuse, domain documents.

1 Introduction

Studies have shown that systematic software reuse offers many benefits [4]. A key step in systematic software reuse is domain analysis. In domain analysis, an engineer studies several related software systems and their documentation to understand their commonalities and variabilities. This is done to determine how to improve the production of systems in that domain including which types of reusable assets can be created.

Several domain analysis techniques have been proposed [4]. One such methodology is the Domain Analysis and Reuse Environment (DARE) [5]. This methodology uses a domain book to document different views of the domain. The book captures useful code components, architectural diagrams, feature tables, facet tables, and a domain vocabulary. The vocabulary is typically one of the first products created during the process, and is also one of the most important as its formation leads to the creation of subsequent models, like a generic facet table and a generic architecture.

While a domain vocabulary can come from many sources, like subject matter experts and code, it is typically drawn primarily from domain documents. These documents, such as requirements documents and user manuals, describe systems in the domain.

I. Schaefer and I. Stamelos (Eds.): ICSR 2015, LNCS 8919, pp. 269–281, 2014.
© Springer International Publishing Switzerland 2014

A domain vocabulary can be selected manually, with the domain engineers reading the documents and selecting the vocabulary. The DARE method, however, suggests using tools that provide basic term frequency analysis as a starting point for selecting a vocabulary. However, not all words that appear frequently are important, and not all important words appear frequently. Domain engineers currently base their decisions on their understanding of the domain. This task is very time consuming and prone to error due to a single human's perspective on what is important in the study of the domain. Domain analysis could greatly benefit from accurate automation of vocabulary selection. Current selection methods rely on term frequency analysis and a human interpretation of the term frequency metrics.

The purpose of this paper is to evaluate various automatic vocabulary extraction methods for domain analysis [11]. Each method gave weights to terms in an experimental text corpus, and those terms were evaluated against a manually selected domain vocabulary. We evaluated $O = f(K,C,S)$, where O is an overlap score for each methodology K. The variable C represents the conflation variable with two values: stemmed with Porter's stemming algorithm [9], or not stemmed. The variable S represents 3 possible stopword list options: no stoplist, short stoplist, or long stoplist. Our hypothesis was that there would be significant differences in overlaps for the different metrics, and that stemming and stopword removal would also significantly affect overlap.

2   Methods

In this paper we evaluate the effectiveness of many statistical test measures and derivatives of them. Our purpose is to find accurate statistics for automatically selecting a domain vocabulary, W_A (A for automatic), from a small corpus of documents D.

Our model is: D → lexer → W → (metrics / stoplist / stemmer) → W'

The process begins with a set of documents D. D is run through a lexical analyzer to extract the set of words in the corpus, W. The process then applies a combination of metrics, stoplists, and stemmers to W to produce W'. The elements of W' are ranked based on the metric used.

From the ranked set W' we create W_A, which contains the first n elements of W', where n is the size of the expert vocabulary W_E (E for expert). In the experiments we are evaluating the effectiveness of W_A by comparing it to W_E. In the case of ties in W_A, the terms are selected arbitrarily. W_A is considered the final automatically constructed domain vocabulary and is measured for overlap with the expert's manually selected vocabulary W_E.

2.1   Overlap Metric

Overlap is measured as the cardinality of the intersection of W_A and W_E, over the cardinality of the union of the same two sets as follows,

$$O = \frac{|W_A \cap W_E|}{|W_A \cup W_E|} \tag{1}$$

As an example, suppose that an expert chose 12 words to be the domain vocabulary. Thus the automatic term extraction algorithm also selects 12 words. Suppose that four of them are in the expert's vocabulary. The intersection of these two vocabulary sets would have a cardinality of four. The size of the union would be 20, because the automatically constructed vocabulary had eight unique terms. The overlap would be 4/20, or .2.

This experiment seeks to determine which of 14 word frequency metrics will best approximate, i.e. have the highest overlap with, the word sets created by domain experts. The paper also discusses whether the overlaps are affected by stemming and stopword removal.

2.2   Test Set and Demographics

The data used in this study was collected over several years in a graduate course on reuse and domain engineering in which students used DARE to analyze domains. Most of the students were professional software engineers. The results of these projects were complete, or partially complete DARE domain books. Each subject bounded their domain [2], selected at least three exemplar systems in the domain, and then selected documents from the systems in the domain. These documents were typically research papers and web pages, but also included system documentation. With the help of those documents, subjects selected terms pertinent to the domain. The instructions suggested that subjects use tools that could automatically provide frequencies for terms in their corpus. The vocabulary was then used to create other artifacts in the domain book. A subset of these domain books, and their corresponding vocabulary selections, were used for our test set. We selected fifteen domain books to analyze. The vocabularies were determined by the students, who were the domain engineers in this study.

Of the 15 subjects, seven chose conflation algorithms as their domain. Four used domains related to application or programming metrics. The remaining four domains were in personal information management, military medical systems, encryption, and sentence alignment. Figure 1 shows the frequency of subjects' chosen corpus sizes, token counts, unique token counts, and the size of their selected vocabularies.

Figure 1.A shows that the median number of documents used by subjects was 5, but that some subjects used 2 to 3 times that many. From these documents, the total number of words extracted by lexical analysis gave a median value of around 15,000 words as shown in Figure 1.C. When duplicates were eliminated, the median number of words was around 2,000 as shown in Figure 1.B. From these unique terms about 40 words were selected on average for the domain vocabulary, as can be seen in 1.D.

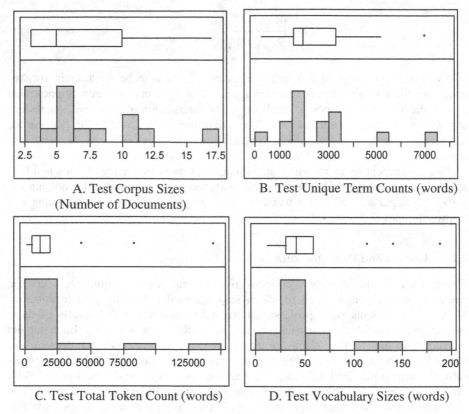

A. Test Corpus Sizes
(Number of Documents)

B. Test Unique Term Counts (words)

C. Test Total Token Count (words)

D. Test Vocabulary Sizes (words)

Fig. 1. Distributions for various metrics for domain engineering projects

2.3   Corpus Preparation

We prepared our corpuses first with tokenization. The frequency with which each word appears in a document was counted and recorded. The recorded frequencies are the number of occurrences of a word in an individual document, not the corpus as a whole. This recorded frequency list was the baseline for an individual document. We created several variations of this baseline. The first two variations were created through stopword removal. Stopwords are terms that occur in language so often that they are generally not associated with a domain. These terms tend to be articles, prepositions, and exclamations. We used two stopword lists, one short and the other large. In addition to the baseline and the two stopword variations, we also created another variation by using a stemmer. Stemming is the process of grouping related terms into one central term, often by removing suffixes and prefixes [3]. The Porter stemmer was chosen because of its popularity, and the convenience of having many implementations available. Stemming was most likely to reduce the number of terms by bringing similar terms into the same grouping, such as plural and singular nouns, and past and present tense verbs.

2.4   Vocabulary Creation

These steps produced large vocabularies that we trimmed down using statistical metrics. We used Java to write several algorithms that use corpus and document statistics to filter the corpus' vocabulary to a few terms that best exemplify the vocabulary of the domain. Although most work in this field has strictly used noun phrases for term candidates, our research used any single word in a corpus, not just nouns, as a possible candidate. There are two reasons for this. Our human produced vocabularies include many verbs (mean = 14.51%), and also some adverbs and adjectives. Domain engineering is different from many of the other fields requiring vocabularies in that the vocabulary is used in domain artifacts, such as a generic architecture. Software projects often use verbs to model methods and transitions.

2.5   Word Frequency Metrics

Using each metric, we weighted each term in a subject's corpus and assigned it a value, w. The term weights were sorted and the top |V| terms were selected (unless otherwise noted), where V is the set of terms in the expert selected vocabulary for the domain corresponding to the corpus. Tables 1-4 summarize the metrics and provide an abbreviation for metric names. The tables also provide a short description of the weighting rationale of each term.

Figure 2 gives a taxonomical view of the metrics in the experiment, showing the four broad categories into which we group the metrics. The Non-normalized, Normalized, and Static Document Allotment categories are all based on term frequencies, while the Frequency Distribution category is based on frequency distributions.

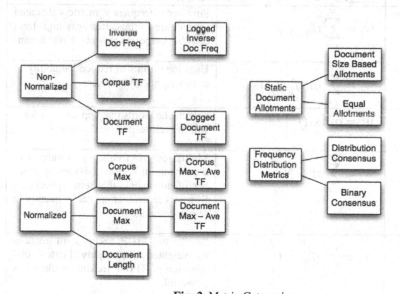

Fig. 2. Metric Categories

Sections 2.5.1 through 2.5.4 give equations and details for each of the four categories of metrics. In the equations, the following variables are used.

- N – Number of documents in a corpus
- T_j – Number of terms in a document
- T_c – Number of terms in a corpus
- V – A set representing the experts vocabulary
- tf_{ij} – Number of occurrences of term i in document j
- tf_{ic} – Number of occurrences of term i in corpus c
- P_j – Number of occurrences of the most frequent term in document j
- P_c – Number of occurrences of the most frequent term in corpus c
- n_i – Number of documents in which term i appears
- w_i – weight of term i in a corpus
- K_j – Number of terms to be selected from document j

2.5.1 Non-normalized Term Frequency Metrics

Most indexing algorithms and term extraction algorithms base their results on some calculation involving term frequency, assuming that words that appear often are likely candidate terms for the vocabulary of the domain. This assumption is justified by [6], although they further their results with restricting candidates to particular patterns. The original paper on the importance of term frequency in selecting index terms for information retrieval dates back to [7]. The metrics in this and the following two sub-sections are all based on term frequency.

Table 1. Non-Normalized Term Frequency Metric Equations

Metric Title	Equation	Notes
Corpus Term Frequency (TF)	$$w_i = \sum_{j=1}^{N} tf_{ij}$$	Pure term frequency metric calculated over entire corpus. Rewards high term counts. Large documents have advantage
Logged Term Frequency (LTF)	$$w_i = \sum_{j=1}^{N} \ln(tf_{ij} + 1)$$	Uses logarithms to reduce variability of term weights in document.
Document Term Frequency (USN)	$$w_i = \max_{1 \le j \le N}(tf_{ij}) / T_c$$	Selects the words that appear most often within their respective document.
Term Frequency and Inverse Document Frequency (TFIDF)	$$w_i = \sum_{j=1}^{N} tf_{ij} \cdot N / n_i$$	Multiplies term frequency by number of documents in corpus. Divides by number of documents that term appears in. Rewards terms that appear frequently in few documents.
Term Frequency and Logged Inverse Document Frequency (TFLIDF)	$$w_i = \sum_{j=1}^{N} tf_{ij} \cdot \ln(\frac{N}{n_i})$$	Similar to TFIDF, except term frequency weighted more highly. Flattens distribution of TFIDF making outliers less powerful.

2.5.2 Normalized Term Frequency Metrics

The concept of term normalization has been a standard metric for information retrieval since the late 1970's [8]. Normalization occurs by dividing the frequency of a term in a document by the total number of terms in a document. By normalizing each document, we remove the effect of size, and each term frequency is now a percentage of another characteristic of the document, the document's term count.

Table 2. Normalized Term Frequency Metric Equations

Metric Title	Equation	Notes
Normalized Term Frequency (NTF)	$$w_i = \sum_{j=1}^{N} tf_{ij} / T_j$$	Normalizes by dividing term frequency by number of terms in document. Rewards high term count but negates large document skewing.
Document Relativized (DR)	$$w_i = \sum_{j=1}^{N} tf_{ij} / P_j$$	Divides by most frequent term in document, then sums the results. Less rewards for large documents; penalizes verbose documents.
Corpus Relativized (CR)	$$w_i = \sum_{j=1}^{N} tf_{ij} / P_c$$	Normalizes by dividing by most frequent term in corpus, then summing results. Less reward for large documents.
Document Relativized Minus Document Average Frequency (DRDA)	$$w_i = \left(\sum_{j=1}^{N} tf_{ij} / P_j \right) - \frac{\sum_{j=1}^{N} tf_{ij}}{N}$$	Normalizes using most frequent term in document, then subtracts average frequency of term i in all documents. Less reward for large documents.
Corpus Relativized Minus Document Average Frequency (CRDA)	$$w_i = \left(\sum_{j=1}^{N} tf_{ij} / P_c \right) - \frac{\sum_{j=1}^{N} tf_{ij}}{N}$$	Normalizes using most frequent term in corpus, then subtracts average frequency of term i in all documents. Less reward for large documents

2.5.3 Static Document Allotment Metrics

The following two metrics use a different approach to term selection. The weights given to each term are specific to individual documents within the corpus and are not summed, nor used in a maximization formula. Each document is allotted some number of terms, K_j, to add to the set of terms to be returned to the user. The scoring internal to each document is a normalized term frequency score. The algorithm, $W_{AG,}$ is as follows:

```
for ( j = 1; j ≤ N; j++ )        // for each document
    rankTermsByWeight();    // sort the terms by their weight, in descending order
    for ( i = 1; i < T_j; i++ )    // for each term in document j
```

if (Tij exists in W_{AG}) **continue;**
else
    $W_{AG} = W_{AG} \neq T_{ij}$
    if ($|W_{AG}| > K_j$)   **break;**

Table 3. Static Document Allotment Metric Equations

Metric Title	Equation	Notes
Evenly Distributed (ED)	$K_j = floor \dfrac{V}{N}$	Each document contributes the same number of terms based on the proportion of most frequent terms from each document, avoiding duplicate terms.
Favor Big Documents (BD)	$K_j = floor \dfrac{T_c}{T_j}$	Each document in corpus is allotted a quota of terms based on its size.

2.5.4 Frequency Distribution Based Metrics

Previous term extraction work that looks at noun phrases has shown that consensus can be an important factor in selecting a suitable vocabulary [10]. This metric will reward terms that have consensus. Consensus is an indication of a term's popularity by many authors. Terms that have an even probability distribution across the documents of the domain have consensus.

Table 4. Frequency Distribution Based Metric Equations

Metric Title	Equation	Notes
Distribution Consensus (DC)	$w_i = \sqrt{\dfrac{1}{N} \sum_{j=1}^{N} \left(tf_{ij} - \left(\dfrac{1}{N} \sum_{j=1}^{N} tf_{ij} \right) \right)^2}$	Rewards terms with consensus – a reflection of a term's popularity by many authors.
Binary Consensus (BC)	$w_i = \sum_{j=0}^{N} bin_{ij}$ where $bin_{ij} = \begin{cases} 0 & \text{if } tf_{ij} = 0 \\ 1 & \text{if } tf_{ij} > 0 \end{cases}$	Measures consensus based on a term's binary distribution. Rewards minimum frequency of one.

3   Results

In this section we discuss how the observed data supports or contradicts our hypothesis that stemming and stoplist methods and variations on term frequency metrics impact the quality of term extraction as measured by overlap as described in section 2.

We used several information retrieval related metrics to select the vocabularies for each project, and then compared the results to the expert vocabularies. As described above, we used overlap as the measure of similarity. After processing each vocabulary through various automatic term extraction algorithms, we compared the metrics' overlap measures against each other using notched box plots [1]. Notched box plots are a variation on normal box plots that provide a simple visual demonstration of an experiment's statistical significance. Variability in these boxplots is measured with midspreads, that is, the difference between the first and third quartile. These are represented in the plot as the top and bottom of the boxes. The line across the middle of the box is the median. The notch (sloping lines) in the box plot represents the 95% confidence interval for the median. If the notches for two datasets do not overlap, this indicates a statistically significant difference. The box plots also show outliers.

3.1   Stemming and Stoplist Impact

It is clear that stemming and stopword removal improved overlaps. While the results are better on the whole, we found that there are cases when improvement is not guaranteed, particularly with stemming. Our experiments used two possible stemming options –stemmed or not stemmed, and three possible stopword list options – no stoplist, short stoplist, or long stoplist. For example, Figure 3 provides the results of six different treatments involving the term frequency metric. BASE is the term frequency metric with no stoplist or stemming. BIGSTEM is the metric with stemming and the use of the big stoplist. BIG is the metric with no stemming and the use of the big stoplist. SHRTSTEM is the metric with stemming and the use of the short stoplist. SHORT is the metric with no stemming and the use of the short stoplist. STEM is the metric with stemming and no stoplist. The notched box plots show that the big-stem and short-stem treatments have significantly higher overlaps than does the base treatment.

In our experiments, stemming improved vocabulary extraction. There are a few problems that did occur however. Many of the preselected vocabularies did indeed contain morphological variants of each other, and stemming eliminated any chance of having two words with the same stem from being selected as terms. For example, subject 5 chose the words "stem", "stemming", and "stemmer" to be three distinct terms in their expert vocabulary. But for results in which a stemmer was used, the terms *stemming* and *stemmer* were eliminated, and only the term *stem* was chosen, resulting in a lower overlap score.

As expected both the short and big stopword lists increased overlap on average, but in some cases stopword list removal can hurt effectiveness. An obvious example is medicine, where vitamin types have short names like 'A' and 'B'. Many stopword removal lists remove single letter words from texts. Most stopword lists also remove articles and prepositions. The first stopword list we used, a short stoplist, removed many of these and improved performance. However, it did not include many words that were on the big stoplist. For instance, "end" and "ending" are both on the big list, but not on the small list. The vocabulary created by expert 15 included both "end" and "ending". The short stoplist performed better than the big stoplist in this case because it allowed these words to be selected.

Both stoplists took away many candidates that scored highly in the base line run, like "the" and "of". The big stoplist found more words than the short stoplist, and therefore received better overlap results. For instance, subject 12 received a 26% overlap score versus a 20% overlap score when using the document term frequency metric alone. Some words that appear in the short stem vocabulary that did not appear in the big stem vocabulary were "I", "our", "you" and "each". In this case, removing these words was very effective.

In most cases, a combination of both stemming and stopword removal was more effective than either filtering method alone. The big stopword removal list was more effective overall than the short stopword list, even in conjunction with stemming. The results of using a big stoplist and stemming were the highest scoring results in our tests.

Our results show that the highest overlaps were typically produced by using the combination of the big stoplist and stemming. This was true for the following metrics: TF, LTF, USN, ED, BD, NTF, DR, CR, CRDA, and TFIDF. For two of the metrics, TFIDF and BC, the big stoplist in combination with stemming produced the highest average overlap but the scores were not significantly different. For two other metrics, DRDA and DC, the combination of the big stoplist and the stemmer did not produce the highest overlaps, nor were the scores significantly different from the baseline. For these two metrics, the overlaps were quite low and roughly the same.

As an example, Figure 3 displays the overlap scores for our filtering methods when the corpus term frequency metric was applied. As discussed above, the baseline performs relatively poorly because common words are not omitted, like 'the' and 'or'. In fact, 'the' was the top word in almost every test. It also performs poorly because words that have several variants are counted individually. The baseline could not overcome the problems of word variants and common terms in almost all runs, and therefore the distribution had a small variability.

The test shows that the big stopword removal (BIG) and the stemming filterer (STEM) had very similar improvements on the baseline, and the big stopword removal and stemming in the same test caused significant improvement. The base run had the smallest midspread because the same set of stopwords caused noise in every run, and unstemmed words were not consolidated into a single variant.

The outliers in the figure belong to two subjects that remain outliers in almost every test. The reasons behind these outliers will be discussed later.

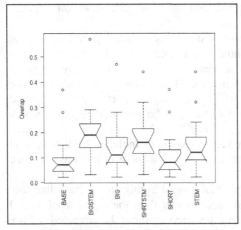

Fig. 3. Overlap Results for term frequency metric

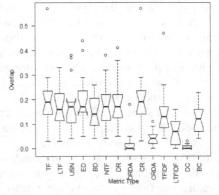

Fig. 4. Metric Overlap Results after applying big stoplist and stemming

3.2   Filtering Methods

Most of the filtering methods produced similar results. For example, Figure 4 displays the overlap scores for our statistical metrics when stemming is applied to the tokens and a large set of stopwords are removed. Most of the methods here produced results of around 20 percent. Four of the metric produce significantly lower results that the others: DRDA, CRDA, LTFIDF, and DC.

3.3   Consistent Outliers

The first consistent outlier was subject 12. The only comment about the expert vocabulary in the domain book is that stemming was not used. The vocabulary terms in the domain book were presented with scores, leading us to believe that some type of statistic was computed to derive the vocabulary. Tokens that would typically be removed by humans, such as "1" and either "used" or "using" were included in the final vocabulary. This indicates that some metric was applied to the corpus, and few, if any, human alterations occurred. If the statistic that was used was term frequency related, that would account for the high overlap scores. Any differences in vocabularies could be accounted for by definitions of allowable tokens, pre-processing of data, and variations of the metric used.

Another possible reason that this subject's overlap score was consistently high could be that the corpus used was heavily text oriented and did not include source code, pictures, or graphs. Source code and diagrams created noise in other subjects' results. Short variable names from source code and abbreviations from diagrams made their way into automatically constructed vocabularies, and these terms did not belong in the expert vocabulary.

The second consistent outlier was subject 9. This subject studied application analysis. It is less obvious why the results were better for this subject than many of the others, but it is most likely due to reasons similar to subject 12. The subject stated that the domain vocabulary was created in less than one hour. This is unusual as many other subjects indicated it took longer than one hour, even though they had significantly less words in their domain vocabulary. This indicates that some quick approach was used. Another note about the domain vocabulary is that it stood out from the other vocabularies in that it used multiple tenses and capitalization in each term. It incorporated present and past tense words, singular and plural words, and upper and lower case words. We can infer that the vocabulary was quickly extracted from the corpus, most likely using automation. If quickness of vocabulary creation and inconsistent tense are indications of automatically constructing a vocabulary, then this would put this subject into similar circumstances with the previous outlier. Unfortunately we cannot judge the validity of their vocabularies, so we cannot state whether the high metric scores for these subjects are the result of poor vocabularies or because these metrics can perform well in certain circumstances.

4   Conclusions

Our results show that the highest overlaps were typically produced by using the combination of the big stoplist and stemming. This was true for the following metrics: TF,

LTF, USN, ED, BD, NTF, DR, CR, CRDA, and TFIDF. For two of the metrics, TFIDF and BC, the big stoplist in combination with stemming produced the highest average overlap, but the scores were not significantly different. For two other metrics, DRDA and DC, the combination of the big stoplist and the stemmer did not produce the highest overlaps, nor were the scores significantly different from the baseline. For these two metrics, the overlaps were quite low and roughly the same.

One obvious conclusion of these experiments is that overlap scores are low, with the medians ranging from 0 and 20 percent. Some of the methods – specifically DRDA, CRDA, and DC – had significantly lower overlaps than the other methods. The DRDA and CRDA metrics both penalize high term frequency. The fact that they performed poorly confirms previous work that suggests term frequency is one of the most important factors in term extraction. Distribution consensus (DC) also scored poorly. The DC metric rewards terms that have a consistent frequency in all documents, regardless of whether that frequency is high or low. This suggests that there should be some minimum frequency threshold used in conjunction with the DC metric. Other than the DRDA, CRDA, and DC metrics, there tended to be no significant differences among the frequency metrics tested. The use of stemming and stopwords did significantly improve overlaps. However, if the performance of the metric was poor enough to begin with – as in the case of DC – stemming and stopwords did not improve overlaps. The practical conclusion would be to use term frequency (TF) as the metric because it is simplest to calculate, and to augment it with a stoplist and a stemmer.

References

1. Crawley, M.J.: The R Book. Wiley, West Sussex (2007)
2. Frakes, W.: A Method for Bounding Domains. In: IASTED International Conference Software Engineering and Applications, Las Vegas, NV, pp. 269–272 (2000)
3. Frakes, W.B.: Stemming Algorithms. In: Frakes, W.B., Baeza-Yates, R. (eds.) Information Retrieval: Data Structures and Algorithms, pp. 131–160. Prentice Hall, Englewood Cliffs (1992)
4. Frakes, W.B., Kang, K.: Software Reuse Research: Status and Future. IEEE Transactions on Software Engineering 31(7), 529–536 (2005)
5. Frakes, W., Prieto-Diaz, R., Fox, C.: DARE: Domain Analysis and Reuse Environment. Annals of Software Engineering, 125–141 (1998)
6. Justeson, J., Katz, S.: Technical Terminology: Some Linguistic Properties and an Algorithm for Identification in Text. In: Natural Language Engineering, pp. 9–27. IBM Research Division, Almadem (1993)
7. Luhn, H.P.: The Automatic Creation of Literature Abstracts. IBM Journal of Research and Development 2(2), 159–165 (1958)
8. Noreault, T., McGill, M., Koll, M.: A performance evaluation of similarity measures, document term weighting schemes and representations in a Boolean environment. In: Proceedings of the 3rd Annual ACM Conference on Research and Development in Information Retrieval, pp. 57–76. Butterworth and Co., Cambridge (1980)
9. Porter, M.F.: An Algorithm for Suffix Striping. Program 14(3), 130–137 (1980)

10. Sclano, F., Velardi, P.: TermExtractor: A Web Application to Learn the Shared Terminology of Emergent Web Communities. In: Gonçalves, R.J., Müller, J.P., Mertins, K., Zelm, M. (eds.) Enterprise Interoperability II, pp. 287–290. Springer, London (2007)
11. Tilley, J.: A Comparison of Statistical Filtering Methods for Automatic Term Extraction for Domain Analysis. Masters Thesis, Computer Science Department, Virginia Tech (2009)

Measures for Quality Evaluation of Feature Models

Carla I. M. Bezerra[1,2], Rossana M. C. Andrade[1,2,*], and José Maria S. Monteiro[2]

[1] Group of Computer Networks, Software Engineering and Systems (GREat),
Campus do Pici - Bloco 942-A - ZIP: 60455-760 - Fortaleza - CE - Brazil
[2] Computer Science Department (DC) Federal University of Ceará, UFC Fortaleza, Brazil
{carlabezerra,rossana}@great.ufc.br,
monteiro@lia.ufc.br

Abstract. In Software Product Lines (SPL), quality evaluation is a critical factor, because an error in a SPL can spread to various end products. However, it is often proved impractical to ensure the quality of all products of a given SPL both for economic reasons and the effort needed due to their large number. In this context, a strategy that can be used is to make quality assessments on the initial phases of the SPL development. This approach avoids having errors that could be propagated to the next SPL phases. So, taking into account the feature model, which is one of the most important artifacts in a SPL since its quality directly affects the quality of the SPL end products, to assure the quality of the feature model is one of the current strategies to assess the quality of a SPL. In this sense, one way to evaluate the feature model is to use measures, which could be associated with the feature model quality characteristics and their quality attributes. This paper presents a measures catalog, which can be used to support the quality evaluation of the feature model. In order to identify these measures, a systematic mapping is conducted and to validate the measures catalog, we perform a peer review with experts in software quality and SPL. Besides that, to evaluate the use of the proposed catalog, we apply the measures in three feature models in the domain of mobile applications. The results show that the proposed measures catalog can be effectively deployed to support the quality evaluation of the feature models.

Keywords: Software Product Lines, Quality Evaluation, Measures, Feature Model.

1   Introduction

Among the techniques for software reuse, one that has gained relevance is Software Product Line (SPL). Clements and Northrop [1] defined SPL as a collection of software intensive systems using and sharing a group of common characteristics, which are managed to meet the needs of a particular segment of the market or mission, and which are developed from a common set of core assets and a predetermined shape.

In this scenario, quality assessment is essential because an error or inconsistency in a SPL artifact can be propagated to all its products. It is important to notice that

---

* Research Scholarship – DT Level 2, sponsored by CNPq.

I. Schaefer and I. Stamelos (Eds.): ICSR 2015, LNCS 8919, pp. 282–297, 2014.
© Springer International Publishing Switzerland 2014

quality assessment in SPL presents greater complexity than in traditional software development due to two aspects: i) different products can be derived from the same SPL; and ii) different products in the same SPL may require different levels of quality [2]. In this context, the quality evaluation of all artifacts and software products of a given SPL proves to be impractical, both for economic reasons and the effort needed [2].

One of the most important assets of a SPL is the feature model. This artifact captures the common features and differences among end applications resulting from a SPL [3]. It models all possible products of a SPL in a given context [4]. Features describe the functional as well as the quality characteristics of the system under consideration [5]. The feature model serves as a basis for a SPL since all features are set in this model and, in general, it is one of the first artifacts to be produced in a SPL. Therefore, evaluating the quality of a feature model is critical to ensure that errors in the early stages do not spread throughout the SPL.

To evaluate the quality of an artifact, a popular strategy is the use of measures. A measure is a mapping from an entity to a number or a symbol in order to characterize a property of the entity. Measures can be part of a quality model. According to the ISO/IEC 25010 standard (SQuaRE) [6], a quality model categorizes software quality into characteristics which are further subdivided into subcharacteristics and quality attributes. Quality characteristics are properties of a software product by which its quality can be defined and evaluated [7]. Quality attributes are measurable physical or abstract properties of an entity. The quality measures are used to reflect the quality characteristics, subcharacteristics or attributes. The SQuaRE model evaluates internal software quality (software intermediate products) and external software quality (software execution) [6]. The feature model is a software intermediate product.

According to Montagud and Abrahão [8], several works have been proposed in order to ensure the quality in SPLs. However, the majority of them focus on the evaluation of quality attributes at the architecture level (e.g., see [9, 10, 11, 12, 13,14]) and a few methods focus on the evaluation of the relevant domain attributes [2, 15].

This paper presents a measures catalog, which can be used to support the quality evaluation of the feature model. In order to identify these measures, a literature review using the technique of systematic mapping was conducted. In this review we identified: quality characteristics, quality attributes, measures and quality models used to evaluate the quality of the feature model. Then, to validate the measures catalog we performed a peer review with experts in software quality and SPL. Next, to evaluate the use of the proposed catalog, we applied the measures in three feature models, in the domain of mobile applications. The results show that the proposed measures catalog can be effectively deployed to support the quality evaluation of the feature model.

The remainder of this paper is organized as follows. Section 2 describes the results of the systematic mapping and the identified measures. Section 3 discusses the peer review executed in order to validate the measures catalog. Section 4 presents the use evaluation of measures in three feature models. Section 5 describes approaches relates to the quality evaluation of the feature model. Finally, Section 6 concludes this paper and points out directions for future research.

2   Identifying Measures

In order to identify a set of measures that could be used to evaluate the quality of feature models, a literature review using the technique of systematic mapping was conducted. A systematic mapping is a type of systematic literature review [16] used when there are a lot of extensive research questions and there is a need to identify a high number of papers related to a research area. More specifically, in this review, we tried to identify: quality characteristics, quality attributes, measures and quality models that could support feature model quality evaluation.

The protocol used to guide the execution of this systematic mapping was based on the guidelines defined by [17]. The following steps compose the protocol: defining research questions, conducting the search for relevant papers, screening of papers, keywording using abstracts and data extraction.

The research questions (RQ) are defined based on the subject of the conducted systematic mapping study as follows:

- RQ1: What measures are used to evaluate the quality of the feature model in a SPL and which of these measures have specifications?

The following secondary research questions are also identified as relevant to our purpose:

- RQ2: What quality characteristics are used to evaluate the quality of a feature model?
- RQ3: What quality attributes are used to evaluate the quality of a feature model?
- RQ4: Which of these quality models use measures for quality evaluation?
- RQ5: What feature model notations are used to represent the SPL domain?
- RQ6: Which studies present a tool to evaluate the feature model?

The following search libraries are chosen because they are reliable sources and also widely used by other studies in the literature: IEEE Computer Society Digital Library; ACM Digital Library; Science Direct; and Springer Link.In order to perform an automatic search in the selected digital libraries, we used a search string as follows:

((Quality OR Attribute OR Metric OR Measure OR Characteristic) AND ("Feature Model" OR "Feature Diagram") AND ("Product Line" OR "Product Family") AND ("Quality Evaluation" OR "Quality Assessment"))

It is important to notice that some papers selected by this work were already well known (e.g. see [5, 18]). Then, based on key terms used by these papers we were able to identify a set of relevant terms to be used in the aforementioned search string. Searches were conducted in the search libraries from January 26 to 31 of 2014. Therefore, this mapping is considering only papers that were indexed up in this period.

We define, for the screening of papers, inclusion and exclusion criteria. The studies that met at least one of the following inclusion criteria were considered: papers that present quality measures to evaluate the quality of the feature model in SPLs; papers that present quality models to evaluate the quality of the feature model in SPLs; and papers that present quality characteristics, subcharacteristics or attributes related with the feature model. The studies that met at least one of the following exclusion criteria were removed: papers that are not related with SPL; introductory papers for special issues and books; and papers not written in English.

In the keywording of abstracts, we apply the criteria of inclusion and exclusion in reading the abstracts of all papers. After the selection of primary studies, it was performed the extraction and analysis of the relevant data to the research, reading each one of the selected papers. In order to guide this data extraction, we examined the research questions and defined the fields to guide the systematic mapping, as shown in Table 1. It was also included the kind of facet classification for primary study proposed by Petersen et al. [15]. Our classification scheme includes two facets. The first facet structured the topic in terms of the research questions. The second one considered the type of research. For this, we used the classification of research approaches proposed by Wieringa et al. [18].

Table 1. Data extraction form

RQ	Item	Possible Answers
-	Research Type Facet	Validation Research; Evaluation Research; Solution Proposal; Philosophical Papers; Opinion Papers; Experience Papers
RQ1	Measures	Extract measures from papers that are related to the assessment of the feature model in SPL (e.g. Cyclomatic complexity, Number of Variants)
RQ1	Specifying Measures	( ) Yes ( ) No
RQ2	Quality Characteristics	Extract quality characteristics that are related to the feature model in SPL (e.g., Maintainability, Reliability, Performance Efficiency)
RQ3	Quality Attributes	Extract the quality attributes that are related to feature model in SPL (e.g., Accuracy, Consistency)
RQ4	Quality Model	( ) Yes ( ) No
RQ5	Feature Model Notation	Extract the feature model notation (e.g. FODA, FORM, Extended Feature Model)
RQ6	Tools	( ) Yes ( ) No

Initially, the search process was performed using the search string in the search libraries defined in section 2. The next step for the selection of primary studies is to apply selection filters on the search results using the inclusion and exclusion criteria defined in section 2. The selection of studies consisted of three selection filters:

- #1 Filter: Refine the search excluding duplicated papers;
- #2 Filter: Apply the selection criteria of inclusion and exclusion, defined in the screening of papers section, in the abstract and title reading; and
- #3 Filter: Apply again the selection criteria of inclusion and exclusion.

Table 2 shows the activities that were performed during the search and selection of the studies and the number of studies that have remained in the mapping after each filter. Therefore, the search returned papers published prior to January of 2014. In the first filter, we found 3 duplicate papers. In the second filter, we read the titles and the abstracts of the articles and applied the inclusion and exclusion criteria, selecting then 40 papers. Finally, we applied the third filter in the complete reading of 40 papers, and, by applying the inclusion and exclusion criteria, we selected 17 papers.

Table 2. Results of the studies search and selection

Source	Search Results	#1 Filter	#2 Filter	#3 Filter
IEEE	22	20	11	3
ACM	16	16	8	4
Springer	19	18	11	7
Science Direct	22	22	10	3
Total	**79**	**76**	**40**	**17**

For distribution of the primary studies by type of facet, we can conclude from this figure that most studies are Evaluation Research (35%), Solution Proposal (41%) and Philosophical Papers (18%). Most studies have proposed measures, quality characteristics, quality attributes and/or quality models to evaluate the feature model, and part of the studies has a Solution Proposal with small application examples [19, 20, 21, 22, 23, 24, 25]. Other studies of the Evaluation Research proposed further experiments to validate their solution, often using cases in the industry [26, 27, 28, 29, 30, 31]. Studies of the Philosophical Papers type were systematic reviews [7, 32, 33], one review is about assessing quality in SPL, another revision is on measures for evaluating SPL and the latest revision involves the study of management of variabilities in SPL. Only one paper was classified as an Opinion Paper [34] and it presents a comparison of methods for assessing quality in SPL.

Based on the results of the selected papers, we elaborate a systematic map relating the studies by facets. We consider a facet the research type and the second facet are the research questions with information extracted from the form. The classification was performed after applying the filtering process, i.e. only the final set of studies was classified. The results of the classification are presented in Figure 1.

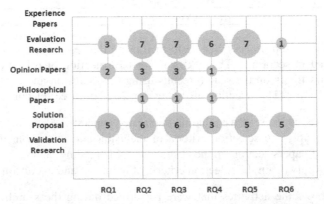

Fig. 1. Visualization of the systematic map in the form of a bubble plot

For the studies classification in a systematic map, each type of facet could answer more than one research question, and not just one research question, which could concentrate the studies. Our goal is to analyze all the research questions and identify opportunities for future work on the subject of quality evaluation of the feature model in SPL. As shown in Figure 3, the research types Experience Papers and Validation Research were not classified in the selected papers. Therefore, the line in the graph in Figure 1 is empty for these two points. The systematic map indicates that the selected studies focus on Evaluation Research and Solution Proposal facet types. These results partially answer the research question RQ1, which is the main subject of our study. Some of the research presents measures to assess the quality of the feature model. However, none of these papers present a specification for these measures.

After analyzing the types of research, the next step was to answer and analyze the facet of the research questions. Table 3 consolidates the results that answer the research questions RQ1, RQ2 and RQ3, and it presents the quality characteristics, quality attributes, and the measures extracted from the selected papers. The quality characteristics extracted were classified according to SQuaRE [6], which sets 8 quality characteristics of the software product: Functional Suitability, Reliability, Performance Efficiency, Usability, Portability, Maintainability, Security and Compatibility. The quality attributes extracted from the papers (see Table 3) are based on the standard SQuaRE [6] (e.g. Functional correctness, Functional appropriateness, Analyzability) and attributes that are specific to the feature model (e.g. Extensibility, Flexibility, Variability). The quality attributes may not have Measures associated with them. We can see that most of the quality attributes extracted are related to the quality characteristic of maintainability (see Table 3), indicating that this characteristic has several factors that impact the quality of the feature model.

Analyzing the result of the mapping we can see that most of the measures focus on the quality characteristic of maintainability. In Table 3, we can also see that some quality attributes have no associated measures (e.g. Ease of use, Accuracy, Resource utilization, Scalability, Security, Availability, Integrity, Authenticity). This allows future research to focus on these attributes and to derive new measures to assess the quality of the feature model. New specific quality attributes were also identified for feature model quality (e.g. Cognitive complexity, Extensibility, Flexibility, Structural Complexity, Variability, Accuracy, Scalability). These new attributes are not represented in the SQuaRE model and they are highlighted in bold in Table 3.

The research question RQ4 is answered by papers that propose quality models that focus on evaluation of the feature model. Such quality models could be represented by methods, approaches, or processes to assess the feature model. We found that most of the papers (65%) proposed a model for quality assessment [12, 19, 20, 21, 22, 23, 24, 25, 26, 30, 34]. Another part of the papers (29%) proposed measures, quality characteristics and/or quality attributes that did not have an associated quality model.

For papers that have proposed models based on quality measures found in the reading, none have developed a specification for these measurements. Some papers present the calculation formula of the measure. Others only present the description of the measures, and others only have the name of the measure. The specification for the measures should contain, according to the ISO/IEC 9126-3 standard [39], the following items: description of the measure, formula, method of application, interpretation of the measurement value, type of scale, and type of measure.

The lack of such information in proposed measures specification makes it difficult to collect and analyze these measures in a standardized way, allowing the Domain Engineer to interpret the measures wrongly, causing collection and analysis errors.

One factor that may affect the quality assessment of the feature model is the type of feature model notation. Some notations for representing the features and variability of SPLs have been proposed (e.g. FODA [3], FORM [35], FeatuRSEB [36], Cardinality-based Feature Model [37]; Extended Feature Model [13], Common Variability Language [38]). The research question RQ5 was included to examine whether there is any impact of the feature model notation in quality evaluation. Results present that 25% of the selected papers do not identify the notation in which the feature model is represented. Most papers (25%) represent the feature model in FODA notation [19, 22, 28, 29, 30]. The second most frequently identified notation in the papers (20%) was Extended Feature Model [25, 29, 30, 31]. The Extended Feature Model incorporates quality attributes in the model. Other notations were also identified (30%), for example: FORM [19, 20], Cardinality-based Feature Model [23, 26], FeatuRSEB [25], and Common Variability Language [24]. However, none of the papers commented on the influence of the feature model notation in its quality evaluation.

The RQ6 research question corresponds to the identification of tools to support the model or specified quality measures. We identified only 35% of the papers mentioned a support tool [20, 26, 27, 28, 29, 30]. The identified tools support the automation of approaches for quality evaluation of the feature model. Tool support is important in the evaluation and data collection to make the analysis regarding the quality of the feature model more precise. Thus, efforts are needed to build tools to support the evaluation of the quality feature model based on measurements.

3   Validating the Measures Catalog

In the previous section we identified a measures catalog (Table 3) that could be used to evaluate the quality of feature models. However, it is important to verify if the measures and the relationships between the measures, the quality characteristics and the quality attributes are correct. So, we used peer review to evaluating and assessing the correctness and quality of the proposed measures catalog. Peer review is a type of software review in which a work product (document, code or other) is examined by its author and one or more experts, in order to evaluate its technical content and quality. The technique of peer review was chosen because it is a technique widely used by academia and industry and has a satisfactory result, because it involves experts.

The peer review was conducted with the following objectives:

- Evaluate if the identified quality characteristics, quality attributes are aligned with the nomenclature of the SQuaRE quality model;
- Evaluate if the relationship between quality characteristics, quality attributes and measures are correct;

Table 3. Measures Catalog: Quality characteristics, quality attributes and measures extracted from the papers

Characteristics	Quality Atributes	Measures	References
Functional Suitability	Functional correctness	Precision / Recall / F-measure	[28]
	Functional appropriateness	Value of the feature importance (VFI)	[20]
Maintainability	Analyzability	Number of leaf Features (NLeaf) Impact of change (IC)	[26, 33]
	Changeability/ Modifiability	Flexibility of change (FC) Maintainability index of a feature (MI) Quantitative impact of functional variable features on quality attributes (QIFVF)	[8, 23, 25, 26, 29, 32, 33, 34]
	Cognitive complexity/ Understandability	Cognitive Complexity of a Feature Model (CogC)	[26, 27, 33]
	Extensibility	Feature EXtendibility (FEX)	[8, 19, 25, 33, 34]
	Flexibility	Flexibility of configuration (FoC)	[24, 26, 29, 32, 33]
	Modularity	Single Cyclic Dependent Features (SCDF) Multiple Cyclic Dependent Features(MCDF)	[19]
	Reusability	Non-Functional Commonality (NFC)	[33]
	Structural Complexity	Cyclomatic complexity (CyC) Configuration Complexity(ConfC) Constraint Complexity (ConsC) Structural Complexity (SC) Compound Complexity (ComC) Complexity Variability (CVy) Complexity Variant (CVt) Cross-tree constraints (CTC) Coefficient of connectivity-density (CoC) Depth of tree (DT) Number of features (NF) Number of top features (NTop)	[26, 27, 33]
	Variability	Multiple Hotspot Features (MHoF) /Multiple Variation points Features Number of variable features (NVF) / Number of variants / Number of PL variants Number of variation points (NVP) / Number of HotSpots Ratio of variability (RoV) / PL Variability Number of valid configurations (NVC) Rigid Nohotspot Features (RNoF) /Rigid No Variation points Features Single Hotspot Features (SHoF) /Single Variation points Features	[19, 26, 27, 30, 32, 33]
Usability	Ease of use	-	[29]
Performance Efficiency	Accuracy	-	[21, 25]
	Resource utilisation	-	[20, 23]
	Scalability	-	[8, 31, 33]
	Time Behaviour	Documentation Time (DT) Time when a feature was included into the scope of the project (TISP)	[20, 22, 29, 33]
Portability	Adaptability	Feature Static Adaptability (FSA) Feature Dynamic Adaptability (FDA)	[10, 26]
Reliability	Availability	-	[8]
	Consistency	Consistency Ratio (CR)	[29, 33]
Security	Authenticity	-	[20, 29]
	Integrity	-	[20, 33]

- Assess if the quality characteristics, quality attributes and measures are in a suitable granularity level. Where the level of granularity of the quality characteristic is high, the quality attribute is medium and the measures is low; and
- Assess if the identified measures make sense in the feature model context.

Four experts conducted the peer review: two experts in software product quality and two experts in software product line. In this review, inconsistencies were found regarding with some aspects: granularity level of quality attributes (e.g. Size and Length was identified as quality attributes, they were excluded), nomenclature not aligned with the SQuaRE standard (e.g. Reuse information was identified as quality attribute, Reusability is the correct use) and incorrect relationships between quality characteristics (e.g. Accuracy quality attribute related to the Functional Suitability characteristic, the correct is Accuracy quality attribute related to the Performance Efficiency characteristic) and measures (e.g. measures that do not assess the feature model as Program Complexity and Complexity of Core Models). The problems found in peer review were analyzed and corrected. So, after the peer review a new version of the measures catalog was produced (see Table 3).

4   Evaluating the Use of the Measures Catalog

In order to evaluate the use of the measures catalog, we selected a subset of the measures in the proposed catalog (showed in Table 4) to apply in three features models. These feature models were extracted from the SPLOT tool [40]. SPLOT has a repository of features models maintained by the SPL academic community. Only a measures subset were selected, as illustrated in Table 4, because other measures identified in the mapping needed more information of the construction lifecycle and the evolution of the feature model, for example, Precision, Recall, F-measure, Value of the feature importance (VFI), Complexity Variability (CVy), Complexity Variant (CVt), Documentation Time (DT), time when a feature was included into the scope of the project (TISP), Feature Static Adaptability (FSA) and Feature Dynamic Adaptability (FDA), or they did not have complete information for collecting, how to change, time, customer decisions, among others (Impact of change (IC), Flexibility of change (FC), Maintainability index of a feature (MI), Quantitative impact of functional variable features on quality attributes (QIFVF), Structural Complexity (SC) and Consistency Ratio (CR)). All the measures calculation formulas are presented in Table 4. Measures calculation formulas were developed according to the descriptions of the papers, being a contribution of our work.

According to the measures in Table 4, some measures were collected in an automatic way by SPLOT tool (e.g., Number of features, Number of leaf Features, Depth of tree, Cross-tree constraints, Number of variable features, Ratio of variability, Number of valid configurations). The other measures not cited in this paper were collected manually using either the calculation formula or the description provided by the paper where the measure was cited.

Table 4. Calculation formulas

Measures	Formula
Number of features (NF)	NF = $\sum$ (Number of features of the feature model)
Number of leaf Features (NLeaf)	NLeaf = $\sum$ (Number of children without features)
Cognitive Complexity (CogC)	CogC = $\sum$ (Number of variants points)
Flexibility of configuration (FoC)	FoC = NO / NF NO - Number of Optional Features
Single Cyclic Dependent Features (SCDF)	SCDF = $\sum$ (Number of participants in features Constraints and daughters of variants points with cardinality [1..1])
Multiple Cyclic Dependent Features (MCDF)	MCDF = $\sum$ (Number of participants in features constraints and daughters of variants points with cardinality [1..*])
Feature EXtendibility (FEX)	FEX = NLeaf + SCDF + MCDF
Cyclomatic Complexity (CyC)	CyC = $\sum$ (Number of integrity constraints)
Compound Complexity (ComC)	ComC = NF^2 + ($Rand^2$ + $2Ror^2$ + $3Rcase^2$ + $3Rgr^2$ + $3R^2$)/9 Rand - Number of mandatory relations Ror - Number relations grouping OR. Rcase - Number relations grouping XOR Rgr - Number relations grouping R = $\sum$(Number relations grouping) + $\sum$(Number of Constraints)
Cross-tree constraints (CTC)	CTC = NFRI / NF NFRI - Number of unique features involved in the integrity constraints of the feature model
Coefficient of connectivity-density (CoC)	CoC= NE/NF NE - Number of edges
Depth of tree (DT)	DT = $\sum$ (Number of features of the longest path from the root of the feature model)
Number of top features (NTop)	NTop = $\sum$ (Number of the descendants of the root)
Non-Functional Commonality (NFC)	NFC = NCNF / NF NCNF - Number of common non-functional features (mandatory)
Multiple Hotspot Features (MHoF)	MHoF = $\sum$ (Number of features daughters of variants points with cardinality [1..*])
Number of valid configurations (NVC)	NCV = $\sum$ (Number of possible and valid configurations of the feature model)
Number of variable features (NVF)	NVF = (NA + NO) / NF NA - Number of alternative features
Ratio of variability (RoV)	RoV = $\sum$ (Average number of children of the nodes)
Rigid Nohotspot Features (RNoF)	RNoF = $\sum$(Number of features not daughters of variants points)
Single Hotspot Features (SHoF)	SHoF = $\sum$ (Number of features daughters of variants points with cardinality [1..1])

The features models used in this paper are related to the domain of mobile applications SPL, as follows:

- Strategy Mobile Game: Dynamic SPL of a multiplayer strategy mobile game;

- Mobile Guide (Mobiline): SPL for mobile and context-aware applications [41]. The feature model is specific for the domain of mobile visits guides; and
- Mobile Media 2: SPL for applications that manipulate photo, music, and video on mobile devices, such as mobile phones.

All measures presented in Table 5 are related to the quality characteristic of maintainability. So, we will discuss the measurement results grouping the measures by quality attribute.

Table 5. Results of measures for each feature model

Measures	Strategy Mobile Game	Mobile Guide (Mobiline)	Mobile Media 2
Number of features (NF)	33	51	43
Number of leaf Features (NLeaf)	22	29	32
Cognitive Complexity (CogC)	8	11	7
Flexibility of configuration (FoC)	43	41	34
Single Cyclic Dependent Features (SCDF)	19	8	0
Multiple Cyclic Dependent Features (MCDF)	2	4	2
Feature EXtendibility (FEX)	43	41	34
Cyclomatic Complexity (CyC)	4	9	3
Compound Complexity (ComC)	1125	3263	2168
Cross-tree constraints (CTC)	4	9	3
Coefficient of connectivity-density (CoC)	0,4	0.53	0,6
Depth of tree (DT)	5	6	5
Number of top features (NTop)	6	12	14
Non-Functional Commonality (NFC)	6	8	10
Multiple Hotspot Features (MHoF)	1	12	11
Number of valid configurations (NVC)	9.198	1123200	2.128.89
Number of variable features (NVF)	21	26	20
Ratio of variability (RoV)	1,07E-04	1,50E-02	2,42E-05
Rigid Nohotspot Features (RNoF)	11	23	21
Single Hotspot Features (SHoF)	7	14	9

For the analyzability quality attribute we have the number of leaf features (NLeaf) measure. Analyzability is the degree of effectiveness and efficiency in which it is possible to assess the impact on a product or system of an intended change for one or more of its parts, or to diagnose a product for deficiencies or causes of failures, or to identify parts to be modified [6]. The higher the NLeaf, the greater the analyzability. Thus, the Mobile Media feature model has higher analyzability (NLeaf=32).

The modifiability quality attribute was not analyzed since all related measures need information about feature models changes. For the modularity attribute, the measures Single Cyclic Dependent Features (SCDF) and Multiple Cyclic Dependent Features (MCDF) were collected. Modularity is the degree to which a system or computer program is composed of discrete components such that a change to one component has minimal impact on other components [6]. The smaller the number of SCDF and MCDF, better modularity. Therefore, the feature model with the better modularity was the Mobile Media.

The reusability quality attribute is related to the Non-Functional Commonality (NFC) measure. Reusability is the degree in which an asset can be used in more than one system or in building other assets [6]. The higher the NFC, greater reusability. Therefore, the feature model that has greater reusability is the Mobile Media (NFC=10).

The other measures are related to quality attributes that are not present in the SQuaRE model [6]. These quality attributes are specific to evaluate the feature model quality (e.g. Cognitive complexity, Extensibility, Flexibility, Structural Complexity, Variability).

The cognitive complexity attribute is related to the Cognitive Complexity of a Feature Model (CogC) measure. Cognitive complexity denotes how easy software can be understood, which relates to traceability of variability in product line engineering [43]. The feature model that showed better cognitive complexity was Mobile Guide (CogC=11).

The extensibility quality attribute is related to the Feature EXtendibility (FEX) measure. Extensibility refers to the ability to extend a feature model and the level of effort required to implement the extension. The higher the FEX, the higher the extensibility of the feature model [8, 19, 25, 33, 34]. Therefore, the feature model that presents better extensibility is Mobile Strategy Game (FEX=43).

The flexibility quality attribute is represented by the Flexibility of Configuration (FoC) measure. Flexibility refers to ability of a feature model to respond to potential internal or external changes affecting its value delivery, in a timely and cost-effective manner [24, 26, 29, 32, 33]. The greater the FoC, the better the flexibility. Therefore, the feature model that has the best flexibility is Mobile Guide (FoC=0,59).

The complexity structural quality attribute is represented by the Cyclomatic complexity (CyC), Compound Complexity (ComC), Cross-tree constraints (CTC), Coefficient of connectivity-density (CoC), Depth of tree (DT), Number of features (NF) and Number of top features (NTop) measures. Structural complexity is related to understanding the structure of the feature model [26, 27, 33]. The lower the value of the measures of complexity, the lower the complexity of the feature model. Thus, the feature model that presents the lowest value of most measures of complexity was Strategy Mobile Game. Therefore, it is the model with the least complexity.

Finally, the variability attribute is represented by the Number of Variable Features (NVF), Single Hotspot Features (SHoF), Multiple Hotspot Features (MHoF), Rigid Nohotspot Features (RNoF), Ratio of Variability (RoV) and Number of Valid Configurations (NVC) measures. Variability refers to the ability of an artefact to be configured, customized, extended, or changed for use in a specific context [44]. The lower the value of the measures of variability, the lower the variability. Therefore, the feature model that presents the lowest variability was Strategy Mobile Game.

We cannot conclude by the measures which model has better maintainability, since all three feature models obtained good results in at least one quality attribute. For this, we would need to investigate which attributes have more impact in the quality of the feature model. It is important to note that we had not identified measures for some quality characteristics, such as usability and security, for example. So, it is necessary to propose new measures for these quality characteristics. Besides, some identified measures do not have specification. Then, it is mandatory to provide a complete specification for these measures. Another complex and relevant problem consists in defining the measure goal, that is, the interpretation of the measurement value. In this sense, it is necessary to build a historical basis of measurements of various features models and perform a statistical analysis to define the measure goal.

5   Related Work

In the last years, several proposals to ensure quality in SPL have been proposed. However, most of these works has focused on the development and validation of product configurations. Just a few of them have been investigated quality assurance aspects, such as the definition of quality measures and internal and external evaluation of quality attributes.

Bagheri and Gasevic [26] proposed a number of structural measures to assess the quality of feature models in SPLs. They validated their measures using measurement-theoretic principles. A controlled experimentation was performed in order to analyze whether these structural measures can be good predictors of the three maintenance subcharacteristics: analyzability, changeability and understandability. However, the measures presented in their study belong only to the maintainability quality attribute, not worrying about other attributes that may influence the quality of the feature model what we have done in our work. In addition, other measures of maintainability mentioned in our work were not covered by Bagheri and Gasevic.

Montagud and Abraham [33] published a systematic review aiming to identify studies that have quality attributes and/or measures for SPL. These attributes and measures were classified using a set of criteria that includes the phase of the life cycle in which the measures are applied. At the end of this study, a catalog was elaborated identifying measures and quality attributes for all phases of SPL. However, different from our work, in this catalog, few measures for evaluation of the feature model were identified. Most measures focus on evaluating the architecture of the domain engineering in SPL. Furthermore, these measures did not provide calculation formula and not performed evaluation of the use of these measures.

Gamez and Fuentes [45] propose to use cardinality-based feature models and clonable features to model and manage the evolution of the structural variability present in pervasive systems, composed by a large variety of heterogeneous devices. Besides, they propose a model driven development process to propagate changes made in an evolved feature model, into existing configurations. Le et al. [46] present an approach to validate the consistency between commonality and variability (C&V) of a SPL, expressed in a feature model, and C&V embedded in an implementation. With this approach, product line engineers can have a method for maintaining C&V consistency across SPL assets systematically. Both studies evaluate only one aspect of the quality of the feature model, structural variability [45] and consistency [46].

6   Conclusion and Future Work

In this paper, we presented a measures catalog, which can be used to support the quality evaluation of the feature model. In order to identify these measures, a systematic mapping was conducted. Then, to validate the measures catalog we performed a peer review with experts in software quality and SPL. Besides that, to evaluate the use of the proposed catalog, we applied the measures in three feature models. We consolidated calculation formulas for maintainability measures of the feature model. The results show the proposed measures catalog can be effectively deployed to support the quality evaluation of the feature model.

As future work we intend to defining a measurement-based approach to evaluate the quality of the feature model; deriving new measures; developing complete measures specifications; building a historical measurements base; performing a statistical analysis; analyzing which measures have the greatest impact on the quality of the feature model and building a tool to support feature model quality evaluations.

Acknowledgments. First, we would like to thank GREat (Group of Computer Networks, Software Engineering and Systems) team for all fruitful discussions throughout this work. Second, we acknowledge that this work is a partial result of the Ubi-Structure project supported by CNPq (MCT/CNPq 14/2011 - Universal) under grant number 481417/2011-7 and the Maximum project supported by FUNCAP (FAPs/INRIA/INS2i-CNRS 11/2011).

References

1. Clements, P., Northrop, L.: Software Product Lines: Practices and Patterns. Addison-Wesley Longman Publishing Co., Inc., Boston (2001)
2. Etxeberria, L., Sagardui, G.: Variability Driven Quality Evaluation in Software Product Lines. In: 12th Software Product Line Conference, pp. 243–252. IEEE, Ireland (2008)
3. Kang, K.C., Cohen, S.G., Hess, J.A., Novak, W.E., Peterson, A.S.: Feature-Oriented Domain Analysis (FODA) Feasibility Study. Technical Report CMU/SEI-90-TR-21, Carnegie Mellon University (1990)
4. Benavides, D., Segura, S., Ruiz-Cortes, A.: Automated Analysis of Feature Models 20 years Later: A Literature Review. Information Systems 35(6) (2010)
5. Pohl, K., Böckle, G., van der Linden, F.J.: Software Product Line Engineering: Foundations, Principles and Techniques. Springer (2005)
6. ISO/IEC 25010: System and software engineering - system and software quality requirements and evaluation (SQuaRE) - System and software quality models, Switzerland (2011)
7. ISO/IEC 9126-1: Software Engineering – Product Quality, Part 1: Quality Model (2001)
8. Montagud, S.: Abrahão. S.: Gathering Current Knowledge about Quality Evaluation in Software Product Lines. In: 13th International Software Product Line Conference (SPLC), San Francisco, USA (2009)
9. Thiel, S.: On the definition of a framework for an architecting process supporting product family development. In: van der Linden, F.J. (ed.) PFE 2002. LNCS, vol. 2290, pp. 125–142. Springer, Heidelberg (2002)

10. Matinlassi, M., Niemelä, E., Dobrica, L.: Quality-driven architecture design and quality analysis method: A revolutionary initiation approach to a product line architecture. Technical Report VTT-PUBS-456, VTT (2002)
11. Olumofin, F.G., Mišic, V.B.: A holistic architecture assessment method for software product lines. Information and Software Technology 49, 309–323 (2007)
12. Kim, T., Ko, I., Kang, S., Lee, D.: Extending ATAM to assess product line architecture. In: 8th IEEE Int. Conference on Computer and Information Technology, Sydney, Australia, pp. 790–797 (2008)
13. Oliveira, E.A., Gimenes, I.M.S., Maldonado, J.C., Masiero, P.C., Barroca, L.: Systematic Evaluation of Software Product Line Architectures. Journal of Universal Computer Science 19(1), 25–52 (2013)
14. Benavides, D., Segura, S., Trinidad, P., Ruiz-Cortés, A.: FAMA: Tooling a Framework for the automated analysis of feature models. In: 1st Internacional Workshop on Variability Modelling of Software Intensive Systems, pp. 129–134. Springer, Berlin (2007)
15. Etxeberria, L., Sagardui, G.: Evaluation of quality attribute variability in software product families. In: 15th Annual IEEE International Conference and Workshop on the Engineering of Computer Based Systems, pp. 255–264 (2008)
16. Petersen, K., Feldt, R., Mujtaba, S., Mattsson, M.: Systematic mapping studies in software engineering. In: EASE 2008, pp. 1–8. IET Publications (2008)
17. Kitchenham, B., Charters, S.: Guidelines for performing systematic literature reviews in software engineering. Technical Report EBSE-2007-01, School of Computer Science and Mathematics, Keele University (2007)
18. Wieringa, R., Maiden, N.A.M., Mead, N.R., Rolland, C.: Requirements engineering paper classification and evaluation criteria: A proposal and a discussion. Requir. Eng. 11(1), 102–107 (2006)
19. Janakiram, D., Rajasree, M.S.: ReQuEst: Requirements-driven quality estimator. ACM SIGSOFT Software Engineering Notes (2005)
20. Zhang, G., Ye, H., Lin, Y.: Quality attributes assessment for feature-based product configuration in software product line. In: 17th Asia Pacific Software Engineering Conference (APSEC). IEEE (2010)
21. Lee, K., Kang, K.C.: Usage context as key driver for feature selection. In: Bosch, J., Lee, J. (eds.) SPLC 2010. LNCS, vol. 6287, pp. 32–46. Springer, Heidelberg (2010)
22. Belategi, L., Sagardui, G., Etxeberria, L.: Model based analysis process for embedded software product lines. In: International Conference on Software and Systems Process, pp. 53–62. ACM (2011)
23. Gonzalez-Huerta, J., Insfran, E., Abrahao, S.: A Multimodel for Integrating Quality Assessment in Model-Driven Engineering. In: 8th International Conference on the Quality of Information and Communications Technology (QUATIC 2012), Lisbon, Portugal (2012)
24. Duan, Y., Kattepury, A., Getahun, F., Elfakiz, A., Du, W.: Releasing the Power of Variability: Towards Constraint Driven Quality Assurance. In: IIAI International Conference on Advanced Applied Informatics (IIAIAAI), pp. 15–20 (2013)
25. Etxeberria, L., Sagardui, G.: Quality assessment in software product lines. In: Mei, H. (ed.) ICSR 2008. LNCS, vol. 5030, pp. 178–181. Springer, Heidelberg (2008)
26. Bagheri, E., Gasevic, D.: Assessing the maintainability of software product line feature models using structural metrics. Software Quality Journal, 579–612 (2011)
27. Patzke, T., Becker, M., Steffens, M., Sierszecki, K., Savolainen, J.E., Fogdal, T.: Identifying improvement potential in evolving product line infrastructures: 3 case studies. In: 16th International Software Product Line Conference, pp. 239–248. ACM (2012)

28. Bagheri, E., Ensan, F., Gasevic, D.: Decision support for the software product line domain engineering lifecycle. Automated Software Engineering 19(3), 335–377 (2012)
29. Zhang, G., Ye, H., Lin, Y.: Quality attribute modeling and quality aware product configuration in software product lines. Software Quality Journal, 1–37 (2013)
30. White, J., Benavides, D., Schmidt, D.C., Trinidad, P., Dougherty, B., Ruiz-Cortes, A.: Automated diagnosis of feature model configurations. Journal of Systems and Software 83(7), 1094–1107 (2010)
31. White, J., Galindo, J.A., Saxena, T., Dougherty, B., Benavides, D., Schmidt, D.C.: Evolving feature model configurations in software product lines. Journal of Systems and Software 87, 119–136 (2014)
32. Chen, L., Ali Babar, M.: A systematic review of evaluation of variability management approaches in software product lines. Information and Software Technology 53(4), 344–362 (2011)
33. Montagud, S., Abrahão, S., Insfran, E.: A systematic review of quality attributes and measures for software product lines. Software Quality Journal, 425–486 (2012)
34. Etxeberria, L., Sagardui, G., Belategi, L.: Quality aware software product line engineering. Journal of the Brazilian Computer Society 14(1), 57–69 (2008)
35. Kang, K.C., Kim, S., Lee, J., Kim, K., Shin, E., Huh, M.: FORM: A feature-oriented reuse method with domain- specific reference architectures. Annals of Software Engineering 5(1), 143–168 (1998)
36. Griss, M.L., Favaro, J., d'Alessandro, M.: Integrating feature modeling with the RSEB. In: Fifth International Conference on Software Reuse, pp. 76–85. IEEE (1998)
37. Czarnecki, K., Helsen, S., Eisenecker, U.: Staged configuration using feature models. In: Nord, R.L. (ed.) SPLC 2004. LNCS, vol. 3154, pp. 266–283. Springer, Heidelberg (2004)
38. Fleurey, F., Haugen, Ø., Møller-Pedersen, B., Svendsen, A., Zhang, X.: Standardizing Variability – Challenges and Solutions. In: Ober, I., Ober, I. (eds.) SDL 2011. LNCS, vol. 7083, pp. 233–246. Springer, Heidelberg (2011)
39. ISO/IEC TR 9126-3: Software Engineering – Product Quality - Part 3: Internal Metrics, Geneva: International Organization for Standardization (2002)
40. Mendonca, M., Branco, M., Cowan, D.: S.P.L.O.T. - Software Product Lines Online Tools. In: 24th ACM SIGPLAN International Conference on Object-Oriented Programming, Systems, Languages, and Applications, Orlando, Florida, USA (2009)
41. Marinho, F.G., Andrade, R.M., Werner, C., Viana, W., Maia, M.E., Rocha, L.S., Teixeira, E., Filho, J.B.F., Dantas, V.L., Lima, F., Aguiar, S.: Mobiline: A nested software product line for the domain of mobile and context-aware applications. Science of Computer Programming (2012)
42. Bosch, J.: Software Variability Management. In: 26th International Conference on Software Engineering, Scotland, UK, pp. 720–721 (2004)
43. Štuikys, V., Damaševicius, R.: Measuring complexity of domain models represented by feature diagrams. Information Technology and Control 38(3), 179–187 (2009)
44. Chen, L., Ali Babar, M., Ali, N.: Variability management in software product lines: A systematic review. In: 13th International Software Product Line Conference, pp. 81–90. Carnegie Mellon University (2009)
45. Gamez, N., Fuentes, L.: Software product line evolution with cardinality-based feature models. In: Schmid, K. (ed.) ICSR 2011. LNCS, vol. 6727, pp. 102–118. Springer, Heidelberg (2011)
46. Le, D.M., Lee, H., Kang, K.C., Keun, L.: Validating consistency between a feature model and its implementation. In: Favaro, J., Morisio, M. (eds.) ICSR 2013. LNCS, vol. 7925, pp. 1–16. Springer, Heidelberg (2013)

A Metric for Functional Reusability of Services

Felix Mohr

Department of Computer Science, University of Paderborn, Germany
`felix.mohr@uni-paderborn.de`

Abstract. Services are self-contained software components that can be used platform independent and that aim at maximizing software reuse. A basic concern in service oriented architectures is to measure the reusability of services. One of the most important qualities is the *functional reusability*, which indicates how relevant the task is that a service solves. Current metrics for functional reusability of software, however, have very little explanatory power and do not accomplish this goal.

This paper presents a new approach to estimate the functional reusability of services based on their *relevance* . To this end, it defines the degree to which a service enables the execution of other services as its *contribution*. Based on the contribution, relevance of services is defined as an estimation for their functional reusability. Explanatory power is obtained by normalizing relevance values with a reference service. The application of the metric to a service test set confirms its supposed capabilities.

Keywords: reusability, metric, semantic descriptions, services, functionality.

1   Introduction

The past years have shown a conceptual shift in software development toward the service paradigm. Services are self contained software components that can be used platform independent and that aim at maximizing software reuse.

A basic concern in service oriented architectures is to measure the *functional reusability* of the services in general or for specific tasks. Such a metric would

- support the analysis of relations among services within a service network,
- allow to estimate the potential impact of new services, and
- serve as a heuristic to determine services that are relevant for a specific task.

The insight that is achieved by such a metric is depicted in Fig. 1. Usually, we have no knowledge about how services in a network are related; they are merely members of a homogeneous set (Fig. 1a). Analyzing their specifications helps us recognize relations between them and identify reuse potential (Fig. 1b).

Measuring the functional reusability of software has been done before, but the used metrics are either unsuitable for services or lack expressiveness. There are two key problems. First, most metrics are based on code analysis, e.g. the Halstead metric and others, but code analysis is contradictory to the service

I. Schaefer and I. Stamelos (Eds.): ICSR 2015, LNCS 8919, pp. 298–313, 2014.
© Springer International Publishing Switzerland 2014

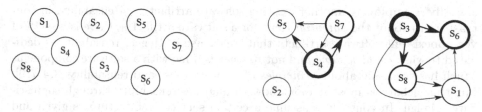

(a) No knowledge about services relations   (b) Insights in how service are related

Fig. 1. A metric for reusability helps us understand how services are related

paradigm [8]. Second, most metrics analyze reuse rather than reusability, but it is unclear what reuse can say about reusability. Reusability metrics for black box components do exist [5,12,13] but are notoriously inexpressive; that is, they do effectively not allow to draw any conclusion regarding functional reusability.

This paper presents a new approach to estimate the functional reusability of services based on their *relevance* . I suppose that the reusability of a service s depends on how many other services can do something with the output of s and on how many other services have outputs that, in turn, make s work. We can then capture the degree to which services contribute to others in a *service contribution graph* similar to the one in Fig. 1b. The contribution graph is then used to estimate the relevance of services: First, we determine the *impact* of a service as its recursive contribution to other services. Second, we determine the *applicability* of a service as the recursive contribution of other services to it. The relevance finally combines the impact and the applicability.

I conducted an experimental analysis of the relevance metric using a service test set and exploit these experiments to discuss its contributions and shortcomings. The experiments show that we can use the metric to (i) make assertions about the suitability of automation approaches, (ii) cluster services into domains, (iii) show relationships among services and their strengths, (iv) reveal isolated services, and (v) give suggestions for the development of new services with high reuse potential. However, we can also see limitations of the relevance metric where service specifications are too vague.

Summarizing, this paper contributes to the question of how functional reusability of services can be measured. I present relevance as a new metric for that purpose based on their impact and applicability. I evaluate the metric with a test set and discuss its capabilities and limitations.

The rest of this paper is organized as follows. Section 2 discusses related work. Section 3 introduces the formal problem definition, and Section 4 explains the relevance metric. The evaluation is described in Section 5.

2   Related Work

This paper is not about reuse but about *reusability*; more specifically, a *metric for functional reusability*. Reuse means that there is a software artifact s_1 that actually *is* employing another existing software artifact s_2. Reusability, in contrast, talks about the *potential* that, for a software artifact s, there is a set S of yet nonexistent software artifacts that *would* use s. Hence, reusability is dedicated to what *could be done* and not to what *is* done with a software component. Much has been said about *principles* of software reuse and reusability [3,4,7,9], but that debate is mostly about how to *increase* reusability through sophisticated design. In contrast, I assume a certain service architecture as given and (try to) *estimate* the reusability under these conditions. In my previous work, I give a corresponding vision statement but do not present a concrete metric [10].

In contrast to classical reuse metrics, metrics that estimate the functional reusability of black box components are alarmingly poorly studied. I briefly discuss three approaches that are closest to what I aim at. A comprehensive and exhaustive survey of these and other works is found in [1]. Note that I use the terms service and component synonymously in this paper, because the distinguishing technical features are irrelevant for the discussion.

Washisaki measures the reusability of a component through the *existence* of meta-information [13]. This binary metric, which is called *Existence of Meta-Information* (EMI), does not take into account the meta-information itself but only whether one exists or not. However, it is highly questionable what can be deduced from this information. My paper, in contrast, analyzes that meta-information itself in order to retrieve reusability information.

Rotaru defines a reusability measure based on the component interface [12]. The problem is that the presented metrics are notoriously vague, because they are completely based on the *number* of parameters in an interface. I acknowledge that reusability metrics always underlie estimations, but the metrics presented in that paper are much too weak to have any explanatory power.

Choi defines functional reusability in terms of *commonality* [5]. The commonality of operation *op* is computed by "the number of service consumers who want to user the functionality of *op*" divided by the "total number of service consumers in the business domain". It is not clear to us how the first number is obtained, but, more importantly, this is a metric for reuse rather than reusability.

A field that is closely related to this research is *specification matching*. Specification matching has been heavily studied [11]. It is related to my approach in that it also compares service descriptions in order to identify similarities. However, there are conceptual differences as visualized by Fig. 2. On one hand, matching addresses the look-up problem of services; that is, which existing services are similar or equal to a desired service (Fig. 2a)? On the other hand, we are interested in determining the "probability" that a service s_1 is used *together with* another service s_2 (Fig. 2b). In fact, we *use* specification matching in order to estimate the contribution of services; still, the examined question is different.

Some approaches for *automated service composition* use *dependency graphs*, which are related to the contribution graph in this paper. Brogi et al. construct a dependency graph consisting of service and data nodes and connects them according to the service description [2]. Apart from their semantic difference, dependency graphs and contribution graphs differ in their purpose: Dependency

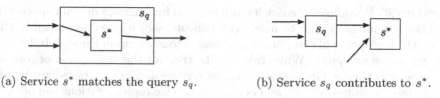

(a) Service s^* matches the query s_q.   (b) Service s_q contributes to s^*.

Fig. 2. Matching and reusability analysis are related but pursue different goals

graphs are used to provide a structural basis for a composition algorithm; hence, the goal is to solve an *individual* composition problem. In contrast, we use the contribution graph as a logical basis for metrics that aim at making assertions about reusability, independent from a concrete problem.

3   Problem Description

The ideal metric for functional reusability is roughly the number of problems for whose solution a service may be used. Considering the probability of their occurrence, we may formalize functional reusability as follows:

$$r^*(s) = \sum_{p \in \mathcal{P}_s} probabilityOfOccurrence(p) \tag{1}$$

where $\mathcal{P}$ is the set of all composition problems, and $\mathcal{P}_s \subseteq \mathcal{P}$ is the set of problems for which there exists a solution that contains s; I refer to [10] for details.

I briefly introduce some formal definitions to obtain commonsense about the problems in $\mathcal{P}$. In this paper, I use a state-based setting, in which services are described through inputs, outputs, preconditions, and effects (IOPE), and where problems are characterized by an initial state and a goal state that must be reached from the initial state through the application of services.

Definition 1. *A **service description** is a tuple* (I, O, P, E). *I and O are disjoint sets of input and output variables. P and E describe the precondition and effect of the service in first-order logic formulas without quantifiers or functions. Variables in P must be in I; variables in E must be in $I \cup O$.*

As an example, consider a service *getAvailability* that determines the availability of a book. The service has one input b for the ISBN of a book and one output a for the availability info; we have $I=\{b\}$ and $O=\{a\}$. The precondition is $P = Book(b)$ and requires that the object passed to the input b is known to have the type *Book*. The effect is $E = HasAvInfo(b, a)$ and assures that the object where the output a is stored contains the info whether b is available.

I acknowledge that this model can and should be discussed, so I briefly point out my positions regarding two frequent topics. First, it is true that the existence of semantic descriptions is currently an issue. However, there is a notable shift in the programming style towards *workflows*, replacing technically oriented programs [6]. Workflows are much more suitable for business domain specific descriptions than the former technical components, which gives new incentives for semantic description of components. Second, a formalization through IOPE may not always be adequate. While this may be true for the description of complex services, it is the by far most established service description paradigm besides finite state machines (FSM), and even FSM service representations can often be efficiently *transformed* into an IOPE representation.

Apart from this discussion, the approach in this paper is not limited to semantic descriptions. In fact, we applied the presented metrics to common Java libraries and obtained interesting insights from that. The explanatory power of the metric, however, is closely related to the explanatory power of the underlying service descriptions and, therefore, the real potential of the proposed method is certainly an environment of semantically described software/services.

The service description in mind, we define a composition problem as follows:

Definition 2. *A **composition problem** is a tuple $(S, pre, post)$ where pre is a precondition that must be transformed into the postcondition post by arranging services from a set S described as in Def. 1. pre and post are first-order logic formulas without quantifiers and functions.*

For simplicity, we leave a knowledge base out of the model. A knowledge base is usually used to express ontological information and logical implications in the model but is not needed to explain the idea of this paper.

It is quite evident that the ideal reusability metric r^* cannot be computed in practice, so the task is to find a function that *estimates* it [10]. This is in part because the number of potential problems is very large and estimating their occurrence is not a trivial task. So, for a set S of services, the task is to find an efficiently computable function $r : S \to \mathbb{R}_+$ that comes reasonably close to r^*. The rest of this paper is dedicated to explain and evaluate such an estimation function based on the relevance of services.

4   Estimating Reusability through Relevance

This section introduces relevance of services as an estimate for their reusability. I argue that a service s is most likely to be reused if there are many other services that can do something with the effect of s; we say that s *contributes* to those services. Likewise, there should be many other services that contribute to the service itself and, thus, enable its execution. We capture these two directions of contribution in terms of *impact* and *applicability* of a service and merge them into the final relevance metric. I argue that the higher the relevance of a service, the higher the number of problems that can be solved with it, and that, therefore, relevance is a reasonable estimator for reusability.

4.1   The Service Contribution Graph

We capture the direct relation of two services in a *service contribution graph*. Given a set of services S with descriptions as in Def. 1, a service contribution

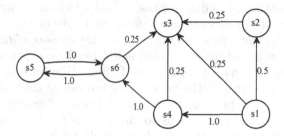

Fig. 3. An exemplary contribution graph for 6 services

graph is a directed (cyclic) graph (V, E) with exactly one node in V for every service in S and with an edge $(s_i, s_j) \in E$ if and only if at least one literal in the effect of s_i and the preconditions s_j can be unified. Intuitively, a link between s_i and s_j means that the effect of s_i has something to do with the precondition of s_j, and, thus, edges indicate a chance that the services represented by the linked nodes may be invoked one after each other in a composition. Note that the contribution graph, since it only relies on completely formalized information, can and should be constructed automatically from the set of specifications.

To give consideration to the fact that contributions of services to the preconditions of other services usually vary, the edges in the service contribution graph should carry a weight. A weight function $w : E \to [0, 1]$ indicates for an edge (u, v) to which *degree* service u contributes to service v. That is, to which extent the effects of u cover the preconditions of v. An example is depicted in Fig. 3. The weight function is usually implemented through a specification matching algorithm [11] and should take into account the *explanatory power* of the different description elements; e.g. it should give more weight to ontological concept matching than to data type matching.

Experiences from the past or expert knowledge should be captured in a second model but not in the contribution graph. Of course, if we already know that a service is already used together with another one, we would want to exploit this knowledge. Likewise, if two services are connected in the contribution graph and we know that they will *never* be used together, we may be tempted to delete the edge from the graph. However, it is the formal specification that allows the deduction that s_2 can do something with the effect of s_1 and that makes the edge between s_1 and s_2 appear in the graph. Instead of modifying the contribution graph, we should refine the semantic description in order to prevent the undesired deduction. Section 5.3 discusses this point in more detail.

4.2   Service Impact

I understand the impact of a service as a product of its contribution to the preconditions of other services and the impact of those services. For example, if a service s_1 only contributes to a service s_2 that does not contribute to any other service, s_1 is probably less reusable than a service s_3 that contributes to a service s_4 that contributes to five services, each of which contributing to another five services. The impact of a service is then a recursive metric.

Additionally, an expert may announce (estimate) an *unconditional impact* for every service. Such an estimation would not depend on other services but be rather a rule of thumb that expresses the "feeling" that an expert has towards the reusability of a service. If the expert does not define this value, it is set to a default constant; the choice of this constant does not matter as long as the expert relates his explicit estimations to this number (cf. Section 4.3).

The fact that the contribution graph is usually cyclic is not a serious issue for the recursive character of the impact metric. When defining impact, we can reasonably assume a recursion cancel if a recursion path considers a service, in particular itself, for the second time. A good argument to do this is that we want to measure the impact of a service by its benefits to *other* services. Otherwise the impact of a service value would be increased only due to the possibility to invoke itself, which does not make sense. There will be compositions that are excluded by this assumption, but this should not be the usual case.

To compute the impact of a service s, I utilize an *impact tree*. Every node in that tree corresponds to a sequence of services, and the root corresponds to the sequence of length 1 that is just the service s itself. There is an edge from node $(s_1, \ldots, s_n)$ to node $(s_1, \ldots, s_{n+1})$ if (s_n, s_{n+1}) is an edge in the contribution graph and if s_{n+1} is not already in $\{s_1, \ldots, s_n\}$. Fig. 4 depicts the impact tree for service $s1$ from the above contribution graph. Taking such a tree, the impact of a service s sums up the expert's impact estimation (or default value) of each node, weighted with the multiplied path weights from that node to the root.

Since the impact tree can be very large, the depth up to which it is computed explicitly should be bound. An edge from u to v is then only inserted if the path from u to the root has length at most a predefined bound $k \in \mathbb{N}$.

We obtain the impact of a service s for depth k by the following formula:

$$impact(s, k) = \begin{cases} uci(s) + \sum\limits_{s' \in c(s)} w(s, s') \cdot impact(s', k-1) & \text{if } k > 0 \\ uci(s) & \text{else} \end{cases} \quad (2)$$

where $uci(s) \in \mathbb{R}_+$ is the experts' estimation for the unconditional impact and $c(s)$ the child nodes of service s in the impact tree[1]. Since the maximal recursion depth k will usually be a parameter that is chosen once and then remains unchanged, we denote the impact value of a service as $impact_k(s) := impact(s, k)$.

Note that the alleged redundancy of execution paths that are merely permutations of each other is intended. For example, a service s_0 may contribute to both s_1 and s_2 while in turn s_1 contributes to s_2 and vice versa. Thereby, the impact of s_0 is increased twice, once by s_1, s_2 and once for s_2, s_1. This may seem unreasonable at first, but it is actually quite what we want. The edge (s_1, s_2) only has a high weight if s_1 contributes for s_2 and vice versa. If one of the paths does not make sense, it will have a low weight anyway and will only marginally affect the impact value of s_0.

---

[1] More precisely, the last service in the child, since nodes are service sequences.

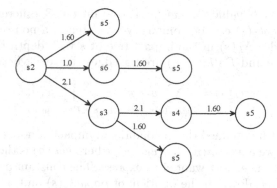

Fig. 4. The impact tree of service $s1$

4.3   Normalized Impact

The impact itself has a low explanatory power, so it makes sense to normalize it. Indeed, there is a good intuition for the absolute values in the contribution graph, but the absolute impact values are quite unintuitive. Without a reference point, it is unclear whether a particular value, say 4.71, is good or bad. In particular, without normalization, the impact strongly depends on the arbitrary choice of the default constant for the unconditional impact.

Therefore, we relate the impact values of service to the impact of a *reference service* s^*. The reference service is a preselected service that is, in the eyes of the experts, considered acceptable with respect to its reusability. There is no need that the reference service is part of the service environment. It may also be part of a different service environment that may, of course, even be artificial. The reference value must be computed with the same measure $impact_k$. Given a service s^*, we denote the normalized impact of a service s as follows:

$$||impact_k||(s) = \frac{impact_k(s)}{impact_k(s^*)} \tag{3}$$

As a result, the normalized impact not only increases the explanatory power but also is agnostic to the choice of the default constant for the unconditional impact. The explanatory power obviously comes from relating impact values to a reference value and makes its interpretation intuitive. In addition, relating the impact value to a reference service makes the concrete value of the default unconditional impact irrelevant. For example, if the default value for the unconditional impact is 1, the expert assigns a value of 2 to a service in order to express that he thinks that the "intuitive impact" of a service is twice as high as the common impact. The same relation would be specified if the default was 10 and the expert would assign a value of 20. While the unnormalized impact of the service is different for the two cases, the normalized impact is identical.

Proposition 1. *The normalized impact of a service is independent from the choice of the default value of the unconditional impact as long as it is not zero.*

Proof. Let the default value for *uci* be a constant $c \in \mathbb{R}$ different from 0. The above metric $impact_k(s)$ can be compactly rewritten in a non-recursive fashion as a sum over nodes $N_k(s)$ in the impact tree of s with depth bound k, where n_0 is the root node and $Path(n_0, n)$ are the edges that exist between n_0 and n:

$$impact_k(s) = \sum_{n \in N_k(s)} uci(n) \cdot \prod_{(u,v) \in Path(n_0,n)} w(u, v) \qquad (4)$$

Since the expert has defined the unconditional impact of nodes n in relation to the default value, we have $uci(n) = c \cdot uci'(n)$, where $uci'(n)$ is the relation to the default value that the expert wanted to express. The constant c can be factored out and then cancels down in the quotient of $impact_k(s)$ and $impact_k(s^*)$. $\square$

4.4 Discounts and Penalties for Subsequent Services

The above formula applies discounts only on the basis of the edge weights in the contribution graph. However, we may want to insert additional discounts.

First, we may want to assign a *fixed discount* per edge in the impact graph in order to make the model more conservative. For example, given a path (s_1, s_2, s_3) in the impact graph of s_1, we may want to reduce the impact of s_2 and s_3 for the impact of s_1, no matter what the contributions are. The reason is that we do not want to blindly trust the specifications of the services with respect to their functional interoperability. Even if s_1 has a contribution of 1 to s_2 and s_2 has a contribution of 1 to s_3, there is still the risk that the model abstracts away aspects that are important for functional reusability. We can consider this risk in our model by discounting the value of each node n by $\delta \in [0, 1]$ for every service before it on the path.

Second, we may want to give a special penalty to leaf services in the impact tree that would not be expanded for a higher depth bound. Due to the depth bound k, we ignore possible compositions of length greater than k. The problem is that we may weight two services s and $s\prime$ equally, while s is a dead end (no outgoing edges in the contribution graph) and s' gives access to several other services. We can consider this problem in our model by discounting the value of a leaf service in depth k by $\epsilon \in [0, 1]$ if it has no successor in the contribution graph. This allows us to make a difference between compositions with a service at position k that enables or prevents to append more services to the composition.

Joining the two modifications, we obtain the following impact formula:

$$impact_k(s) = \sum_{n \in N_k(s)} uci(n) \cdot \left(\prod_{(u,v) \in Path(n_0,n)} w(u, v) \cdot (1 - \delta) \right) \cdot (1 - \epsilon)^{leaf(n)} \qquad (5)$$

where $leaf(n)$ is 1 if n is a leaf node and the corresponding service has no outgoing edge in the contribution graph and 0 otherwise.

Note that the metric in (4) is just a special case of the parametrizable metric (5). We obtain the initial metric by setting both δ and ϵ to zero, which hence means to deactivate these discounts.

4.5   The Counterpart of Impact: Applicability

The impact of a service captures the number of possibilities that are opened by it, but reusability also depends on the chance that a service can be used at all. For example, two services s_1 and s_2 may have the same impact, but there are no services that contribute to s_1 while there are many services that contribute to s_2; then s_2 has obviously a higher reusability because the goals reachable from s_2 can be reached from more initial situations.

I describe this indicator as the *applicability* of a service and compute it in the same recursive way as the impact. That is, for each service s, we define an applicability tree that has (s) as its root and with edges defined as follows. There is an edge from node $(s_1, \ldots, s_n)$ to node $(s_1, \ldots, s_{n+1})$ if (s_{n+1}, s_n) is an edge in the contribution graph and if s_{n+1} is not already in $\{s_1, \ldots, s_n\}$. In other words, the applicability tree is defined through the backward application of edges in the contribution graph. The formula to compute the applicability of a service, which we denote by $applicability_k(s)$, equals the impact $impact_k(s)$, including the discounts and penalties, but with the underlying graph being the applicability tree instead of the impact tree.

4.6   Merging Impact and Applicability Into Relevance

In order to obtain a metric that estimates reusability, I combine impact and applicability and merge them into the *relevance* of a service. That is, I define $relevance_k(s)$ that aggregates the indicators $impact_k(s)$ and $applicability_k(s)$.

There are lots of possibilities how the relevance can be computed, but it is reasonable to use a multiplicative aggregation. On one hand, low applicability of a service means that it only occurs at the beginning of compositions, because there are no services that enable it. On the other hand, low impact of a service means that it only occurs at the end of compositions, because it does not enable other services that could follow it. Consequently, the relevance of a service should be high if both its impact and applicability are high, it should be medium if one of the two is high and the other is low, and it should be low if both are low. For example, a reasonable choice is the product of the applicability and the impact.

In the following, I compute the relevance as the geometric mean of the applicability and the impact. That is, $relevance_k(s) = \sqrt{applicability_k(s) \cdot impact_k(s)}$. Obviously, for this choice of $relevance_k$, the normalized relevance $\|relevance_k\|$ is the relevance $relevance_k$ applied with the normalized applicability and normalized impact.

5   Preliminary Evaluation

In this section, I explain the evaluation setting, describe the observations made and explain them where necessary, and finally interpret and discuss the observations. Impact, applicability, and relevance refer to their normalized value. Note that the evaluation is based only on synthetical data and, therefore, should be considered preliminary; a deep analysis requires exhaustive case studies.

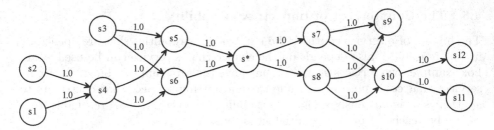

Fig. 5. Contribution graph for an artificial network with reference service s^*

5.1 Evaluation Setting

I applied the metric to the publicly available set of service descriptions *OWL-S TC4* [2]. This set contains 1083 semantically described services, which belong to different domains (book ordering, localization, etc). As the name suggests, the services are described in OWL-S and, hence, fit into the IOPE service model. The service model is special in the sense that it has no "complex" preconditions and effects that exceed ontological concepts and that preconditions and effects are literal conjunctions.

To obtain a reference service, I created an artificial service environment where every service completely enables the preconditions of two other services. This network is computed for a particular $k \in \mathbb{N}$ that shall be used for the computation of the metrics. An example of this network for $k = 2$ is depicted in Fig. 5 with s^* as reference service. The graph is extended by $s1, s2, s11$, and $s12$ in order to test the penalty ϵ. It would have been an option to just choose a service from the *OLW-S TC4* set, but the idea was to evaluate that set according to my understanding of good relevance.

I computed the metric with $k = 3$ and different values for δ and ϵ. I chose $k = 3$, because the computation for $k = 4$ was too resource intensive and interesting conclusions could also be drawn with this small depth bound. I ran the experiments for all configurations $(\delta, \epsilon) \in \{0.0, 0.1, \ldots, 0.9\}^2$ and $uci = 1$.

5.2 Observations

Our first observation is that a significant part of the services is completely isolated from any other service. There are 286 (26.4%) services that have neither an outgoing nor an ingoing edge in the contribution graph; it is safe to say that these services are useless for composition [3]. The following results are based on the adjusted service repository that does not contain these services.

Fig. 6 summarizes the values for impact, applicability, and relevance of the remaining 797 services according to the choices of δ and ϵ respectively. The gray

---

[2] At time of writing, this data set is available at
    http://projects.semwebcentral.org/frs/?group_id=89&release_id=380

[3] Of course, they *may* be used in a composition, but its *specification* does not give reason to believe that this would make sense.

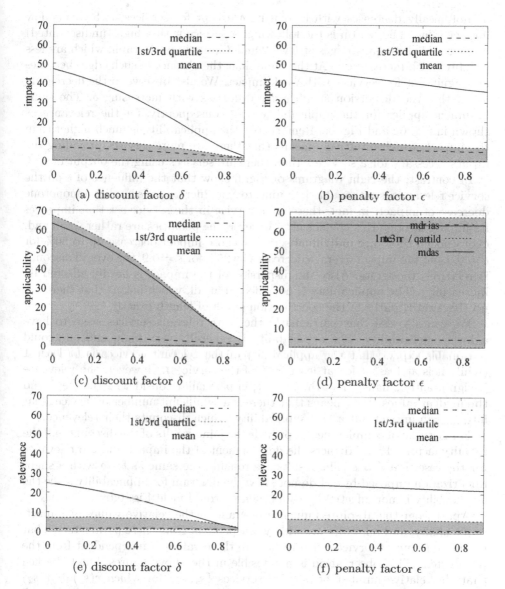

Fig. 6. Summary of relevance values depending on discount and penalty factors

area is the inter-quartile range (contains 50% of the services for the respective factor) and reveals a moderate dispersion of impacts among the majority of the services. However, there is a significant increase of impact in the upper quartile. We use the mean instead of a maximum to avoid out-scaling implied by this dispersion, but I shall mention that the maximum impact for $\delta = \epsilon = 0$ is 596,54. Figures on the left assume $\epsilon = 0$, and figures on the right assume $\delta = 0$.

The left diagrams of Fig. 6 show that the choice of δ has a huge implication for the relevance. Fig. 6a summarizes the fact that the impact of a service monotonically decreases with increasing δ except for services with a very low impact value. The reason is the following: A service with a high (undiscounted) impact value has many edges at level 2 and 3 in its impact graph, which are less weighted with increasing δ. At the same time, the absence of such edges becomes less significant for services with weak impact. We also observe in the decreasing mean that the dispersion significantly decreases with increasing δ. The same argument applies for the applicability and, consequently, for the relevance as shown in Fig. 6c and Fig. 6e. Remarkably, the applicability is much higher than the impact, which intuitively means that there are more services providing the inputs necessary for a service s than there are services using the output of s.

In contrast, the right diagrams of Fig. 6 show that the influence of ϵ on the service relevance is rather small. Similar to δ, an increase of ϵ implies a monotone decrease of impact; in fact, there is no service in the service set that improves its impact through this coefficient[4]. However, the penalties are rather small and, even though there are individual services whose impact decrease up to 50% for $\epsilon = 0.9$ and the impact average decreases by 25% for $\epsilon = 0.9$, the overall discount is relatively moderate. Also, the dispersion of the impact is hardly affected by increasing ϵ. The applicability is not affected at all, which means that there are no (backward) paths in the contribution graph of length exactly k.

We can also see that particularly the more relevant services seem to have a lower applicability. The applicability is generally very high, and one could reasonable expect that the applicability of the relevant services is at least 1 (while it is at least 4 for at least 50% of the services). However, the relevance is significantly smaller than the impact, in particular considering the mean and the median values. This means that there is a significant number of services that have a high impact but a bad applicability, which discounts their relevance.

For the sake of completeness, I provide the joint results of the discount and the penalty factors. Fig. 7 depicts the development of the impact and the relevance for the case that $\delta = \epsilon$. The results are roughly the same as for δ with a slight linearization imposed by ϵ. I do not show the diagram for applicability since the applicability is not affected by ϵ and, hence, would yield Fig. 6d.

Apart from the absolute influence of δ and ϵ, the relative values of impact, applicability, and relevance are widely independent from these parameters. That is, the *ordering* of services with respect to these values is independent from the parameters. This observation is not visible in the above figures, but I checked that the relative number of pairs of services $\{s_1, s_2\}$ for which $r(s_1) \geq r(s_2)$ (for applicability and relevance respectively) has the same truth value for all configurations (δ, ϵ) is between 90% and 99%. While this result holds for the particular dataset, I do not claim that it is also valid for other repositories.

5.3   Discussion

Some of the services have very high relevance values, which may generally have both a positive or negative meaning. A high relevance value implies that,

---

[4] This would be possible because also the reference service is discounted by ϵ.

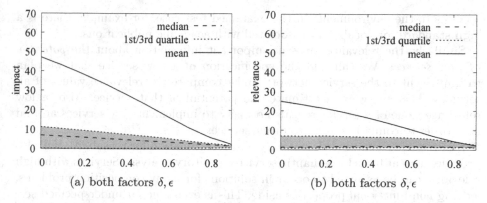

Fig. 7. Impact and relevance of the examined repository for the case $\delta = \epsilon$

according to the specification, the service has probably a very high functional reusability. This can mean that the service has really a very high reusability or that it is *underspecified.* For example, a service s_1 may have a contribution of 1 for service s_2 even though they would never be used together; the precondition of s_2 is underspecified. Of course, it can also be a mixture of the two.

In our case, it is in fact a mixture of the two reasons. A brief look at the services shows that many of them could be used together. However, the preconditions and effects of the services are merely (semantic) types and do not really specify what computation they perform. This implies that many services fit together according to their specifications, but they would not necessarily be used together in practice.

This does, of course, not mean that the metric is useless in this scenario; quite the contrary. First, without the metric, the very discovery and analysis of the underspecification is cumbersome. Second, even if services are underspecified, it still helps derive insights about the applicability of automated service composition. The good relevance values for many of the services tell us that there *are* many service compositions constructable by automated approaches. The only problem is that we must expect that the results of such a composition may not always be satisfactory due to underspecification of services; so, automation techniques are applicable with *concessions* regarding the quality of composition results. Concludingly, the metric provides valuable information about reusability that becomes even more valuable with increasing quality of service descriptions.

Apart from this, we can see that the presented concepts give great insights into the relations within a service network. The domain detection as a side-effect of the contribution graph allows us to partition the service set according to topics. It may be interesting to analyze how this domain analysis can be refined by an analysis of the coupling within a domain in order to identify sub-domains.

Also, we can derive interesting information about the *vocabulary standard* in the service environment. Services with high impact or applicability values, even if underspecified, define a de facto standard of predicates for what they do. This serves as a very important orientation for developers who want to add new services to the environment. In the examined test case, for example, there is a high standard for vocabulary associated with academic publications.

Similarly, the relevance gives us important information about the *potential of new services*. We can add the specification of a new service that we plan to implement to the service network and recompute the relevance values of all services. Thereby, we can estimate the potential of that service. Also, a low relevance value of a service reveals necessity to implement new services around it in order to connect it more to other services.

Summarizing, relevance is not only a good estimation for reusability but also provides a great basis for semantic service repository analysis. Services with high relevance can be assumed to occur in solutions for many composition problems, leaving non-functional properties aside. This is even true for underspecified services, only that the obtained compositions in this case may not be as satisfactory as for detailed specifications; this, however, is not an issue of the metric. In addition to this core benefit, the metric gives important insights about domains, vocabulary standards, and the potential of new services.

5.4   Practical Usage of the Approach

If applied to a service repository, the described metric must be understood as a guideline rather than a hard measurement of facts. The goal of the metric is to give a *feeling* of reusability of components, but the results of the (and any such) metric are inherently subject to interpretation and discussion. For example, the quality of the descriptions cannot be recognized by the approach. Consequently, applying this metric in practice means to do it in an interactive way and to compare the results to the rough expectations and adjust the parameters if necessary. For example, if the impact metric is unreasonably high for $\delta = 0$, as in our example, this is a signal that the services are underspecified; increasing the "mistrust" factor δ helps purify the metric to a certain extend.

Regarding the *choice* of δ and ϵ, it seems reasonable to start with low values and increase them if necessary. The influence of the penalty factor is rather small and, due to its semi-linear nature, it may be reasonable to initialize it with 0.1. The "mistrust" factor δ should be set according to the estimation of the doubt that two services are not used together even if the contribution would allow to do so; a default value may also be 0.1. If the relevance values of services are much higher than we think they should be, then we can still increase the parameter. For example, in the above case, a reasonable choice could be $\delta = \epsilon = 0.75$. However, there is no general "correct" choice of the parameters, but they should be interactively adjusted considering the respective scenario.

6   Conclusion

In this paper, I presented and evaluated service relevance as a metric that estimates the reusability of services. Service relevance combines the impact and the applicability of services in their environment to estimate the number of compositions that may contain a service. The evaluation shows that the presented metric not only provides reusability estimations but also gives important conceptual insights, which are knowledge about domains within the service environment, possible underspecifications of services, vocabulary standards, and the applicability of automatization approaches. The quality of service descriptions limits its explanatory power.

This paper is a first step into the direction of analyzing functional reusability, so there is great potential for future work; I just mention some options. First, it would be intersting to estimate the reusability of services in a completely different way; for example, we could use a simplification of the service model that makes the number of composition problems tractable. Second, the proposed metric could be integrated with a learning approach that collects information about how services are used together. This integration of reuse with reusability could make the metric more robust to poor service description quality.

Acknowledgements. This work was partially supported by the German Research Foundation (DFG) within the Collaborative Research Centre "On-The-Fly Computing" (SFB 901).

References

1. Fazal-e Amin, A., Oxley, A.: A review of software component reusability assessment approaches. Research Journal of Information Technology 3(1), 1–11 (2011)
2. Brogi, A., Corfini, S., Popescu, R.: Semantics-based composition-oriented discovery of web services. ACM Transactions on Internet Technology 8(4), 19 (2008)
3. Caldiera, G., Basili, V.R.: Identifying and qualifying reusable software components. Computer 24(2), 61–70 (1991)
4. Cheesman, J., Daniels, J.: UML components. Addison-Wesley, Reading (2001)
5. Choi, S.W., Kim, S.D.: A quality model for evaluating reusability of services in soa. In: Proceedings of the 10th IEEE Conference on E-Commerce Technology, pp. 293–298. IEEE (2008)
6. Frakes, W.: Software reuse research: Status and future. IEEE Transactions on Software Engineering 31(7), 529–536 (2005)
7. Frakes, W., Terry, C.: Software reuse: metrics and models. ACM Computing Surveys (CSUR) 28(2), 415–435 (1996)
8. Gill, N.S., Grover, P.: Component-based measurement: few useful guidelines. ACM SIGSOFT Software Engineering Notes 28(6), 4 (2003)
9. Krueger, C.W.: Software reuse. ACM Computing Surveys 24(2), 131–183 (1992)
10. Mohr, F.: Estimating functional reusability of services. In: Proceedings of the 12th International Conference on Service Oriented Computing (ICSOC). IEEE (2014)
11. Platenius, M.C., von Detten, M., Becker, S., Schäfer, W., Engels, G.: A survey of fuzzy service matching approaches in the context of on-the-fly computing. In: Proceedings of the 16th International ACM Sigsoft Symposium on Component-based Software Engineering, pp. 143–152. ACM (2013)
12. Rotaru, O.P., Dobre, M.: Reusability metrics for software components. In: Proceedings of the 3rd ACS/IEEE International Conference on Computer Systems and Applications, p. 24. IEEE (2005)
13. Washizaki, H., Yamamoto, H., Fukazawa, Y.: A metrics suite for measuring reusability of software components. In: Proceedings of 5th Workshop on Enterprise Networking and Computing in Healthcare Industry, pp. 211–223. IEEE (2003)

Revealing Purity and Side Effects
on Functions for Reusing Java Libraries

Jiachen Yang, Keisuke Hotta, Yoshiki Higo, and Shinji Kusumoto

Graduate School of Information Science and Technology, Osaka University
1-5 Yamadaoka, Suita, Osaka, 565-0871, Japan
{jc-yang,k-hotta,higo,kusumoto}@ist.osaka-u.ac.jp

Abstract. Reuse of software components requires the comprehension
of the behavior and possible side effects among APIs of program components. Meanwhile, identifying problematic usage of these components
is difficult with conventional static analysis. Purity and side effects are
important properties of methods that often are neglected by the documentations of the object oriented languages such as Java. In this paper,
we studied these properties by using a static analysis technique to automatically infer the state dependencies for the return value and side
effects of methods. As a result, the effect information reveals purity of
methods as well as well-defined state interactions between objects. We
have implemented the analyzer targeting Java bytecode and tested it on
some open source Java software libraries with different scale and characteristic. From our experimental results, we found that 24–44% of the
methods in the evaluated open source Java libraries are pure, which indicates that a large percentage of the methods are suitable for high level
refactoring. Our study can help programmers to understand and reuse
these libraries.

Keywords: static analysis, pure function, state boundary, state dependency, object-oriented, design by contract.

1   Introduction

It is difficult for programmers to reuse software components without fully understanding their behavior. The documentation and naming of these components
usually focuses on *intent*, i.e., what these functions are required to do, but fails
to illustrate their *side effects*, i.e., how these functions accomplish their task [4].
For instance, it is rare for API function[1] signatures or documentation to include
information about what global and object states will be modified during an invocation. It is hard to reuse the modularized components, because of the possible
side effects in API libraries. For instance, it is usually unclear for programmers

---

[1] We interchange the term *function* with the term *method* throughout this paper
referring to the same thing. We use *function* to refer the ideas that originate from
the functional paradigm, and *method* to refer the ideas that originate from object-
oriented paradigm such as Java.

I. Schaefer and I. Stamelos (Eds.): ICSR 2015, LNCS 8919, pp. 314–329, 2014.
© Springer International Publishing Switzerland 2014

whether it is safe to call the APIs across multiple threads. In addition, undocumented API side effects may be changed during software maintenance, making debugging even more challenging in the future [16].

By understanding of side effects in the software libraries, programmers can perform high level refactoring on the source code that is using the functional part of the libraries. For instance, the return value of math functions such as sin will be the same result if the same parameter is passed, therefore the result can be cached if the same calculation is performed more than once. Moreover, the calculation without side effects are good candidates for parallelization [9]. However, the purity information is usually missing in external libraries, therefore programmers would risk introducing bugs with such refactorings, for example, caching the result of a function which depends on the mutable internal state.

In this paper, we present an approach to infer a function's purity from byte code for later use. Programmers can use effect information to understand a function's side effects in order to reuse it. For example, the approach can help to decide whether it is safe to cache or parallel a time-consuming calculation. The contributions of this research include:

- An approach to automatically infer purity and side effects,
- A concrete implementation for Java bytecode,
- Experiments on well-known open source software libraries with different scale and characteristic.

In our experiments,we found that 24–44% of the methods in the evaluated open source Java libraries are pure. Also, we observed methods that should be pure in theory but not in the implementation, and revealed tricks or potential bugs in the implementation by a case study of our approach.

We achieved the same percentage of pure functions with the existing study without a manually created white-list, and we revealed which side effects these functions were generating which would not found in the existing studies. We focused on revealing these side effect information on real world software libraries to be used by the programmers and tools.

2 Related Work

The idea of verifiable imperative programs has been used in the Euclid language [10] and its descendants [6] since the 1970s. However, modern OO languages such as Java and C# have not implemented these ideas. The proposed research checks side effects and purity in legacy source codes written in these modern OO languages.

Many previous efforts on combining pure functional style into an OO paradigm concentrate on introducing immutable restrictions on existing type systems, as in functional programming languages. Tschantz, et al. [19] proposed Javari as a new programming language that adds readonly and other keywords into Java syntax to indicate the reference immutably of variables. Based their work, Quinonez [8] proposed an analyzer called Javarifier to automatically infer reference immutability in Javari syntax. Huang, et al. [7] proposed a much simpler but more restricted design, called ReIm and ReImInfer, as they only modified the type system of Java by adding three extra qualifiers in the type declaration, and their implementation is more unified in comparing Javari with Javarifier. A similar approach has been taken by extending the syntax of C# in [5]. All these type-system-based approaches require syntax modification of the source code. Although they can be applied in newly developed projects, it is much more difficult for these approaches to be adopted in legacy libraries, and existing tools such as IDE support need to be extended to accept their new syntax.

There are studies of automatic purity analyzers on unmodified syntax. Sălcianu, et al. present a purity analyzer for Java in [18], which uses an inter-procedural pointer analysis [17] and escape analysis to infer reference immutability. Similar to our approach, they verify the purity of functions, but their pointer and escape analysis relies on a whole program analysis starting from a main entry point, which is not always available for software libraries. We have compared the purity result of our approach with their study using the same benchmark in Section 5.2. JPure [14] eliminated the need for reference immutability inference by introducing pure, fresh and local annotations, which lead to a more restrictive definition of purity, and loses the exact information for effects. Both studies focus on analyzing of purity only, and does not expose effects informations outside their toolchain. Compared with these studies, our approach uses lexical state accessor analysis, which will hopefully combine the modularity of JPure by illuminating the need for inter-procedure analysis, and the flexibility of reference immutability with the availability of effect informations. Also neither of these two studies further classify the pure functions into *Stateless* and *Stateful* as we do. Further, we provide a heuristic approach to detect cache semantics in member fields, thus eliminating the need of a manually provided white-list.

Mettler, et al. [13] take a different approach. Instead of extending the syntax of an existing language, they created a subset of Java called Joe-E. As one application of Joe-E, they proposed [3] to verify the purity of functions by only permitting immutable objects in the function signature. Kjolstad, et al. [9] proposed a technique to transform a mutable class into an immutable one. They utilized an escaping and entering analysis similar to [18]. These two studies are similar to each other as they completely eliminate the mutable states from target source codes, which is not always acceptable in general programming scenarios, thus limits their application. Comparing to these two studies, our technique can be performed on the real world software libraries, even without the source code. Therefore we are more suitable for comprehension the legacy code bases.

3   Automatic Inference of Purity and Side Effects

In this section, we first define the concepts of purity and side effects on the functions in Java. Then we present our approach to automatically infer the purity and side effects. Lastly, we will describe how to utilize our approach during the reusing of software components.

3.1   Stateless and Stateful Purity of Functions

The notion of purity on functions does not match well with other OO paradigm concepts. In OO languages such as Java, program states are usually encapsulated within objects, which use well-defined boundary functions called methods to interact with each other. This is the opposite of a pure functional paradigm where states of the program are passing through function arguments. Moreover, we noticed that most objects have a life span pattern of creation, use and destroy. Many objects will not change their states after properly created, and the methods called on them simply query these internal states. We would like to distinguish these state-querying methods from those methods that modify the states. Through our research we have observed that Java libraries can contain around 24-44% of functional code that does not modify the program's state.

Based on the above observation, we defined a function as *pure* if it does not generate side effects such as modifying the state outside the object. Note that this definition is slightly different from the traditional definition of pure functions by return value dependencies [15]. Meanwhile, many existing studies such as [11, 14, 18] share the same purity definition with us. To illustrate the difference of two definitions, we divide our definition of a *pure* function into *stateless* and *stateful* functions:

Definition 1 (Stateless). *If the return value of a pure function is only determined by the state of its arguments.*

Definition 2 (Stateful). *If the return value of a pure function is also determined by the states of member fields.*

All other non-*pure* functions generate side effects. Although the notion of a stateful pure function may seem like a contradiction, we can view the state of field members as extra arguments, so that they can be converted into the mathematical form of a pure function. An example of a stateful pure function is `equals` method in Java, which compares the value equality of two objects. Although they depend on an object's state, well-formed `equals` methods do not change the state.

3.2   Lexical State Accessors and Side Effects

The main purpose of this research is to reveal the effects of functions. Therefore we need to define what is a side effect of a function.

Definition 3 (Effect). *We define the effects of a function as the modifications to the states of the program, including the return value.*

Definition 4 (Side Effect). *We define the side effects of a function as the modifications to the states of the objects or performing I/O operations.*

The effects of a functions are all the side effects plus the return value. According to the *single response principle* in [12], a function should have exactly

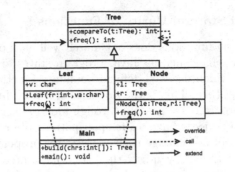

Fig. 1. Class Diagram with Call Graph

one effect, either calculating a value and return it, or doing one kind of modification to the state of the program. Disobeying this practice usually leads to problematic, unmaintainable coding style.

Definition 5 (Lexical State Accessor). *We define a lexical state accessor to be any variable that is directly accessible within a function's lexical scope before the execution.*

All possible modifications to the state of a program are achieved by accessing the aforementioned lexical state accessors. There are two forms of modification: changing the values of these accessors directly, or modifying indirectly though the use of lexical state accessors. These modifications are considered to be the side effects of executing the function. Additional side effects include directly or transitively calling system routines to perform I/O operations.

3.3   Call Graph and Data Analysis

The analyzer identifies method targets by using a class diagram and call graph. The class diagram records the inheritance relationship of classes (including interfaces) and the overriding relationship between methods in a class hierarchy. The call graph records the invocation instructions inside the method body, which points to another method defined in the class diagram. An example class diagram is shown in Fig. 1.

Our analyzer traverses all of the methods in the class diagram, inferring possible effects including side effects. We capture only the dependencies of lexical state accessors, during these three analysis stages:

data flow analysis estimates the return value dependency.

reference alias analysis identifies possible modifications to lexical state accessors that are side effects.

control flow analysis supports data dependence calculations on conditional branches.

There are three kinds of lexical state accessors as defined in Section 3.2, which are the *static fields* (shortened as S) of a class, the *member fields* (shortened as F) of an object, and the *arguments* (shortened as A) passed to the function.

Definition 6 (Data Dependency Set). *We define a data dependency as the value of a lexical state accessor before a function executes, and a dependency set (DS) as the set of data dependencies such that* $DS \subset \{x | x \in S \cup F \cup A\}$.

The above definition of *dependency set* is used in both our data flow analysis and reference alias analysis. The difference between the *dependency sets* used in these two analyses is that we only consider reference type dependencies in reference alias analysis, and value type dependencies in data flow analysis. All dependencies suitable in reference alias analysis are also suitable in data flow analysis, but not vice versa. We define two *dependency sets* used in these two stages of analysis as:

reference dependency (rd) is a DS of the possible reference aliases.

value dependency (vd) is a DS that affects the value.

Our analyzer interpret the code, follow the instructions in the given function, and apply the aforementioned three analysis. The analyzer begins its interpretation by breaking the code of a given function into statement *blocks* using control flow analysis, where we define a *block* to be a sequence of statements. The *block* can be associated with a value of its condition if it is nested in a *if* or *while* statement. Next, the analyzer interprets each *block*'s instructions to evaluate the value dependencies and obtain a list of effects. During the interpretation stage, each value is represented as a triplet of its static type, a reference-dependency set, and a value dependency set ($V = (\text{type}, rd, vd)$).

At the beginning of the interpretation of the given function, the argument values are assigned with value and reference dependencies of themselves. Next we interpret each instructions of the function by following the transfer functions in Table 1. The input of a transfer function is V before the execution of the instruction, and the output is the new V after the execution. Besides the reference and value dependency sets in this table, the static types of these values should also be calculated as defined in the language specifications. Note that the "merge" instruction in this table merges the branches of statements during the interpre-

Table 1. Transfer Functions for Values and Instructions

Type of Instuctions	Code Pattern	Reference Dependency	Value Dependency
new object	new τ	$\emptyset$	$\emptyset$
parameter	x	$\{x\}$	$\{x\}$
local variable	y	$\emptyset$	$\emptyset$
member field	this.field	$\{\text{field}\}$	$\{\text{field}\}$
static field	Class.field	$\{\text{field}\}$	$\{\text{field}\}$
object field	V.field	V_{rd}	V_{vd}
unary operation	$op\,V$	$\emptyset$	V
binary operation	$V_1\,op\,V_2$	$\emptyset$	$V_{1vd} \cup V_{2vd}$
array access	$V_1[V_2]$	V_{1rd}	$V_{1vd} \cup V_{2vd}$
type cast	$(\tau)\,V$	V_{rd}	V_{vd}
assignment	$V_1 = V_2$	V_{1rd}	V_{2vd}
return value	return V	$\emptyset$	$\emptyset$
merge		$V_{1rd} \cup V_{2rd}$	$V_{1vd} \cup V_{2vd}$

```
boolean f(int[] a, int b) {
  if(a.length > 0){ // condition depends on arg a
1:  int [] local = a;    // copy reference
2:  a = new int[1];      // overwrite reference
3:  a[0] = local[0];     // not modification
4:  local[0] = b;        // modify arg a
5:  b = a[0];            // not modification
6:  return true;
  }else{
    return false;        // depend on arg a
  }
}
```

Fig. 2. Example of Data and Control Analysis

tation. Besides the instructions listed in the table, there is another important kind of instructions, the function invocations, described in Section 3.4.

During interpretation, possible function effects are collected when processing assignment instructions. We initially mark two kinds of dependencies: *modification behavior* for reference dependencies and *return statement* for value dependencies. Both dependencies are merged with the value dependency set for the current block.

An example of the interpretation stage is represented in Fig. 2. At the beginning of interpretation, the reference dependency of a is assigned as argument a, and the value dependency of a and b are assigned as corresponding argument names. There are two blocks in this code colorized as red (above) and green (below), which are associated with the branch condition a.length > 0. Since the value dependency of this condition is argument a, both two blocks depend on the state of a. Then, during the interpretation of the red block:

1. The reference of a is copied into local, which implies that the reference dependency of local is {a}
2. The reference dependency of a is now ∅
3. A *modification behavior* is performed on the reference dependency of a, which is ∅, and thus has no side effects.
4. A *modification behavior* is performed on the reference dependency of local, with a value dependency of {b}. An @Argument effect on a is generated with a data dependency on b and a control flow dependency on a.
5. A *modification behavior* is performed on ∅.
6. A *return statement* generates a Depend effect with a value dependency of ∅ and an value dependency of the constant true, which is then merged with the control dependency on a.

The analysis on the green block generates the same Depend effect, and these two Depend effect are then merged.

3.4   Effects from Function Invocations

We refer to the function containing an invocation as a *caller*, and the function being called as a *callee*. When the analyzer sees a function invocation instruction during interpretation, it generates possible effects by examining the data flow across the invocation boundaries. Fortunately, this cross-function analysis is possible with the generated effect information on the callee, so that we do not need to examine the codes of the caller and callee at the same time.

There are two kinds of invocation instructions in Java: static and dynamic dispatch. Dynamic dispatch is used to call virtual methods, and static dispatch is used to call non-virtual methods and special cases such as calling overridden methods defined in a super class.

All of the invocation instructions share the same form as V_{obj}.function$(\overline{V_{arg}})$. All side effects on static fields are transferred from callee to caller. If there are argument effects generated on the callee method, i.e., when the callee is modifying the state of a passed argument, then the analyzer will generate a modification behavior on the reference dependencies of corresponding position, as if the modification occurred inside the caller method.

The V_{obj} is the object that owns the method, which could be this, ClassName or a certain dynamically calculated value during the interpretation. Static member methods on ClassNames are guaranteed not to generate modification side effects on member fields. If a reference dependency of V_{obj} is this, all the modification side effect information on member fields will be copied, otherwise a single modification effect on the reference dependency of the current V_{obj} will be recorded. This behavior of analyzer follows the definition of lexical state accessors described in Section 3.2 to distinguish between directly and transitively accesses of these accessors.

Finally, if the interpreted invocation expression returns a value, we need to determine the reference and value dependency of its return value. The reference dependency of the invocation expression is the reference dependency of return value from callee, and the value-dependency of this expression is the merged value dependencies of all V_{arg}.

With the effect information on the functions, we can simply determine whether a function is a *pure function*, and further, whether it is *stateful* or *stateless*. A function that has no modifications is considered to be a *pure function*. A pure function whose return value depends only on arguments is considered to be a *stateless* pure function.

3.5 Iteration to a Fix-point of Class Diagram

A function's effects depend on the effects of its callees as well its overriding functions, potentially causing a function to be analyzed several times. In addition, recursive functions may also be analyzed multiple times. We continue analyzing until the effects are inferred. We set a flag in each function on the class diagram to indicate whether the effects for this function need to be inferred or updated.

We also differentiate two sets of effects: *static effects* and *dynamic effects*, because we differentiate between static and dynamic dispatch invocations.

Firstly, we initialize all methods in the class diagram with both *static effects* and *dynamic effects* as $\emptyset$. Next we mark the flags for all of these methods as "need to be analyzed". Then, for each method whose flag is marked, the analyzer:

1. Merges the *static effects* with the result of the data analysis on this method.
2. Sets the *dynamic effects* to be the merge of *static effects* and all *dynamic effects* of the overridden methods.
3. Clears the flag on this method.
4. If the effects have changed since last analysis, marks the flags of all methods that depend on this method.

We continue iterating until none of the methods in the class diagram are marked, which means a fix-point of the analysis is reached. Note that during the execution of this algorithm, the size of both *static effects* and *dynamic effects* only increases and never decreases. There is an upper limit on the size, which is the sum of numbers of all possible modifications to the fields and arguments in the program. With the monotone increasing property and the upper bound of the algorithm, we can guarantee that it will halt.

3.6   Applications in Reusing Software Components

We have described how our analyzer infer the effect information. Next, we will briefly introduce how to use our analyzer from a programmer's point of view.

Suppose a programmer is facing a reusable software component, either in distributed binary form or in source code form, and the programmer would like to know whether it is safe to reuse this component in his new code. The programmer can apply our analyzer on the candidate component, together with all its dependent libraries, to obtain a list of side effects on each functions from the component. The programmer can then decide whether it is safe to reuse the component based on the side effects.

For example, if the programmer is writing a multi-threaded program, and the candidate component is accessing some global states, then the programmer may need to introduce a thread lock to synchronize the accesses to these global states. As another example, if the candidate function is a pure function reported by our analyzer, then it is usually safe to reuse this function in the new source code without introducing hidden data dependency.

Moreover, the output of our analyzer can help the debugging and understanding of the behavior of software components. It is reported [1] that some bug will appear only if the programmer execute the unit test separately. Understanding the side effects could reveal these bugs even before executing the test cases.

4   Implementation Details

We discuss some of the implementation details of our analyzer in this section. We chose Java bytecode defined by the Java Runtime Environment (shortened as JRE) version 6 as our target language, and implemented the described analyzer based on the widely used ASM library [2]. There are several advantages in targeting an intermediate language rather than source code. First, the analyzer is syntax neutral, so we can automatically analyze all languages targeting the Java Virtual Machine. Second, the analyzer can be applied on binary libraries without source code. Finally, the type safety is assured by the JRE's compiler and bytecode verifier.

```
class String{
  /** Cache the hash code for the string */
  private int hash; // Default to 0
  ...
  public int hashCode() {
    int h = hash;
    if (h == 0 && value.length > 0) {
      char val[] = value;
      for (int i = 0; i < value.length; i++) {
        h = 31 * h + val[i];
      }
      hash = h;
    }
    return h;
  }
}
```

Fig. 3. Example of Cache Semantic in `java.lang.String`

4.1 Detection of Cache Semantics

Although the described analysis works well for identifying modification behaviors in theory, we find a difficulty to apply it in practice when member fields are used solely to cache the calculation results. We refer to the member fields that are used to cache the calculation results as having cache semantics. We found that the implementation of `HashMap.equals` modifies its member field `HashMap.entrySet`, and the implementation of `String.hashCode` caches the result in its member field `String.hash`, as shown in Fig. 3. By our definition, these methods change the state of internal member fields, and thus are no longer pure functions. As a result of these two methods not being pure, callers of these methods were also marked as generating side effects.

This caching semantic is not only found by us, but also described in previous literatures such as [18]. A widely accepted solution to this problem was to accept a white-list of functions from the user (called *special* methods in [18]), indicating that they are proven to be pure by the user manually. For the reason that the selection of the white-list will impose great impact on the precision of the analyzing result, and they involve human judgments, we do not consider this as an ideal solution.

To preciously and automatically analyze this kind of methods that have caching semantics, we extend our analyzer to detect the cache semantics using a heuristic approach. More precisely, we consider a member field of a class having the cache semantic if all the following preconditions are true:

P1 The field is assigned either by a constant value, or in only one member function.
P2 The non-constant assignment on the field occurs within a branch block.
P3 The right-hand value of the non-constant assignment is only depended on other fields.
P4 The branch condition of the block checks that the value of the modified member field is a constant value.

We consider the following values as constant values: constant literals, null pointers and values of `static final` member fields that have a primitive type. The assignment with a constant value is considered as re-initializing the state of the cache field. The checking with a constant value is considered as checking the initialized state. In either cases, the value of the field is determined by other fields, therefore, it cannot be used to store a mutable state of the object.

In the example of `String`, the member field `hash` is assigned by `hashCode` with a calculation result and by its constructor with a constant value, therefore P1 is true. The assignment to `hash` occurs in a `if` condition block, therefore P2 is true. The value of the assignment is depend on the member field `value`, therefore P3 is true. Lastly in the condition block, the value of `hash` is assured to be zero by the condition check `h==0`, therefore P4 are true. The member field `hash` meets all the preconditions, therefore it is considered to be a caching field by our analyzer.

The modification behavior on the detected caching fields are suppressed from the effects, and the return value dependencies on these caching fields are ignored.

5   Experiments

We implemented our analyzer with name *purano*[2], and evaluated it on real world software components in terms of accuracy, performance, and the distribution of different kinds of effects in different scale of software components. During the experimentation, we expected to answer the following research questions:

RQ1 What is the distribution of pure and side effect methods in the software libraries?

RQ2 How is the accuracy of our analysis comparing with an existing study? How is the heuristic approach in the detection of cache semantic compared to the white-list approach?

RQ3 How to utilize the revealed information during reusing the software components?

Firstly, we will answer the 2 research questions by experiments. Then we will demonstrate how would our study help programmers in RQ3 as a case study.

5.1   R1: Distribution of Effects

To show the distribution of purity and side effects of the methods in real world software libraries, we experimented on 4 target software projects, listed in Table 2. These experiments were executed on an octo-core Xeon E5520 with a 2GB heap size limitation. *purano* is the implementation of the analyzer of this paper, which includes a modified version of the ASM library. Both *htmlparser*, *tomcat* and *argouml* are well-known open source Java projects, and we used their latest stable binary distributions. Note that all of these software projects were analyzed together with the JRE standard libraries, because the analyzer need the purity

---

[2] We have published *purano* at `https://github.com/farseerfc/purano`.

Table 2. Experiment Target and Analysis Performance

Software	Analyzed Classes	Target Classes	Target Functions	Time (sec.)	# Passes
purano	2,942	253	2,372	148	16
htmlparser	5,795	156	1,645	112	17
tomcat	7,673	772	8,824	186	18
argouml	11,608	2,545	20,167	233	22

and side effect information for all functions being called including the ones in the libraries. This lead to the much greater number of analyzed classes than the number of the target classes. According to the Javadoc for JRE 7, there are 3,793 public classes altogether, and more private ones in the JRE library. The analysis time of *argouml* was around 4 minutes, which is reasonable for large scale software. The number of analysis passes ranged from 16 to 22, which was depended on the longest invocation and overriding chain in all analyzed methods. Based on the analysis times in Table 2, we can conclude that the performance of our analyzer is reasonable within a daily programming environment, although it could be further optimized by caching the result of the standard libraries.

The purity of functions of the experimental result is listed in Table 3. From the output, we find that around 24%–44% of the methods in these software projects were marked as *stateless* or *stateful* pure functions. We manually confirmed the generated result for *purano* to make sure it matched our expectation. The *argouml* project contains many non-pure graphical code percentage and the htmlparser project have more pure functional code percentage.

5.2   R3: Comparison with an Existing Approach

While there are none of existing studies to identify the side effect informations within our knowledge, there are studies that only infer the purity of the functions based on different approaches. Therefore, we compare our purity result with one of the existing studies to examine the accuracy of our analysis. We ran our tool against the JOlden benchmark used in [18]. The result from the benchmark is shown in Table 4, comparing with the result from their study. Also we run our analyzer in two different configurations. One configuration is using a white-list which is similar to the configuration of [18], with the detection of cache semantic disabled. Another configuration is using the detection of cache semantics.

Table 3. Percentage of Effects

Software	Pure Functions		Side Effects	Modifying		
	Stateless	Stateful		Member	Static	Arg.
purano	382 (16.1%)	192 (8.0%)	1,798 (75.9%)	1,548	1,087	485
htmlparser	363 (22.1%)	358 (21.8%)	924 (56.2%)	679	462	143
tomcat	1,260 (14.3%)	1,861 (21.1%)	5,703 (64.6%)	4,346	3,990	1,288
argouml	5,019 (24.9%)	1,744 (8.6%)	13,404 (66.5%)	7,057	11,849	3,255

Table 4. Comparison on JOlden Benchmark. Function numbers are different because our approach analyzes all functions while Sălcianu's approach analyzes only the functions invoked transitively from the `main` entry point.

| Application | Our (White-list) | | | | Our (Cache Semantic) | | | Sălcianu's | |
	Total	Stateless	Stateful	Pure	Stateless	Stateful	Pure	Total	Pure
BH	73	14	17	31	13	13	26	59	28
BiSort	15	6	0	6	5	0	5	13	5
Em3d	23	7	3	10	5	2	7	20	8
Health	29	8	1	9	8	0	8	27	13
MST	36	8	11	19	5	9	14	31	17
Perimeter	50	28	11	39	28	9	37	37	33
Power	32	2	4	6	2	4	6	29	9
TSP	16	5	1	6	4	1	5	14	5
TreeAdd	12	3	1	4	2	1	3	5	2
Voronoi	73	11	31	42	12	33	45	70	50

Their approach relies on a whole program analysis starting from a `main` entry point, and thus they covered fewer functions than our tool. They chose a set of functions for the white-list by viewing all the source code manually in advance, a time-consuming task in practice, while our approach automatically identifying the cache semantics. We were unable to compare precision and recall due to challenges in executing their tool in our environment. Therefore we compared with their result from the published literature [18]. As we can see from the result table, we achieved a similar result on the number of pure functions. In addition to the number of pure functions shown in the result, we identified all the side effects and the type of purity, which is the main purpose of our study and cannot be found in their result.

Comparing our result with different configurations, we can see that the detection of cache semantics result to a slightly lower pure percentage than the white-list approach. This is excepted, as the heuristic detection approach cannot find all the fields that are used for caching purpose without increasing the false positive rate. For example, we cannot detect the cached result within an entry of a hashmap instead of a single field. We consider the heuristic detection approach is more applicable for the existing software libraries because the programmers usually do not have a clue of which API functions are the libraries using and whether they are pure functions. Revealing this information is the main purpose of the purity analysis in the first place. An automatic technique like our approach will break the chicken or the egg dilemma and enable the purity analysis to be adopt in practice.

5.3 RQ3 A Case Study: Purity of `equals` and `hashCode`

Different programmers may use our tool for their own usages. Therefore, we conducted a case study to illustrate one possible usage of our tool. We examined the inferred effects on two methods, namely `equals` and `hashCode`. These two

```
package java.io;
public final class FilePermission ... {
  public boolean equals(Object obj) {
    ...
    return (this.mask == that.mask) &&
      this.cpath.equals(that.cpath) &&
      (this.directory == that.directory) &&
      (this.recursive == that.recursive);
  }
  public int hashCode() { return 0; }
}
```

Fig. 4. A Potential Problem in `FilePermission`

methods are related with the value equality of objects in Java, and they are used by collection classes such as `HashMap`. The programmer must ensure that the return values of these methods reflect their value equalities, and hence these return values should depend on the state of the objects. Therefore, we expect these methods to be *stateful* pure functions if they contain member fields. The purity types of these two methods are listed in Table 5.

To further understand the result, firstly we focused on the existence of *stateless* pure functions in Table 5 by manually examining their source code. Most of these methods are defined in interfaces or abstract classes. There were also 2 `equals` and 6 `hashCode` methods defined in the classes that do not have member fields. There were 9 `equals` that compares referential identities defined in classes, while these classes have member fields that are not accessed in the `equals`. These were used in unusual cases when comparing by referential identity rather than value identity is desired. An example of this kind of special design can be found in `DefaultCaret.equals`, where the author explicitly documented in the Javadoc as *"The superclass behavior of comparing rectangles is not desired, so this is changed to the Object behavior"*. In addition, most of these classes are inner classes in Java with their names containing a "$" character. These inner classes are supposed to be used internally, where programmers control the creation of all objects. We found 3 `hashCode` that return a constant, whereas their corresponding `equals` compared the states of member fields. An example is

Table 5. Purity of `equals` and `hashCode`

Software		All	Pure Functions		Side Effects
			Stateless	Stateful	
purano	`equals`	518	19 (3.7%)	165 (31.9%)	334 (64.5%)
	`hashCode`	499	14 (2.8%)	176 (35.3%)	306 (61.9%)
htmlparser	`equals`	359	14 (3.9%)	141 (39.3%)	204 (56.8%)
	`hashCode`	355	10 (2.8%)	147 (41.4%)	198 (55.8%)
tomcat	`equals`	477	65 (13.6%)	282 (59.1%)	132 (27.7%)
	`hashCode`	473	52 (11.0%)	245 (51.8%)	176 (37.2%)
argouml	`equals`	426	55 (12.9%)	219 (51.4%)	152 (35.7%)
	`hashCode`	416	55 (12.2%)	214 (51.4%)	162 (28.9%)

shown in Fig. 4, that `FilePermission.hashCode` will always return 0. The user of these classes must be aware of their respective behaviors, in order to avoid putting them in a `HashSet` or `HashMap`, or comparing them using equals.

Next we examined the functions in Table 5 that generate side effects. Some classes such as `Date` and `Calendar` normalized their internal representation before comparing equality or calculating the hash code. Classes used in reflection at runtime, such as `java.lang.reflect.Class`, used a lazy loading technique to optimize general performance, which is similiar to the caching technique but will change the observable state of the object.

All of these implementation details revealed by our analyzer require special care in both development and maintenance of the software. We hope our research can aid the development in the situations like we have studied in this case study.

6   Future Work and Conclusions

The current implementation of our analyzer works on Java bytecode rather than source code. Besides all the advantages described, this decision is also made to ease the development, because it is easy to generate bytecode from source code by a compiler but not vice versa. However, targeting source code format is still important for integrating as an IDE plugin. We plan to add a source code analyzer in the future.

Moreover, we plan to further evaluate the usability of the generated effect information, by programmers as well as by analysis tools. Currently we output the effect information as annotations. The format of these annotations needs to be more readable and understandable to be used by programmers. We will also further investigate the applications of these effect annotations other than identification of pure functions. We will apply this approach to more software projects for further evaluation.

To conclude, in this paper we presented a study on the purity and side effects of the functions in Java, helping programmers to reuse the software libraries. We proposed a technique to automatically infer the purity and side effect informations from Java bytecode. We implemented and experimented the proposed analyzer on real world Java software libraries, and found that around 24%–44% of all the methods of a Java libraries are made of pure functions. We compared the accuracy of distribution of pure functions with an existing study. Also, we demonstrated how programmers will use our technique to understand the behavior of library APIs by a case study.

Acknowledgment. This work was supported by MEXT/JSPS KAKENHI 25220003, 24650011, and 24680002.

References

1. Bell, J.S., Kaiser, G.E.: Unit test virtualization with vmvm (2013)
2. Bruneton, E., Lenglet, R., Coupaye, T.: Asm: A code manipulation tool to implement adaptable systems. Adaptable and Extensible Component Systems 30 (2002)
3. Finifter, M., Mettler, A., Sastry, N., Wagner, D.: Verifiable functional purity in java. In: Proc. of the 15th ACM Conference on Computer and Communications Security, pp. 161–174. ACM (2008)
4. Goetz, B.: Java theory and practice: I have to document that (2002), http://www.ibm.com/developerworks/java/library/j-jtp0821/index.html
5. Gordon, C., Parkinson, M., Parsons, J., Bromfield, A., Duffy, J.: Uniqueness and reference immutability for safe parallelism (2012)
6. Holt, R.C., Cordy, J.R.: The turing programming language. Communications of the ACM 31(12), 1410–1423 (1988)
7. Huang, W., Milanova, A., Ernst, W.: Reim & reiminfer: Checking and inference of reference immutability and method purity. In: OOPSLA (2012)
8. Javarifier, J.Q.: Inference of reference immutability in Java. Ph.D. thesis, Massachusetts Institute of Technology (2008)
9. Kjolstad, F., Dig, D., Acevedo, G., Snir, M.: Transformation for class immutability. In: Proceedings of the 33rd International Conference on Software Engineering, ICSE 2011, pp. 61–70. ACM, New York (2011), http://doi.acm.org/10.1145/1985793.1985803
10. Lampson, B.W., Horning, J.J., London, R.L., Mitchell, J.G., Popek, G.J.: Report on the programming language euclid. ACM Sigplan Notices 12(2), 1–79 (1977)
11. Leavens, G.T., Baker, A.L., Ruby, C.: Preliminary design of jml. Technical Report 96-06p, Iowa State University (2001)
12. Martin, R.C.: Clean code: A handbook of agile software craftsmanship. Prentice Hall (2008)
13. Mettler, A., Wagner, D., Close, T.: Joe-e: A security-oriented subset of java. In: Network and Distributed Systems Symposium. Internet Society (2010)
14. Pearce, D.J.: JPure: A modular purity system for java. In: Knoop, J. (ed.) CC 2011. LNCS, vol. 6601, pp. 104–123. Springer, Heidelberg (2011)
15. Peyton Jones, S.L., Wadler, P.: Imperative functional programming. In: Proceedings of the 20th ACM SIGPLAN-SIGACT Symposium on Principles of Programming Languages, pp. 71–84. ACM (1993)
16. Raymond, C.: The importance of error code backwards compatibility (2005), http://blogs.msdn.com/b/oldnewthing/archive/2005/01/18/355177.aspx
17. Sălcianu, A.: Pointer analysis and its applications for Java programs. Ph.D. thesis, Citeseer (2001)
18. Sălcianu, A., Rinard, M.: Purity and side effect analysis for java programs. In: Cousot, R. (ed.) VMCAI 2005. LNCS, vol. 3385, pp. 199–215. Springer, Heidelberg (2005)
19. Tschantz, M., Ernst, M.: Javari: Adding reference immutability to Java, vol. 40. ACM (2005)

Mining Software Components
from Object-Oriented APIs

Anas Shatnawi[1], Abdelhak Seriai[1], Houari Sahraoui[2], and Zakarea Al-Shara[1]

[1] UMR CNRS 5506, LIRMM, University of Montpellier II, Montpellier, France
shatnawi,seriai,alshara@lirmm.fr
[2] DIRO, University of Montreal, Montreal, Canada
sahraoui@iro.umontreal.ca

Abstract. Object-oriented Application Programing Interfaces (APIs)
support software reuse by providing pre-implemented functionalities. Due
to the huge number of included classes, reusing and understanding large
APIs is a complex task. Otherwise, software components are admitted to
be more reusable and understandable entities than object-oriented ones.
Thus, in this paper, we propose an approach for reengineering object-
oriented APIs into component-based ones. We mine components as a
group of classes based on the frequency they are used together and their
ability to form a quality-centric component. To validate our approach,
we experimented on 100 *Java* applications that used *Android* APIs.

Keywords: Reuse, reusability, component, API, object-oriented,
reengineering, mining, understandability, frequent usage pattern.

1 Introduction

Nowadays, the development of large and complex software applications is based
on reusing pre-existing functionalities instead of developing them from scratch
[1,2]. Application Programming Interfaces (APIs) are recognized as the most
commonly used repositories supporting software reuse [1]. APIs provide a pre-
implemented, tested and high quality set of functionalities [2,3]. Consequently,
they increase software quality and reduce the effort spent on coding, testing and
maintenance activities [2].

In the case of object-oriented APIs, e.g., *Standard Template Libraries* in *C++*
or *Java SDK*, the functionalities are encapsulated as object-oriented classes. It
is well known that reusing and understanding large APIs such as *Java SDK*,
which contains more than 7.000 classes, is not an easy task [4,5]. Consequently,
several approaches have been proposed, such as [6,7,8], in order to facilitate
the understandability and the reusability of APIs by discovering frequent usage
patterns of APIs. This is based on the API usage history of software applications
(i.e. API clients). Despite the value of frequent usage patterns, these are not
sufficient to provide a high degree of API reusability and understandability.
These are used as guides for reusing API classes and are not themselves reusable
entities [9].

Otherwise, software components are admitted to be more reusable and understandable entities than Object-Oriented (OO) ones [10]. This is because components are considered coarse-grained software entities, while OO classes are

I. Schaefer and I. Stamelos (Eds.): ICSR 2015, LNCS 8919, pp. 330–347, 2014.
© Springer International Publishing Switzerland 2014

considered fine-grained ones. In addition, components define their required and provided interfaces. This means that the component dependencies are more understandable compared to the dependencies among objects. Consequently many approaches have been proposed to identify components from OO software applications such as [11,12]. Nevertheless, no approach has been proposed to identify components from object-oriented APIs. Thus, in this paper, we propose an approach to mine components from object-oriented APIs. This does not only improve the reusability of APIs themselves, but also supporting component-based reuse techniques by providing component based APIs. The approach exploits specificities of API entities. We statically analyze the source code of both APIs and their software clients to identify groups of API classes that are able to form OO components. This is based on two criteria. The first one is the probability of classes to be reused together by API clients. The second one is related to the structural and behavioral dependencies among classes and thus their ability to form a quality-centric component. In order to validate the proposed approach, we experimented on a set of 100 *Java* applications that use three *Android* APIs. The evaluation shows that structuring object-oriented APIs as component-based ones improves the reusability and the understandability of these APIs.

The rest of this paper is organized as follows. The subsequent section, Section 2 puts in context the problem of component identification from APIs. It presents the goal of the proposed approach, the background needed to understand our proposal and the problem analysis. Section 3 presents the foundation of our approach. Then, in Section 4 we present the identification of component interface classes. Section 5 presents how APIs are organized as component-based libraries. Experimentation and results of our approach are discussed through three APIs case studies in section 6. Next, the related work is discussed in Section 7. Finally, concluding remarks and future directions are presented in section 8.

2 Putting Problem in Context

2.1 The Goal: Object to Component

Our goal is to reengineer object-oriented APIs into component based ones. Based on [10,13,14], we consider a component as, "a software element that (a) can be composed without modification, (b) can be distributed in an autonomous way, (c) encapsulates the implementation of one or many closed functionalities, and (d) adheres to a component model". According to this definition, we derive three quality characteristics that should be satisfied by a component; *Composability*, *Autonomy* and *Specificity*. *Composability* of a component refers to its ability to be composed through its interfaces without any modification. *Autonomy* refers to that a component can be reused in an autonomous way because it encapsulates the strongly dependent functionalities. *Specificity* refers to that a component implements a limited number of closed functionalities, which makes it a coarse-grained entity. Based on that, we consider as OO components those implemented as a group of OO classes.

In the context of our approach, the identification[1] of a component means identifying OO classes that can be considered as the implementation of this

---

[1] Component identification is the first step of the migration process of object-to-component.

component. Thus we consider that a component can be identified from a cluster of classes that may belong to different packages. Classes that have direct links (e.g. method call, attribute access) with classes implementing other components compose the interfaces of the component. Provided Interfaces of a component are defined as a group of methods implemented by classes composing these interfaces. Required interfaces of a component are defined as a group of methods invoked by the component and provided by other components. Figure 1 shows our object to component mapping model.

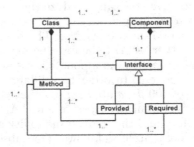

Fig. 1. Mapping object to component

2.2 Background

Identifying Components in Software Applications : Synthesis of Previous Work. We have proposed in our previous works related to ROMANTIC[2] approach [11,15] a set of metrics to measure the ability of a group of classes in a software application to form a component. These metrics are defined based on the main characteristics of a component (i.e. *Composability*, *Autonomy* and *Specificity*). Similar to the software quality model ISO 9126 [16], we proposed to refine the characteristics of the component into sub-characteristics. Next, the sub-characteristics are refined into the properties of the component (e.g. number of required interfaces). Then, these properties are mapped to the properties of the group of classes from which the component is identified (e.g. group of classes coupling). Lastly, these properties are refined into OO metrics (e.g. coupling metric). This quality refinement model is shown in Figure 2. According to this model, a quality function has been proposed to measure the component quality. This quality function is used as a similarity metric for a hierarchal clustering algorithm [11,15] as well as in search-based algorithms [17] to partition the OO classes into groups; where each group represents a component.

Frequent Usage Patterns. In the domain of data mining, a Frequent Usage Pattern (FUP) is defined as a set of items, subsequences or substructures that are frequently used together by customers [18]. It provides information that helps decision makers (e.g. customer shopping behavior) by mining associations and correlations among a set of items in a huge data set. An example of FUP mining is a market basket analysis. In this example, the customer buying habits are

---

[2] ROMANTIC: Re-engineering of Object-oriented systeMs by Architecture extractioN and migraTIon to Component based ones.

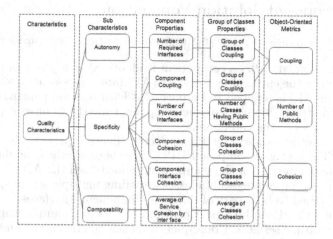

Fig. 2. From component characteristics to object-oriented metrics

analyzed to identify items that are frequently bought together in the customer shopping baskets, for instance, milk and bread form a FUP when they bought frequently together. The identification of FUP is based on *Support* quality metric that is used to measure the interestingness of a set of items. *Support* refers to the probability of finding a set of items in the transactions. For example, the value of 0.30 *Support*, means that 30% of all the transactions contain the target item set. The following equation refers to *Support*:

$$S(E1, E2) = P(E1 \cup E2) \tag{1}$$

Where *E1*, *E2* are sets of items; *S* refers to *Support*; *P* refers to the probability.

2.3   Component and Frequent Usage Pattern

FUPs are observations made based on the analysis of previous uses of APIs. They aim to help users of APIs by identifying recurring patterns, composed of classes frequently used together.

FUPs and components serve the reuse needs in two different ways. Components are entities that can be directly reused and integrated into software applications, while FUPs are guides for reuse and not entities for reuse. In addition, components and FUPs are structurally different. Related to *Specificity* characteristic, classes composing a component serve a coherent body of services, while classes composing a FUP may be related to different services. Concerning *Autonomy* characteristic, dependencies of component's classes are mostly internal, which forms an autonomous entity. FUP's classes can be very dependent on other classes that are not directly used by clients of APIs. Concerning *Composability* characteristic, a component is structured and reused via interfaces, while FUPs are not directly reusable entities.

3 The Proposed Solution Foundations

Based on the observations made in the previous sections, we consider that:

- In object-oriented APIs, a component is identified as a group of classes.
- To reengineer the entire object-oriented API into component-based one, each class of the API is mapped to be part of at least one component. Each class is mapped either as a class of the component interfaces or as a part of the internal classes of the component.
- Classes directly accessed by the software clients represent the end-users' services. These classes compose FUPs. These ones are the candidate to form the provided interface of the components mined from the API.
- As a FUP can be composed of classes providing multiple services, its classes can be mapped to be a part of different component interfaces.
- A class of an API can be a part of several FUPs and can participate to implement multiple services. Consequently a class can be mapped into multiple component interfaces.

Figure 3 shows our mapping model which maps class-to-component through FUPs. According to this mapping model, we propose the following process to mine components from APIs (c.f. Figure 4):

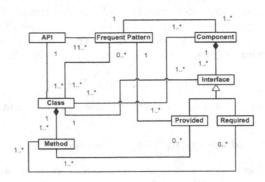

Fig. 3. Mapping class to component through FUP

- **Identification of frequent usage patterns.** FUPs are identified by analyzing the interactions between the API and its application clients.
- **Identification of the interfaces of components.** We partition the set of classes of each FUP in subgroups, where each is considered as related to the provided interfaces of one component (c.f. Figure 5). The partitioning is based on criteria related to dependencies and lexical similarity of classes and their frequency of simultaneous reuse.
- **Identification of internal classes of components driven by their provided interfaces.** Classes forming the provided interfaces of a component form the starting point for identifying the rest of the component classes. To identify these classes we rely on the analysis of structural and behavioral dependencies between classes in the API with those forming the interfaces. We check if these classes are able to form a quality-centric component.

- **Organizing API as Layers of Components.** As we previously mentioned, the API classes can be categorized according to whether they are directly reused by the API clients or not. Classes that are not directly used by API clients can also be organized into two categories. This is based on whether they belong to components identified from the classes that are directly used by API clients or not. As each class of the API must be a part of at least one component, we associate classes that do not compose any of the already identified components to new ones. Based on that, we organize component-based APIs as a set of layers describing how their components are organized. This organization is used-driven. The first layer is composed of components that are used by the software clients, while the second layer is composed of components that provide services used by components of the first layer, and so on. As a result, the API is structured in N layers of components (c.f. Figure 6).

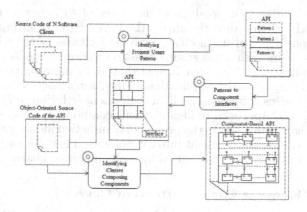

Fig. 4. The process of mining components from an object-oriented API

4 Identification of Component Interfaces

The identification of classes forming an API component is driven by the identification of classes composing the provided interfaces of this component. Classes composing these interfaces are those directly accessed by the clients of the API. Classes belonging to the same interface are those frequently used together. Therefore they are identified from frequent usage patterns. Classes of the API composing frequent usage patterns are identified based on the analysis of how API classes were used by the API clients. API classes used together constitute transactions of usage.

4.1 Extracting Transactions of Usage

A transaction of usage is a set of interactions between an API and a client of this API. These interactions consist of calling methods, accessing attributes, inheritance or creating an instance object based on a class of the API. They are identified by statically analyzing the source code of the API and its clients.

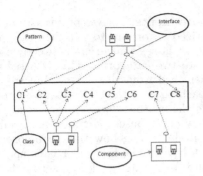

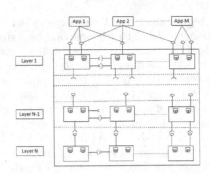

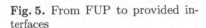

Fig. 5. From FUP to provided interfaces

Fig. 6. Multi-layers component-based API

Transactions are different depending on the choice of API clients. Therefore the choice of the API clients directly affects the type of the resulting patterns. A client can be considered either a class, a group of classes or the whole software application. We define a client as group of classes forming a functional component in software applications. The idea behind that is to mine patterns related to functionalities composing the applications. Thus, a transaction is a set of API classes used by classes composing a client component (c.f. Figure 7). To this end, we use ROMANTIC approach to identify client components composing software applications. Algorithm 1 shows the process of transaction identification. It starts by partitioning each software client into components. Then, for each component, it identifies API classes that are reused by the component classes.

4.2   Mining Frequent Usage Patterns of Classes

In the previous step, the interactions of all client components with the API are identified as transactions. Based on these transactions, we identify FUPs. A FUP is a set of API classes that are frequently used together by client components. It allows the detection of hidden correlations of usage among classes of the API. We mine FUPs based on the FPGrowth algorithm [18]. In this algorithm, a pattern is considered as frequent if it reaches a predefined threshold of interestingness metric. This metric is known as *Support*. The *Support* refers to the probability of finding a set of API classes in the transactions. The use of the *Support* metric separates the classes of API into two groups according to whether they belong to at least one FUP or not. Classes that do not belong to any of the identified FUPs are the less commonly used classes. As each API class that belongs to a transaction is a class that has been accessed by the clients of the API, therefore it must be a part of the classes composing the interfaces of at least one component. We propose assigning each class of the less commonly used classes to the pattern holding the maximum *Support* value when they are merged together.

4.3   Identifying Classes Composing Component Interfaces from Frequent Usage Patterns

We identify classes composing component interfaces from those composing FUPs. Each FUP is partitioned into a set of groups, where each group represents a

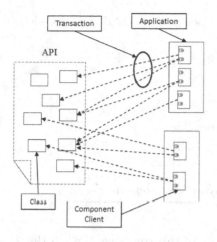

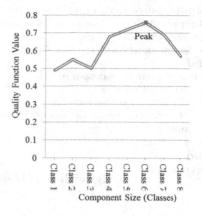

Fig. 7. Client components using API

Fig. 8. Identifying classes composing components

component interface. Classes are grouped together according to three heuristics that measure the probability of a set of classes to be a part of the same interface. The first is the frequency of simultaneous use of these classes by the same client. The second is the cohesion of these classes. This measures the strength of sharing data (e.g. attributes) between these classes. The third heuristic is the lexical similarity between these classes based on the textual names of the classes, their methods as well as their attributes. Based on the above heuristics, we propose a fitness function, given below, measuring the ability of a group of classes to form a component interface. We use LCC metric [19] to measure the cohesion of a set of classes, *Conceptual Coupling* metric [20] to measure classes' lexical similarity and *Support* metric to measure the association frequency of a set of classes. The partition of each pattern into groups of classes is based on a hierarchical clustering algorithm which uses this function as a function of similarity.

$$I(E) = \frac{1}{\sum_i \lambda_i} \cdot (\lambda_1 \cdot LCC(E) + \lambda_2 \cdot CC(E) + \lambda_3 \cdot S(E)) \qquad (2)$$

Where E is a set of OO classes; $LCC(E)$ is the *Cohesion* of E; $CC(E)$ is *Conceptual Coupling* of E; $S(E)$ is the *Support* of E; and λ_1, λ_2, λ_3 are weight values, situated in [0-1]. These are used by the API expert to weight each characteristic as needed.

5   API as Library of Components

5.1   Identifying Classes Composing Components

As we mentioned before, the component identification process is driven by the identification of its provided interfaces. This means that API classes forming a component are identified in relation to their direct or indirect structural and behavioral dependencies with the classes forming provided interfaces of the component. The selection of a class of the API to be a part of the component classes

Input: Source Code of a Set of Software Clients(*clients*), API Source Code(*api*)
Output: A Set of Transactions(*trans*)
for *each c in clients* **do**
  | *components*.add(ROMANTIC(*c*));
end
for *each com in components* **do**
  | *transaction* = ∅;
  | **for** *each class in com* **do**
  | | *transaction*.add(class.getUsedClasses(*api*));
  | **end**
  | *trans*.add(*transaction*);
end
return *trans*

Algorithm 1: Identifying Transactions

is based on the measurement of the quality of this component, when this is included. The identification of these classes is done gradually. In other words, we start to form the group of classes composing the interface ones, and then we add other classes to form a component based on the component quality measurement model. Classes having either direct or indirect links with the interface ones represent the candidate classes to be added to them. At each step, we add a new API class. This is selected based on the quality value of the component, formed by adding this class to the ones already selected. The class that maximizes the quality value is selected in this step. This is done until all API classes are investigated. Each time we add a class, we evaluate the component quality. Then, we select the peak quality value to decide which classes form the component. This means that we exclude classes added after the peak value. As an example, *Class*7 and *Class*8 in Figure 8 are excluded from the resulting component because they were added after the quality value reached the peak.

5.2   Organizing API as Layers of Components

As we previously mentioned, the API is structured in N layers of components. To identify components of layer L, we rely on components of layer $L-1$. We proceed similarly to the identification of the components of the first layer. We use required interfaces of the components already identified in layer $L-1$ to identify the interfaces provided by components in layer L. This continues until reaching a layer where its components either do not require any interface or they require ones already identified. Each interface defined as a required for a component of layer $L-1$ is considered as a provided by a component of layer L except ones provided by the already identified components. All interfaces provided in layer L are grouped into clusters to identify those provided by the same component of layer L. The clusters are obtained based on a hierarchical clustering algorithm. This algorithm uses a similarity function that measures: (i) the cohesion of classes composing a group of interfaces, (ii) the lexical similarity of these classes and (iii) the frequency of their simultaneous use. Clusters that maximize this function are selected. The interfaces composing each cluster are considered as provided by the same component. Analogously to the identification of the components of the first layer, the other classes composing each component are identified starting from classes composed of its already identified provided interfaces.

6 Experimentation and Results

6.1 Experimental Design

Data Collection. We collected a set of 100 *Android − Java* applications from open-source repositories[3]. The average size of these applications in terms of number of classes is 90. The application names are listed in the Appendix. These applications are developed based on classes of the *android* APIs[4]. In our experimentation, we focus on three of these APIs. The first is the *android.view* composed of 491 classes. This API provides services related to the definition and management of the user interfaces in android applications. The second API is the *android.app* composed of 361 classes. This API provides services related to creating and managing android applications. The last API is the *android* composed of 5790 classes. This API includes all of the android services.

Research Questions and Evaluation Method. The approach is evaluated on the collected software applications and APIs. We identify client components independently from each software application. Each component in software is considered as a client of the APIs to form a transaction of classes. Then, we mine Frequent Usage Pattern (FUP) from the identified transactions. Next, from classes composing each FUP, we identify classes composing a set of component interfaces. Then, we identify all component classes starting from ones composing their interfaces. Lastly, the final results obtained by our approach are presented.

We evaluate the obtained components by answering the three following research questions.

- **RQ1: Does the Approach Reduce the Understandability Efforts?** This research question aims at measuring the saved efforts in the API understandability that are brought by migrating object oriented APIs into component-based ones.
- **RQ2: Are the Mined Components Reusable?** As our approach aims at mining reusable components, we evaluate the reusability of the resulted component. This is based on measuring how much related classes are grouped into the same components.
- **RQ3: Is the Identification of Provided Interfaces Based on FUPs Useful?** The proposed approach identifies the provided interfaces of the components based on how clients have used the API classes (i.e. FUPs). Thus, this research question evaluates how much benefit the use of FUPs brings by comparing components identified by our approach with ones identified without taking FUPs into account.

To answer the second question that related to the reusability, we use the $K −$ *fold* cross validation method [18]. The idea is to partition the client applications into K parts. Then, the identification process is applied K times by considering, each time, $K − 1$ different parts for the identification process and by using the remaining part to measure the reusability. Next, we take the average of all K trail results. In our experiment, we set K to 2, 4, and 8.

---

[3] sourceforge.net, code.google.com, github.com, gitorious.org, and aopensource.com

[4] We select android API level 14 as a reference

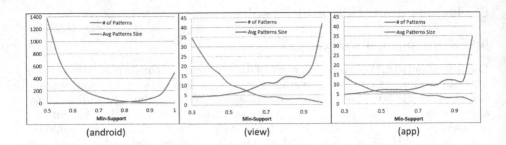

Fig. 9. Changing the support threshold value to mine FUPs of classes

6.2 Results

Intermediate Results and Identified Components. The average number of client components identified from each software is 4.5 and the average number of classes composing each component is 18.73. Table 1 shows the average number of transactions per software application ($ANTIC$), the average of transaction size in terms of classes (ATS), and the percentage of components that have used the API (PCU). The last column of this table shows an example of transactions.

The results show that *android, view,* and *app* APIs have been used respectively by only 54%, 29% and 32% of client components. In addition, we note that each client component has used the API classes intensively compared to the number of classes composing it. For example, the transaction size is 17.91 classes for the *view* API, where the average number of classes per component is 18.73. This is due to the fact that classes that serve the same services in software applications, and consequently depend on the same API classes, are grouped together in the same client component.

Table 1. The Identification of Transactions

API	ANTIC	ATS	PCU	Example
android	2.61	64.82	0.54	Bitmap, Path, Log, Activity, Location, Canvas, Paint, ViewGroup, MotionEvent, View, TextView, GestureDetector
view	1.51	17.91	0.29	MenuItem, Menu, View, ContextMenu, WindowManager, MenuInflater, Display, LayoutInflater
app	1.58	10.90	0.32	ProgressDialog, Dialog, AlertDialog, Activity, ActionBar, Builder, ListActivity

The identification of FUPs relies on the value of the *Support* threshold. The number and the size of the mined FUPs depend on this value. For all application domains where FUPs are used (e.g. data mining), this value is determined by domain experts. In our approach, to help API experts to determine this value, we assign the *Support* threshold values situated in [30%-100%]. We give for each *Support* value the number of the mined FUPs and the average size of the mined

FUPs for each API (c.f. Figure 9). The results show that the number of mined FUPs is directly proportional to the *Support* value, while the average size of the mined FUPs is inversely proportional.

Based on their knowledge of the API, API experts can select the value of the *Support*. For example, if the known average number of API classes used together to implement an application service is N, then the experts can choose the *Support* value corresponding to FUPs having N as the average size. Based on the obtained results and our knowledge on android APIs[5], we select the *Support* threshold values as 60%, 45%, and 45% respectively for the *android*, the *view* and the *app* APIs.

Table 2 shows examples of the mined FUPs. For instance, the FUP related to *view* API contains 10 classes. The analysis of this FUP shows that it corresponds to three services: animation (*Animation* and *AnimationUtils* classes), view (*Surface, SurfaceView, SurfaceHolder, MeasureSpec, ViewManager* and *MenuInflater* classes), and persistence of the view states (*AbsSavedState* and *AccessibilityRecord* classes). These services are dependent. Animation service needs the view service and the data of animation view needs to be persistent.

Table 2. Examples of the Mined FUPs

API	Example
android	Intent, Context, Log, SharedPreferences, View, TextView, Toast, Activity, Resources
view	Surface, Animation, AnimationUtils, AccessibilityRecord, ViewManager, MenuInflater, AbsSavedState, SurfaceView, SurfaceHolder, MeasureSpec
app	Dialog, Activity, ProgressDialog

In Table 3, we present the results of interface identification in terms of the average number of component interfaces identified from a FUP ($ANCIP$), the average number of classes composing component interfaces ($ACIS$) and the total number of component interfaces in the API ($TNCI$). The last column of this table presents examples of component interfaces identified from the FUPs given in Table 2. For instance, the analysis of classes composing the component interfaces identified from the FUP related to the *view* API shows that they are related to surface view services.

Table 3. Identification of Component Interfaces from FUPs

API	ANCIP	ACIS	TNCI	Examples
android	1.57	5.62	232	Activity, View, TextView, Toast
view	2.17	2.94	19	Surface, SurfaceView, SurfaceHolder
app	2.50	4	10	Dialog, ProgressDialog

Table 4 presents the results related to the mined components composing the first API layer. For each API, we give the number of the mined components (NMC) and the average number of classes composing the mined components (ACS).

---

[5] The authors of this paper are experts on the android APIs.

The last column of this table shows examples of classes composing components identified started from classes composing provided component interfaces presented in Table 3. The results show that the services offered by classes of *android*, *view* and *app* APIs are identified as 232, 19 and 10 components respectively. This means that developers only require to interact with these components to get the needed services from these APIs.

Table 4. Identifying Classes Composing Components

API	NMC	ACS	Example
android	232	19.99	Activity, View, TextView, Toast, Drawable, GroupView, Window, Context, ColorStateList, LayoutInflater
view	19	7.49	Surface,SurfaceView, SurfaceHolder, MockView, Display, CallBack
app	10	5.86	Dialog, ProgressDialog, AlertDialog

Table 5 shows the final results obtained by our approach. For each API, we firstly give the size of the API in terms of the number of OO classes composing the API and the number of the identified components. Secondly, we present the total number of used entities (classes and respectively components) by the software clients. The results show that classes participating in providing related services are grouped into one component. Furthermore, the total number of cohesive and decoupled services is identified for each API. For instance, *android* API consists of 497 components (coarse-grained services), while *view* and *app* APIs contain 43 and 55 components respectively.

Table 5. The Final Results

API Name	API Entity	API size	No. of used Entities
android	OO	5790	491
	CB	497	54
view	OO	491	42
	CB	43	17
app	OO	361	45
	CB	55	5

Answering Research Questions. *RQ1: Does the Approach Reduce the Understandability Efforts?* The efforts spent to understand such an API is directly proportional to the complexity of the API. This complexity is related to the number of API elements and the individual element's complexity. On the one hand, the reduction in the number of elements composing the API is obtained by grouping classes collaborating to provide one coarse-grained service into one component. The results show that the average number of identified components for the studied APIs is 11% (((497/5790) + (43/491) + (55/361)) /3) of the number of classes composing the APIs. This means that the API size is significantly reduced by mapping class-to-component. On the other hand, the reduction in the individual element complexity is done by migrating object-oriented APIs into component-based ones. Meaning, components define their required and provided interfaces, while OO classes at least do not define required interfaces (e.g. a class may call a large number of methods belonging to a set of classes without an explicit specification of these dependencies). The results show that the average number of used components for the APIs is 4% (((54/491) + (17/42) + (5/45)) /3) of the number of used classes. This means that the effort spent to understand API entities is significantly reduced in the case of software applications developed based on API components compared to the development based on API classes. Note that, developers only need to understand the component interfaces, but not the whole component implementation.

RQ2: Are the Mined Components Reusable? We consider that the reusability of a software component is related to the number of used classes among all ones composing the software component. Thus, we calculate the reusability of the component based on the ratio between the numbers of used classes composing the component to the total number of classes composing the component. To prove that our resulted component-based APIs could be generalized to another independent set of client applications, we rely on $K - fold$ cross validation method. Table 6 presents the results of this measurement. These results show that the reusability results is distributed in a disparate manner. The reason behind this disputation is the size of the train and test data as well as the size of the API. For instance, the average reusability for the *app* API is 37% when the number of train clients is 50 application clients, while it is 51% when the number of train clients is 88 application clients. Thus, the reusability of the components increases when the number of train client applications increases. The results show that our approach identifies reusable components, where the average reusability for all APIs is 47%.

Table 6. Reusability Results

API	*android*			*view*			*app*		
K	2	4	8	2	4	8	2	4	8
Reusability	40%	43%	57%	46%	48%	56%	37%	41%	51%

RQ3: Is the Identification of Provided Interfaces Based on FUPs Useful? To prove the utility of using FUPs during the identification process, we compare the components mined based on our approach with ones mined using ROMANTIC approach, which does not take FUPs into consideration. This is based on the density of using the component provided interfaces by application clients. The density refers to the ratio between the number of used interface classes to the total number of interface classes for each component. Table 7 shows the average density for the two identification approaches. These results show that our approach outperforms ROMANTIC approach. For instance, the application clients need to reuse a larger number of components of ones mined based on ROMANTIC with less density of provided interface classes compared to component mined based on our approach. For instance, the average usage density of classes composing provided interfaces of ROMANTIC components is 21%, while it is 61% for components mined by our approach for all APIs.

Table 7. The Results of Interface Density

API	ROMANTIC	Our Approach
android	20%	69%
view	18%	58%
app	26%	55%

7   Related Work

To the best of our knowledge, no approach has been proposed to identify components from object-oriented APIs. However, we present two research areas that are related to our approach. The First one aims at identifying components from OO software applications. The second area aims at mining frequent patterns of API usage.

Concerning the identification of software components from the source code of software applications, numerous approaches have been presented. Garcia et al. provide a survey of some of these approaches [21]. In [22], Detten et al. presented the Archimetrix approach, which aims at mining the architecture of the legacy software. It relies on a clustering algorithm to partition the system classes into components. This algorithm depends on name resemblance, coupling and cohesion metrics as a fitness function. In [11], Kebir et al. presented an approach to extract components from a single OO software system. Classes composing the extracted components form a partition. Mined components are considered as a part of the component-based architecture of the corresponding software. In [12] Allier et al. depended on dynamic dependencies between classes to recover components. Based on the use case diagram, the execution trace scenarios are identified. Classes that frequently occur in the execution traces are grouped into a single component. Cohesion and coupling metrics are also taken into account during the identification process. Weinreich et al. proposed, in [23], an approach to recover multi-view architecture model of software applications implemented based on service oriented architecture. The authors classified software artifacts based on the information from source code, configuration files and binary codes. In [24], an approach has been presented to mine reusable components from a set of similar software applications. A component is considered as more reusable, when it is reused many times by the software applications. The authors firstly identified components independently from each software application. Then, based on the lexical similarity between the classes composing these components, they identified reusable ones.

In the context of API mining, many approaches have been proposed to mine frequent usage patterns of APIs based on the usage history of APIs. Robillard et al. provide a survey of these approaches [25]. These approaches can be mainly classified based on four main criteria. The first one is related to the goal, which can be either giving examples and recommendations of how to use API entities (e.g. [7,5]), supporting the documentation of APIs (e.g. [7,6]), or improving the bug detection task (e.g. [8]). The second criterion is related to the pattern ordering, where some approaches mine ordered patterns (e.g. [7,6]), while other ones mine unordered patterns (e.g. [8,26]). The third one concerns the granularity of the elements composing a pattern. For examples, in [7,6]), the approaches mine patterns composed of methods, and the approach in [26] mines patterns composed of classes. The fourth one related to the technique that is used to identify the patterns. The used technique can be association rules mining (e.g. [26]), clustering algorithms (e.g. [6]) or a heuristic defined by the authors such as [7,8]. Some approaches combines many techniques, e.g., Unddin et al. used Principle Component Analysis with Clustering algorithm [5], and Buse and Weimer combined the clustering algorithm with their own proposed heuristic [27].

8 Conclusion and Future Work

In this paper, we presented an approach aimed at mining software components from object-oriented APIs. It is based on static analysis of the source code of both the APIs and their software clients. The mining process is used-driven. This means that components are identified starting from classes composing their interfaces. Classes composing the provided interface of the first layer components compose FUPs. We experimented our approach by applying it on a set of open source *Java* applications as clients for three android APIs. The results show that our approach improves the reusability of the API.

As our approach is used-driven, the results depend on the quality and the number of usages of the API. This means that identified FUPs rely on the considered software clients. Therefore the identification of provided interfaces and then their corresponding components depends on API clients. Consequently it is essential to select clients having the largest number of usages of the API.

Our future work will focus on migrating the identified OO components into existing component models such as OSGI model, and developing a visual environment that allows domain experts to interact with the approach at each step of the identification process, thus modify the obtained results as needed.

Appendix

These are the names of the applications that considered as clients of the APIs.

ADW Launcher, APV, ARMarker, ARviewer, Alerts, Alogcat, AndorsTrail, AndroMaze, AndroidomaticKeyer, AppsOrganizer, AripucaTracker, Asci-iCam, Asqare, AugmentRealityFW, AussieWeatherRadar, AutoAnswer, Avare, BansheeRemote, BiSMoClient, BigPlanetTracks, BinauralBeats, Blokish, BostonBusMap, CalendarPicker, CH-EtherDroid, CVox, CamTimer, Chan-ImageBrowser, CidrCalculator, ColorPicker, CompareMyDinner, ConnectBot, CorporateAddressBook, Countdown, CountdownTimer, CrossWord, Cus-tomMaps, DIYgenomics, Dazzle, Dialer2, DiskUsage, DistLibrary, Dolphin, Doom, DriSMo, DroidLife, DroidStack, Droidar, ExchangeOWA, FeedGoal, File-Manager, FloatingImage, Gcstar, GeekList, GetARobotVPNFrontend, GlTron, GoHome, GoogleMapsSupport, GraphView, HeartSong, Hermit, Historify, Holoken, HotDeath, Introspy, LegoMindstroms, Lexic, LibVoyager, LiveMusic, LocaleBridge, MAME4droid, Look, LookSocial, Macnos, Mandelbrot, Mathdoku, MediaPlayer, Ministocks, MotionDetection, NGNStack, NewspaperPuzzles, On-MyWay, OpenIntents, OpenMap, OpenSudoku, Pedometer, Phoenix, PhotSpot, Prey, PubkeyGenerator, PwdHash, QueueMan, RateBeerMobile, AlienbloodBath, SuperGenPass, SwallowCatcher, Swiftp, Tumblife, VectorPinball, WordSearch.

References

1. Frakes, W.B., Kang, K.: Software reuse research: status and future. IEEE Transactions on Software Engineering 31(7), 529–536 (2005)
2. Zibran, M.F., Eishita, F.Z., Roy, C.K.: Useful, but usable? factors affecting the usability of apis. In: 18th Working Conf. on Reverse Engineering (WCRE), pp. 151–155 (2011)
3. Monperrus, M., Eichberg, M., Tekes, E., Mezini, M.: What should developers be aware of? An empirical study on the directives of api documentation. Empirical Software Engineering 17(6), 703–737 (2012)
4. Ma, H., Amor, R., Tempero, E.: Usage patterns of the java standard api. In: 13th Asia Pacific Software Engineering Conf. (APSEC), pp. 342–352 (2006)
5. Uddin, G., Dagenais, B., Robillard, M.P.: Temporal analysis of api usage concepts. In: Proc. of the 2012 Inter. Conf. on Software Engineering (ICSE), pp. 804–814. IEEE Press, Piscataway (2012)
6. Wang, J., Dang, Y., Zhang, H., Chen, K., Xie, T., Zhang, D.: Mining succinct and high-coverage api usage patterns from source code. In: Proc. of the 10th Working Conf. on Mining Software Repositories (MSR), pp. 319–328. IEEE Press, Piscataway (2013)
7. Montandon, J.E., Borges, H., Felix, D., Valente, M.T.: Documenting apis with examples: Lessons learned with the apiminer platform. In: 20th Working Conf. on Reverse Engineering (WCRE), pp. 401–408 (2013)
8. Monperrus, M., Bruch, M., Mezini, M.: Detecting missing method calls in object-oriented software. In: D'Hondt, T. (ed.) ECOOP 2010. LNCS, vol. 6183, pp. 2–25. Springer, Heidelberg (2010)
9. Maalej, W., Robillard, M.P.: Patterns of knowledge in api reference documentation. IEEE Transactions on Software Engineering 39(9), 1264–1282 (2013)
10. Szyperski, C.: Component Software: Beyond Object-Oriented Programming. Pearson Education (2002)
11. Kebir, S., Seriai, A.-D., Chardigny, S., Chaoui, A.: Quality-centric approach for software component identification from object-oriented code. In: Joint Working IEEE/IFIP Conf. and European Conf. on Software Architecture (WICSA)/(ECSA), pp. 181–190 (2012)
12. Allier, S., Sadou, S., Sahraoui, H., Fleurquin, R.: From object-oriented applications to component-oriented applications via component-oriented architecture. In: 2011 9th Working IEEE/IFIP Conf. on Software Architecture (WICSA), pp. 214–223 (2011)
13. Lüer, C., Van Der Hoek, A.: Composition Environments for Deployable Software Components. Citeseer (2002)
14. Heineman, G.T., Councill, W.T.: Component-Based Software Engineering: Putting the Pieces Together, vol. 17. Addison-Wesley, Reading (2001)
15. Chardigny, S., Seriai, A., Oussalah, M., Tamzalit, D.: Extraction of component-based architecture from object-oriented systems. In: Seventh Working IEEE/IFIP Conf. on Software Architecture (WICSA), pp. 285–288 (2008)
16. ISO. Software Engineering – Product Quality – Part 1: Quality Model. Technical Report ISO/IEC 9126-1, International Organization for Standardization (2001)
17. Chardigny, S., Seriai, A., Oussalah, M., Tamzalit, D.: Search-based extraction of component-based architecture from object-oriented systems. In: Morrison, R., Balasubramaniam, D., Falkner, K. (eds.) ECSA 2008. LNCS, vol. 5292, pp. 322–325. Springer, Heidelberg (2008)
18. Han, J., Kamber, M., Pei, J.: Data mining: Concepts and techniques. Morgan Kaufmann (2006)
19. Bieman, J.M., Kang, B.-K.: Cohesion and reuse in an object-oriented system. In: Proc. of the 1995 Symposium on Software Reusability (SSR), pp. 259–262. ACM, New York (1995)

20. Poshyvanyk, D.: A Marcus. The conceptual coupling metrics for object-oriented systems. In: 22nd IEEE Inter. Conf. on Software Maintenance (ICSM), pp. 469–478 (2006)
21. Garcia, J., Ivkovic, I., Medvidovic, N.: A comparative analysis of software architecture recovery techniques. In: IEEE/ACM 28th Inter. Conf. on Automated Software Engineering (ASE), pp. 486–496 (2013)
22. von Detten, M., Platenius, M.C., Becker, S.: Reengineering component-based software systems with archimetrix. Software & Systems Modeling, 1–30 (2013)
23. Weinreich, R., Miesbauer, C., Buchgeher, G., Kriechbaum, T.: Extracting and facilitating architecture in service-oriented software systems. In: Joint Working IEEE/IFIP Conf. on Software Architecture (WICSA) and European Conf. on Software Architecture (ECSA), pp. 81–90 (2012)
24. Shatnawi, A., Seriai, A.-D.: Mining reusable software components from object-oriented source code of a set of similar software. In: IEEE 14th Inter. Conf. on Information Reuse and Integration (IRI), pp. 193–200 (2013)
25. Robillard, M.P., Bodden, E., Kawrykow, D., Mezini, M., Ratchford, T.: Automated api property inference techniques. IEEE Transactions on Software Engineering 39(5), 613–637 (2013)
26. Bruch, M., Schäfer, T., Mezini, M.: Fruit: Ide support for framework understanding. In: Proc. of the 2006 OOPSLA Workshop on Eclipse Technology Exchange, pp. 55–59. ACM, New York (2006)
27. Buse, R.P.L., Weimer, W.: Synthesizing api usage examples. In: Proc. of the 2012 Inter. Conf. on Software Engineering, ICSE 2012, pp. 782–792. IEEE Press, Piscataway (2012)

Adapting Collections and Arrays: Another Step towards the Automated Adaptation of Object Ensembles

Dominic Seiffert[1] and Oliver Hummel[2]

[1] University of Mannheim, Germany
`seiffert@informatik.uni-mannheim.de`
[2] Karlsruhe Institute of Technology, Germany
`hummel@kit.edu`

Abstract. An important challenge of reuse in object-oriented development is that objects or more generally components often cannot be plugged together directly due to interface mismatches. Consequently, automating the adaptation of software building blocks has been on the research agenda for quite a while. However, after various attempts based on (semi-)formal specifications, only recently, adaptation approaches based on test cases have demonstrated that practically useable implementations of this idea are feasible. This paper addresses the adaptation of arrays and collections in order to bring the associated challenges into the center of attention and to increase the applicability of existing test-based adaptation approaches.

Keywords: Object adaptation, signature mismatches, test-driven adaptation.

1 Introduction

Decomposing large problems into smaller, more manageable, is a well-known principle in computer science that has been successfully applied in software development as well. Let it be in object-oriented, component-based, or service-based approaches, all are decomposing a monolithic system into smaller building blocks that are easier to handle and not to forget supposed to be more reusable in different contexts. Not surprisingly, however, the sheer complexity of software development makes system composition and reuse of existing building blocks a challenging undertaking, because even if a building block provides exactly the right functionality it often cannot be used in a given environment because it's provided interface does not match the one required due to signature mismatches. A classic solution for overcoming such mismatches in the object-oriented programming is wrapping the provided interface with an adapter [1], which, however, is often a time-consuming and error-prone manual activity. One potential solution to this problem is fully automated adaptation, which has hence been gaining increasing importance in various research communities in recent years. Unfortunately, and to the best of our knowledge, a practically usable solution for adapting objects, based on test-cases, has only been presented very recently [2]. In order to increase the application range of automated adaptation in object-oriented programming languages this paper addresses the challenge of adapting

I. Schaefer and I. Stamelos (Eds.): ICSR 2015, LNCS 8919, pp. 348–363, 2014.
© Springer International Publishing Switzerland 2014

complex parameter objects which are more difficult to adapt than primitive data types, as they may provide their own functionality.

The contribution of this paper is that we present an upgraded prototype implementation of an existing test-based adapter generation tool [3] that is able to adapt collections and arrays, as a subset of existing object types, on examples taken from the Commons Math: The Apache Commons Mathematics Library [16].

The remainder of the paper is structured as follows: Section 2 gives background information on adaptation in object-oriented development. Section 3 provides a motivation for providing automated conversion mechanisms. Section 4 gives an overview on selected literature from related fields. Section 4 introduces the Java Collections Framework and briefly describes the term of test-driven reuse where the adaptation approach happens. This section also specifies the challenges that need to be overcome in detail. Section 5 provides an evaluation on "in-vitro" and "in-vivo" examples. Section 6 states the Conclusion and Outlook.

2   Background

In order to overcome mismatches on the signature level (cf. to Becker et al. [4] for an overview of other mismatch levels) a well-known solution is to add an adapter that handles message "forwarding" from one interface to the other. In every object-oriented programming language like Java the Object Adapter Pattern as documented e.g. by the Gang of Four [1] is a well-known approach for the implementation of an adapter. Figure 1 illustrates a typical object adapter where a Client would like to use the functionality provided by the Adaptee, but is not able to do so, as it depends on a different Target interface. Therefore, an Adapter gets interposed in order to implement the Target interface and forward incoming messages. In this example messages arriving at the request method of the Adapter are forwarded to the specificRequest method of the Adaptee.

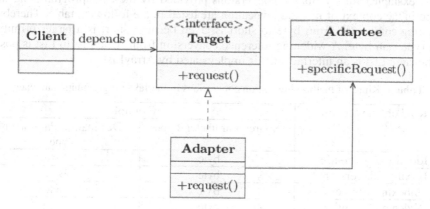

Fig. 1. The Gang of Four Object Adapter Pattern

Again according to Becker et al. [4], mismatches on the signature level can be furthter categorized into the following mismatch types.

- Deviating Method Names and Parameter Names
- Different Parameter Types and Return Types
- Parameter Permutations
- Different Numbers of Parameter (through the use of record types)
- Deviating Types of Exceptions
- Attribute Sequence in Complex Types (e.g. structures)

This means that the adapter has to fulfill tasks such as "translating" between methods with different names and different parameter orders. In order to specify the semantics that the adapter must fulfil the idea of Hummel and Atkinson [2] is that the Client specifies a test case. Out of this test case the required interface can be extracted in the first step, which is used then to find potential matchings on the Adaptee's provided interface. Through the assertions defined in the test case the Adapter can control if the semantics for the matchings are fulfilled during the adaptation process.

In order to increase the range of automated adaptation approaches, with the ultimate goal of providing fully automated adaptation on arbitrary objects, however, it is necessary to tackle the challenge of different parameter and return types that may even contain even different complex types. Unfortunately, this has not been solved in literature so far as further illustrated in the section of related work. This challenge needs to be distinguished from simple conversion mechanisms which are already provided by a common programming language such as Java, for instance. According to the Java language specification [5], in the context of a method invocation, Java allows the use of such implicit conversions, which means that the Java programming language handles necessary conversions such as "Boxing" and "Unboxing", e.g. converting a provided parameter of type int to an expected parameter of type Integer and vice versa, automatically. The latter represents a wrapper class for the primitive data type int. Wrapper classes are used when objects are expected and the primitive data type itself cannot be provided. It encapsulates the value of the primitive data type. Other examples for automated conversions provided by the Java programming language in the context of method invocation are listed in the following table. Thereby a widening conversion from byte to short is given because short is a larger primitive data type than byte. A widening reference conversion from ArrayList to List is possible because List is an interface that is implemented by ArrayList.

Table 1. Kinds of method invocation conversions in the Java programming language

Kind of Conversion	Example	
	Source Parameter Type	Destination Parameter Type
Identity Conversion	byte	byte
Boxing Conversion	byte	Byte
Unboxing Conversion	Byte	byte
Widening Primitive Conversion	byte	short
Widening Reference Conversion	ArrayList	List

The listed conversion mechanisms happen automatically, i.e. there is no need for an adapter to provide such conversions programmatically. But given two types of a Stack for instance, namely MyStack and YourStack which are assumingly not connected by type hierarchy, no conversion mechanism can be applied. That is, although both do semantically the same an instance of the one can not be provided if an instance of the other is expected. Such conversion needs to be provided by the Adapter. To distinguish automatically provided conversion mechanisms from those that need to be fulfilled by the adapter we use the term transformation instead. Since the transformation of arbitrary type instances in each other can be a quite complex task we start with a subset, namely arrays and collections from the Java Collections Framework. The reason for this is that arrays and collections are data structures that show common semantics as explained in the next section.

The Java Collections Framework and Arrays

The interface List and the class ArrayList both belong to the Java Collections framework, which distinguishes between different kinds of collections, such as the general purpose implementations like ArrayList, LinkedList, or HashSet, for instance. Table 2 gives an overview on these collections that are considered in this paper, categorized by the interfaces they implement.

Table 2. General-purpose implementations

Interfaces	Implementing Classes				
	Hash table based	Resizable Array based	Tree based	Linked list	Hashtable + Linked List
Set	HashSet		TreeSet		LinkedHashSet
List		ArrayList Stack Vector		LinkedList	
Deque		ArrayDeque		LinkedList	
Map	HashMap		TreeMap		LinkedHashMap

In general, Java knows five different strategies for implementing collections with different idiosyncrasies: Classes that implement the Map interface rely on a key value mapping, where each key can map to at most one value and the Map may not contain duplicate keys. Classes that implement the List interface represent ordered sequences and may contain duplicate elements. Classes that implement the Set interface do not allow duplicate elements. Classes that implement the Deque interface allow the insertion and removal of elements at both ends. All the listed interfaces – except for the Map interface - inherit from the super interface Collection. This interface provides for example the add(Element) method to its sub-interfaces.

As collections, arrays are data structures that are used to store elements. For arrays, once initialized, the length never changes which is different to collections. For example, for the array Integer[] arrayInt = {1,2,3} the variable arrayInt points to an array of element type Integer which keeps three elements. In order to keep four elements instead the array needs to be re-initalized by arrayInt = {1,2,3,4} for instance. Whereas for an ArrayList instance the addElement method can be invoked.

3   Motivation

Obviously, collections and arrays share similar semantics, namely to store elements. Therefore automated conversion of those in each other should make life easier for developers, and hence should be supported during – potentially automated – adapter creation as well. However, especially in the context of collections and arrays, there exist a large number of other relatively straightforward conversions that are not supported by current automated adaptation approaches.

The example following in figure 2 illustrates a situation where a Client depends on the Target interface that allows him to sort an array of numbers. But the Client wishes to use the sortIt method provided by the Sorter instead, because it sorts faster. Thus, Sorter plays the role of the Adaptee. The sortIt method is programmed against the List interface and therefore can take any class implementing this interface as an argument, like LinkedList or ArrayList, for intance. Since a direct match between both methods is not possible, the Adapter needs to translate an array of primitive component type int to a List implementation with argument type Integer (which is the wrapper class for int). The other way around happens for the return type argument delivered by the Sorter back to the Client.

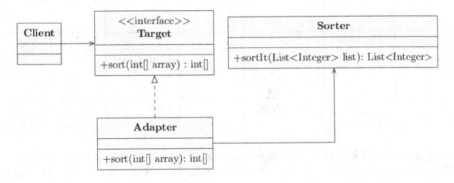

Fig. 2. Object adapter pattern example

The transformation from the array to the List and vice versa is not that difficult a task as will be illustrated in the next section. But writing such a transformation manually can be effortful and time-consuming. Therefore, it should happen automatically as detailed in the reminder of this paper.

4   Related Work

Various approaches in literature are concerned with the adaptation of software building blocks. In the following we concentrate on literature that tackles adaptation on the signature level.

The work by Reiss [6] is based on the idea of test-driven reuse [7] where simple test-cases are used as input for a component search engine, which takes the extracted required interface out of the test-case as an input for an interface-based search. If components are delivered that do not fit the requirements, as parameter and return types do not match, a modification is attempted to the components in order to fit the requirements. However, when components get modified invasively on source level or even on binary level this may lead to license problems because the vendor of the component may not allow the modification of the component's source code [8], or may not allow the re-compilation of it. The second problem are dependency problems: If a method of a component's interface gets renamed for instance, all other components that use the method must be modified. If parameter types are changed this might require an even more propagated deep adjustment of type changes.

Kell [9] proposes a formal and rule-based language named Cake for automated wrapper generation. The mapping rules used for defining interface relations thereby must be written manually. Applying these rules, transformation on object structures are possible. Nevertheless, we believe that transformation should happen automatically since it is a clear overhead for a developer writing mapping rules, especially for unknown complex objects. The approach proposed by Nita and Notkin [10] is concerned with adapting programs to alternative APIs. The user must still have knowledge of the new API in order to write mapping rules. The approach works best when the differences between the APIs are small and it considers not-straightforward structural correspondences as out of scope, which we believe are the main challenge for providing transformation. The work presented by Hummel [11] is based on the Identity Map Pattern from Fowler [12] and solves the problem of the Gang of Four adapter pattern when the parameter or return type has the type of its own interface. For example, given the expected interface of type Matrix which provides a method getMatrix():Matrix. Let the provided interface be of type OtherMatrix, playing the role of the Adaptee, and providing a method getMatrix():OtherMatrix. Then both methods can get matched on each other if OtherMatrix could be transformed to Matrix. But such a transformation is not considered, since what is actually returned to the Client is an adapter of type Matrix which delegates messages to the Adaptee OtherMatrix. Therefore this approach does not consider the transformation of complex data types as proposed in this paper. The approach is integrated into another work by Hummel and Atkinson [2] that provides relaxed-signature matching for primitive data types. But again, it does not provide a transformation mechanism as proposed in this paper.

The work by Janjic [13] overcomes the problem of the signature mismatches for different method names, but again, it does not consider the transformation of complex data types. The work by Seiffert and Hummel [3] tackles the challenge overcoming signature mismatches on method and parameter-names, relaxed signature matching for primitive data types, and parameter permutations, on the basis of efficient run-time behavior in the context of test-driven reuse (where test-cases are used as an input [7]). But again, it does not consider the transformation of complex data types.

In the context of web-services Cavallaro et al. [14] present an approach that only requires WSDL as an input to automatically derive a script that maps the correct operation sequence from the expected to the provided service. The approach uses schema matching and ontology-based reasoning. This is not appropriate for object types because of the following reasons: First, ontologies for ordinary programming language APIs do not exist. Second the provided interfaces of a web-service are described in a Web Service Description Language (WSDL) by XML. Parameter or return types described as complex data types in such a WSDL are abstract data types which do not provide any functionality through methods. Such a complex data type in WSDL is therefore quite different from a complex data type forming an object or a component.

As this overview reveals, literature is lacking a transformation mechanism for complex data types (in the context of adaptation) for objects and components that cannot be matched on each other. But we believe it is a need tackling this challenge in order to realize McIlroy's [15] idea of a component supermarket from where components can simply plugged together to create new functionality.

5   Implementing Transformations

The general idea for creating adapters that are able to deal with collections and arrays as parameters or return types should have become clear already. It is necessary to generate routines that are able to transform instances of every type from table 2 to instances of every other one contained there while taking the requirements for the different implementations into account. Moreover, the transformation mechanism should also consider arrays.

The adaptation tool presented in the following which supports the transformations on collections and arrays is written in Java and is executed as a stand-alone application with a graphical user interface. For each adaptation it takes a test-case as an input from which the required interface gets extracted. Furthermore, the Adaptee needs to be available out of which the provided interface gets extracted. When the adaptation process finishes either the final adapter or a summary of exceptions is provided.

The following sequence diagram gives an overview on the adaptation process. The TestCoordinator is responsible for managing the process. The test case is executed until all the tests in the test case are executed successfully or the testing failed. The adapter built for the process is temporary and able to change its "wirings" dynamically. This is different from the final adapter which will be available if the process finishes successfully. If the temporary adapter needs to transform parameter and return type instances during the process it uses methods which are provided by the Transformer class.

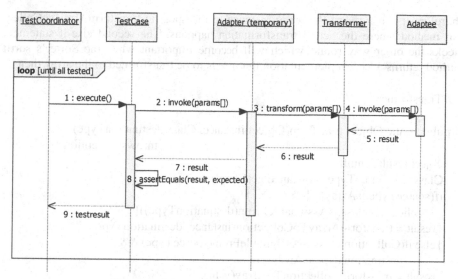

Fig. 3. Sequence diagram of the testing process

The following code snippet illustrates how the transformation is implemented by the adapter for the example from the last section. These transformation methods will eventually also be part of the final adapter.

```
//Adapter

public void sort(int[] param0){
    try{
        adaptee.sortIt(java.util.LinkedList<Integer>)
                Transformer.transform(param0,
                                java.util.LinkedList<Integer>));
    }catch(Exception e) { }
    return ;
}
```

When the adaptation process gets initiated the tool recognizes that the sort method required by the Client potentially matches the sortIt method provided by the Sorter. It identifies that the parameter of the sort method is an array and the parameter of sortIt is a List. Second, the primitive component type of the array is int which matches the parameter type Integer of the List. Therefore the appropriate transformation can be applied. When the array instance provided by the Client as an input arrives at the Adapter's sort method it first forwards it to a transform method which is provided by the class Transformer. The transformed result is casted then to the expected destination type List which gets forwarded then to the Sorter's sortIt method.

The Transformer's transform method is described in the following for the previous example. In the first step it detects that the type of the provided instance is actually an array and that the destination type is a List, i.e. its super-interface Collection.

Therefore it can forward the array instance to the specific transformArrayToCollection method where the actual transformation happens. The second else-if statement checks the other way round which will become important when the Sorter's sortIt method returns a List implementation that needs to be transformed to the array then.

```
//Transformer

public static Object transform(Object instance, Class destinationType)
                                              throws Exception {
  Object result = null;
  Class<?> sourceType = instance.getClass();
  if(sourceType.isArray() &&
      Collection.class.isAssignableFrom(destinationType)){
    result = transformArrayToCollection(instance, destinationType);
  }else if(Collection.class.isAssignableFrom(sourceType) &&
          destinationType.isArray()){
    result = transformCollectionToArray(value,
                                  destinationType.getComponentType());
  }
  return result;
}
```

Before the actual transformation starts it is important to check if the destination type is an interface type, such as List, or its super-interface Collections, or a class type, such as ArrayList implementing the List interface. If it is one of the interface types then a default List implementation is chosen, which is LinkedList in this case. Any other implementation could be chosen instead. Since a LinkedList implements the List interface which inherits from the Collection interface the created instance can be casted to Collection. The helper class Array is then used to iterate over the array instance's elements and to insert these elements into the Collection. This Collection is then returned to the adapter where it is casted to List again, since this is expected by the Sorter's sortIt method. If on the other hand an exception occurred during the transformation it will be displayed on the GUI to the Client appropriately.

```
private static Object transformArrayToCollection(Object array,
                              Class collectionType) throws Exception{
  Collection collection = null;
  try{
  if(collectionType.isInterface()){    //any kind of Collection is default a List
    if(collectionType == List.class || collectionType == Collection.class){
        collection = (Collection) LinkedList.class.newInstance();
    }
  }else {
    collection = (Collection) collectionType.newInstance();
  }
  for(int i=0; i< Array.getLength(array); i++){
```

```
      collection.add(Array.get(array, i));
   }
}catch(Exception e){
   throw new TransformationException("Could not transform array to Collection:
                                    "+e.getMessage());
}
return collection;
}
```

The transformation the other way round from the List implementation to an array is realized by the following transformCollectionToArray method provided by the Transformer again. The second parameter contentType specifies the content type of the array to create. In the first step the Object instance is casted to a Collection. That collection instance is a Collection that was already checked before in the transform method accordingly. In the next step the array instance is created with the help of the class Array. Then it is checked whether the Collection is empty. If so, the empty array instance can be returned. If not, we need to check if another transformation is necessary for the content type. This is the case for example, when the Collection contains elements of type Short and the array expects elements of type Integer on the other hand. That is, the elements of the Collection of type Short are then transformed to elements of type Integer. No automated conversion is provided in this case by the Java language.

```
private static Object transformCollectionToArray(Object collectionInstance,
                                    Class contentType) throws Exception{
Collection collection = (Collection) collectionInstance;
Object array = null;
try{
array = Array.newInstance(contentType, collection.size());
int i = 0;
Object firstElement = (collection.isEmpty() == true) ?
                     null : collection.iterator().next();
if(firstElement == null) {
 return array; //empty array
}else if(needToTransform(firstElement.getClass(), contentType) == true){
   Class<?> elementType = firstElement.getClass();
  for(Object o : collection){
  Object collectionWrapperElement = getWrapperConstructor(getDataType(
    elementType)).newInstance(o.toString());
  Object transformedObject = getWrapperConstructor(getDataType(
    contentType)).newInstance(collectionWrapperElement.toString());
  Array.set(array, i, transformedObject);
  i++;
  }
}else {
for(Object o : collection){
```

```
        Array.set(array, i, o);
        i++;
      }
    }
  }catch(Exception e){
   throw new TransformationException("could not transform collection to array:
                                "+e.getMessage()));

  }
  return array;
  }
```

Due to space restrictions we cannot list all the kinds of transformations, as for example the transformation from a LinkedList to an ArrayList for instance. But the procedure is obviously similar. For transforming Map instances on Collection or array instances, however, some more obstacles need to be overcome. For example, an array or Collection does not use key value mappings for its entries as the Map does. The idea is therefore to use the index positions where the elements are stored in the Collection or the array as the keys for the Map. Since an index position is a numeric type this requires that the Map instances expect such a type instance as a key, however. The other way round, if keys of a Map are of numeric type, they can be used as the index position in a Collection or an array. If this is not the case, a more sophisticated transformation such as using a hash function in order to transform String keys to integer keys is currently not implemented, but theoretically possible.

The following code snippet shows the transformation from a Collection instance to a Map instance, provided that the check if the transformation is possible validated true.

```
private static Object transformCollectionToMap(Object value, Class destinationType)
                                                        throws Exception{
Map destinationMap = null;
 try{
   if(destinationType != Map.class) {
      destinationMap = (Map) destinationType.newInstance();
   }else{
      destinationMap = (Map) HashMap.class.newInstance();
      //take HashMap as default.
   }
   Collection sourceCollection = (Collection) value;
   int indexAsKey = 0;
   for(Object element : sourceCollection){
    destinationMap.put(indexAsKey, element);
    indexAsKey++;
   }
 }catch(Exception e){
  throw new TransformationException("Could not transform Collection to Map");
 }
 return destinationMap;
 }
```

6 Experiments

The adapter generation tool can be downloaded at our homepage[1]. It is supplied with a comprehensive documentation and samples of JUnit test cases and adaptees that easily allow the verification of its adaptation capabilities. Some of them are described in a former publication [3]. The tool is completely written in Java and is executable as a standalone application. It is equipped with a GUI where different adaptation projects can be created. Each project needs to specify the class to adapt, the test case where the required interface gets extracted from, and the result directory where the final adapter should be written.

The evaluation described in the following consists of two parts. In the first part an "in-vitro" evaluation is provided by constructed examples. In the second part mathematical components get adapted which are taken from the "wild".

Concerning the first part of the evaluation: In order to verify the newly integrated ability to transform arrays and collections different projects exist, which can be executed to verify the adaptation capabilities. The test cases for each project correspond to the adaptation example where a Client would like to use a sorting mechanism by an Adaptee but is prevented from this because he depends on an interface. That is Sorter plays the role of the Adaptee again, sort represents the required interface and sortIt the provided interface. For example, the following test method belongs to the testcase from the project *ArrayListTransformationTest* where the transformation from an ArrayList to a Vector instance is necessary. More exactly, it is the task of the adapter to match the sort(ArrayList<Integer>):Vector<Integer> method on the sortIt(Vector<Integer>):ArrayList<Integer> method provided by Sorter. The second test method tests the transformation from an ArrayList to a LinkedList. For each of the introduced collection classes and for arrays a test method exists.

The helper class Generator is used to generate a random ArrayList and a sorted Vector instance. The latter is what is expected by the Client. If the assertEquals statement validates true, both instances have the same sorted content. The test case finishes successfully for this test method then. If all test methods finish the same the whole test case does. All test cases equipped with the projects pass successfully.

```java
import generator.Generator;

public class ArrayListTransformationTest extends TestCase {

    public void testArrayListToVector(){
        Sorter sorter = new Sorter();
        ArrayList<Integer> delivered = Generator.getRandomArrayList();
        Vector<Integer> expected = Generator.getSortedVector();

        assertEquals(expected, sorter.sort(delivered));
        //transform ArrayList to Vector (on forward)
        //transform ArrayList to Vector (on return)
    }
```

---

[1] http://oliverhummel.com/adaptation/tool.zip

```
public void testArrayListToLinkedList(){
    ...
}
}
```

Besides this in-vitro evaluation on constructed examples the new integrated ability to transform arrays and collections was also tested on real world examples. Thereby classes from the Commons Math: The Apache Commons Mathematics Library [16] were selected, namely those where its methods expect arrays or collections as parameter or return types. The selected classes play the role of the Adaptee during the adaptation process.

As the name of the library implies the classes offer mathematical functionality. Since they are equipped with test cases its functionality can be easily verified.

After the classes were selected the test cases were modified, i.e. clones were created manually, such that the test cases threw compilation errors. This happened in the following way: The type of provided method parameters and expected return types were changed appropriately, as for example, when an array was expected by the Adaptee, the test cases was changed to provide an ArrayList instead. This problem should be solved by our adapter generation tool then.

After the adaptation process succeeded successfully the modified test case was executed again, but this time using the final adapter instead of the Adaptee directly. Since the test case executed successfully the adapter's transformation capability was verified. For example, in the following test case the compute method of the selected class EuclideanDistance from the org.apache.commons.math3.ml.distance package is tested. It takes as an input two vectors, represented by an array of type double each, and calculates the distance between them. If the same vector is provided as the first and second parameter, as in this example, the distance should be zero. The interface of the compute method is public double compute(double[], double[]).

```
package org.apache.commons.math3.ml.distance;
//skipping imports

public class EuclideanDistanceTest {
    final DistanceMeasure distance = new EuclideanDistance();

    @Test
    public void testZero() {
        final double[] a = { 0, 1, -2, 3.4, 5, -6.7, 89 };
        Assert.assertEquals(0, distance.compute(a, a), 0d);
    }
```

After verification that the original test case executed successfully the array of type double was replaced with an LinkedList<Float> and the expected name of the method was changed from compute to calculate. The required interface in the test case therefore changed to public void double calculate(LinkedList<Float>). The adapter generator had therefore to overcome a parameter type and method name mismatch, namely from LinkedList<Float> on double[] and calculate on compute.

In the next step, the modified test case and the candidate to adapt, in this case EuclidDistance, was used as an input for our adapter generation tool. The following table provides an overview on the required interfaces, the selected components, and their provided interfaces to adapt. The first column names the required interface of the modified test case. The second column names the component to adapt from the Commons Apache Mathematics library. The third column names its provided interface that must be adapted in order to match the required interface.

Table 3. Adaptation testing overview

Required Interface	Name of the Adaptee adapt	Provided Interface
calculate(float[],float[]):float	EuclidDistance	compute(double[], double[]): double
calculate(int[], int[]): int	CanberraDistance	compute(double[], double[]): double
calculate(ArrayList<Byte>, ArrayList<Byte>): int	Chebyshev-Distance	compute(double[], double[]): double
calculate(Stack<Float>, Vector<Float>): float	ManhattanDis-tance	compute(double[], double[]): double
Calculate(double[][]):double	OneWayAnova	anovaPValue(List<double[]>): double

All the modified test cases passed successfully when the final adapter was tested. Therefore, the adaptation capabilities could be verified.

7   Conclusion

We have presented in this paper matching possibilities for a subset of complex data types that share common semantics, namely arrays and collections from the Java Collections Framework. These matching possibilities are realized through simple - but automated - transformation mechanisms which are a clear overhead for a developer writing them manually. These mechanisms were implemented in our adapter generation tool.

We have provided experiments on that tool by an "in-vitro" evaluation that uses constructed examples, as well as an evaluation on selected examples taken from the "wild".

Although the tool was improved by the presented matching possibilities it is not able to adapt arbitrary candidates, because the problem of matching unknown complex data types still exists. Therefore, from matching collection classes and primitive data types, the next step would be to further improve the adaptation capabilities towards complex data types that do not represent known data structures, in order to further improve the adaptation capabilities concerning signature mismatches.

Tackling the challenge of signature mismatches by more research and tools is necessary to further push fully automated adapter generation, which we believe should have a great benefit for ordinary developers and the communities of self-adapting and component based systems.

References

1. Gamma, E., Helm, R., Johnson, R., Vlissides, J.: Design Patterns: Elements of Reusable Object-Oriented Software. Pearson Education (1994)
2. Hummel, O., Atkinson, C.: Automated Creation and Assessment of Component Adapters with Test Cases. In: Grunske, L., Reussner, R., Plasil, F. (eds.) CBSE 2010. LNCS, vol. 6092, pp. 166–181. Springer, Heidelberg (2010)
3. Seiffert, D., Hummel, O.: Improving the Runtime-Processing for Component Adaptation. In: Favaro, J., Morisio, M. (eds.) ICSR 2013. LNCS, vol. 7925, pp. 81–96. Springer, Heidelberg (2013)
4. Becker, S., Brogi, A., Gorton, I., Overhage, S., Romanovsky, A., Tivoli, M.: Towards an engineering approach to component adaptation. In: Reussner, R., Stafford, J.A., Szyperski, C.A. (eds.) Architecting Systems with Trustworthy Components. LNCS, vol. 3938, pp. 193–215. Springer, Heidelberg (2006)
5. Gosling, J., Joy, B., Steele, G., Bracha, G. Buckley, A.: The Java Language Specification, Java SE 7 Edition (February 28, 2013), http://docs.oracle.com/javase/specs/jls/se7/html/index.html (accessed November 14, 2014)
6. Reiss, S.P.: Semantics-based code search. In: IEEE 31st International Conference on Software Engineering, ICSE 2009, pp. 243–253 (2009)
7. Hummel, O., Janjic, W.: Test-Driven Reuse: Key to Improving Precision of Seach Engines for Software Reuse. In: Finding Source Code on the Web for Remix and Reuse, pp. 227–250. Springer (2013)
8. Hölzle, U.: Integrating independently-developed components in object-oriented languages. In: Nierstrasz, O.M. (ed.) ECOOP 1993. LNCS, vol. 707, pp. 36–56. Springer, Heidelberg (1993)
9. Kell, S.: Component adaptation and assembly using interface relations. In: Proceedings of the ACM International Conference on Object Oriented Programming Systems Languages and Application, OOPSLA 2010, pp. 322–340 (2010)
10. Nita, M., Notkin, D.: Using twinning to adapt programs to alternative apis. In: Proceedings of the 32nd ACM/IEEE International Conference on Software Engineering, ICSE 2010, vol. 1, pp. 205–214 (2010)
11. Hummel, O., Atkinson, C.: The Managed Adapter Pattern: Facilitating Glue Code Generation for Component Reuse. In: Edwards, S.H., Kulczycki, G. (eds.) ICSR 2009. LNCS, vol. 5791, pp. 211–224. Springer, Heidelberg (2009)
12. Fowler, M.: Patterns of Enterprise Application Architecture. Addison-Wesley (2003)
13. Janjic, W., Atkinson, C.: Leveraging software search and reuse with automated software adaptation. In: 2012 ICSE Workshop on Search-Driven Development - Users, Infrastructure, Tools and Evaluation (SUITE), pp. 23–26 (2012)

14. Cavallaro, L., Di Nitto, E., Pelliccione, P., Pradella, M., Tivoli, M.: Synthesizing adapters for conversational web-services from their WSDL interface. In: Proceedings of the 2010 ICSE Workshop on Software Engineering for Adaptive and Self-Managing Systems, pp. 104–113 (2010)

15. McIlroy, M.: Mass-Produced Software Components. In: Software-Engineering: A Report on a Conf. Sponsored by the NATO Science Commitee, pp. 138–155 (1969)

16. Apache Software Foundation, Commons Math: The Apache Commons Mathematics Library (2014), http://commons.apache.org/proper/commons-math/ (accessed August 2014)

Author Index